Gender in Applied Communication Contexts

We would like to dedicate our book . . .

To the women and men of OSCLG, and to our families, especially our children and grandchildren, who must carry on our work . . .

Patrice: For my partner, Steve Wilson, and our children, Sgt. Brendan Sheahan (and his wife, Ashley Sheahan), Sheridan Sheahan, Ashlee Sheahan, Lisette Sheahan, Annie Grace Sheahan, and Robyn Wilson.

Helen: For my husband, Mark Van Halsema, and our children, Gerard and Katie.

Lynn: For my family (named and unnamed)—Roberta, Jerry, Ted III, Sabrina, Billy, Sophie, Leila, Russ, Zoe, Dylan, Ted IV, Sally, and Ely.

Gender in Applied Communication Contexts

Edited by

PATRICE M. BUZZANELL
Purdue University

HELEN STERK
Calvin College

LYNN H. TURNER
Marquette University

SAGE Publications
International Educational and Professional Publisher
Thousand Oaks ■ London ■ New Delhi

For information:

Sage Publications, Inc.
2455 Teller Road
Thousand Oaks, California 91320
E-mail: order@sagepub.com

Sage Publications Ltd.
6 Bonhill Street
London EC2A 4PU
United Kingdom

Sage Publications India Pvt. Ltd.
B-42, Panchsheel Enclave
Post Box 4109
New Delhi 110-017 India

Printed in the United States of America on acid-free paper

Library of Congress Cataloging-in-Publication Data

Gender in applied communication contexts / Patrice M. Buzzanell,
Helen Sterk, and Lynn H. Turner, editors.
    p. cm.
Includes bibliographical references and index.
ISBN 0-7619-2864-2 — ISBN 0-7619-2865-0 (pbk.)
    1. Communication-Social aspects. 2. Sex role. 3. Women-Communication.
4. Feminist theory. I. Buzzanell, Patrice M. II. Sterk, Helen M., 1952-
III. Turner, Lynn H.
HM1206.G46 2004
302.2—dc21

                        2003013375

03   04   05   06   07   08   09   10   9   8   7   6   5   4   3   2   1

Acquiring Editor:	Todd R. Armstrong
Editorial Assistant:	Veronica K. Novak
Production Editor:	Claudia A. Hoffman
Typesetter:	C&M Digitals (P) Ltd.
Copy Editor:	Meredith L. Brittain
Indexers:	Rebecca J. Meisenbach and Robyn V. Remke

Contents

Foreword

I n 1992, the *Journal of Applied Communication Research*, in the wake of the Clarence Thomas Supreme Court hearings, published a special issue that provoked a good deal of discussion within the communication discipline. The issue featured stories of sexual harassment from members of the discipline, presented as written, along with critical analyses of those stories from the perspective of organizational communication and performance studies. I was privileged to edit the journal at that time and to work with Professor Julia Wood of the University of North Carolina, Chapel Hill, to execute her idea. Looking back, I believe that issue provided a turning point for feminist scholarship in communication. The articles in that special issue demonstrated that feminist theory could be used to analyze and provide correctives for the lived experiences of those in the discipline.

If anything, the communication discipline has become even more gendered since 1992. Women far outnumber men in both graduate and undergraduate programs in communication. The Women's Caucus is the largest unit within the National Communication Association, and the Feminist Studies in Communication Division is the third largest of the substantive units in membership, behind only Rhetorical and Communication Theory and Interpersonal Communication. Clearly, the contributions of both women and feminist scholars to the communication discipline are substantial.

The hallmark of gendered applied communication scholarship is a focus on social issues, the content of which serves either to reveal gender discrimination or to highlight the empowerment of women in a variety of settings. This development particularly pleases me because it coincides with a call I issued following the conclusion of my *JACR* editorship. In that call (Eadie, 1994) I indicated that the communication discipline could achieve its goal of becoming a greater part of the public consciousness by producing a body of research that presented insight into the solution of social problems. To do so, I argued, the discipline needed to become more deliberate about pursuing collective research agendas and about synthesizing and publicizing the research conducted as part of those agendas.

The National Communication Association (NCA), where I served as Associate Director from 1993 to 2001, created a research agenda for studying the impact of communication technologies on people's lives. In a booklet describing that agenda (Poole & Walther, 2002), the participants at an NCA-sponsored conference identified four "scientific and social challenges" to study. These challenges included the following:

1. To maintain and enhance a vigorous, self-renewing democracy

2. To promote the health and well-being of all

3. To help our organizations and institutions change in ways that enable our society to prosper in the emerging global economy

4. To enable people to live happy, meaningful lives and to have fulfilling relationships

The research reported in this volume responds to several of these challenges. Part I presents papers on telecommuting, the subtle linguistic features of sexual harassment, and alternative approaches to organizing, all of which respond to NCA's third challenge. Part II presents research that can certainly assist in the promotion of the health and well-being of all. Parts III and IV present research that can easily be construed as responding to the fourth challenge in the NCA brochure. Moreover, these contributions are not formed simply as a collection of studies. Their findings, several of which challenge conventional wisdom, are synthesized and commented upon by a series of expert scholars in each area. In my opinion, the structure of this volume enables the discipline to move forward in a more systematic manner than we have done previously.

Finally, these studies demonstrate the value of smaller, more specialized, scholarly organizations as vehicles for carrying out scholarly research agendas. Although I would be the last person to denigrate the value of discipline-wide associations such as NCA, their very nature does not lend itself well to systemic research. As groups such as the Organization for the Study of Communication, Language and Gender (OSCLG) demonstrate, having a concentrated period of time each year in which an "invisible college" of colleagues can be created is a key to doing the sort of intellectual work that produces agenda-driven research. These organizations are usually operated through the "sweat equity" of volunteers and take a great deal of time and energy to manage. Nevertheless, they promote a set of common research values, and they generate a set of questions that excite the scholars who participate year in and year out. In addition, the level of identification with and commitment to the organization produces excellent results.

My congratulations and thanks to all of the scholars whose work is represented in this volume. You have done a great service to the communication discipline by producing this work.

—*William F. Eadie*

Acknowledgments

We would like to extend our sincere appreciation to the following 43 editorial board members who reviewed chapters for our edited book.

Michael Arrington, Ohio University

Karen Ashcraft, University of Utah

Deborah Ballard-Reisch, University of Nevada at Reno

Judy Berkowitz, ORC Macro

Sandy Berkowitz, University of Maine

Nancy A. Burrell, University of Wisconsin at Milwaukee

Judi Dallinger, Western Illinois University

Debbie Dougherty, University of Missouri-Columbia

Alice Deakins, William Patterson College

Paige Edley, Loyola Marymount University

Laura Ellingson, Santa Clara University

Marlene Fine, Simmons College

Patricia Geist Martin, San Diego State University

Annis Golden, State University of New York at Albany

Steve Goldzwig, Marquette University

Beth Haslett, University of Delaware

Kate Hawkins, Clemson University

Sandra Herndon, Ithaca College

Jane Jorgenson, University of South Florida

Jeff Kassing, Arizona State University West

Madeline Keaveny, California State University-Chico

Joann Keyton, University of Kansas

Erika Kirby, Creighton University

Kim Kline, Southern Illinois University

Elisabeth Kuhn, Virginia Commonwealth University

Diane Martin, University of Portland

Marifran Mattson, Purdue University

Jill McMillan, Wake Forest
   University

Caryn Medved, Ohio University

Marcy Meyer, Ball State University

Wendy Morgan, Purdue University

Bren O. Murphy, Loyola University

Elizabeth Nelson, University of
   Minnesota at Duluth

Linda A. M. Perry, University of San
   Diego

Felicia Roberts, Purdue University

Amardo Rodriguez, Syracuse
   University

Lisa Skow, WatchMark Corporation

Patty Sotirin, Michigan
   Technological University

Patricia Sullivan, State University of
   New York at New Paltz

Angela Trethewey, Arizona State
   University

Paige Turner, St. Louis University

Richard West, University of
   Southern Maine

Steve Wilson, Purdue University

We would also like to thank our editorial assistants:

Rebecca Meisenbach, Purdue University

Robyn Remke, Purdue University

Introduction
Challenging Common Sense

Patrice M. Buzzanell,
Helen Sterk,
and Lynn H. Turner

C ommon sense, in terms of gender, tells us that men will be men and women will be women. This supposes that femininity and masculinity are stable, essential qualities inscribed in our genes that make women and men very different from one another. Further, this commonsense belief explains communication dilemmas between women and men by pointing to those seemingly essential differences. Sandra Bem (1993), in *The Lenses of Gender,* describes essentializing as one of the three culturally constructed ways that people use to understand gender. The other two are acting as if maleness were the norm for humanity and seeing women and men as polar opposites. Because people tend to believe that these three lenses answer all questions concerning gender, they are taken as normal and commonsensical.

Our book challenges culture's common sense. We illustrate some of the many and varied ways in which gender plays out in applied communication contexts, arguing through example that gender is best analyzed in specific historically and culturally situated places. In our book we offer examinations of gendered difficulties, struggles, and tensions in specific settings. These analyses include managing relationships with adolescent daughters, coping with intimate violence, communicating with health care providers, balancing work and home responsibilities, and integrating feminist practices in school settings.

Our two main goals are *first,* to illustrate how commonsense dichotomies fail to hold in the applied communication contexts of organizations, health institutions, educational settings, and family life; and *second,* to show how gender infuses and influences our everyday, ongoing communicative choices in these contexts. Our desire to reveal the complexity and importance of gender as an organizing and explanatory construct underlies and unites both these goals.

Four Critical Threads in *Gender in Applied Communication Contexts*

With these two goals in mind, we wove four critical threads throughout this book: (a) the importance of context, specifically the contexts of organizational, health, family, and instructional communication; (b) the ongoing tensions about how to frame central processes of gender, discourse, and context; (c) the necessity of keeping praxis visible in communication research; and (d) the critical task of advocating feminist transformation of communication practices.

The first thread, *the importance of context,* is exemplified in our belief that "difference" research (which assumes men and women are different and searches for general differences) oversimplifies situations because gender is not given, but enacted. Gender tests and creates as well as responds to contexts, and it is best analyzed as situated in specific times and places. Seeing gender in action in educational, family, organizational, and health contexts clarifies the ongoing process of gendering. We observe how gendering occurs through our linguistic choices, ordinary interactions, policies, routine ways of handling situations, and so on. Further, we view context as constitutive of gender. As people engage each other, they enact gender in ways that respond to and are shaped by situations.

Our foci on the complex interplay of gender, context, and discourse and the ways in which these processes shape and are shaped by each other are consistent with ongoing interdisciplinary feminist research and theorizing. Work by Karen Lee Ashcraft (in press) provides a schematic for organizing and critiquing gender, communication, and organizations. She suggests that there are four frames encompassing contemporary gender research: (a) discourse as outcome: gender identity organizes discourse; (b) discourse as performance: discourse (dis)organizes gender identities; (c) discourse as text-conversation dialectic: organizing (en)genders discourse; (d) discourse as social text: societal discourses (en)gender organization. We adapt her outcome, performance, dialectic, and social text lenses to focus on gender in applied communication contexts. The first thread of our analysis, and the chapters that reflect it, is reminiscent primarily of Ashcraft's third frame of gender. In it, Ashcraft establishes how applied communication contexts act as gendered discourse communities that suggest gendered scripts for members to enact and/or contest. In this frame, contextual discourses interpellate with gender. Although context may direct member practice, it does not determine it. Rather, gender and power narratives are constructed collectively. Buzzanell's chapter analyzing sexual harassment in academe (Chapter 2) is one example of research that emphasizes this sort of collective construction. Fink and Tucker's chapter (Chapter 17), which describes male abusers in domestic violence episodes and the interventions designed to break the gendered (masculine) scripts that they routinely follow, provides another example of gender's collective construction. Further, Fink and Tucker explore cultural contexts that foster certain kinds of masculinities, evolving legal (and other) remedies, and political controversies about defining violence and funding intervention programs. And Hylmö (Chapter 3) foregrounds telecommuting and in-house work arrangements in a hybrid (governmental and private sector) agency to show that where and how labor is performed can produce particular work, gender, family, and status identities.

Our second thread of *ongoing tensions about how to frame central processes of gender, discourse, and context* suffuses the chapters. Chapter authors are *not* writing about applied communication as either a prescriptive set of recommendations or a static entity. Instead, most are describing ways in which gender, discourse, and applied contexts intersect, shift, and form varied communication practices. In many of the essays in this collection, gender identities and communication structures have been destabilized, emerging as relatively fluid.

This thread of ongoing tensions resonates with Ashcraft's (in press) second frame, attending to the ways in which discourse (dis)organizes gender identities. Ashcraft focuses on the ways in which mundane interactions and situated discourse construct gender. Because the emphasis is on how individuals "do gender," the production and reproduction of gender differences, identity(ies) construction, and shifting power relations are central. In our collection, Meyer and O'Hara's chapter (Chapter 1) on the diverse interconnections between traditional institutions and temporary organizations (i.e., Ball State University and the National Women's Music Festival), heterosexual and lesbian identities, and co-opted discourses of dominant and subaltern groups portrays a revealing and exciting picture of behind-the-scenes negotiations among permanent and temporary residents of a particular site as they go about their activities. In addition, Ellingson's chapter (Chapter 5), about the ways women cope with the physical and emotional aftermath of disfiguring and disabling illnesses, shows how institutional norms and cultures both enable and constrain gendered identities, acting as underlying dynamics in the construction and resolution of identity dilemmas. Sotirin echoes this theme in Chapter 7 when she examines the cultural baggage related to women's bodies, specifically their breasts. Sotirin illustrates the tension between a woman's sense of her identity and cultural messages about the breast.

The third thread that pervades our edited collection is *the necessity of keeping praxis visible in communication research*. From the beginning, we envisioned this book as one that uses theory and research as a starting place for not only describing, but also challenging, everyday practices. This commitment to praxis infuses each chapter, connecting theoretical insights and contributions with pragmatic situations. The situations described in these chapters are those confronted by our students, ourselves, our family members, and our friends in daily life. For instance, Penington and Turner's chapter (Chapter 16), which focuses on mother-adolescent daughter interactions, challenges the accepted idea that mothers and their daughters are at odds during adolescence. Their respondents provided a fresh look at differences and commonalities within gender and across race and generations.

The central theme of praxis cuts across chapters concerned with different sites of communication, showing that feminist change need not be only at the level of formal or macro-level interventions. Rather, possibilities for change may take place in spontaneous conversations about body image (Russ, Chapter 12), in explorations of figurative language in a classroom (Buzzanell, Chapter 10), in interactions with family members while conducting paid work at home (Edley, Chapter 15), and in the talk and procedures of gynecological exams (Brann & Mattson, Chapter 8) and music festivals (Meyer & O'Hara, Chapter 1). Our authors use research/discovery, teaching/learning, service/active engagement as means of bettering the world for women and men (see Calás & Smircich, 1996). They explicitly state what can be done by whom with their theoretical insights, data analyses, and findings.

The fourth thread woven throughout the book is our hopefulness that the research promoted through the Organization for the Study of Communication, Language and Gender (OSCLG) will contribute to *feminist transformation of communication practices*. Specifically, *Gender in Applied Communication Contexts* uses feminist theory to analyze situations and construct realistic interventions for achieving greater workplace equity, for enhancing women's health outcomes, for developing more inclusive and thought-provoking classroom (and training workshop) practices, and for constructing family relationships that enable positive enactment of masculinities and femininities. This collection of essays reflects optimism about the possibilities for improving the lives of women and men.

Consciousness of our options enables us to bring the possibility for feminist transformation to the forefront. When people comprehend what is going on in a given situation, they possess the ability to challenge, contest, and sometimes change it. As such, our chapter authors are grounded in advocacy. We wish to change gendered practices in the direction of greater equity between women and men. We wish to challenge everyday assumptions about institutions such as health care, family, organizations, and schools, and transform them into spaces where women and men exercise their strengths and develop their sense of individuality.

We wish to explore local pockets of resistance to traditional thinking and practice. In so doing, we hope to give insight into how transformational processes begin. The chapters explore such transformational processes as social movements against domestic violence (Fink & Tucker, Chapter 17), Web sites and chat rooms where entrepreneurial mothers find and create empowerment (Edley, Chapter 15), friendships and interactions that can (re)assess women's body shaping discourses (Russ, Chapter 12; Sotirin, Chapter 7), legitimation of alternative health care practices and understandings of women's bodies (Ellingson, Chapter 5; Brann & Mattson, Chapter 8; Quintanilla, Cano, & Ivy, Chapter 6), alternative work locations (Hylmö, Chapter 3), and innovative classroom strategies based on feminist theory and engagement (Meyer, Chapter 11; Buzzanell, Chapter 10; Jaasma, Chapter 13; Russ, Chapter 12).

Insofar as research brings about awareness of some social or cultural issue, the implied next step is to motivate toward change. As Bowers and Buzzanell (2002) state,

> The process of translating awareness into advocacy often requires assistance of others not only to determine which of the many change strategies might be useful in a given situation but also to continue the process of interpreting and evaluating lived experiences in light of feminist commitments. (p. 29)

We invite you, as readers of this book, to be part of the process. We believe a fundamental task for feminist research involves not only describing communication situations and choices, but making sense of them within a feminist worldview and suggesting meaningful change strategies.

Gender in Applied Communication Contexts—Our Organizational Pattern

We developed four sections for *Gender in Applied Communication Contexts* based primarily on the applied communication context in which authors positioned their work. Because chapters share commonalities of framing and reframing discourse, applied contexts, gender, and identity construction, they could have been partitioned in a number of different ways. For instance, Meyer's discussion about feminist transformation in an organizational communication classroom (Chapter 11) could logically be placed in either Part I, "Organizing Gender," or Part III, "Constructing Pedagogy." Similarly, Edley's analysis of entrepreneurial mothers' discourse and practices as located on their Web sites and chat rooms (Chapter 15) provides insight into both "Organizing

Gender" (Part I) and "Empowering Family" (Part IV). Fink and Tucker's description of male abusers and the group-based interventions developed to prevent domestic violence (Chapter 17) could be placed within "Constructing Pedagogy" (Part III) as well as in "Empowering Family" (Part IV). So, our choice of where chapters should be situated displays some level of arbitrariness. However, our choices also indicate the ways gender, context, identities, and discourse shift depending on how one examines each process.

All the chapters view gender as socially constructed in ways that restrict opportunities for expression by both sexes, but they reflect a partial view of all the different points that could be made. For example, we could have focused more on men and masculinities and different sexual-social orientations. However, we do include masculinities and varied orientations in our chapters on domestic violence and male abusers (Fink & Tucker, Chapter 17) and lesbian music festival participants and organizers (Meyer & O'Hara, Chapter 1). Yet, because we believe that most applied communication theory and research still focuses more on men and traditional ways of constructing health, organizations, pedagogy, and families than on women and alternative perspectives of processes and issues, this book fills an important gap in the field's literature.

We also could have chosen to publish only empirical research articles. However, we wanted to portray the varied ways by which we come to know about and experience human nature, communication processes, identity construction, and the shifting boundaries around reason/emotion, work/family, masculine/feminine, and so on. Presentational formats range from traditional literature reviews and empirical studies to interviews, stories, autoethnographic sketches, and essays. We think the variety of methodological and theoretical approaches represented in this volume does justice to the many faces of current feminist research.

We acknowledge that we opted for depth rather than breadth in our collection. We maintain that most chapters in each section provide detailed and richly contextualized views of some ways women and men construct their identities, challenge public-private boundaries, and discursively (re)frame and (re)construct their lives.

In **Part 1:Organizing Gender** (editor: Patrice Buzzanell), we challenge the beliefs that organizational communication must focus on corporate America and on work prioritization. Instead, we look at the ways in which our different gendered, professional, familial, and organizational identities come into play as we try to figure out positive courses of action in our everyday interactions and in institutional policies. We highlight the ways in which our conceptualizations of and remedies for sexual harassment have proven woefully inadequate. We see how dominant and subaltern members exert agency while simultaneously feeling as though their options are constrained. We pull apart advice and procedures for alternative work arrangements, such as telecommuting, to locate different lenses that both undermine the possibilities for workplace change and that push organizational members to do work differently.

In **Part II: Gendering Health** (editor: Lynn Turner), we interrogate the beliefs surrounding medical practices: the supremacy of the physician, the passivity of the patient, and the benevolence of the system. This section explores the communication behaviors that may deconstruct these beliefs and bring better health care to women. The chapters focus on the ways in which gender is embodied and constructed through discourse: discourse with physicians, with supportive friends, and in the media. Further, discourse is viewed as a way to (re)construct gender in a more productive and healthful manner. The chapters in this section challenge commonsense responses to disease and health and, in so doing, they situate alternatives in language and practice.

In **Part III: Constructing Pedagogy** (editor: Helen Sterk), we argue that educational settings provide a key site for enacting feminist ways of knowing, teaching, and learning. The authors use their own experiences or research studies to suggest that sharing one's life with students, taking the risk of creating a safe space for discourse about gender and life, engaging in discourse about body shape, and intervening in middle school violence through gendered pedagogy flip ordinary ideas about how to educate. Instead of endorsing the notion of professor as the source of disembodied, objective knowledge, this section provides visions of feminist classrooms.

In **Part IV: Empowering Family** (coeditors: Patrice Buzzanell and Lynn Turner), we break from hegemonic constructions of family to delve into both the hopeful and the dark, tension-filled sides of close connections with others. Instead of concentrating only on white, middle-class families and assuming generational differences and problems, we look at racial/ethnic influences and commonalities in talk between black and white mothers and their adolescent daughters. Instead of focusing only on women and on positive aspects of relationship development or family life, we direct attention to men caught in unproductive masculinities and cultural directives that can prompt domestic violence. We describe some complexities in designing group-level interventions that emphasize choice and agency for male abusers. Instead of detailing corporate women's work-family dilemmas, we present resourceful groups of ordinary women who negotiate family and paid work time (and space) while conducting their businesses from their homes. In their daily struggles, they use technology to learn from, support, and assist each other in their work-life balancing and in their desire to be role models for their children.

To support the insights of the four sections and the chapters contained in each, four well-known scholars developed **commentaries** that respond to, interpret, and extend each section. In each commentary, the author talks about what is theoretically and pragmatically significant about the work in a particular section and how the ideas could be extended. We are pleased that Connie

Bullis, Gary Kreps, Richard West, and Kathleen Galvin provided thoughtful, provocative commentaries for the organizational, health, instructional, and family communication sections, respectively.

How This Book Came to Be

This collection of essays had its inception when the three editors planned the October 2000 conference for the Organization for the Study of Communication, Language and Gender (OSCLG) in Milwaukee, Wisconsin. Patrice Buzzanell, at that time President of OSCLG, designed breakfast discussion tables (at 7:30 a.m. with more than 60 people attending!) and panel sessions, workshops, and program details. Lynn Turner and Helen Sterk planned the conference program together, which meant not only a stimulating program of paper presentations but also an inviting social atmosphere with plenty of fabulous food and breaks for conversation between panels, art exhibits, and other events. We three worked to create a context for creative interaction and productive research.

We were so taken by the quality of the manuscripts presented at the conference that we began talking about a book immediately. We heard our themes articulated throughout the conference presentations and discussions and we realized that we had the basis for a collection focusing on gender enactment in applied contexts. The submissions coalesced around several main areas of applied communication—organizational, health, instructional, and family communication. Further, we saw in the papers ongoing tensions about how to frame central processes of gender, discourse, and context. We noted that the papers shared the basic value of keeping praxis visible in communication research. Finally, we believed that the research promoted through OSCLG could contribute to feminist transformation of communication practices. These observations coalesced into the four central themes that now inform our book.

These factors led us to propose an edited volume to Sage Publications— not just an anthology of the papers presented at the program, but a coherent set of essays that are tied to a central vision. To ensure the highest quality of chapters and the greatest opportunity for involvement, we opened up the submission process. In addition to OSCLG conference papers, we solicited manuscripts by placing a call for papers in outlets frequented by feminist communication researchers. To safeguard the high quality, coherence, and transformative nature of the book, the submitted papers underwent a rigorous and masked review process.

With the exception of two solicited essays in the family section—one on mother-adolescent daughter interactions and one on men charged with domestic violence—all chapters were sent out to two or more reviewers for recommendations and decisions. (In addition, reviewers provided extensive comments on the two chapters written by the first editor while knowing her identity. Since Patrice Buzzanell managed the review process, it would have been impossible to maintain reviewer anonymity in the case of her papers.) Forty-three percent of the competitively selected manuscripts are published in this book. Including the two invited essays, we are pleased to offer our readers 15 original chapters that have not been published elsewhere.

The 43 editorial board members who participated in this review process are listed at the beginning of this book. We selected these board members based on their subject matter expertise and/or feminist orientation to scholarship and practice. We are very grateful for their generosity in providing challenging and constructive commentary in a timely fashion. We could not have asked for a better group of advisors on this project.

Expressing Our Appreciation

As we have already noted, we are grateful for the detailed and helpful suggestions made by the 43 editorial board members and for the commentaries developed by Connie Bullis, Kathleen Galvin, Gary Kreps, and Richard West. In addition, Bill Eadie wrote a perceptive foreword to the volume, focusing on how feminist research in applied contexts can advance theory and provide correctives for troubling gendered experiences. We appreciate his thoughtful contribution to this work. We also want to extend our appreciation for the insightful recommendations of our proposal reviewers: Debbie Dougherty (University of Missouri at Columbia), Kathleen Galvin (Northwestern University), Steven Goldzwig (Marquette University), Linda Putnam (Texas A&M University), and Julia Wood (University of North Carolina at Chapel Hill). Finally, some of our student-colleagues contributed to the processing of this work. Rebecca Meisenbach and Robyn Remke from Purdue University volunteered to help Patrice send manuscripts out for review, track responses, and correspond with Lynn and Helen. As her editorial assistants, they helped create indices—a job that actually was fun because of their presence, laughter, and desire for lots of pizza and chocolate! Lynn's research assistant at Marquette, Jaime Leick, was an incredible proofreader and reference checker for the health communication section. We'd also like to thank Todd Armstrong at Sage for moving so quickly on our proposal and for his great suggestions.

Final Thoughts

The mark of productive theory and research is that we learn something new every time we pick up materials and reread them. In working on this book project, we have enjoyed exploring the different theoretical insights, personal stories, and concrete details in pragmatic applications that authors developed in their chapters. A first reading just scratches the surface of possibilities for theoretical extensions and directions for feminist advocacy. Repeated readings may enable readers to uncover different ways to enact change that may build upon or contest the findings of these chapters. We welcome the opportunity to facilitate this kind of transformational process and hope that this edited collection indeed enables our readers to challenge common sense.

Part I

Organizing Gender

1

When They Know Who We Are

The National Women's Music
Festival Comes to Ball State University

Marcy Meyer and Laura Shue O'Hara

D espite compelling calls for scholars to engage in diversity-related research within organizations (e.g., B. Allen, 1995; Fine, 1996; Wood, 1998a), the organizational communication literature on diversity remains relatively scarce (B. Allen, 1995; Fine, 1996). Of the few studies that do focus explicitly on diversity (e.g., the special issues of the 1996 *Journal of Business Communication* and the 1994 *Journal of Business and Technical Communication*), most conceptualize diversity in terms of sex-gender or race-ethnicity. Although these demographic definitions are useful in bringing attention to obvious and important aspects of diversity, they run the risk of reducing a multidimensional construct to a single variable. If we define diversity more broadly as "a variety of personal and social bases of identity, including race-ethnicity, gender, age, socioeconomic status, religion, sexual orientation, country of origin, etc." (B. Allen, 1995, p. 144), we are able to "recognize interplay among specific aspects of personal and social identity" (Wood, 1998a, p. 174). By exploring how multiple, often overlapping components of social and personal identity affect diverse interactants' communication with and about each other, we can develop a more nuanced understanding of what constitutes diversity in organizations, and thus hope to help organizations address diversity in more enlightened and appropriate ways.

According to Fine (1996), most organizational literature treats diversity as a resource that is "available to managers for their use in enhancing organizational effectiveness" (p. 487). From this perspective, intercultural communication theory is used primarily as a tool to achieve productivity through assimilation.

Because this approach glosses over power differences, it can have devastating consequences for individuals. Fine suggested that we reconceptualize diversity research as the study of "cultural voices in the workplace" (p. 486). We embrace Fine's approach because it allows us to explore discourses of resistance that marginalized group members use to undermine existing power arrangements and to nurture "multiple cultural identities" (p. 497). In addition, conceptualizing diversity as multiple, often marginalized voices allows us to rethink how we define organization. If we agree that marginalized voices should be the starting point for inquiry, then we can view organizations as diverse discourse communities, rather than interrelated systems of structures, roles, and responsibilities (Mumby, 2000).

Theoretical Groundings

Consistent with our conceptualization of diversity, we use feminist standpoint theory and the literature on subaltern counterpublics to examine gender and power in organizations.

STANDPOINT THEORY

Many feminist researchers (e.g., B. Allen. 1995; P. Collins, 1986; Dougherty & Krone, 2000; Harding, 1991; Mumby, 1996, Wood, 1992a) invoke standpoint theory to investigate the experiences of marginalized individuals, noting how distinct societal positions provide subjective vantage points "from which persons interact with themselves and the world" (Orbe, 1998, p. 5). Standpoint theorists (e.g., Buzzanell, 1995; O'Brien Hallstein, 2000) contend that, despite some commonalties in the standpoints among members of any given social group, differences still exist. Thus, of key importance is "the notion that no Archimedean point exists from which to objectively survey other standpoints; in essence, all 'truths' are standpoints" (Orbe, 1998, p. 5).

Some central convictions guide standpoint researchers. First, studies must originate from the lives and experiences of marginalized group members. Such positioning identifies varied standpoints among and within diverse social groups. Second, "knowledge always arises in social locations and is structured by power relations" (O'Brien Hallstein, 2000, p. 5). Indeed, marginalized members have the ability to see dominant societal structures from an "outsider-within" position (P. Collins, 1986), thus making insightful contributions to knowledge that traditionally has represented only the dominant, white, male perspective. Finally, standpoint theory is visibly political and action oriented, existing ultimately to make a positive impact on the lives of marginalized people as well as on society in general.

In this chapter, we use standpoint theory to explore marginalized and privileged voices that exist within and between two diverse organizations. In addition, Fraser's (1990-1991) concept of subaltern counterpublics offers us a heuristic model for examining organizational members' standpoints because it illustrates the ways in which discourse is central to identity construction.

SUBALTERN COUNTERPUBLICS

Fraser (1990-1991) defined *subaltern counterpublics* as "parallel discursive arenas where members of subordinated social groups invent and circulate counterdiscourses, which, in turn, permit them to formulate oppositional interpretations of their identities, interests, and needs" (p. 67). Maguire and Mohtar (1994), who defined *counterdiscourses* as discursive moves that reinforce community members' positions as counter to the practices and structures of the dominant culture (p. 241), applied Fraser's framework in an ethnographic study that demonstrated how members of a women's center engaged in counterdiscourses to create a positive group identity and to express resistance to stereotypes generated about them by members of the dominant public.

Although Maguire and Mohtar (1994) provided an excellent description of the ways that women working at the shelter articulated their identity in opposition to patriarchal discourse, their work (and Fraser's) reified a false dichotomy between powerful and powerless. By focusing on unified discourses of oppression and resistance, Fraser exaggerated the effect of societal forces over individual agency. Moreover, her framework failed to explore fully potential disunities that exist within *any* discourse. Her choice to focus exclusively on subaltern counterpublic resistance to oppression downplayed the dialogic communicative position that domination is mobile, situational, and not "done by" anyone (Deetz, 1996, p. 203).

To bridge this gap, we extend Fraser's framework by adding the concepts of marginalization/privilege and commonality/difference, drawn from feminist standpoint literature (e.g., K. Bell, Orbe, Drummond, & Camara, 2000; Carillo Rowe, 2000; P. Collins, 1986; Dougherty & Krone, 2000; Harding, 1991; O'Brien Hallstein; 2000; Wood, 1992a). In particular, we suggest that members of subaltern counterpublics may, at times, reproduce discourses of oppression. Moreover, in failing to acknowledge their positions of privilege, dominant group members may respond to members of subaltern counterpublics by co-opting subaltern discourses of resistance.

In our study, we examine the discursive interface between the National Women's Music Festival (NWMF) and Ball State University (BSU). For a short time each year, the NWMF becomes a "tenant organization" on BSU's campus, renting time and space to host a festival for several thousand women. Given that the NWMF is a women's music festival organized principally by lesbian feminists, NWMF members may appropriate some discursive moves of a subaltern counterpublic. In turn, given BSU's status as a state-supported, bureaucratic institution run primarily by and for dominant publics, BSU citizens may appropriate discursive moves of dominant publics. However, subaltern counterpublic members may co-opt the discursive moves generally associated with the dominant public (and vice versa).[1] Thus, we ask four questions:

1. What counterdiscursive moves do NWMF members, as citizens of a subaltern counterpublic, use to express resistance to the dominant public?

2. What discursive moves do BSU citizens, as members of the dominant public, employ to oppress NWMF members?

3. To what extent do NWMF members reproduce discursive moves of the dominant public?

4. To what extent do BSU members appropriate the counterdiscursive moves of a subaltern counterpublic in their own discourse?

Method

PARTICIPANTS AND CONTEXT

To offer a clearer picture of the discursive interstices between two diverse cultures, we provide brief descriptions of both groups (NWMF participants and BSU observers).

Research Participants. For interviews, we selected 25 *NWMF participants* *(festigoers)* who represented a diverse population of women. The festigoers ranged in age from 21 to 71, although most were in their 40s. Most also were lesbians. We recruited 20 *BSU students* who were enrolled in summer courses or who were working as assistants at the housing complex where the festival was headquartered. Students included an even number of males and females between the ages of 19 and 40, although most were in their 20s.

The Context. According to Eder, Staggenborg, and Sudderth (1995), the *NWMF* is the oldest women's music festival in the United States.[2] Organized primarily by lesbian feminists to promote women's music, the festival is also designed to help women network, provide educational opportunities, and create a safe, fun space where women can share their experiences. First organized at the University of Illinois at Champaign-Urbana in 1974, the festival moved to Indiana University in Bloomington in 1982. More recently, in 1998, the festival relocated to BSU in Muncie, Indiana, where it was held at the time of this study.

BSU is located in Muncie, Indiana, a mid-sized city about 60 miles northeast of Indianapolis. According to the Office of the Vice President for Student Affairs (2000), BSU was founded as Indiana State Normal School in 1918 when the Ball brothers (five Muncie industrialists) purchased a private teacher's college and donated it to the state of Indiana. By 1965, the institution had evolved into a state-supported university, at which point it adopted its present name. BSU currently serves approximately 17,500 students, 44% male and 56% female, including 2,000 graduate students. The students' ethnic and racial composition is homogeneous: 91% are European American; 7% are African American, Native American, Asian American, Hispanic, or Pacific Islanders; 2% are international students. About 15,500 are from Indiana.

PROCEDURES

We conducted an investigation of the discursive moves that NWMF and BSU members employed as they expressed their identities in shared organizational space. We used feminist ethnographic methodology to ground the data collection procedures, which included interviews, focus groups, and participant observation. We analyzed the data by categorizing and recategorizing emerging patterns, finally achieving consensus on the reported categories.

Feminist Ethnography. According to Lengel (1998) and DeVault (1999), feminist ethnography challenges theoretical, methodological, epistemological, and political assumptions that undergird traditional (patriarchal, elitist, capitalist, colonialist) ethnography and offers an alternative form of inquiry that examines the power relations of self and other in a self-reflexive manner. Feminist ethnographic research extends phenomenological methodology in a number of important ways (Langellier & Hall, 1989). In feminist research, women's everyday experiences play a central role in theory construction, making women's voices valid epistemological and theoretical sources. In addition, feminist research strives to minimize the power distance between researcher and researched, such that researchers have a moral obligation to involve participants. Finally, feminist researchers are politically committed to improve women's lives.

Consistent with standpoint theories, feminist ethnographic research begins with women's experiences and seeks positive social change. As Langellier and Hall (1989) noted, "Research *on* women views women as objects of research, whereas research *for* women conducts research for the purpose of empowering women" (p. 195). By viewing women's experiences as valuable resources for theory construction, research practice, and social action, feminist ethnography not only provides unique opportunities to generate new knowledge from women's standpoints, but also challenges researchers to go "beyond

the task of studying 'an other' and involve themselves in the life of 'another'"
(Frey, 2000, p. 181).

Paramount to redefining relationships between researchers and the
researched is a commitment to self-reflexivity. As Carillo Rowe (2000)
encourages white feminists to "find ways to examine, undefensively, how
whiteness both privileges and contains them" (p. 77), we self-reflexively
examine how, as participant-observers, we managed dialectical tensions of
privilege/subordination and inclusion/exclusion in the research process.

Data Collection Procedures. We conducted qualitative *interviews* with festigoers
from June 22 through June 25, 2000. We began the interviews by introducing
ourselves and our project, then asked about festigoers' demographics,
knowledge of the festival, and perceptions of the festival. Because these 15- to
30-minute interviews were recorded using pencil and paper, rather than
audiotape, we included interview data in our 40 pages of field notes.

During the 2-week period following the festival, we conducted both *interviews and focus groups* with BSU students and student workers who observed
the festival. We recruited students enrolled in summer classes as well as
students who were working at the conference. Although we attempted to
obtain accounts from food-service personnel, their supervisors did not grant
us permission to do so. We took notes during our interviews and audio-taped
the focus groups, resulting in 52 pages of transcriptions.

We used *participant observation* as a data-gathering technique during the
summers of 2000 and 2001. In particular, we participated as work-exchange
volunteers and festigoers to gain access to the festival culture, to establish
unique vantage points from which we could observe and interact with other
festigoers as they engaged in discourse about the festival, and to de-emphasize
power differences between researcher and the researched. We gathered *observational data* over the entire course of each festival. We observed formal and
informal interactions in the food court and in workshops, performances,
presentations, and the marketplace at varied times of day and night. We used
unobtrusive pencil-and-paper methods to record our informal interactions
and, as Fine (1996) suggested, journal accounts to preserve observations and
feelings about the festival and our positions as participant observers. Finally,
we gathered *archival data* about the festival "herstory," mission, and program
from the "Women in the Arts" Web site, which provided details about the
festival and 2000-2001 programs (see National Women's Music Festival
[NWMF], 2000a, 2000b, 2001).

Data Analysis Procedures. After we transcribed our field notes and audiotapes,
we carefully and repeatedly combed through our data to gain an understanding
of festigoers' and BSU students' reflections. After these initial readings, we used

thematic analytic techniques (Lindlof, 1995; Owen, 1984) to categorize our observations into broad semantic patterns.

Because our research questions required us to explore discursive moves made by members of different discourse communities (e.g., dominant public vs. subaltern counterpublic), we used standpoint theory as another analytic lens (e.g., P. Collins, 1986; Harding, 1991; Wood, 1992a). Congruent with feminist ethnography, this position assumes "interpretation in the interest of women" (Langellier & Hall, 1989, p. 194). However, given that standpoint theory "suggests ways to recognize what unites and differentiates women without essentializing them" (Wood, 1992a, p. 11), we also looked for divergent discourses. We identified counterdiscursive and discursive moves that festigoers and BSU observers used to construct their identities. We examined how social positioning informed festigoers' and BSU observers' responses. We attended to discursive constructions that varied systematically across social boundaries of sex/gender, race/ethnicity, sexual orientation, class, age, and able-bodiedness. We shared preliminary discursive and counterdiscursive moves with one another, highlighting complementary findings. Finally, we critically assessed the consistency of our interpretations, recategorizing examples and collapsing categories of discursive moves until we achieved consensus on all analytic decisions.

Results and Interpretations

As we interpreted festigoers' and BSU members' festival accounts, "places" and "spaces" emerged as powerful themes, evidenced by discursive and counterdiscursive moves that they used to construct their own and each other's identities (for politics of space and place in identity constructions, see Aden, 1999; Buzzanell, 1995; de Certeau, 1984; Flores, 1996; Harvey, 1990; P. Collins, 2000; Massey, 1994; Moraga & Anzaldúa, 1983; Rakow, 1988; Spain, 1992; Spigel, 1989; Spitzack & Carter, 1987). In this section, we explore how festigoers and BSU citizens employed discursive moves to embrace and resist diversity in the festival milieu.

A PLACE FOR BUILDING COMMUNITY

Theorists such as Conquergood (1994), Flores (1996), and Moraga (1983) have emphasized the significance of being part of a safe, welcoming community: a place where marginalized group members can experience the sense of identity confirmation and cohesion that is largely absent from other areas of their lives. Conquergood articulated the importance of community among gang members who rely on the rhetoric of family and safe home spaces to symbolically create trust, intimacy, and community in the midst of "a mainstream world where residents of the inner city have been marginalized socioeconomically and stripped of human dignity" (p. 43). A strong community identity sustained through members' discourse is a response to social structures that disaffirm those in gangs. Similarly, Maguire and Mohtar (1994) found that women's center members enact countercultural discursive moves to carve out space for their own subaltern counterpublic.

Consistent with this research, festigoers used counterdiscursive moves to highlight the communal spirit of their own subaltern counterpublic, wherein their lesbian identities and values are affirmed. Many festigoers expressed relief and joy at being able to safely declare their sexuality and women-centeredness among like-minded individuals. As one festigoer noted, the NWMF was about "community more than anything. It's nice to have an atmosphere where you can be open about sexuality." A group of three festigoers agreed that they experienced a community feeling from the start and reveled in the "openness" they felt from the group. One of these festigoers remarked that feelings of community and acceptance have been a primary feature of all of her NWMF experiences, "from the first one [in Bloomington] until now."

Counterdiscursive moves deconstructing the typical hierarchy that exists in the dominant public discourse were important expressions of lesbian community values within this women-centered space. One young festigoer, who was also a performer in the festival's smallest venue, "The Bloomington Café," noted that even more meaningful to her than her own performance were her interactions with other performers and participants. She observed that there was "camaraderie and support for each other" among performers. She was surprised and happy to learn that, in contrast to her usual performances, there was no competition, especially among new performers: "I feel like everyone wants genuine success [for every performer]." Another young woman said that her backstage work with well-known artists such as Dar Williams at the main stage concerts was "like an extension of women's studies programs" with "no power struggles."

Our observations confirmed these festigoers' claims: Constructions of hierarchy were consciously and constantly "leveled" by performers as they lessened the social distance between "fan" and "celebrity." For example, well-known lesbian activist and playwright Carolyn Gage and singer-songwriter Lucie Blue Tremblay (headliners at the festival) hosted personal empowerment workshops to give festigoers a chance to interact with them in more intimate settings. Tremblay and Chris Williamson (another headliner) spent much stage time telling audience members of personal travails. These accounts positioned these stars in a down-to-earth light to which, judging by audience reactions, many festigoers related.

Counterdiscursive moves within the NWMF supported the value of collectivity and rejected individualism and hierarchy, which define patriarchal discourse (for similar discussions of marginal group communication, see Alarcón, 1990; Conquergood, 1994; Flores, 1996; Padilla, 1992). However, some festigoers indicated that the festival was not community-oriented enough. One participant observed that there was "no central feeling of 'festival.'" She felt that it was "less intimate—less sense of community [than other festivals she had attended]," adding that there was "no other communal space if someone were alone," making it "very isolating." Others described the site as "disconnected spatially," commenting that the marketplace was "not a real marketplace [because the] open space is missing."[3] For them, the ideal community was constrained by segmented physical facilities built to satisfy institutional needs. This articulation of unrealized ideals is a reminder that the NWMF is an ephemeral organization that inscribes its identity tenuously on space and time leased from a bureaucracy that serves the dominant public.

Despite these women's views, most festigoers' comments reflected appreciation of the NWMF space to enact alternate (lesbian) ways of being in the world. This finding echoes Eder et al.'s (1995) observation that attendees imbued the NWMF with a sense of "unity" associated with "women's space" and values. Closely linked to their perceptions that the NWMF was a place for community, festigoers used counterdiscursive moves to construct the festival as a safe space where they could express their lesbian identities. For many festigoers, such free expression stands in stark contrast with how they express themselves in the dominant culture, where many believe they must hide their identities. (According to Dwyer and Slaybaugh, 2001, results from a 2000 member survey revealed that 43% of lesbians attending the festival were not "out.") Although both festigoers and BSU students articulated the safety theme, it was understandably more salient for festigoers.

In one festigoer's words, the festival is a "women-only space . . . and because it gives women their own space I feel safer here." In comparing the "women's space" of the NWMF to "life outside," she remarked, "We live in a rat race. . . . Where can you go? I tend to get lost in bullshit, in economic abuse, social abuse." This festigoer noted that "women's space is sacred and extremely empowering." Origins of her empowerment were related to her joy at being able to express her identity, a sentiment manifest in her comment that she was being mirrored by another festigoer: "I see myself in her, she sees herself in me, and I say, 'Ain't I pretty?'" Another festigoer echoed the sense that there is an "atmosphere of acceptance and safety I can't feel in the real world."

Although many festigoers voiced such views, one workshop facilitator perceived things differently, commenting that "I don't feel quite safe." Ironically, the festival was "not scary, challenging, overwhelming enough" for her. As she observed, "There's no liberation here." This apparent contradiction seems less a criticism of the NWMF than an indictment of BSU. Given her standpoint as a radical lesbian feminist, the ideal festival would be situated in a place that rejects all elements associated with male-identified culture. Thus, in her view, real liberation cannot occur at this festival because it is situated within BSU, a bureaucracy embedded in a larger culture that we (the authors) satirically dubbed "Man-see," Indiana, to invoke an image of a patriarchal panopticon where lesbians are under constant scrutiny by members of the dominant (het-erosexual) public and "the oppression of women is linked to the oppression of deviant sexualities" (Harding, 1991, p. 261).

BSU students also discursively constructed the festival as a safe place. One noted that the festival is "an opportunity [for festigoers] . . . to come together without a fear of being insulted or demeaned in any way." Another student per-ceived the NWMF event as a site where festigoers "can be free, where they can take those masks down that they constantly have to wear on a daily basis they have to put up in our society, and they were able to free themselves." A lesbian student who attended BSU during the rest of the year, when it's "unsafe for lesbians," commented that she felt as if the whole campus were relatively safe during the NWMF.

Most narratives constructed the festival as a safe place for women and lesbians to escape multiple forms of oppression (e.g., sexism, heterosexism, feminism, ablism) that are prevalent in the larger society. Yet, this "safe space" was circumscribed: In one student's view, women displaying lesbian identities in the fairly confined geographic area of the festival were safer than lesbians displaying their value system in a public place away from campus.

A Political Place

The festival provided opportunities for festigoers to escape the constraints of dominant discourse and to engage in teaching and learning about lesbian feminist politics—a risky activity in most public arenas. Indeed, a number of festigoers used counterdiscourse to frame the festival as a place where older festigoers taught their young counterparts about the importance of ongoing political struggles. An older festigoer admonished, "You gotta pass the torch on. We are fucking burnt out!" Another explained, "It's our responsibility to teach them 'herstory.' . . . It's a teach and learn situation—they're reminding me that I was in their shoes, but they don't have to be underground." Younger festigoers shared the emphasis on learning. A member of a younger couple commented, "this whole experience . . . felt like a rite of passage" in which they were "gaining wisdom from older women's stories" and were given a chance to relate history to women of their own generation. Another younger festigoer observed that it was "neat to see older women who have walked the walk—those responsible for us and our ability to be a bit more open and accepted."

Although these younger women considered learning from older women a terrific opportunity, they also acknowledged that it could be challenging: One couple felt uncomfortable because they were "not used to interacting as peers to older women." Another woman felt frustrated that the learning was one-way: "All I can do is gain from older women, [but] I have little to share."

Some BSU students discursively constructed the festival in political terms by acknowledging its importance to the festigoers. As one noted, the festival was "a way for women to congregate and talk about women's issues, and learn from each other and grow strength off each other." Another student explained that "the festival is where women come together all across the world to do a lot of arts, crafts, music, education about lesbianism, programs about . . . What's the word I'm looking for? . . . women's rights." Another student extended this idea:

> Uh, it was my understanding that it was a festival that celebrated the awareness of basically what it meant to be a woman in any direction that a female wanted to take in our society . . . or any capacity. Just a celebration of independence as a gender . . . I think it's a good feminist thing.

BSU students' linguistic choices indicated denotative hesitancy (Clair, 1993c), or difficulty in labeling the festival aspect that dealt with feminist politics. Hesitancy may reflect observers' lack of personal experience with feminist activism, their perception of "feminist politics" as unpopular, or their attempts to remove themselves rhetorically from knowledge of the issue.

Festigoers' and students' framing of the festival as "a political place" provides only partial clues to explain how it was discursively constructed as a subaltern counterpublic. Festival programs also reveal the myriad ways counterdiscourses were used to raise awareness of lesbian feminist political issues. For example, Chastity Bono, the keynote speaker at the 2000 festival, addressed the challenges in "coming out" in a largely homophobic society. At the 2001 festival, former congresswoman Sabrina Sojourner's keynote address focused on "building bridges of understanding across differences, including race, gender, and sexual orientation" (NWMF, 2001, p. 34). Most performance artists, musicians, poets, and comediennes satirized dominant Western cultural attitudes toward lesbian and feminist issues. Many workshops discussed political issues. For example, "Grrrrls in Action" invited participants "to share experiences and advice with other activists, young and old" (NWMF, 2000b, p. 33). Main stage performance artists used song and comedy to explore social issues that many lesbian women face. Indeed, for the past 15 years, festival organizers have marked the official commencement by opening the first main stage performance with a video montage that dramatically highlights the struggles, defeats, and victories of lesbian feminist social movements. Accompanied by the feminist anthem, "One Fine Day," this video is a particularly powerful counterdiscursive move that reminds festigoers of the importance of continued social action.

In addition to performers' counterdiscursive moves, large tables near festival headquarters—the heart of NWMF—overflowed with literature encouraging festigoers to become more actively involved in political issues affecting lesbian communities. Included were advertisements for other women's festivals; lists of local and national support groups for lesbians; flyers announcing gay pride events; and publications, such as *Take Action* and *Lesbian Connection,* which urged readers to support anti-hate-crime and human-rights legislation. Embedded within this literature were thousands of powerful counterdiscursive moves. For example, one Human Rights Campaign brochure displayed virulent antigay quotes from right-wing religious and political leaders. In this counterdiscursive move, lesbian activists co-opted dominant conservative rhetoric to promote human-rights legislation.

To invoke an often-used mantra of feminist politics, for many festigoers the "personal is political." In one festigoer's words, the NMWF "focuses on what's real for me as a woman." Another added, "It's a reminder of work we have to do to make the world better." These women's observations are supported by workshops dedicated to such varying life issues as alternate spiritualities, "taboo" sexualities, financial and legal concerns, domestic violence, substance abuse, coming out, and strategies for children of lesbians to manage heterosexuals' inquiry about their family structure (NWMF, 2000b).

Festigoers also used their bodies as highly charged political canvases, upon which they displayed innumerable counterdiscursive moves that simultaneously resisted patriarchy and affirmed lesbian identity. A quick tour of the festival site revealed women wearing lesbian pride fashions. The brightest and most omnipresent were rainbows. This universal symbol of gay pride was manifest in necklaces, earrings, shoes, bracelets, headbands, eyeglass lanyards, and so on. Most festigoers also sported jewelry depicting ancient goddesses, crones, and Amazon warriors. Particularly prevalent was jewelry adorned with the *labrys,* a double bladed axe symbolizing female independence from patriarchy and tribute to ancient matriarchies.

Other counterdiscursive moves were apparent in festigoers' grooming. Although some festigoers wore stereotypically feminine hairstyles and makeup, the vast majority did not—one festigoer even sported a beard. Also missing from festigoers' appearance were the types of constraining fashion (e.g., high heels, form-fitting clothing, short shorts) typically associated with Western women's wear. Instead, festigoers tended to wear comfortable clothing (e.g., loose-fitting jeans with baggy T-shirts, or "goddess wear" consisting of bright-colored shirts and pants or long, flowing dresses). Finally, some women's large physiques could be interpreted as clear moves to counter patriarchal discipline of the female body (e.g., Banet-Weiser, 1999; Bordo, 1993; Shapiro, 1998; N. Wolf, 1991).

Perhaps the most attention-getting counterdiscursive moves were festigoers' public displays of romantic affection (PDAs). Lesbian couples held hands, hugged, kissed, and snuggled together on the campus green. These lesbian PDAs made many BSU students uncomfortable. Harding (1991) explains such discomfort as a reflection of the patriarchal belief that "feminism is 'unnatural' . . . just as are homosexuality and any attitude toward sex and gender that male supremacy chooses not to legitimate" (p. 263).

Thus far, we have demonstrated how subaltern counterpublic members use particular discursive moves to construct their political identities in opposition to dominant public discourse. Festigoers' social positioning and past festival experiences provide a schema for their critiques of the extent to which the festival's social, physical, and political characteristics contributed to and, in some cases, detracted from their notion of an ideal festival. Contrary to our expectations, most BSU students were extremely supportive of the festival and were not overtly hostile to festigoers. However, as we probed more deeply, we noted that BSU students did indeed use discourse to subtly sequester subaltern counterpublic members.

A Contested Space

As Fine, Weis, Addelston, and Marusza (1997) observed in their study of white working-class males who experienced an erosion of economic and cultural privilege, "identities [are] carved inside, and against, demographic and political territories" (p. 65). When festigoers and observers described their interactions with one another, they recalled numerous conflict episodes reminiscent of organizational culture stories (see Bartunek & Moch, 1991; E. Young, 1989) in which subcultural members struggle to maintain identities and claim cultural spaces.

One way in which these conflicts surfaced during the festival was through "turf wars" between festigoers and BSU students and personnel. Festival security workers described tensions that arose when festigoers shared space with other groups on the BSU campus, notably teenagers attending camps. When asked how conflicts arose, one security worker explained that sometimes boys or their fathers would make inflammatory comments (e.g., "I can't believe that *she*'s security"). Similarly, a student conference assistant noted, "A couple of times in the past, I saw members of a boy's junior high basketball camp yelling 'fucking lesbians' or 'dykes' at lesbians who were walking outside during the day holding hands." Other times, it was festigoers who provoked teenage girls in the cafeteria with comments such as "mmm . . . now *there's* a buffet."

Just as the conflicts themselves were clear moves to claim territory and assert identity, so too were the strategies festigoers and BSU citizens used to frame these conflicts. Humor was the most prevalent strategy invoked by festigoers. When asked about ways to respond to "ignorant" comments from teenage boys, one security worker suggested the retort, "You know, I bet I've had more pussy this week than you have had in your whole life." Her coworkers responded to her remark with peals of laughter. However, one student worker, who reported a similar conflict to his supervisor, treated the incident much more seriously: He noted that a Ball State basketball player who was walking with the boys chose not to confront them about their heterosexist behavior. Expressing anger about the player's inaction, he lamented that such incidents perpetuated for outsiders an undesirable image for BSU. He suggested that confrontation and education were preferred conflict-management strategies, but he admitted that he was at a loss as to how these strategies could be taught. Finally, BSU citizens employed separatism as a strategy to minimize dominant public and subaltern counterpublic conflicts. For example, one BSU adminis-trator, who asked not to be identified, used the term *isolationism* to describe the university's position on the festival, remarking that the goal was to keep festigoers largely "confined to an indoor space" and "discretely away from others." Ironically, in embracing containment, BSU citizens co-opted the sepa-ratist dimension of radical feminism as a means to "manage diversity" while privileging institutional goals (i.e., containment minimizes diversity-related conflict). As Lindsley (1998) observes, social isolation, like containment, clearly communicates prejudice.

However, as with prejudice, conflicts over space and identity do not always manifest themselves in obvious ways (de Certeau, 1984). For example, one student's articulation of public space as "heterosexual turf" was a subtle discursive move that sequestered festigoers. Although he disclosed that two of his good friends were a lesbian couple, he exposed his discomfort with visible lesbian sexuality when he described his uneasiness as several lesbian couples danced and "made out" at a local club: "It was . . . kind of weird. . . . I'm not used to seeing that out in public, you know. If I was going to a gay bar, then I'd expect it." Despite some statements to the contrary (e.g., "it's not that big of a deal"), his discursive moves constructed lesbian sexuality as deviant (Harding, 1991) and supported the sequestration of lesbian culture to places invisible to those in the dominant culture (e.g., gay bars). His discursive move echoes one female student's earlier assertion that lesbians' "safe space" was a "little circle" far removed from the public eye.

A Liminal Space

Chicana feminists (e.g., Anzaldúa, 1987; Flores, 1996; Moraga & Anzaldúa, 1983) have written extensively about the difficulties they experience as marginal citizens caught between clashing value systems. As we explored our data, we noticed that some of us constructed festival experiences as liminal—that is, balancing acts performed at the threshold of two cultures. For example, one festigoer mentioned that this was her first festival and that she found it to be "fun, but strange." When asked to elaborate, she mentioned that although her mother was a lesbian, she was straight and felt as though she did not belong. This sentiment resonated strongly with both of us as researchers who had political and identity stakes in both BSU and the NWMF.

In particular, Laura struggled with the ethics of identity management, becoming keenly aware of how boundaries guided her discursive choices:

> I could literally feel the culture shift. One afternoon . . . I took off my NWMF badge, not wanting the students [away from the festival] to identify me as a festi-goer or as a lesbian. For them to have done so might threaten my privileged BSU identity as heterosexual and as a faculty member. . . . It wasn't until I was fully back on NWMF turf that I put my badge back on. . . . I felt like I was "cheating" on the festigoers and betraying all my lesbian friends.

In addition, Marcy recalled a festival experience when she was "outed"[4] as a heterosexual:

> Although I had initially been perfectly comfortable with the ambiguity surround-ing my sexual orientation, I became equally uncomfortable when Tina asked me point-blank if I were gay. After being "outed" as a heterosexual I realized that I held outsider/insider status at the festival. . . . In some senses, I have never felt like I really belong at Ball State. . . . In contrast, I felt immediately embraced by the warmth of the festival culture. I felt like I shared a special bond of sisterhood with everyone around me and that my sisters would accept me as I was. Suddenly, after being outed, I wasn't so sure.

When Marcy disclosed her feelings about her "in-between group" mem-bership status, a middle-aged security worker divulged that sometimes she felt like she did not belong because she was a lesbian who was also married to the man who fathered and co-parented their teenage daughters. She added that some people think that you're not a "real" lesbian if you don't fit their defini-tion of what a lesbian is. She derided the exclusivity of the Michigan Women's Festival "women-born women only" admission policy, pointing out that the NWMF was made up of women-born women, men-born women, hetero-sexuals who have become lesbians, and those who are unsure about their sexuality. She emphasized that "the most important part of the festival is that we're all women."

As this exchange reveals, dialogue is a way that privileged and marginal-ized citizens can come together to construct a common philosophical ground. Through empathetic dialogue, respondents reframed their isolating experiences as shared experience to propel themselves out of the margins and into the center.

Festigoers' accounts also illustrated how they felt marginalized by BSU students and workers. In one festigoer's words, some BSU members seemed "a little snippy—like they were nervous about lesbians. They had very little eye contact, which makes you wonder." Another participant observed "urban behaviors, like no eye contact." Although she thought that the staff was very friendly, "they seem scared [and] can't understand Bit [her bearded friend]." Such discursive moves by members of the dominant public made these festigoers feel unwelcome and invisible.

In a parallel fashion, BSU students' narratives illustrated how they felt marginalized by festigoers. One student talked about how he felt out of place as a man at the festival:

> Um, from what I understand, from what I saw, there were quite a few, what's the word I'm looking for . . . lesbians. There were a lot of women, actually mostly women. Actually I didn't see any men . . . I felt pretty much like . . . out of place a little bit (laughs).

Similarly, another male student noted, "One thing is that I felt the presence of them hating me. A lot of times I felt like a minority—they didn't want me around." Next, he reframed and downplayed the experience, adding, "I haven't often felt like a minority. . . . This was one time when I did feel that way—I was like, oh my god, what do I do? I was fine, though—it was just a new experience." He added: "When I felt that they didn't want me around—well, I didn't know for sure . . . I just assumed—I felt like it was silly to think that. . . . I was just stereotyping them. . . ." Although both men downplayed the extent to which they felt uncomfortable, their descriptions indicate their recognition of the discursive strength of subaltern counterpublic numbers on BSU's campus. Indeed, the sheer number of festigoers "spooked" (to borrow M. Daly's, 1978, term) dominant members, forcing them to feel marginalized on their own turf.

In addition, one of these students—a European American male—talked about feeling "unwanted," "hated," and "upset." However, he dismissed his feelings as "silly," "just a new experience," and a product of "stereotyping." Thus, he simultaneously validated and invalidated his feelings. He framed feelings of being marginalized as natural consequences of being a minority group member. Reminiscent of sexually harassed female workers in Clair's (1993c) study, this student employed trivialization and reification as framing devices to sequester harassment, thereby perpetuating his own perceived subordination. Although he recognized his position of privilege, he quickly constructed a victim identity for himself. In this way, he, as a member of the dominant public, successfully co-opted discourses of marginalization and oppression traditionally associated with subaltern counterpublic members.

Another male student, who described the performers and the workers as "so kind . . . especially to my daughter," went on to recount a negative experience that he had: "I did hear three or four comments like, 'What are the breeders doing here?,' which shocked me that they would say anything within earshot. And I felt intimidated that I couldn't, you know, turn around and say anything." This story expressed the observer's discomfort at being labeled as a "breeder" (a slang term for heterosexuals used by some gay and lesbian people). He did not confront his harassers because of his (perceived) powerlessness. Ironically, by ignoring the harassment because he "couldn't . . . say anything," he perpetuated his (imagined) subordination and co-opted discourses of marginalization and oppression traditionally employed by subaltern counterpublic members. Yet, he failed to reflect on the singularity of this incident that occurred outside of his "normal" everyday life. As a white, straight, married graduate student, he did not seem cognizant of his own privileged position.

In counterpoint, an African American male student reflected on his minority status: "I'm normally the minority anyway. So that kind of didn't faze me. . . . It was fun." Perhaps his minority standpoint in a mostly white community enabled him to relax and enjoy the festival experience, because being "the other" was not new to him.

Conclusions and Beginnings

We investigated how members of the NWMF (as a subaltern counterpublic) and BSU (as an organization whose members represent a dominant public) discursively constructed their own and each other's identities as they shared space on BSU's campus. Our analysis and interpretation of participant narratives, observational data, and archival documents uncovered a variety of ways in which festigoers and BSU students employed discursive and counterdiscursive moves that both embraced and resisted diversity. In this section, we summarize these moves, discuss our theoretical contributions, reflect on our own positions as feminist researchers, and articulate how we can contribute to the activism that is such an integral part of feminist research.

SUMMARY

Festigoers, as subaltern counterpublic members, frequently engaged in counterdiscursive moves that expressed resistance to dominant discourses. Festigoers expressed joy, pride, and relief that a "safe," "sacred," "women-only" (albeit temporary) space allowed them to celebrate their communal and personal identities. Many festigoers constructed the festival as a forum where participants could openly engage in feminist political activity. Yet, this notion of a prefigurative feminist community was not a unified discourse, given that other participants expressed disappointment because, from their points of view, the space lacked community.

As liberating as the festival space was, it was also sequestered. In some cases, BSU citizens enacted discursive moves to keep the NWMF hidden from the view of students and campus visitors. There were also contested spaces between festigoers and BSU citizens: Both students and festigoers expressed accounts of discomfort or hostility in interactions with each other. These accounts indicate how dominant public members used discursive moves to oppress festigoers and how festigoers resisted such moves. Ironically, festigoers sometimes reproduced the very discourses of oppression that they railed against, whereas BSU students co-opted discourses of oppression to protest their marginalization by festigoers.

Despite the differences expressed by members of each organization, there were shared spaces that promoted feelings of connection. Yet, as researchers with political stakes in both organizations, we often occupied liminal spaces, unsure of our own positions as we negotiated our way through the festival, a space that was both welcoming and unfamiliar. As we managed dialectical tensions of privilege/subordination and inclusion/exclusion, we learned about the personal and political process of developing our standpoints.

THEORETICAL AND PRACTICAL CONTRIBUTIONS

This study fuses feminist standpoint theory with Fraser's (1990-1991) work on subaltern counterpublics to generate new knowledge about discursive constructions of organizational diversity. It also makes a valuable contribution to feminist ethnography by extending Eder et al.'s (1995) work examining collective identity and diversity in the NWMF. Using participant observation and interviews, Eder et al. documented how the festival helped most participants (primarily white, middle-class, lesbian feminists) create a positive collective identity. At the same time, they pointed out how this strong collective identity marginalized nonlesbian and minority women. This dialectic of inclusion/ exclusion was also evident in our analysis. Although Eder et al.'s analysis uncovered racial and sexual orientation tensions among festigoers, their study examined neither how participants managed tensions discursively nor how festigoers and dominant members negotiated identities and space. By analyzing these strategies, our work offers a more nuanced understanding of how members of diverse groups discursively articulate their often contrasting worldviews and how organizations operate as "important public spheres in which identities and worldviews are fundamentally shaped" (Mumby, 2000, p. 4).

In addition, our study provided a valuable opportunity to create dialogue about diversity at BSU. Although BSU's leadership expresses commitment to promoting acceptance and understanding among culturally diverse people, BSU is situated within the larger context of Muncie, Indiana, a relatively homogeneous, conservative community (Middletown Area Studies, 1994, 1998).

In contrast, the NWMF culture is liberal, lesbian, and women-centered (Eder et al., 1995). Given these cultural differences, it is not surprising that BSU citizens and NWMF members experienced surprise and discomfort when their cultures intersected. By gaining greater knowledge about discursive moves used by diverse cultural members, our work enhances understanding of the ways in which tensions may be exacerbated or defused through interaction.

Promoting Collaborative Partnerships

Many feminist scholars have failed to include accounts of their own positions of privilege in contrast to the positions of those whom they study (B. Allen, 1995; Carillo Rowe, 2000). In attending to this criticism, we acknowledge that the story we have told is filtered though our eyes. We are middle-class, European American, heterosexual, Ph.D.-holding women in various stages of understanding feminist possibilities for our research. What we see and interpret is very much a relic of our own privileged (and evolving feminist) standpoints. But, this should be more than a confession. How can we integrate this insight into future research?

We are committed to improving the lives of the women at the festival as well as the lives of students at BSU. Therefore, our goals for future research include returning "our interpretations to the persons whose communicative experiences we seek to give voice in our research" (K. Bell et al., 2000, p. 57), including diverse others who possess the multiple consciousnesses about which we write as coauthors, and balancing our academic agendas with coresearchers' agendas, taking care not to commodify relationships we have built with our campus colleagues and students, nor with our friends and co-researchers. Toward these ends, we envision using electronic technologies (e.g., interactive Web sites) to foster the critical exchange of ideas with geographically dispersed coresearchers during future projects. At present, we invite our readers to join us in critical reflection about extant organizational communication research practices.

Fostering Dialogue About Diversity

The NWMF provides a crucial network for many women who are marginalized in the larger public discourse. We are committed to helping them pursue the festival's mission to promote "the creative talents and technical skills of women in the visual, performing, and fine arts [and to facilitate] the growth, knowledge, and empowerment of women in the varied aspects of their lives" (NWMF, 2000a). Our knowledge of organizational communication provides us with certain tools that are needed by but are too costly for nonprofits (Droge & Murphy, 1999).

As we mentioned earlier, the NWMF is at a challenging crossroads in its "herstory." Members are getting older and have been unable to recruit enough young women to ensure the organization's future. In addition, the NWMF continually encounters fiscal problems that threaten its viability. We are in an excellent position to apply organizational communication theory to help the NWMF manage change effectively. Further, we can use our positions as BSU faculty to help BSU citizens embrace diversity by building stronger connections between BSU and the NWMF. The members of numerous student groups that might be considered "subaltern counterpublics" might forge mutually beneficial links with the NWMF.

In addition, we are compelled to carry the tenets of feminist scholarship to points of greater social impact (see Dougherty & Krone, 2000; O'Brien Hallstein, 2000) precisely *because* we are educators and teach in varied educational arenas, such as consulting (Fine, 1996). We have opportunities to bring various dominant and subaltern publics together to engage in dialogue and learning. Specifically, teachers or consultants might use standpoint theories to help students or organizational members engage in more meaningful dialogues about diversity by encouraging reflection, articulation of standpoints, and coauthoring narratives that discuss *in depth* commonalities and differences (Dougherty & Krone, 2000). Through the use of "invitational rhetoric" (S. Foss & Griffin, 1995), participants can embrace social issues from various standpoints.

Standpoint theory is just one model that we can use to teach others to reflect thoughtfully on issues of diversity. Through dialogue and discursive reconstruction of our public and private organizations, we can fortify the social, political, and economic well-being of people who have remained marginalized by those discourses in the past. For those who remain pessimistic about achieving such lofty social aims, we invoke the words of feminist songwriter Jamie Anderson:

> Things are changing, see it all unfurl
>
> Gay and straight together in acceptance in this world . . .
>
> The world will change when they know who we are . . . (Anderson, 1995)

Anderson's lyrics evoke images of a world where diverse people value rather than mistrust each other. In this spirit, we hope that our work enhances knowledge about communication among diverse people within organizations. We invite our readers to join us in using our roles as teacher-scholar-consultants to create spaces where organizational members can engage in reflection and dialogue about diversity. Ultimately, we hope that these processes will form the foundation for more competent and compassionate communication among diverse people.

Notes

1.   We use "subaltern counterpublics" to examine discursive moves made by members of two diverse organizations as they express and contest their respective identities within shared space. However, there are other ways to frame these discursive negotiations. For instance, NWMF can be labeled in a variety of ways, such as feminist, women-centered, alternative, contrabureaucratic, value-rational, and women-owned organization (e.g., Bate & Taylor, 1988; Buzzanell et al., 1997; Edley, 2000; Feree & Martin, 1995; Rothschild-Whitt, 1979). Other writers talk about the hybrid nature of alternative and bureaucratic principles and structures that occur in a tension-filled dynamic relationship (e.g., Ashcraft, 2001; Gottfried & Weiss, 1994).

2.   Also see B. Morris (1999) for a description of American women's music festival culture.

3.   In the "NWMF Marketplace," nearly 60 vendors sold varied products aimed at festigoers (e.g., jewelry, CDs, clothing, massages, and art). This quotation was taken from 2000 NWMF data, when the "marketplace" was relegated to an empty residence hall wherein each "booth" was in its own room. Based on a member survey, the marketplace location was changed in 2001.

4.   Our use of the term "outed" is not meant to co-opt experiences of many gay and lesbian people who keep their sexual orientation secret to avoid discrimination. We use it because we do not have a word in the English lexicon for heterosexual people who are called out to reveal their sexual orientation in a predominantly gay environment.

2

Revisiting Sexual Harassment in Academe

Using Feminist Ethical and Sensemaking Approaches to Analyze Macrodiscourses and Micropractices of Sexual Harassment

Patrice M. Buzzanell

In late spring 2001, I guest lectured in a women's studies class about gender and the workplace. The students and I analyzed a *Wall Street Journal* article about teasing, attractiveness, and young (presumably white, heterosexual, middle-class, able-bodied) women's career success. The columnist, Pollock (2000), suggested that women could act stereotypically feminine in the workplace because women have achieved both equality with men and critical mass in managerial and professional occupations. She also wrote that some men feel as though women are behaving in a sexually harassing manner and that these men express confusion about how they should respond.

During our discussion, a student began talking about the routine comments of her male teaching assistant (TA) about her appearance and about his assignment of extra points to her quizzes based on how she looked on a particular day. Her male TA's comments made her uneasy, and she avoided him. She reported that a female friend taking the same multisection course went to a different TA for assistance and found herself graded down based on her lesser attractiveness (in the eyes of her male TA).

The timing of these comments was ironic. The class discussion happened midsemester in a women's studies course, just as students were initiating their activist projects. In addition, a couple of days earlier I heard from a university administrator that the sexual harassment committee on my campus no longer regularly met. The administrators assumed that no complaints meant no sexual harassment and that regular dissemination of brochures meant that university members would know where to go and what to do if they experienced harassment.

Besides the fact that sexual harassment still is occurring on our university campuses in the 21st century, there are other issues embedded in this case that are disturbing. First, the student never labeled the incidents as harassment. She simply brought up her own and her friend's interactions with their TAs as examples of how people relate on our campus in sex-stereotypical ways. Her female instructor did not know about these incidents prior to the class discussion.

The fact that the student did not name these incidents as examples of sexual harassment is not surprising given the discrepancy between experiencing and labeling behaviors as sexual harassment (D. Lee, 2001; Magley, Hulin, Fitzgerald, & DeNardo, 1999), the differential nature of responses depending on harassees' personal vulnerabilities and sophistication in recognizing power plays (Wood, 1993, pp. 20-21), and the underreporting of sexual harassment instances in academic organizations (Rubin & Borgers, 1990). But the lack of labeling has political implications. Until the instructor and I talked about the discussion immediately after class, it did not occur to her that this incident might be worth reporting (and in subsequent discussions, it became obvious that the student did not consider reporting the incidents either). Gill (1993) notes that educational institution members have minimal knowledge of legal issues surrounding sexual harassment. Even if the student and/or instructor recognized the incident as harassment, either or both of them may not have considered the incident worth pursuing. The incident may not have been serious enough. "Serious" forms of sexual harassment are given more attention than, and thus trivialize, the more common sexual innuendoes and degrading remarks (Benokraitis & Feagin, 1986; Clair, 1993b; Townsley & Geist, 2000).

In addition to not naming the repeated incidents with her male TA as sexual harassment and not perceiving the incidents as serious enough to report, the women's studies student did not consider taking collective action. She was handling the circumstances in the best way she knew how—by avoiding her male TA and by commenting to others about the practice, but not by confronting the harasser. She had hoped that the problem would simply go away. She was not forming any kind of overt or hidden individual or collective resistance even though she knew that at least one other woman was living through similar experiences (for the range of resistance/complicity, see Clair, 1998; A. Murphy, 1998). Although the student's effort to ignore the harassment and hope that it would resolve itself over time is the typical response to these incidents (Payne, 1993), this response can encourage additional acts of harassment because the harasser feels increasingly powerful and immune to retribution (see "commitment" cycle in Cleveland, Stockdale, & Murphy, 2000; see also Kreps, 1993b). Moreover, lack of confrontation perpetuates cultural norms in which men are expected to dominate women and sexual harassment is seen as an inevitable rite of passage in academic institutions that subordinates must bear (Faludi, 1999; Payne, 1993; Phillips & Jarboe, 1993; Taylor & Conrad, 1992).

Finally, administrators' assumption that no complaints indicates no problems perpetuates superficial modifications that do not transform the micropractices of disenfranchisement. Myths of communication abound (see Redding, 1972; for myths of sexual harassment, see Feary, 2000; Payne, 1993). The assumption that telling people something (or publicizing a policy) is tantamount to ensuring that they know about, understand, and comply with the message does not take into consideration the complexities of intent and unanticipated consequences, constrained agency, contextual demands or opportunities, relative benefits of clarity and strategic ambiguity, and so on (see E. Eisenberg, 1984; O'Brien Hallstein, 1999). The "no complaints" assumption, or lack of adherence to a sexual harassment policy, may say more about the institutional culture that normalizes sexualized interactions and silence (see J. Hearn, Sheppard, Tancred-Sheriff, & Burrell, 1989) than about the specific incident. It may indicate that the organization does not recognize that sexual harassment is a moral issue (Feary, 2000). Lack of policy use may signify that the organization is running at such a fast pace that there is little time for rethinking processes and consequences of (in)actions (see Perlow, 1998).

Whatever the reason(s) that the student and her instructor did not classify the incidents as sexual harassment and plan to take some form of immediate or delayed action, my concern is that university members, researchers, and practitioners seem to be revisiting the same issues that have been discussed for decades. In the next section, I explore these issues in higher education settings and provide an overview of different theories used to predict and explain sexual harassment. Next, I examine public/private dimensions, particularly justice and care ethics, to derive some of the reasons why we have not made as much progress as one would imagine. I integrate and extend poststructuralist and standpoint analyses of sexual harassment to develop an overarching feminist ethical and sensemaking approach to sexual harassment that can redress some of the problems in research and practices. I conclude by specifying pragmatic applications of this approach.

Sexual Harassment in Academe

To begin, I describe some of the issues in research and thinking about sexual harassment, particularly the pervasiveness of this phenomenon in institutions of higher education and the difficulties in defining and evaluating harassment in these contexts. Next, I briefly review some of the main theories used to illuminate sexual harassment. I argue that these theories have not captured the intricacies of the phenomenon. As a result, sexual harassment research, thinking, and practice have not made progress toward resolving problems of identifying, evaluating, and constructing viable solutions.

ISSUES INVOLVED IN SEXUAL HARASSMENT

Although 30 years have passed since sexual harassment was first named, documented, and aligned with legal and institutional solutions (Aggarwal, 1987; Fitzgerald et al., 1988; Loy & Stewart, 1984; Popovich, 1988; Wood, 1993), sexual harassment is still a common occurrence in educational institutions (e.g., Bogart & Stein, 1987; Faludi, 1999; Fitzgerald et al., 1988; Galvin, 1993; Martin, 2000; Paludi, 1990; Payne, 1993; Shedletsky, 1993; S. Strauss, 1988; Till, 1980; Townsley & Geist, 2000). In those 3 decades, researchers still have not been able to untangle sexual harassment from "normal" cross-sex exchanges; to make sense out of individuals' different reactions to the same behaviors; and to account for the differential perceptions of mixed and same race and status, of relational dynamics, and of attractiveness levels in harasser-harassee interactions (e.g., Jansma, 2000; Kramarae, 1992; Kurth, Spiller, & Travis, 2000; LaRocca & Kromrey, 1999; Magley et al., 1999; Paetzold & O'Leary-Kelly, 1993; Shelton & Chavous, 1999; Tyler & Boxer, 1996; Waldron, Foreman, & Miller, 1993; Wayne, 2000; Witteman, 1993; Wood, 1993). Especially problematic in understanding sexual harassment is the category of the hostile work environment.

Although quid pro quo sexual harassment appears fairly straightforward (in that the harassee is required to provide sexual favors to the harasser for employment purposes), hostile work environment sexual harassment (in which the harassee must prove that organizational members' conduct inter-feres with work accomplishment and/or creates an offensive or intimidating working or educational environment) seems vague (Paetzold & O'Leary-Kelly, 1993; Rubin & Borgers, 1990; Taylor & Conrad, 1992; Till, 1980; Wood, 2001). The definition of a hostile work environment stipulates that conduct must be unwelcome to the harassee but that he or she need not experience economic loss for the interactions to be labeled as sexual harassment (Paetzold & O'Leary-Kelly, 1993). Moreover, in educational institutions, hostile environment incidents start early in life, as Dougherty's (1999) personal account of sexual harassment during grade school exemplifies.

In addition to the pervasiveness and difficulty of identifying hostile work environment sexual harassment, there also are different parties that could be involved in harassment. Although this chapter focuses on professor-student sexual harassment, cases differ according to parties' race/ethnicity, sexual-social orientation, able-bodiedness, and class. Despite differences, academic sexual harassment displays troublesome patterns because of (a) power imbalances between professors and students—especially graduate students, (b) tenure processes, and (c) the nature of teacher-graduate student contact.

First, professors hold incredible power and influence. The power imbalances associated with sexual harassment in academe are especially bothersome because of differing opinions on rights to privacy and on meanings of consensual relationships when faculty and students are involved in supervisory and nonsupervisory academic relationships. Keller (2000) reviews the legal developments surrounding Title VII of the Civil Rights Act of 1964, Title IX of the Educational Amendments of 1972, the first United States Supreme Court case on sexual harassment (i.e., *Meritor Savings Bank, FSB v. Vinson;* for overviews of recent Supreme Court rulings, see Greenhouse, 2001; Stepp, 2001), and numerous federal court cases. She concludes that faculty and students involved in consensual, nonsupervisory relationships in public universities and colleges should be able to form close personal relationships based on their constitutional rights to privacy. She recommends that universities establish a situational boundary (a "bright-line test") between those relationships considered permissible and those that demand regulation:

> Intimate associations between faculty and students arising within the "zone of instruction" carry the presumption of coercion and render the consensual nature of the relationships suspect. Here the university has a compelling interest in preserving academic integrity and safeguarding students from duress and exploitation. (Keller, 2000, p. 35)

Although Keller suggests that this test could establish some boundaries, she concedes that definitional issues surrounding amorous, consensual, and power relationships, as well as the appropriate role of universities in the lives of students, are ambiguous.

In contrast, Fitzgerald (2000) argues that Keller's "bright-line test" remedy is naïve and problematic. Fitzgerald maintains that professors in nonsupervisory relationships still hold considerable influence and authority over students' careers and lives. Professors have disciplinary knowledge or expertise, professional experience, and scholarly reputations that may make students particularly vulnerable to professors.[1] Professors also have social, institutional, and scholarly/professional networks that enable students to interact with other professors and administrators on a collegial (if not friendship) basis. Based on analyses of the many kinds of power imbalances in professor-student relationships, Fitzgerald concludes that *any* professor-student intimate relationship can be inappropriate or dangerous.

First, to counter arguments that policies against faculty-student consensual relationships patronize women who should be able to make informed decisions about their lives, Fitzgerald says that this emphasis on adult rights does not fully take into consideration either the power of professors or the responsibilities of faculty. Fitzgerald illustrates her points by presenting and critiquing the scenario of a male professor and a female graduate student involved in a long-term consensual relationship that eventually leads to engagement, then a breaking of the engagement when the professor decides that he no longer wants to marry the student. Fitzgerald concludes,

> *But what Keller's analysis ignores is that there are many forms of power, and the professor has them all—whether he acknowledges it or not, or even wishes to or not. It is a fact of life that all of us in academia recognize, if we are truthful, but often wish or choose to ignore.* It is disingenuous to pretend that because we do not chair someone's dissertation committee, act as advisor, or have the opportunity to give a grade in a particular class, a sexual relationship has no influence on a student's academic life, for good or ill. The truth, of course, is that such a relationship colors not only all of her professional interactions with her "partner," but also with every other professor in (at least) her academic department. (Fitzgerald, 2000, p. 46; emphasis in original)

Second, tenure can safeguard known harassers for years. When professors are tenured, they often must demonstrate a developing or full-blown national reputation. Even when incidents of sexual harassment are documented, involve physical contact, and are repeated with other students, a strong research reputation may mean that the harasser is accorded leniency by administrators. In a recent case, Indiana University at South Bend's President Myles Brand argued, "My judgment was that the incident did not rise to the level of detenurization. . . . There was one instance of unwanted touching and kissing. We don't fire faculty members—or even longstanding employees in the corporate world—for that" (Cox, 2001, p. A15). Besides "unwanted touching and kissing," the harasser, H. Daniel Cohen, also offended and intimidated women in his classes as well as readers of the *South Bend Tribune* when he wrote in an op-ed piece that sexual harassment accusers were "physically ugly" (Cox, 2001, p. A16). Even so, it took years to fire this professor.

Third, different forms of teacher-student contact make both parties vulnerable to sexual harassment accusations.[2] In academe, there may be First Amendment or free speech issues as well as questionable immediacy cues in the learning process (Leatherman, 1994; Mongeau & Blalock, 1994; Townsley & Geist, 2000; C. Williams, 1999). Discussions of sensitive topics that some students might consider inappropriate might well fit within the faculty member's class. Of course, *how* these topics are integrated into lectures and discussions has a bearing on students' responses to these materials. In addition, *immediacy cues*, defined as nonverbal and verbal behaviors that are associated with teacher-student physical and psychological closeness (Mongeau & Blalock, 1994), can be troublesome. Students appear to be able to distinguish sexual harassment and immediacy behaviors and to differentially evaluate them as negative and positive, respectively. However, females judge harassment descriptions as more inappropriate than men (Mongeau & Blalock, 1994). Females also feel negatively about teacher-student touch when the touch is unexpected (with males reacting differently; see Lannutti, Laliker, & Hale, 2001). Females react in varied ways depending on who initiated the touch and where it occurred (for touch in coworker relationships, see J. Lee & Guerrero, 2001). In short, free speech, First Amendment, and immediacy can make hostile work environment sexual harassment difficult to identify.

Adding more difficulty to judging instances as sexual harassment is context. Context "frames interpretation of the instructor's intentions and relational meanings" (Mongeau & Blalock, 1994, p. 267). Although context frames interpretations, typical faculty-student scenarios can contain circumstantial characteristics with a high potential to develop into sexual harassment. Scenarios include "the communication instructor leading an interpersonal exercise involving personal self disclosure," "a design instructor driving off-campus with a student to find costumes and props," and "a journalism teacher supervising interns at off-campus sites" (Galvin, 1993, p. 261). Especially troublesome are contexts such as intercollegiate debate and individual events in which students often leave campus with faculty advisors, graduate students, and others to compete in forensics tournaments (Stepp, 2001). Stepp finds that women forensics participants are harassed more than the general university female population and male forensics competitors, and that women in intercollegiate debate are harassed more than women in individual events.

Besides the specific scenarios and extracurricular activities just mentioned, ordinary activities can contain warning signs for potential sexual harassments. For example, the routine practice of faculty members closing their doors when students are in their offices (Payne, 1993) can, and probably should, arouse suspicion. Taylor and Conrad (1992) note that faculty may humiliate and seduce students while acting as counselors, confidantes, and power brokers (p. 405). Faculty teaching and advising roles are ambiguous enough to permit inquiry into students' personal lives and to tolerate eccentric behavior that may be associated with harassment.

Yet, students sometimes come to office hours and classes extremely upset about illnesses or deaths of family members, relational disintegrations, pressures to succeed, and other life events. Closing the door and offering students a tissue and a sympathetic ear would seem to be a compassionate thing to do. However, in reading these and other scenarios, any faculty member who is actively engaged in student learning would become uncomfortable—not because these scenarios constitute sexual harassment—but because analogous circumstances occur routinely across disciplines and campuses.

In short, some issues still being debated in our institutions of higher education focus on what constitutes sexual harassment, what are the rights to privacy or academic freedom, and what behaviors under what conditions comprise sexual harassment.

Theories of Sexual Harassment

There are numerous theories of why sexual harassment occurs and with what consequences.[3] I start with three broad models used frequently in harassment thinking and research, then delve into communication models. The three models seek to predict who are potential victims and harassers, what each party is likely to do, what outcomes are probable, and which organizational characteristics are associated with harassment. These three approaches, or *macro theories*, are the natural (also called biological), organizational, and sociocultural models (Cleveland et al., 2000; Tangri, Burt, & Johnson, 2000).

THE NATURAL MODEL

Depending on which version of the model one prefers, the biological model maintains either that sexual harassment is the result of men's naturally stronger sex drive or that attraction on the part of both sexes could lead to harassment even though the intent was not to harass. The implications of this model are that sexual harassment is trivialized because it is seen as normal and harmless ("boys will be boys," and women should not be offended). However, Tangri et al. (2000) point out that all variations on this model discriminate: "This is a critical characteristic. A failure to find any systematic pattern of harassment, or any evidence of harmful effects on women, would support the natural model of sexual harassment" (p. 117). If there are no systematic patterns or harmful effects on women, research would *not* repeatedly find that females perceive instances to be sexual harassment more often than men, that females are more troubled by these exchanges than men, and that cases remain underreported because women fear sanctions against them—including the assumption that no one will believe them and that organizational members will enact revenge (e.g., Benokraitis & Feagin, 1986; Dougherty, 2001b; Dunn & Cody, 2000; Gill, 1993; Ivy & Hamlet, 1996; Matchen & DeSouza, 2000; McKinney, 1990; Payne, 1993; Rubin & Borgers, 1990).

THE ORGANIZATIONAL MODEL

The organizational model argues that differential opportunity structures may be conducive to sexual harassment. Infrastructure aspects that provide opportunities for sexual aggression include visibility and contact in sex-integrated jobs (e.g., token status), job tasks and requirements (e.g., business trips), and access to grievance procedures. Victims usually are low in power, status, income, and marketability.

THE SOCIOCULTURAL MODEL

The sociocultural model says that sexual harassment is a mechanism whereby men seek to (consciously or unconsciously) dominate women in the workplace and the economy: "Male dominance is maintained by cultural patterns of male-female interaction as well as by economic and political super-ordinancy" (Tangri et al., 2000, p. 121). The premise is that sexual harassment continues because status (such as manager or faculty member over secretaries or students) and gender (such as male/masculine over female/feminine) replicate societal patterns of subordination, vulnerability, and power.[4] Sexual harassment from feminist perspectives assumes that harassment reflects the status of women in society (Gutek, 1985).

CONSISTENT FINDINGS

In examining data from a survey of federal employees (i.e., the U. S. Merit Systems Protection Board), Tangri et al. (2000) found that no single model accounted for sexual harassment within or across the sexes. However, there were consistent findings. Women had negative reactions to incidents they labeled as harassment, with highly vulnerable and dependent women experiencing more harassment than others. Sexual harassment is widespread but seems to "approximate a random event in women's working lives—something which is highly likely to happen at some time, with just when, where, and how being so multidetermined that prediction is difficult" (Tangri et al., 2000, p. 131).

COMMUNICATION APPROACHES

Besides these three models, in the last decade, communication has become an operative framework from which to study and propose recommendations for sexual harassment. Wood (1993; see also Hickson, Grierson, & Linder, 1990; Kreps, 1993a) argues that sexual harassment is inherently communicative because it is symbolically constructed through culturally formed and legitimated definitions and because it is enacted through verbal and nonverbal communication. The variety of communication approaches for investigating sexual harassment attests to its complexity. I explore some of these communication approaches in the next major section.

SUMMARY

Theories of sexual harassment have tried to account for how and why harassment occurs and why issues surrounding this phenomenon continue to be so problematic. Although definitions of sexual harassment appear straightforward, there still is confusion about what constitutes harassment in particular environments and in long-term and power-imbalanced relationships (e.g., faculty-graduate students). What is appropriate for academic professionals also is disputed because some harassment charges may be countered by rights to privacy, academic freedom, and free speech. Communication approaches to sexual harassment that probe into the complexities of and macrodiscourses that frame harassment may be able to account for why sexual harassment research, thinking, and practice have not resolved the problems associated with these behaviors.

Communication Approaches to Sexual Harassment

Although prior research and definitions still cannot enable individuals in many real-life cases to determine whether sexual harassment has occurred and how to respond adequately, communication approaches can move past an outcome-oriented approach to look at why and how sexual harassment continues to perplex researchers. Like Tangri et al. (2000), I do not offer one definitive theory. Instead, I discuss two perspectives (poststructuralist and standpoint) and offer an additional approach based on feminist ethical (public/private and justice/care) tensions and sensemaking that enables researchers to study the interplay of sexual harassment macro- and microdiscourses.

POSTSTRUCTURALIST AND STANDPOINT PERSPECTIVES

Poststructuralist and standpoint perspectives represent competing visions of gender and harassment. Poststructuralists insist that there is no single "right" truth and no fixed understandings. The meaning of sexual harassment operates as a site of struggle in which women's interests are at risk. Poststructuralist perspectives present the parties involved in sexual harassment as constructing their subjectivities and knowledge within the real material and historical locations of their lives and cultures. In contrast, standpoints privilege commonality while folding in (or clarifying) difference (O'Brien Hallstein, 2000). Although standpoint theorists accommodate difference, they still retain commonality "to preserve the analytic and political force of feminist theory" (p. 4).

Both feminist poststructuralist and standpoint researchers contribute to richly nuanced understandings of sexual harassment tensions. Communication researchers and those involved in harassment episodes construct multiple

emotions within women's and men's organizational experiences. She does not state that all women and men experience sexual harassment in exactly the same manner but that there may be some common gender-based fears that warrant further examination. Dougherty maintains,

> Specifically, men hold a *power over* standpoint that serves as a basis for a fear of marginalization through accusations of sexual harassment and organizational policies that men perceive may lead to a silencing of their voices. The masculine standpoint clashes with women's *power with* standpoint and the related fear of physical harm. (p. 439; emphasis in original)

Dougherty's (2001b) additional research in a health care organization found that women's greatest fear was that they would not be believed if they reported harassment. Ironically, the women themselves did not believe victims of sexual harassment. Dougherty (2001a) extended her analysis of these participants to examine the functional and dysfunctional (as parts of organizing processes) nature of sexual harassment. She found that functional aspects seemed to divide along gender lines in such a way that what men identified as functional (for coping, for comforting coworkers, and for building camaraderie), women identified as dysfunctional (as stressful, as something to be endured, and as potentially isolating).

The consequences of gendered standpoints are that men were less likely to both label behaviors as sexual harassment and envision problematic aspects or consequences of their behaviors. Both men and women view sexual harassment as normative, but men consider sexualized behaviors as part of organizing, whereas women simply tolerate what they perceive as unacceptable but unchangeable. Dougherty (2001a) noted pragmatic applications of her findings. She said that men's and women's divergent perspectives on this phenomenon and the myths surrounding sexual harassment in general continue to deserve training session time. She also noted that general policies about sexual harassment will continue to fail because harassment is not understood as part of a larger problem. Until stress and coping mechanisms are discussed as part of organizing processes, other means of handling pressures cannot evolve in the group. Thus, standpoint approaches to sexual harassment can assist researchers and practitioners in focusing on commonalities useful for changing policies and training.

SUMMARY

Communication studies, particularly those from feminist discourse perspectives, have derived complicated understandings of harassment tensions that are not solved easily by legal and institutional remedies. From poststructuralists, researchers find that individuals negotiate identities in complex ways to account for macrodiscourses and micropractices. From standpoint researchers, they note that commonalities among groups' under-standings of and responses to harassment form bases for change in policies and practices. The contradictory aspects of these perspectives are useful for a feminist ethical (public/private and justice/care) and sensemaking approach to sexual harassment.

Feminist Ethical and Sensemaking Approach to Sexual Harassment

Difficulties with sexual harassment interventions and research occur because many researchers focus on individuals' response patterns rather than looking broadly at tensions in human thinking, feeling, and behaving. Often, prior analyses juxtapose rational thinking (e.g., if people could label the phenomena and know legal recourses, then harassment would not occur) with the messiness of sexual harassment.[8] These analyses specify what *not* to do rather than con-structing visions of equitable organizing.

In contrast to traditional as well as postmodern and standpoint perspectives on sexual harassment, a feminist ethical system can enable stakeholders to con-sider policies and practices guided by visions of equitable processes. Feminist ethics strive to enact several interrelated goals: describe and label forms of oppres-sion, critique experiences of group members rendered vulnerable in specific situations, locate means of resistance, create visions of desirable alternatives, and establish advocacy plans. These feminist goals differ from feminine ethics that position feminine traits as criteria for decision making (see Jaggar, 1991; Tong, 1993). It is the *struggle* to construct and sustain visions of equity for women and other marginalized people within everyday circumstances that differentiates feminist ethics from other ethical approaches (Haney, 1994).

At the heart of tensions in contemporary harassment research, thinking, and practice are public/private and justice/care manifestations in macro- and microdiscourses. Public/private translates into distinctions between work-places with masculine discourse and homes with feminine conversation. However, separation of genders and issues into separate spheres does not account for the friction and opportunities between and within these discourses (e.g., justice/care, reason/emotion, moral theory/situated ethics, agency/communion, universal other/concrete individual, and standard procedures/specific cases; see Gilligan, 1982; T. Haas & Deetz, 2000; P. Sullivan & Turner, 1996; Tronto, 1992, 1993;

Wood, 1994). Although considered gendered, public/ private and justice/care priorities may center on contextualized understandings of situations (and not necessarily sex differences; Crandall, Tsang, Goldman, & Pennington, 1999; Friedman, 1985, 1993a).

In sexual harassment, these tensions partly explain difficulties in identifying problematic aspects and in resolving issues. Although theorists say that consensual sexual relationships between faculty and graduate students fall (or do not fall) within adults' rights to privacy based on certain criteria (see Fitzgerald, 2000; Keller, 2000), these kinds of decisions attempt to draw boundaries around shifting definitions of what is admissible (as evidence, connecting logics or warrants, and claims) within private and public concerns. These decisions also try to delimit the contradictory plural identities of relevant parties, the sociohistorical locations of parties, and the evolving narratives of specific situations. Drawing boundaries around public/private or justice/care concerns has proven nearly impossible. Using knowledge created through ethical decision making and through poststructuralist and standpoint findings, researchers and practitioners can create feminist ethical and sensemaking approaches to harassment. In these approaches, sexual harassment, particularly hostile work environments, becomes a site of political struggles in which claims are adjudicated. What is appropriate for the different spheres is of less importance than how, when, and why (i.e., under what circumstances) public/private and justice/care are (re)constituted discursively (Mumby, 2000). Dualities drawing boundaries between what is and is not harassment disappear.

In revisiting sexual harassment as a contested site of politicized and malleable discourse, an analytic scheme similar to Steiner's (1997) and others' discussions of feminist ethics (e.g., Haney, 1994; Mattson & Buzzanell, 1999) can be devised. The advantage of this analytic framework is that it does not assess harassment factors in isolation but, instead, poses a series of interrelated questions that require reconsideration over time. Responses to questions and development of context form a narrative in which persons, plot turning points, and other story elements come into play. This narrative resembles a sensemaking account—that is, a retrospective and ongoing construction of pivotal and mundane events arranged in various ways at different times to make sense to the storyteller(s) (see Arthur, Inkson, & Pringle, 1999; Weick, 1995). As the narrative evolves, certain people and events move into the foreground while details change as individuals attempt to gain support for their versions (e.g., Cooren, 2001). By combining feminist ethics and sensemaking, a story is (re)told in multiple ways so that a highly contextualized account of justice/care and public/private communication emerges.

Using feminist ethical frameworks, we can examine (a) loyalties, (b) values, (c) visions, and (d) responses (adapted from Steiner, 1997). Although there are other qualities in, and finer distinctions in characteristics of, ethical decision making, these four processes address much of the negotiation that underlies feminist visions of equity.

LOYALTIES

Loyalties demand scrutiny of feelings, biases, allegiances, and responsibilities about the well-being of self and others. The unfoldings of ethical dilemmas during examination of socio-historical-economic-relational contextualizations are difficult to summarize, as C. Williams (1999) found out. When confronted with actual details and a need to comment on a campus investigation, she felt ill-prepared to deal with the moral dilemmas and to determine appropriate courses of action despite her background in gender harassment and legal remedies. Her experiences are not surprising because supervisors and administrators charged with investigating cases and providing formal responses to charges often have difficulty deciding what to do (Shedletsky, 1993).

Although justice may seem clear-cut to an outsider, persons reflecting on "facts" and divided loyalties may make different assessments about their own and others' circumstances. For instance, in deriving responses to consensual sexual relationships based in unequal hierarchical relationships (e.g., male professor with female graduate student), academic community members may attempt to balance shifting case aspects, including affection and/or respect for the professor, affection and/or respect for the student and her adult status, dislike of being cognizant of emerging inequities or past relational patterns of one or both parties, awareness that what is said to one may find its way to the other (and the accompanying isolation of one or both relational partners), fear that relationship termination could result in harassment charges, and genuine desire to see both partners happy. Feminist ethics can enhance our understandings of these micropractices. Feminist ethics also can illuminate macrodiscourses (e.g., professional, gendered, and other identities; see Townsley & Geist, 2000) and rhetoric designed to portray organizations sympathetically within their sociopolitical contexts (Finet, 2001).[9]

In cases such as faculty-student relationships, the power imbalances that act as a backdrop to all relational dynamics surface uneasily in discussions about what is private, (in)appropriate, sexual harassment, and so on. How skilled the partners are in alleviating observers' fears, particularly fears that the inequities might explode into a harassment case, enter into the narrative. Questions about loyalties and contextualizations have to address the real material circumstances of people's lives that make resistance and silence tensions difficult to sort and that indicate ways in which agency often is constrained (see O'Brien Hallstein, 1999; Townsley & Geist, 2000).

VALUES

Loyalties blend into the second criterion for judging (in)action, *values.* Values of human dignity, rights to an unobstructed education, and ending subordination demand constant creation and evaluating of alternatives not only to formulate but also to commit to moral principles (Jaggar, 1994). C. Williams's (1999) difficulties with the harassment case did not derive from lack of procedural knowledge or of conviction that harassment is wrong. Her difficulties arose because abstract morals and ethical considerations pose dilemmas in everyday cases (see Friedman, 1985, 1993a). Moreover, in developing fluid sensemaking stories, attention must be paid to the often divergent male and female perspectives and fears that inform case participants' actions (Dougherty, 1999, 2001b).

Attention also needs to be devoted to the different interests, circumstances, and values experienced by harasser and harassee. With regard to harassers, those who are accused of harassment encounter high levels of uncertainty and shame (Leatherman, 1994; Shedletsky, 1993), with accusations as well as silence potentially destroying lives and careers (see "Our stories," 1992). With respect to harassees, male as well as female victims can experience long-term devastating effects (Clair, 1998). Harassment degrades harassees as human beings through violation of their expectations to be treated fairly and respectfully (Kreps, 1993a; Payne, 1993; Quina, 1990). From an outsider's perspective, harassees may disempower themselves through trivialization, denotative hesitancy in the use of legal terms intended to empower them, and invocation of private issues rather than responding to harassment as a complex social process (Clair, 1993b). Harassees may joke about incidences as though they were misguided expressions of affection, romance, teasing, or playfulness (Booth-Butterfield, 1989; Driscoll, 1981; Kramarae, 1992; Kreps, 1993b; Martin, 2000; Shotland & Craig, 1988; Witteman, 1993). They may be too ashamed to speak about their plight and may blame themselves (E. Collins & Blodgett, 1981; Pryor & Day, 1988; Quina, 1990; K. Williams & Cyr, 1992).

VISION

A third consideration, *vision,* involves creation of an ideal vision or standard against which researchers and practitioners can contrast the embodied, daily struggle of redefining and reframing discourse to focus on the ironies, paradoxes, and contractions in "doing ethics" (Haney, 1994). In this vision, transformation can account for resistance and complicity, empowerment and disempowerment, and justice and care. For instance, although Townsley and Geist (2000) focused on women's individual responses (as would be appropriate with their poststructuralist theoretical and analytic lens), their research does not address the connections individuals have with their academic communities and what these communities would look like if they truly were constructed along the lines of gender equity, freedom to explore ideas, and care for members' professional and personal development. They make one mention of community connections—when "Beatrice" describes her disappointment that others are so immobilized by institutional rhetoric that they ignore her harasser's behaviors and her organizational exit (Townsley & Geist, 2000, p. 207).

RESPONSES

Fourth, if researchers and practitioners value an ethical academic community, then community-enhancing *responses* (messages and practices) should be pursued (Buzzanell, 1995). These exchanges assist in dialectical processes of valuing relationships, delving into issues contextually, and working toward meeting self and others' needs. Community and dialogue integrate diverse standpoints and provide the overarching goal of and method for reaching visions of ethical living.

SUMMARY

In short, a feminist ethical and sensemaking approach to sexual harassment transcends public/private and justice/care stances by stipulating that feminist visions guide iterative processes involving both halves of these stances. Friedman (1985) comments that case complexities may produce resolutions that seem inconsistent but that are necessary to develop adequate responses to ethical dilemmas. Thus, an analysis of sexual harassment in academe by examining public/private and justice/care tensions in everyday episodes can account for how and why sexual harassment, particularly hostile work environment, is so difficult to name and to align with adequate solutions. Although policies are on the books, the complexities cannot be handled solely from justice perspectives. In most organizational dilemmas, justice considerations align with procedural (rules and procedures), distributive (outcomes), and interactive (interpersonal) justices (e.g., Tepper, 2000). Combining justice and care ethics opens discussion for public/private considerations, ambiguities about cases, and stakeholder responsiveness.

Conclusion

This chapter provides a different means of analyzing sexual harassment cases and of exploring the tensions that emerge when policies and lived experience collide. Care-private and justice-public are insufficient criteria on which to evaluate real cases. To handle harassment in academe, processes and content of feminist ethical frameworks (iterative thinking and question cycling with specific questions) need to be combined with sensemaking (process of retro-spective storytelling with temporary closure). Although communicative analy-ses derived from poststructuralist and standpoint perspectives provide heuristic means for revisiting harassment policies and practices, *they fail to create a sustainable feminist vision of what academic communities could look like if sexual harassment did not exist in macrodiscourses and micropractices.* These communities would be embedded in ongoing and often contradictory con-structions of narratives, identities, and knowledge about sexual harassment.

Several implications can be derived from this discussion. Sexual harass-ment narratives show how interpretations of actions can lead to recurrent pat-terns of harassment in particular interactions and in academic cultures. Using the discursive framework of justice/care can enable training-session partici-pants to construct highly contextualized accounts that not only situate events along timelines but also incorporate emotions and reactions to episodes. These accounts can provide trainees with an appreciation for the difficulties in deal-ing with real cases. These sessions should be conducted in small groups because many women prefer informality (Brown, 1993).

The notion of evolving and contextualized narratives as training, counseling, and grievance processes is consistent with Waldron et al.'s (1993) findings on women's daily relational maintenance strategies with supervisors. They found that women construct evolving strategies (mostly through trial and error) to handle their emerging knowledge about hierarchical relation-ships and sexual harassment. Women develop four main relational mainte-nance strategies from their own experiences and can adjust their use depending on their organizational interactions and situations (e.g., through training).

In addition, Berryman-Fink (1993) recommends specific training pro-grams in which human resource managers can *facilitate* learning processes. Berryman-Fink argues that managers alone cannot combat power imbalances. They and other administrators need to work with employees and members of educational institutions to effect change. They recommend periodic (at least annual) discussions about harassment and other topics.

In closing, the student in my opening story was contacted by her instruc-tor and asked if she was willing to report the incident. The student responded that she had been sexually harassed before and did not want to initiate another grievance. Because she is not my student and is adamant about not pursuing a complaint, I can only hope that she constructs a narrative for herself that infuses loyalties/contextualization, values, vision, and tensions within an adequate response for herself. The benefits of the classroom and outside-of-class discussions were that she could make sense of her experiences and know that she had the support of academic community members in how she chose to tell her story. Although some might advocate that every instance of sexual harassment should be reported, individuals operate within multiple identities, conflicting discourses, and agency constrained (and enhanced) by the material circumstances of their lives (see O'Brien Hallstein, 1999; Weedon, 1999). This student was caught up in a myriad of conflicting, situated tensions (as are all people when confronted by difficult decisions). Being able to construct a sensemaking story about these issues is one of the benefits of the type of approach advocated in this chapter. I hope that this student's sensemaking about this and other harassment events will provide her with some peace.

Although she has not filed a grievance, she has not silenced herself. She and her instructor have opened a conversation in their class, making an entire group of women and men from different university majors aware of hostile work environment sexual harassment. Perhaps they will take this and other discussions from their women's studies class with them as they enter the workplace as full-time employees.

Notes

1. Benokraitis and Feagin (1986) describe forms of psychological intimidation as "setting the stage for seduction" through extra help, false praise, and other rewards (p. 75). They describe forms of subtle harassment as emotional because harassers prey on some women's inexperience and self-doubt (i.e., harasser-as-scavenger or harasser-as-confidante roles).

2. Both parties are vulnerable to sexual harassment behaviors and accusations. Although most reports and research involve superior-subordinate and male-female dyads, reverse harassment can occur (e.g., when female professors harass male students), with harassees' responses differing from those typically described. For instance, female students report lower self-confidence when male faculty sexually harass them (Martin, 2000; Strine, 1992; Townsley & Geist, 2000; Wood, 1992b), but male students may view sexual harassment by female professors as a phenomenon that enhances their self-esteem (Payne, 1993). Sexual harassment of faculty by coworkers (peer harassment) and students (contrapower harassment) display different forms of, attitudes toward, and definitions of harassment (Grauerholz, 1989; Matchen & DeSouza, 2000; McKinney, 1990).

3. These macro theories are some of the broadest and most-used perspectives on sexual harassment, although none account fully for harassment (Tangri et al., 2000). Micro theories focus on personality and situational factors (Cleveland et al., 2000). They examine such issues as who is likely to harass (e.g., Bingham & Burleson, 1996) and how "normal" expectations about women's sex roles "spill over" into their work roles such that male-female interactions, particularly in numerically male-dominated contexts, are sexualized (Cleveland et al., 2000; Gutek, 1985). Subtle sex discrimination and harassment rely on gender socialization and expectations (Benokraitis & Feagin, 1986).

There are other ways of discussing sexual harassment research in general and specifically in interpersonal and organizational communication. Keyton and Rhodes (1999) use experimental, work experience, victim, and sexualized work environment perspectives. Jansma (2000) summarizes organizational, legal, and academic aspects, then reconceptualizes sexual harassment as a multidimensional phenomenon in which formal power and perceived harasser intent influence behaviors and outcomes.

In addition to these overviews, different data-gathering and analytic techniques enable researchers to study sexual harassment from varied communication perspectives. Bingham (1991; see also Bingham & Burleson, 1996) focuses on verbal message strategies for managing sexual harassment situations and on survey data for providing training session attendees with feedback on their proclivity to sexually harass. Lannutti et al. (2001) use expectancy violation theory to explain positive and negative influences of touch in faculty-student interactions. Organizational communication studies that capitalize on context and qualitative data include narrative analyses of victim's harassment accounts (Brown, 1993); and feminist critiques of discursive framing devices that individuals (Clair, 1993b, 1993c), educational organizations (Clair, 1993a), and governmental institutions (Chapman, 1993) use to silence harassment and controversy. Rhetorical-cultural investigations look at formal responses to harassment (e.g., the U.S. Navy's responses to the 1991 Tailhook sexual harassment scandal; Violanti, 1996).

4. I use the term *status* to refer to several different statuses. *Organizational and hierarchical status* means authority that managers or professors have over direct reports or graduate students within the same professional career ladder. *Prestige status* involves cultural evaluations of occupations, such that managers or professors are classified as more prestigious than secretaries or students. Status also refers to decision-making premises and presumptions (e.g., desires to retain more valuable members; tendencies to believe or to trust professional colleagues). Furthermore, managers and professors accrue status because of occupational and scholarly reputations that may be considered more valuable than local status (external and internal *reputational status*, respectively).

These status forms are different from power, which ranges from authority over grades to less overt control, in which individuals and groups may comply with dominant interpretations, members, and policies regardless of whether these are in the individuals' and groups' best interests. Different types of status and power factor into explanations that sexually harassed individuals give for not reporting incidents. Explanations include fear of negative consequences, "just world" hypothesis, escalation of commitment, sex differences in appraisal of coping effectiveness, and sex differences in dispute resolution preferences (Cleveland et al., 2000, p. 225). Payne (1993) finds that students often do not consider the power that they potentially wield in harassment episodes, whereas Keller (2000) reports survey results indicating that 75% of students believe that most female students would hesitate to report professors' harassing behaviors. Masculine cultures, sexualized work environments, expectations about appropriate feminine and masculine behavior, and so on act against sexual harassment reporting (see J. Hearn et al., 1989).

5. Townsley and Geist (2000) label their female research participants as "victims" but do not mention whether these women label themselves in this way. By providing an evaluative label rather than "harassee," the authors underscore the pain, frustration, and helplessness that these women feel. Ironically, this label also connotes passivity. As such, the authors have inadvertently fixed the meanings of, denied harassees' agency within, and privileged one understanding of their harassment experiences over others.

6. Differences between postmodern and standpoint theories and their possible incommensurability remain unresolved (see Dougherty & Krone, 2000).

7. With regard to black women's experiences, P. Collins (2000) says that just because some women share common group oppressions does not mean that they will develop consciousness or that understanding of oppressions will be articulated (p. 25).

8. The cause-effect linear thinking that underlies this example is associated with traditional masculine approaches that fail to address complex organizing processes in specific contexts (see Buzzanell, 1994). Clair (1993a) underscores how typical advice in Big 10 University policies (e.g., "keep a record") fits within rational approaches. Sexual harassment discourses of taken-for-granted meaning systems, strategic ambiguity, and exclusionary language and interactions cannot open space for alternative explanations and contextualizations. Furthermore, conventional wisdom to follow procedures may neither contain problems nor produce desirable outcomes (see Mattson & Buzzanell, 1999). While rationality establishes orderly and dispassionate behavior as desirable, spontaneous and non-goal-oriented emotions are discouraged (Putnam & Mumby, 1993).

9.   Finet (2001) identifies issues related to institutional harassment rhetoric, such as desires to situate organizations favorably in discourses about sexual harassment as a social problem and institutional rhetoric that aligns employers with employees (i.e., the organization determines which behaviors are sexual harassment). Media organizations contribute to macrodiscourses about what constitutes harassment and how definitions change over time. For instance, media reports still fail to differentiate sexual harassment, illicit behavior, and flirting (e.g., Bordo, 1999; Buzzanell, 2001; Pollock, 2000). On micro levels, Finet expresses concern that everyday accounts may help people sort through complexities but offer little hope for collective action.

3

Women, Men, and Changing Organizations

An Organizational Culture Examination of Gendered Experiences of Telecommuting

Annika Hylmö

Many organizations are initiating programs to meet employees' expectations of assistance in work-family balance, including eldercare, leaves, flexibility for family activities, and alternative work arrangements (see Kirby, Golden, Medved, Jorgenson, & Buzzanell, 2003). Alternative work arrangements are those work contracts between employer and employee that deviate from traditional 9-to-5 structures. Telecommuting is one arrangement in which workers complete most of their work-related tasks away from company headquarters or other centralized offices rather than being co-located among colleagues. Lack of co-location means that telework necessitates a reliance on technology to transfer completed projects (Nilles, 1988; Qvartrop, 1998).

Telecommuting brings with it a number of unanswered questions about organizational life that may affect teleworkers' experiences, including new issues regarding gendered relationships and expectations within and outside the workplace. Women and men may draw different boundaries between paid work and home life (Nippert-Eng, 1996; Perlow, 1998). Men may be able to take work home but leave the family at the door when going to work, whereas women may be expected to prioritize family over work (Perlow, 1997; Wiley, 1991). Furthermore, male telecommuters may have support systems at home that female teleworkers do not have (Haddon, 1998; Haddon & Silverstone, 1995; Kompast & Wagner, 1998). This chapter considers telecommuting from the vantage point of gender as it is socially constructed by both men and women in the organizational context (Buzzanell, 1995). Ashcraft and Pacanowsky (1996) point out that standard organizational practices are rooted in traditionally masculine frameworks of meaning that have become reified as "normal" ways of doing things. When these frameworks become established as norms, they often mask existing power asymmetries and limit communicative opportunities for change. Because these frameworks are embedded in organizational cultures that continue to reproduce established practices and expectations even after (presumably) new patterns of interaction have been implemented (Buzzanell, 1995; Meyer, 1997), connections between gender and organizational culture need to be explored through the lenses of different epistemological assumptions (see Martin, 1992). The first lens presumes that all cultural members strive for coherent, unified views of organizational activities and members. The second assumption maintains that unified, coherent views are not possible but that, within distinct subcultures, there is clarity. The third lens contends that coherence is impossible. Instead, there always are fragmented, disparate attributional patterns that offer contradictory, ironic, and diverse cultural interpretations. By using these three lenses, this chapter provides a thick, multilayered description of telework and gender in a specific organizational context. Other discussions of gender in telecommuting processes have not interrogated the multifaceted ways in which gender is both manifest in and constructs telework discursively. At the end of this chapter, I present specific ideas for implementation by individuals and organizations that are derived from this study's findings.

Telecommuting Organizations and the Role of Gender

Being physically apart from the employing organization creates a complex set of tensions and opportunities for both employee and organization. Telecommuters are apt to feel lonely and disconnected from coworkers (Hylmö & Buzzanell, 2002; Kugelmass, 1995; Schepp, 1990), which may cause telecommuting employees to have a lower sense of identification with their coworkers and cause their employers to be adversely affected by high turnover rates. With increased telework, employees may not only be invisible to coworkers and bosses, but they may also lack the traditional respite that home provides from the office (and vice versa) (Hochschild, 1997; Perin, 1991). Although telecommuting may lead employees to feel disconnected, at the same time telecommuting may lead to higher job satisfaction (Bredin, 1996) and feelings of support in employee efforts to balance home and work life (Maiwald, Pierce, Newstron, & Sunoo, 1997; Rose, 1996). Many telecommuters appreciate the high levels of autonomy and personal control over work interruptions that telecommuting allows (Olson & Primps, 1984).

Although these issues seem to face all telecommuters, the ways that gender factors into these concerns has not been considered fully. Feminist scholars such as Perin (1998) point out that home-work balancing may be different for men and women. How that balance is negotiated is rooted in power relations and long-established patterns of domination (Kompast & Wagner, 1998). Gendered patterns of domination manifest themselves differently over space and time. In the 1930s, the development of the Fair Labor Standards Act in the United States was an attempt to outlaw the potential exploitation of women and children who labored at home (Boris, 1986; Boris & Daniels, 1989; Olson, 1988). More recently, similar concerns have been expressed regarding telecommuting and female clerical workers, who may be losing their company benefits as their jobs are outsourced to independent telecontractors (Matheson, 1992). Moreover, concerns have been raised regarding the additional burden on women who telecommute while taking on an even greater proportion of home-related tasks in comparison to men (Perin, 1998).

To better appreciate the complexity of gender and telecommuting in today's organizations, it may be useful to view the puzzle from the lens of organizational culture. Martin (1992) argues that organizations should be studied from three epistemological assumptions: integration, differentiation, and fragmentation. The three views allow us to fully appreciate the power dynamics and subtle nuances within organizational cultures. In *integration,* culture is manifest as a form of consensus. Both men and women may be expected to share similar interpretations of the role that telecommuting plays in organizing. *Differentiation* allows researchers to consider subgroups within the larger monolith and consensus within these smaller units. Men and women may form different subgroups that have contrasting, gendered experiences with telecommuting and that affect work-home boundaries. Finally, *fragmentation* enables researchers to consider a multiplicity of views. From this perspective, both genders experience ambiguity and complexity. Ambiguity may be fostered by *strategic ambiguity* (i.e., deliberately unclear exchanges that allow people to accomplish both stated and unstated goals; E. Eisenberg, 1984), which subtly upholds and reinforces patriarchal frameworks of power in specific organizational cultures. Taken together, the nexus of these three assumptions reveals the complex nature of organizational culture while enabling us to examine specific power relations in context. A feminist lens can bring power relations to the forefront in ways that enable theorists and practitioners to locate shifting and often ironic patterns that may prove useful for promoting greater gender equity and quality of life. Because these intersections have not been explored fully in organizational communication theory and research, the research question that guides the rest of this chapter is: *How does the opportunity to telecommute affect organizational cultural expectations of gender equality and perceived quality of life?*

Method

PARTICIPANTS AND CONTEXT

I first describe my research participants and then provide an overview of Federal Systems Integration and Management Center (FEDSIM), the agency in which my study was conducted. Out of 162 possible participants, 38 indicated interest in this research, and 37, or 97% of those interested (23% of all employees), were able to schedule and participate in interviews held at their convenience in August and September, 2000. Telecommuting is officially available to all FEDSIM employees, and 45% telecommute on formal and informal bases.

Out of the 37 interviewees, 21 (57%) were men and 16 (43%) were women; their average age was 46 years with a range of 24 to 60 years. There were 13 full-time telecommuters (35% of the participants). Although another 24 (65% of the sample) were not part of a formal, written telework contract, several indicated that they occasionally work at home. Because FEDSIM human resources (HR) personnel estimated that 11% of employees telecommuted full time at the time of data collection, this sample overrepresents teleworkers. Research respondents had worked at FEDSIM for an average of 8 years with a range of a few months through 27 years, compared to an average length of employment across FEDSIM of 7.5 years. (No other comparisons between teleworkers and in-house employees are available from FEDSIM's HR personnel.) Respondents' job titles were: contracting officers ($n = 2$), directors ($n = 4$), project managers ($n = 20$), and senior project managers ($n = 11$).

FEDSIM does not have an appropriated budget provided by the government; instead, the organization receives its funds from the government agencies it services. In other words, it is a cost-reimbursable organization where the project managers are billable for their hours. Each project manager is responsible for maintaining a 70% billability rate. Most employees have relatively high grades (Government Schedule or GS 13-14 on a scale from 1 to 15), with salaries reaching $110,000 in the government's system for determining rank and pay.

PROCEDURES

An interview script that contained mostly open-ended questions was designed. Questions dealt with FEDSIM as a whole and the work-related tasks in which employees engaged. Additional questions requested data about the organization's culture, subcultures, and interviewees' experience with telecommuting.

The participants self-selected themselves for this study by responding to an e-mail invitation to participate from the director of FEDSIM. Interested employees were asked to respond to the researcher by e-mail or telephone. After 38 people responded, the researcher phoned or e-mailed the volunteers to set up appointments, explain the project further, and begin gathering data. Thirty-seven were interviewed and completed a written questionnaire developed to gather background information, such as demographic data, the participant's FEDSIM role, and his or her telecommuting experience.

Each of the 37 interviews lasted anywhere from 20 minutes to 2 hours (average time: 45 minutes). Immediately following the verbal interview, participants filled out the written questionnaire and then chose pseudonyms to protect confidentiality. The signed participation protocols, interview audiotapes, transcribed interviews, and written questionnaires were marked with the same pseudonym to ensure material coordination. Next, the audiotapes were transcribed with the assistance of voice recognition software, ViaVoice for the Macintosh. ViaVoice yields an initial accuracy rate of about 95%, with increasing accuracy as the software continues to develop a voice model for the user (Pogue, 2000). After the ViaVoice transcriptions were completed, I ensured the accuracy of the transcriptions by reviewing them against the audiotapes. Transcriptions yielded 423 pages of single-spaced text.

After the text was transcribed, the data were analyzed using the Nonnumerical Unstructured Data Indexing Searching and Theorizing software, or NUD•IST (QSR International, 1999). NUD•IST was developed specifically for analyzing qualitative data. The software allows text, such as the transcribed interviews, to be imported. After the text is imported, it is possible to read and assign markers to specific segments that indicate what thematic category that segment of text falls within (for more extended discussions of NUD•IST uses, see QSR International, 1999, and Witmer, 1997). I explored themes across participants' interviews and within clusters identified with the assistance of NUD•IST. Using a grounded theory approach (A. Strauss & Corbin, 1998), themes were allowed to emerge from the data as opposed to imposing preset categories. Initial themes were re-examined and clustered using Martin's (1992) three cultural lenses: integration (overarching unifying themes), differentiation (themes distinguished by gendered subgroups), and fragmentation (themes identifying ambiguity or confusion).

Results and Interpretations

My research question was: *How does the opportunity to telecommute affect organizational cultural expectations of gender equality and perceived quality of life?* Analyses of FEDSIM employees' discourse yielded different results depending on the cultural lenses through which data were viewed. From an integrationist viewpoint, FEDSIM appeared as a monolithic organization with values rooted in patriarchal norms and expectations. The differentiation lens revealed distinctions based on space and time but also on gendered value systems. Finally, the fragmentation lens brought to the foreground the typically negated importance of emotions in telework contexts.

AN INTEGRATIONIST VIEW OF FEDSIM AND TELECOMMUTING

The integrationist perspective approaches the question of organizational relationships in the context of telecommuting by looking for expressions of consistency and clarity. These expressions span the content themes, or common threads of expressed concern, as well as the actions and symbolism of which content themes are indicative. Common concerns serve to consistently reinforce one another (Martin, 1992) as, in this study, three discourses of FEDSIM and telework construct and are shaped by a patriarchal ideology that is embraced throughout the organization. First, respondents emphasized billability and productivity as sources of identification, thereby creating an environment based on measurability and transactional exchanges. Numbers were considered more important than relationships. Second, employees emphasized work over family obligations. Even telecommuting was considered in terms that prioritize work over family. Third, telework became a material practice that prioritizes separation over connectedness and community. Telecommuters are separated by technology and have little opportunity for social interaction. Taken together, these three factors display how FEDSIM embraces a stereotypical masculine ideology that was reified through worker discourse and practices.

A shared emphasis on the importance of billability and productivity. Management was often construed in patriarchal terms that emphasize objective forms of measurement and rationality (see Davies, 1998; Mumby & Putnam, 1992). At FEDSIM, measurement and rationality were represented through the monetary means of productivity and billability. The emphasis placed on money meant that employees could view FEDSIM as unique among government agencies because it was, as many employees described it, a "billion-dollar business." The importance of money also meant that they could view FEDSIM as well as their individual contributions to it in terms of measurability. Both men and women described measurability as a form of determining success and individual value. In other words, the employer-employee relationship was expressed in terms of traditional exchange values, where the employee's labor becomes the commodity that takes on value only as determined by organizational criteria for success—that is, his or her ability to maintain billability rates of 70% or more (Sayer, 1991).

The emphasis on billability went hand in hand with the emphasis on productivity. Being billable meant that employees had to account for all of their hours. A 49-year old male telecommuter with the pseudonym "Grizzly" described billability as follows: "You're on the clock. . . . every hour is accounted for." To employees such as "DS," a 44-year-old male telecommuter, billability and productivity became synonymous because productivity meant that workers had to show that they were busy: "You can show that you were not twiddling your thumbs . . . all day." Just as in other wage work contexts (e.g., Perin, 1998; Perlow, 1995, 1998; Zucchermaglio & Talamo, 2000), paid work becomes a priority that takes precedence over other life activities and that is expected to maintain that stature over extended periods of time.

A shared emphasis on the prioritization of work over family. A second integrationist theme is that FEDSIM emphasized quality of life or, as many employees phrase it, *employeecentrism.* Employees often describe employeecentrism in terms of telework. FEDSIM was employeecentric because it allowed employees to choose their own location of paid work. For many employees, the fact that FEDSIM was employeecentric meant that the company allowed employees to balance work and private life better than other organizations did. "Tigger," a 41-year-old female employee, telecommuted from the West Coast so that she could raise her kids in an environment with a quality of life that she considered to be better than on the East Coast. "Allison," a 43-year-old female employee, found that quality of life meant a liberal policy in taking leave when her kids were sick, and to "Frodo," a 48-year-old male telecommuter, it meant being able to take two weeks of vacation in a row. These and other descriptions support the more feminized discourse that current management literature espouses (Fondas, 1997).

However, even as employees noted the importance of quality of life, they also said that their ability to achieve that goal came only by adapting their lives to their paid work rather than adapting work to their private lives. In contrast to espoused benefits of work-life balance (see Hill, Miller, Weiner & Colihan, 1998; Shaw, 1996; F. Wolf, 2001), many employees described telecommuting as a situation in which they were expected to work harder and longer than they did while in the office. Many teleworkers would get up in the middle of the night to work, while others would be reluctant to take vacations ("Bing," a 51-year-old male, noted that he would take a vacation only because he was "forced to" by his kids). For many teleworkers, family life took a secondary role to work life (Haddon & Silverstone, 1995).

However, Allison said that being able to telecommute on an occasional basis meant that "if my kids are sick, I can come home early for whatever reason and work at home, too. It means I don't have to take leave. I can still get the work done." "Clint," a 48-year-old telecommuter, found himself working on weekends because he had important FEDSIM projects to complete. When his family would complain, he would "just ignore them" instead of interacting with his children. Although telework was presented as a work arrangement that supported both organizational and employee needs, in reality, telecommuting supported the employees' ability to do paid work so that FEDSIM was not inconvenienced by the needs of the family.

A shared reality of the material practice of telecommuting and separation. As Clair and Thompson (1996) point out, material and discursive practices coexist in dynamic, intertwined processes that support prevailing ideologies. The material practice of telework through technological connection coexists with the discursive practice of encouraging and normalizing separation among people. Billing by the hour tends to lead to longer hours (and time away from relationships) rather than more efficient performance (which can provide time for more leisure and family activities) (Bailyn, 1993). Not only were FEDSIM telecommuters encouraged to commit more time to work by the very system through which they were paid, but they also were physically distanced from their peers and unable to develop new relationships or to sustain existing ones. Yet they never questioned how the material conditions of their lives fostered lack of flexibility or connection. Employees would often describe themselves as "independent contractors" rather than as coworkers (e.g., "Money," a 58-year-old in-house employee, said that "we're all supposed to function as independent contractors"). Because independence, autonomy, and billability were central to telework at FEDSIM, these values and this work arrangement served to reinforce a patriarchal working environment with limited options for truly alternative organizing processes (e.g., Davies, 1998; Mumby, 2000).

To all employees—teleworkers and in-house employees alike—telecommuting was considered to be normal and the same as working side-by-side in the office because employees remained focused on productivity and adaptability to client and organizational needs. "Fedsim SPM," a 51-year-old female teleworker, always kept her telephone line open even during her off hours because "I've noticed that it's really beneficial to [the clients] to see me be available [to them]." Thus, although telework and other alternative work arrangements espouse flexibility for work, personal, and family concerns, flexibility exists only in the ways paid work and increased productivity are accomplished.

Summary of integration themes. From an integration perspective, work at FEDSIM was masculinized in that what mattered was that it was observable and measurable (Mumby, 1988; Nadesan, 1997; Perlow, 1995), regardless of whether employees were participating in traditional or alternative forms of work. Few people questioned the normalcy of measurability. They went to great lengths to exhibit their commitment to measurable, observable, billable hours even when working from other locations, such as home. At home, family was secondary even when employees claimed that they desired balance between work and private life. As a result, the traditional patriarchal value systems of numeric order and structure remained intact despite the portrayal of telework in feminine terms of family and employee friendliness by all members (Fondas, 1997).

A DIFFERENTIATION VIEW OF FEDSIM AND TELECOMMUTING

From a differentiation lens, inconsistency between expressed content themes and members' actions or practices formed differences between subgroups (Martin, 1992). If the integration analysis left an impression that FEDSIM was a unified culture with a shared focus on billability as a rational measurement of performance, a prioritization of work over family, and an alignment of material practices and socially constructed meanings of telework, then the differentiation lens demolishes these impressions through its emphasis on inconsistencies. Different subcultures emerged from discourses describing anticipated advancement opportunities as well as individual assessments of what would be required for an employee to gain a promotion. Expressed inconsistencies were grounded in gendered expectations and experiences of work life, including those regarding time and space.

Differentiating on the basis of promotability. Interviews revealed a subcultural demarcation based on participants' expectations of their own advancement potential. One group of employees clearly anticipated advancement; indeed, their nonadvancing coworkers anticipated advancement for this group as well. Promotion often appeared to be the result of preselection, with fast trackers or highly promotable individuals rapidly moving through the system either because of qualifications (according to the directors or official discourse) or sociability (according to members' accounts) (for career discourse, see Buzzanell & Goldzwig, 1991; Gowler & Legge, 1989). For many employees, promotions came to be associated with whom they knew rather than objective performance criteria. Promotions were linked closely to networking opportunities with superiors and upwardly mobile coworkers (rather than billability— an irony unnoted by respondents).

Both in-house and telecommuting employees expressed an interest in advancing and, according to the managers, work form (that is, whether an employee is a telecommuter or in-house worker) should make no difference in promotion processes. Furthermore, although women at higher levels remained in the minority, many had advanced at FEDSIM (e.g., the deputy director and several division directors were female) and saw opportunities for further growth. The perception that such opportunities were available to all is important. Even when many signs pointed to increased female participation at the highest levels, women still were faced with glass-ceiling processes embedded in patterns of interaction and participation. For example, women were encouraged by coworkers and supervisors alike to leave work on time to pick up their children, whereas men were encouraged to stay after hours to work overtime. In other cases, lack of participation in meetings because of flexible work hours may have prevented women from being considered for promotions because they were viewed as less committed than men (e.g., Bailyn, 1993; Perlow, 1997). Glass ceilings may have been (re)created in part through the actions of women themselves in addition to those of well-meaning individuals who believe that encouraging women to leave for family reasons while continuing meetings is helping women (Bailyn, 1993; Buzzanell, 1995; Ruether & Fairhurst, 2000). Telecommuting presents an interesting challenge in this context. On one hand, telework has been viewed as an option that enables people to balance demands of work and home life (e.g., Hill, Hawkins, Ferris, & Weitzman, 2001). On the other hand, balance may be achieved at the cost of reinforcing glass ceilings (Duxbury, Higgins, & Neufield, 1998; Mirchandani, 1998; Perlow, 1997). Participants' discourse illuminated an opportunity-cost paradox (for more on paradoxes, see Stohl & Cheney, 2001).

Differentiating on the basis of relationship to space and time. In addition to differentiated subcultures on the basis of advancement opportunities, FEDSIM's employees also differed on the basis of gendered relationships to time and space. Although the boundaries were not unbreachable, they were significant, especially in terms of the divisions that were drawn between men and women's advancement expectations and their work-home balance attempts.

The first division entailed a *feminine attitude toward time and space enacted by men.* For many of FEDSIM's employees, telework did enable them to balance work and family. Teleworkers who found that their lives had been enhanced by flexible work schedules tended to have attitudes toward time and space that were very fluid. For example, Frodo valued being able to spend time at home with his daughter while still being productive. Grizzly appreciated the ability to "time shift some things. Just like right now, if I needed to follow my son over there and pick up my daughter, I could just do that." For many employees with children, telecommuting allowed them to be physically available to family members.

What is significant about this group, however, was that it was *mostly* made up of men with older children, and most members of this group accepted the idea that they could be penalized for their lack of face time or work prioritization. Grizzly said, "By telecommuting, I'm invisible to upper management. I'm more of a statistic, and not interacting, and not going up there and playing golf with the boss and interacting with him personally." These employees had given up opportunities to interact with superiors, which would likely lead to advancement possibilities (Rapoport & Bailyn, 1996), in favor of time and space that enabled more contact with family and friends.

Ironically, many of the people who belonged to this group actually engaged in career-enhancing activities, although not for reasons of increased visibility. "Rose," a 42-year-old female telecommuter, and Grizzly maintained contact by having lunch with people in the office, whereas Fedsim SPM (the 51-year-old female telecommuter mentioned previously), dealt with potential isolation by staying in touch through instant messaging. These people made an effort to maintain contact with colleagues because they enjoyed others' company. Their discourse and attendant behaviors exhibited the value they placed on family, friends, and colleagues and may also have displayed later career stages, when relationships become more important in many men's and some women's work and personal lives (Gordon & Whelan, 1998).

Male teleworkers usually welcomed the ability to enact flexible hours and work locations. In contrast, for the most part, the *female teleworkers enacted a masculine attitude toward time and space.* They took every precaution to ensure that their workdays reflected "normal" work hours (thus negating one of the potential benefits of telework), and they also voiced appreciation for the ability to telework (thus utilizing one benefit of telecommuting—i.e., choice of work space). Interestingly, these women desired advancement in FEDSIM even though they were working outside the main office and had less potential for interaction with supervisors and other managers. As a group, the telecommuters with a fluid relationship to space but a fixed relationship to time were diligent about the way in which they structured their time. Many of these employees emphasized the distinct difference that they saw between work and family life. "Diana," a 45-year-old female telecommuter, drew distinct boundaries in the following way:

> [It's] just like I'm coming in here to work. I go and take a shower, put on my clothes, put on my make-up, I go downstairs into my office and I work the allotted time that I am scheduled to work or if I have to do a little overtime.

Diana's ritualized actions, like the behaviors of many other teleworkers wanting to retain a sense of clear boundaries, served to normalize her nontraditional workplace. To that end, she would turn on her home answering machine when she started to work in the morning, meaning that family members who "want to reach me during the day during work hours, you have to call me on my work number, because I don't answer my home phone number." The importance that teleworkers such as Diana placed on the distinctness of boundaries was rooted in the belief that by maintaining clear lines between work and home life, they could create the impression of being a hard worker who was a valuable organizational member. The impression that workers are efficient and valuable is one that is especially difficult for female employees to attain (Bailyn, 1993). That challenge may be exacerbated by tensions between home and work life that are made visible by the implementation of alternative work programs, particularly for women (Mills, Duncan, & Amyot, 2000; Mirchandani, 1998, 1999; Wiley, 1991). Although all telecommuters in this second group emphasized the need to draw lines between work and home life, the women were more stringent when it came to boundary maintenance work than men. In all cases, telecommuters physically marked their different life spheres by, at a very minimum, closing a door. Male telecommuters, not only in this group but overall, were more inclined to permit the "intrusion" of family members on work activities. DS appreciated being part of his son's early developmental years, noting that "you don't miss a moment." "Joseph," a 45-year-old male telecommuter, saw such interruptions as a normal part of the day: "You just have to be aware of the family. You . . . have to be sure that you're tuned into the family and not just say, 'well, I have to go to work.'"

Some telecommuters in the advancement-oriented group felt that it was important to maintain a relationship with their supervisors, if no one else. DS even went so far as to schedule 2 days a week that he would spend in-house on a regular basis. However, many teleworkers in this group, most typically the women, tended to downplay the importance of interacting socially with coworkers even as they recognized the value of relationships in the organization. Diana repeatedly stated that "I don't need that face-to-face [interaction]" even though she also noted that when she comes in to the office, "There's so many people that I want to talk to and I have, like, 5 minutes between rounds around from this person to that person." "Goldfish," a 32-year-old female telecommuter noted that she did not need to be a part of "the rumor mill." By de-emphasizing the importance of face-to-face interaction, the telecommuters' narratives established ideological inconsistency, or contradictory content themes (Martin, 1992), in relation to in-house employees' narratives, where the importance of face-to-face interaction was established both for those employees who sought advancement and those who did not. Furthermore, the attitude that the women displayed when de-emphasizing the importance of interpersonal relationships may well be to the detriment of obtaining advancement opportunities (Aryee, Wyatt, & Stone, 1996; Davies, 1998; Seibert, Kraimer, & Liden, 2001). In addition to the telecommuting groups, there were two groups of in-house employees at FEDSIM who also valued coworker relationships. Their reasons for valuing these relationships were different and in many ways reflected masculine and feminine attitudes toward work. Although one group, who viewed time as fluid but space as fixed, considered their relationships with coworkers and upper management as essential to advancement, the other group, who viewed both time and space as fixed, saw their relationships from the vantage point of friendship.

Many in-house employees—mostly men—enacted *a masculine attitude toward time and space aligned with their advancement orientation.* They viewed their days in terms of temporal fluidity, where tasks would change as the days went on. The in-house employees who wanted to be promoted viewed that fluidity in positive terms and as something that was exciting. As "Pete," a 37-year-old male in-house employee, put it, "anything can happen," a sentiment echoed by "Nando Jones," a 24-year-old male in-house employee, who noted, "Being here, you don't come in at 8 and leave at 5." In many ways, the in-house promotion-oriented employees adhered to an integrationist view of adaptability to work when it came to time and task processes. However, what distinguished the in-house employees from the telecommuting groups was their emphasis on the need to be co-located to develop collegial connections. They considered such connections crucial to further advancement—therefore, they did not want to telecommute full time. As Money, the 58-year-old male in-house employee mentioned previously, said, "I would not want to isolate myself." "Kevin," a 39-year-old in-house employee, agreed, noting that it is "the face-to-face interaction. There's something about being visible. Them seeing you and you seeing them. That's very important." The men in this group were fully aware of the importance of connections in the development of mentorships and promotion opportunities (Aryee et al., 1996; Seibert et al., 2001).

The directors reinforced the perceptions that in-house advancement-oriented employees had about the importance of face-to-face interactions. Although the directors fully endorsed the benefits of telecommuting to the whole organization, they themselves were unwilling to commit to full-time telework. Many managers suggested that part of their jobs was to be there for their subordinates. "Molly," a 50-year-old director who wanted to keep advancing, indicated that, "being a director . . . people are always going to need to have the ability to walk in and sit down and say, 'listen I need to talk to you about something.'" Bailyn (1993) and Kirby (2000) have pointed out that such comments may be problematic because of the inconsistency between the espoused values (i.e., allowing better work-home balance) and the actual practice of those values, especially as modeled by managers.

A third group with upward mobility aspirations exhibited a *masculine attitude with feminine proclivities.* The in-house employees who did not have further aspirations to advance at FEDSIM were similar to the previous group in that both groups emphasized interpersonal relationships. What made members of the third group different, however, was their focus on camaraderie (rather than connections for the purpose of advancement) as well as their ongoing attempts to fix temporality in addition to space. In other words, this third group greatly emphasized friendships that they developed in their work as a means of support (Sias & Cahill, 1998). Much as in the case of the telecommuters who did not view advancement as an option, this group tended to stress the need for clearly demarcated boundaries between home and work in a stereotypically male way (Mills et al., 2000; Wiley, 1991). "Food Guy," a 58-year-old director who expected to retire in a few years, found it important that "the office is one place, home is another place." "Minimal," a 60-year-old male employee, agreed: "I don't want it [home life] polluted by office life." As a group, these employees tended to keep relatively fixed hours, during which they worked and attempted to keep a fairly strict schedule.

Although this group of in-house employees did not consider promotions to be an option, they still regarded the immediacy of face-to-face communication an essential part of work life. "Alpha," a 51-year-old male employee, found that "oftentimes when [there are] emergencies, the face-to-face always has a much better feel. It may not in fact improve the product, but it improves the crisis person's disposition when there's face-to-face interaction." To "Susan," a 55-year-old female employee, being co-located in the office meant that "there's more sharing . . . of the good stuff as well as the bad stuff." The emphasis on co-locatedness led some employees to question why people would want to telework. As "Frog," a female employee (age undisclosed), asked, why would anyone "want to isolate yourself at work in that environment as opposed to getting involved with things [that] are going on here?" As Perlow (1998) points out, alternative work forms are often developed in organizational contexts that have established work cultures not conducive to new arrangements. When workers begin to telework, in-house employees who view telecommuters as less committed and loyal than themselves may ostracize them.

Thus, in-house employees who were not anticipating promotions still saw co-location as imperative—if not for advancement then for development of camaraderie and ease of work collaboration. The expressed values and necessities of co-location set up a conflictual relationship with telecommuters. Many in-house employees who viewed themselves as not due for promotions dealt with these tensions by distancing themselves from teleworkers. "Ariel," a 29-year-old female in-house employee, noted, "I don't talk to a lot of telecommuters." Minimal, a 60-year-old male in-house employee, felt that, "I have not much interaction with those that are telecommuting now. So my interaction with them is business; it's minimal." Telecommuters were rendered invisible, or ostracized (Perlow, 1997). In Frog's words, "You might as well not exist."

Summary of differentiation themes. The differentiation lens reveals four subgroups divided by perceived promotion opportunities but also by varied relationships to space and time that appear rooted in gendered expectations.

1. Teleworkers who did not view themselves as promotable developed flexible boundaries between home and paid work, thereby adopting what may be construed as a more feminine approach to work life. Ironically, this group was composed predominantly of males with older children and women who did not have children living at home.

2. Paradoxically, telecommuting women with younger children would seem to be the ones who would most benefit from adopting an attitude of work-home boundarylessness. Yet these individuals managed boundaries based on patriarchal values of measurability (Davies, 1998; Mumby & Putnam, 1992) or based on strict temporal boundaries and accountability as foundations for advancement. Measurability as the assumed means to gain promotions meant that these female teleworkers did not interact with their in-house coworkers.

3. The telecommuting employees (primarily female) who wanted to be promoted retained such strict boundaries mirroring traditional organizational temporal structures that they could, in fact, be jeopardizing their own opportunities to advance. The literature on leader-membership exchanges has shown us the importance of interactions between supervisors and subordinates for employee advancement opportunities (e.g., Fairhurst, 1993; Lee, 1999), which the strict adherence to boundaries did not allow. Because coworkers may be promoted in the future, the teleworkers' lack of interaction could inhibit advancement. Furthermore, the tendency to maintain such strict boundaries tended to be particularly widespread among women who accepted the organizational myth of career advancement based on factors other than interpersonal interactions (Buzzanell & Goldzwig, 1991).

4. Teleworkers who did not consider themselves promotable tended to engage in important relationship-building by going to lunch with colleagues and participating in group activities. Ironically, the telecommuters who did not see a promotion in their future might actually be more likely to advance than the telecommuters who wanted to be promoted.

Subgroups' lack of interaction is inconsistent with overall cultural messages because *all* in-house workers stressed the need to connect with other FEDSIM members.

A FRAGMENTATION VIEW OF FEDSIM AND TELECOMMUTING

Whereas the integration narrative constructed FEDSIM as coherent and unified with a dynamic future, and the differentiation narrative described the organization as segmented into promotable/nonpromotable or in-house/teleworker subgroups, the fragmentation lens reveals a FEDSIM that was inherently equivocal to many employees. One way in which employees expressed that equivocality was through their emotions. The expression of emotion is significant because telework literature rarely addresses feelings associated with alternative work forms (as well as traditional work forms, see Fineman, 1996), although emotions are an integral part of organizational life (see Hercus, 1999; Mumby & Putnam, 1992). As such, emotions can often reveal information about organizational life that otherwise would remain hidden. FEDSIM's employees experienced emotions that cut across all organizational experiences but remained distinctly individual expressions. Although there were several emotions that the employees discussed, this chapter focuses on loss, the coexistence of joy with confusion, and fear.

Experiences of loss. The expression of loss in employees' discourse revealed not only profound sadness associated with telecommuting but also the silencing of sadness (see Clair, 1997; Ehrenhaus, 1988). A masculine, rational view of telework as beneficial for workers, clients, and for FEDSIM in general superseded emotional displays. Those who were no longer co-located because they had become teleworkers and those who were left behind implied loss in their discourse and practices—loss not unlike that experienced by job-loss individuals and downsizing survivors. By recognizing the experience of loss and grief, it may be possible to unveil opportunities for positive actions that may help all organizational members to regroup and reconstitute themselves under the new organizational structures that telecommuting represents (Guiniven, 2001; Mossholder, Settoon, Armenakis, & Harris, 2000). Moreover, as Frost, Dutton, Worline, and Wilson (2000) have pointed out, understanding the role of pain and loss in organizations can help point researchers and practitioners in the direction of finding ways to express compassion.

Tensions arise when employees grieve for lost or transitioning relationships (Bensimon, 1997). "Scott," a 56-year old in-house worker, felt frustrated when he transitioned one of his projects to a telecommuter following FEDSIM's reorganization:

> I made the appointment at 1:00 [p.m.] on Wednesday, and she [the telecommuter] said that "I'm going to be doing something." I wanted to strangle her. And she had been right here [visiting the office], we couldn't just sit down when she was here, but I was having an identity crisis losing clients.

As FEDSIM was moving toward a boundaryless organization that included telecommuting, the old targets of identification no longer existed (see Russo, 1998; Scott & Timmerman, 1999). The loss of identification targets was exacerbated by employees' decreased levels of interaction. FEDSIM employees did not realize that they felt detachment as well as loss during times when coworkers left the office to work off site. Gone were routine patterns and rituals of greeting and saying good night to friends after a day's work. Gone were the hallway or cubicle conversations about clients, colleagues, changing practices, and other events and issues.

Although employees recognized the loss of informal interaction, the losses usually went unnoted or were swept aside. But these losses still led to disconnectedness among members. Minimal said the only way that he had been affected by telework was missing "their personal appearances in the office. Other than that, it has not impacted me at all." Still, there was no mistaking the sense of loss when he said that "probably right about 30% vanished. You just don't see those faces. And when you walk around the office, it's empty. They left one by one." Fedsim SPM experienced a different sense of loss since leaving the office:

> I notice that I don't—*belong* is too strong a word, because I do belong to FEDSIM, but I don't belong in that space anymore. I kind of feel funny when I leave there; it's like it's not home anymore? I guess I expected [that it] would be the same—an analogy would be that you moved out of your home, and you go and visit, and a room is there, but it's now a den. You kind of feel funny. You still belong to the family, but you don't belong to the house anymore.

As Fedsim SPM pointed out, the grief that employees experienced was left unattended, and there were no mechanisms in place to help members to deal with loss. Furthermore, there is nothing in management or communication literature that comments on grief associated with telework. Instead, the grief of losing close friends even as both parties remain in the same organizational context remains unspoken. As FEDSIM grew, new employees were brought on board, but the new employees and the telecommuters never had a chance to develop relationships because teleworkers often did not spend time at headquarters. "Number 1," a 40-year-old female teleworker, discovered that

> I no longer know the people on the third floor. I used to know everyone there! Now they're just faces. And some daily, mundane things I used to know about my colleagues, I don't know anymore, because I'm not around.

Although respondents spoke about loss, they also described other emotions, such as joy and confusion. They felt joy about new possibilities and confusion about how to carry them out.

Experiences of joy and confusion. Any experience may give rise to several feelings simultaneously (Basch & Fisher, 2000). Rather than being diametrically opposed, emotions appeared along a continuum (for discussion of bipolar and monopolar dimensions of emotions, see Zerbe, 2000). Employees at FEDSIM experienced both joy and confusion over changes in FEDSIM's structure.

Throughout employees' discourse, it was very evident that they experienced joy in their jobs. Molly, a 50-year-old director who would like to advance, referred to FEDSIM as "the happiest, most professional place anybody could ever want to work." Frodo, the 48-year-old telecommuter mentioned previously, was content at his current level and described himself as being "foaming at the mouth in love with the job." The sources of the employees' positive expressions were very different. In Molly's case, joy came from being validated personally by others through a procedural change. Other people were thrilled about specific experiences. Diana, the 45-year-old telecommuter mentioned previously, described how excited she still felt about a work-related trip to Africa, whereas Fedsim SPM, the 51-year-old female teleworker already introduced, felt joy over her "13 step commute [upstairs to her office]. I really love that! I can see all these poor cars leaving the driveway, and I know that everyone is going to work. . . . Yes, some 13 steps!" Rather than these emotions being forms of ideological ambiguity, as Martin (1992) would suggest, they were connected through ideological complexity, whereby multiple emotional experiences addressed specific organizational values with which each individual could identify. However, employees' experiences did not necessarily address the same ideological theme even as they shared in the same emotion. As such, each individual experienced ideological complexity differently.

Although participants experienced joy, they also felt confused. They voiced concerns about losing control as a familiar environment passed into new structures. Since the restructuring of the organization along client lines, many employees such as Goldfish were constantly trying to "get a feel for exactly what is it that the culture is set up [to be]." Other employees, including "Robert," a 59-year-old teleworker, said that FEDSIM "now looks like it's a plate of very ugly scrambled eggs. It's not a pretty sight." Employees struggled with new expectations surrounding project transfers and new directorates (i.e., projects that they had under the old system now fell under different divisions with new project managers). "Joan," a 33-year-old female in-house employee, pointed out that, "right now, every program manager does things differently."

Experiences of fear. Confusion often leads to feelings of disconnectedness. As a result of the recent reorganization, many people felt distanced from the organization. Robert said that "everybody is an island." Susan questioned, "When you have almost a hundred projects, what kind of quality are you giving to anybody?" Underlying these statements were fears of not being able to keep up with evolving procedures and of not being able to do the job well on behalf of clients. These fears were rooted in action ambiguity, or lack of consistency experienced between content themes and actual practices (Martin, 1992). The actions that employees needed to take to do a good job for the client frequently appeared to be inadequate or not valued. For example, because she did not perceive her work to be valued by others, Susan dealt with ambiguity by distancing herself: "I'm not one of the key people around here."

Many employees said that they did not know how to do their jobs well enough. Goldfish felt "inadequate with where you are, searching to find a way to pay more attention to my technical skills materials, taking more classes, or backing off on some projects and grabbing onto other types of projects." There never seemed to be a good time to catch up; as teleworker Clint said, "Every time that you think that you're okay, they come up with something new!" Employees seemed to have problems with supposedly clear information because they had no basis to understand fully what the information meant. They became frustrated with their inability to interpret data (see Weick, 1995). Furthermore, employees associated fear with telework and the possibility of becoming invisible to the rest of FEDSIM. "Oracle," a 31-year-old male in-house worker, even suggested,

> [The telecommuters would] cease to exist in the minds of management and your boss. If nothing goes wrong, they won't bother you, but at the same time, yours is not the first name that springs to mind when they need somebody to do a new job, a project, or to be promoted, or be on the bowling team, or whatever. That's probably the main reason why I would never [telecommute].

Oracle was not alone in his perception. As in-house employees distanced themselves from their telecommuting coworkers and teleworkers downplayed the importance of social interactions with their in-house counterparts, both sets of workers created emotional tensions that were not resolved.

Summary of fragmentation themes. The fragmentation analysis reveals an abundance of unexpressed emotions. FEDSIM employees experienced deep senses of loss resulting from changing work arrangements, including telework. Many employees felt disconnected when their coworkers telecommuted, but they were reluctant to acknowledge the emotional impact of this loss. However, they did express joy because they could control their own work life and work independently. Many FEDSIM employees asserted traditional values, strengthening connections to paid work, independence, billability, and individual rewards through their declarations of joy. This exuberance masked the loss of feminine values, such as connectedness with others. There were no communal expressions or actions taken to work through feelings, leaving workers feeling isolated.

Discussion

This study of FEDSIM drew upon Martin's (1992) tripartite cultural framework of integration, differentiation, and fragmentation to discuss telework from a gendered perspective. The integration analysis revealed an organization that expressed shared values very much rooted in patriarchal meaning systems. But differentiation analyses uncovered subgroups divided by promotion expectations and preferred locations of and times for work. The differentiation analysis further revealed that female and male teleworkers at different life and career phases navigated home-work boundaries differently. As a result, although members hoped for positive results from telecommuting, they also believed that it was unlikely that productivity (billable hours) would yield promotions without the day-to-day contact that in-house workers experienced.

Furthermore, the fragmentation lens showed the importance of emotions for all members. Although many members talked about emotions associated with telework, the patriarchal integrationist value system that they embraced meant that the importance of their feelings typically was rejected (and unvoiced) in favor of maintaining productivity and billability. All members—male and female—participated in the reproduction of a masculine system of interpretation that emphasized assertiveness and measurable rationality while de-emphasizing emotionality and caring for each other (see Ashcraft & Pacanowsky, 1996). These values were learned and enacted by all employees through everyday work processes and communicative practices.

Taken together, the three analyses point to some significant issues that need to be resolved in practice. Telecommuting could be an opportunity for feminist organizing to be implemented in mainstream organizations (i.e., fluid spatio-temporal boundaries around paid work and family or individual concerns; agency in deciding when and how to enact paid work while finding time to engage in friendships and family activities; collective action and self-help groups to avoid erosion of telework benefits by paid work demands, such as billable hours and in-house members' beliefs that telecommuters are not working). However, FEDSIM members' discourse and practices reveal that attempts to change organizational values and work beliefs are not easily implemented (see also Meyerson & Kolb, 2000). As several researchers (e.g., Bailyn, 1993; Coleman & Rippin, 2000; Mallia & Ferris, 2000) have pointed out, traditional values and work cultures must be changed to devise truly equitable workplaces and innovative work arrangements that can facilitate work-life balance. To accomplish these goals, organizations would need to engage in two interventions.

First, this analysis shows how employees build walls rather than bridges between different groups. Few, if any, employees made concerted efforts to interact with other groups. Lack of such interaction can be particularly damaging to telecommuting women who believed that by working hard, they would be able to advance. Unfortunately, this is not likely to happen. Research shows that social relationships are essential to advancement opportunities (Davies, 1998; Seibert et al., 2001). The advancement myth, which suggests that it is possible to get promoted just by working hard and by embracing masculine standards (Buzzanell & Goldzwig, 1991), is alive and well. Women need to be aware that although telework might offer them flexibility, work-life balance is likely to be achieved at the cost of advancement. Women can and should ask their HR specialists to track women who telecommute and those who work in-house to compare and verify promotion routes and employability criteria. In the meantime, HR specialists can address promotion expectations explicitly and work through practices that contradict written policies. Additionally, organizations should present their membership with opportunities to interact and strongly encourage participation. Such opportunities may include large gatherings for business and/or social purposes (e.g., company picnics), free lunches that pair in-house and telecommuting colleagues, and credit toward billable hours (billable to agency headquarters) for workers who train and/or mentor others.

Second, this study found that emotions were important in telecommuting contexts. Organizations with existing or impending telework programs would do well to make the membership aware of the importance of emotions in organizational environments, especially in telecommuting contexts. Acknowledging emotions and working through feelings are significant themes of job loss and downsizing survivor literature (Buzzanell & Turner, 2003; Guiniven, 2001; Mossholder et al., 2000) that also need to be included in telecommuting research. Formal and informal training programs, brown-bag lunches, Web sites, and farewell gatherings can provide safe spaces for workers to express feelings and gain help if feelings of detachment and sadness become intense and damaging to relationships.

Although the current analysis suggests that certain applied practices would be effective, questions about telework as a gendered process and practice remain unanswered. First, the present study is a case study that cannot make any claims about generalizability or the longitudinal consequences of telecommuting. Second, this study does not consider the possibility that telework might be associated with different experiences and interpretations for people with different demographic backgrounds. For example, it is likely that marital and family status could lead to different expectations for both men and women who telecommute. Similarly, other factors, such as race/ethnicity, class, age, and able-bodiedness could play roles in the negotiated meaning systems for organizational members. Finally, feelings of loss, confusion, fear, and joy should be explored further, not just in the telecommuting context but in all situations of organizational change. Including feelings in organizational change literature would enable researchers to name the emotions that are present and thereby enable more emotion-based interventions.

In conclusion, telecommuting is an alternative work form that presents opportunities to challenge existing organizing processes but, as this study of

FEDSIM reveals, it is a practice that can just as easily reproduce and reinforce existing gendered realities. To FEDSIM's employees, telework was another way to enact and embrace masculine rationality and efficiency without question. Telecommuting opens opportunities to challenge the gendered nature of existing norms and structures as long as researchers and practitioners remember that it is a socially constructed phenomenon rooted in real material conditions. For employees to structure their work (and home) lives in ways that serve their own best interests, they need to envision their organizational cultures, telework, and other work forms as evolving and changeable processes.

4

Commentary

Lessons Learned and Possibilities Revealed From Feminist Scholarship

Connie Bullis

Feminist scholarship, traditionally understood, aims to improve women's lives. To do so, such scholarly work is grounded in women's lives and utilizes processes that diverge from mainstream social science methods. The products are pieces of knowledge that are beneficial to women. By adopting a feminist frame, the chapters in Part I of this book serve to exemplify the purposes, processes, and products of feminist scholarship. First, given the trend toward considering feminism as having achieved its goal of gender equality, let us ask whether there is a need for feminist scholarship. Second, we consider processes through which feminist scholarship proceeds. Third, we consider the products or ends. Fourth, we examine the ways scholarly research improves women's lives. In doing so, I suggest that recent discussions of "civically" engaged scholarship may be valuable.

Is There a Need?

The Introduction of this book compellingly illustrates both that women are subjected to sexist treatment and that theorizing needs to better account for this concern. In Chapter 1, accounts given by festival goers in Marcy Meyer and Laura Shue O'Hara's study suggest the need for feminism; women attending

Author's Note: I would like to extend my appreciation to Karen Rohrbauck Stout for her contributions to this commentary.

the festival report that they attend to feel safe, to be open about their sexuality, and to feel supported. The political struggle that constitutes much of the festival content further illustrates the need for feminism. And the counterdiscursive moves identified, such as affection display among lesbian women and the discomfort with such display reported by university students, remind us that struggles with marginalization continue. Similar to the work of Marcy Meyer and Laura Shue O'Hara, Patrice Buzzanell's Chapter 2 is grounded in a university setting, where we might expect to encounter somewhat progressive attitudes and patterns of interaction. Yet we encounter clear cases in which women are graded differently from men while the institution ignores the troubling dynamics. Although the accounts in Chapters 1 and 2 are worrisome because of their campus settings and their analyses of the roles of higher-education institutions in these cases, Annika Hylmö's case is at least as troubling because it reveals how some women are harmed through an apparently family-friendly practice: telecommuting. In all three chapters, we are introduced to compelling reminders that, in spite of several decades of feminism and the many ways in which women have improved their lives, normal routines continue to harm women.

In Chapter 2, Patrice Buzzanell asks why we have been re-examining the same issues for decades. The cases here provide sad and potent reminders that we do need to continue to examine the same issues and that much has not changed. These chapters remind us of just how pervasive gender dynamics continue to be in our lives and institutions. Further, each of these accounts illustrates women's lives in the context of particular institutional contexts and how these gendered dynamics harm women in particular ways.

What Processes Are Useful?

Rather than reviewing feminist methods in this section, let us consider these chapters as a group. Although there is much to be gleaned from each chapter's unique contributions in the understanding of feminist theory, methods, and guidance for feminist transformation, here I focus on their similarities. Marcy Meyer and Laura Shue O'Hara present a feminist ethnography and integrate complementary theories as a way to understand the counterdiscursive moves made by lesbian feminist discursive community members, as well as the ways in which dominant and suppressed groups adopt one another's discursive moves as they interact. Focusing specifically on sexual harassment, Patrice Buzzanell suggests that we have yet to adequately theorize the gendered situations that harm women. By rethinking our theories and by integrating complementary theories in ways that provide a more comprehensive theoretical frame, she suggests that we may be better able to understand and thereby address sexual harassment in particular and gender problems more generally.

She develops an integrative framework for examining sexual harassment and suggests how her framework might be used. Annika Hylmö uses an integrative framework that includes three theoretical lenses previously identified and applied in organizational studies so that she can develop a comprehensive analysis of the gender dynamics surrounding telecommuting in a particular organizational context. Each chapter, then, illustrates that our individual theories have been inadequate. We often need to integrate theories with complementary strengths to reveal dynamics that warrant attention.

Each chapter develops multiple levels of analysis. In particular, in each chapter, individual lives are revealed through detailed accounts offered by the individuals themselves. These accounts are then understood in terms of the institutional contexts and power dynamics within which they occur. Marcy Meyer and Laura Shue O'Hara contrast the lesbian women's festival purpose and experiences with the patriarchal institutional surroundings within which the festival is situated. Patrice Buzzanell juxtaposes the sexual harassment experiences revealed in her chapter with the report that her institution decided not to have its sexual harassment committee continue to meet regularly. Annika Hylmö provides individual accounts and experiences with telecommuting while illustrating the organizational context that suggests different meanings and important outcomes for women who telecommute. In each case, by embedding experiences and particular interaction dynamics within institutional surroundings, the analysis is meaningfully enhanced. We are able to consider how institutional dynamics serve to produce particular experiences and, in some instances, how institutional dynamics serve to conceal and/or deny those same experiences.

Relatedly, it is disturbing to encounter so many instances in which women are harmed and, according to feminist interpretations, unaware of the harm. These analyses may be useful because they encourage us to question whether we are sometimes overly cautious in our reliance on direct participant sensemaking accounts. In contrast, these analyses are grounded in women's lives but extend to institutional and theoretical analyses.

All three case analyses reveal the value of irony as an analytic logic for discerning complex (and ironic) relationships among levels. In Patrice Buzzanell's chapter, she argues for complicating understandings. In doing so, she both uses irony in her own analyses and reviews literature that relies on irony. For example, she draws on irony in considering the temporal juxtaposition of the sexual harassment she reports with the activist project initiation occurring in the class and the lowered level of administrators' concerns about sexual harassment on the campus. She also relies on irony as she reviews pertinent studies. For example, in analyzing Townsley and Geist's (2000) analysis, she comments that the authors connote passivity in labeling their research participants as "victims." Marcy Meyer and Laura Shue O'Hara rely on a logic of irony as they interpret discursive ways in which the marginal group sometimes reproduces dominant exclusionary practices—for example, by insisting on admitting only those with certain lesbian identities to a certain festival, excluding those who are not "real" lesbians. At the same time, their analysis reveals how the dominant group reproduces identity constructions used by the marginalized group as the dominant group relies on the importance of a safe space and political place in their accounts. Annika Hylmö identifies *employeecentrism* as the organization's interest in facilitating balance between employees' work and private lives. She also points out that telecommuting employees who choose to balance their work and private lives often ironically ignore their private lives in favor of working longer hours at home while telecommuting. Further, although her participants identified billability (a particular form of productivity) as an important integrative theme throughout the organization, they also pointed out that, ironically, networking rather than billability was the known way to be promoted.

This logic of irony may be needed in feminist analyses to reveal gender dynamics. Possibly, theoretical lenses that don't include irony may be unable to identify the kinds of forces that are so potently revealed in these analyses. The three chapters reveal rich and varied ways in which irony was employed to construct insightful analyses.

What Is Learned?

In addition to the many unique and complex results of each study, we encounter at least three similar findings. First, all three chapters report detailed, situated analyses resulting from close attention to participants and complex, multileveled analyses that provide insight into how participants' experiences are ironically related to the institutional dynamics within which they are located.

Second, isolation repeats itself as a theme throughout these cases. Although a cursory review suggests very different uses of the theme from chapter to chapter, a second look suggests that there may be more commonality than is at first evident. Marcy Meyer and Laura Shue O'Hara discern isolation as a strategy employed both by the lesbian feminist marginalized group and by the administrative campus managers. Just as the festival goers (and, presumably, the organizers) value the opportunity to express themselves while isolated from their usual contexts and from the normal campus spaces, the administrators value isolation and use it as a means of managing the diversity inherent in the festival. Marcy Meyer and Laura Shue O'Hara's case study suggests that community is a means of overcoming isolation. Their analysis shows how this isolated community was liberating for its members while, at the same time, its sequestered nature limited its liberating potential. This analysis adds an ironic commentary in showing how the dominant culture was able to ignore difference by facilitating this isolation while supporting the community.

In Patrice Buzzanell's analysis, isolated women experience sexual harassment as an individual experience. Further, situations in which women are isolated with potential harassers, such as in closed-door sessions with faculty members and in situations where women are accompanied by faculty members to off-campus events, create contexts in which harassment sometimes occurs. Harassment is analyzed by focusing on individual responses, a further means of isolation. Other theoretical approaches isolate masculine and feminine public/private and justice/care contexts. As in Marcy Meyer and Laura Shue O'Hara's chapter, in Patrice Buzzanell's analysis, overcoming isolation in favor of community is an antidote to sexual harassment. She hopes that a woman who was harassed is able to make sense of her experiences through discussions with her supportive academic community, and that the woman will generate a helpful account while those around her become more aware of hostile work environment sexual harassment. At the same time, by integrating feminist ethics into sensemaking about sexual harassment, a community discussion is an essential antidote. In other words, isolation facilitates ongoing sexual harassment, while community discussion facilitates an end to such harassment.

Feelings of isolation were a consequence of telecommuting for some workers in Annika Hylmö's analysis. Both traditional employees and telecommuters reported that telecommuters were isolated from the organization. In this case, isolation seems to be an unintended consequence of flexible working arrangements, and it also isolates some employees from the promotion-enhancing networking operative in the organizational context. In all three analyses, isolation both protects and harms, while community is understood as a complexly connected entity. Together, these chapters suggest that the varied and complex connections between isolation and community may be important dynamics in future explorations.

Third, the individual findings and the set of findings from these studies act as exemplars of careful feminist scholarship that uncover insights into women's and men's everyday lives so that we see oppressive situations within the material or situated experiences of their lives. We might also continue to seek ways for scholarship to directly benefit lives. Next I suggest that feminist scholarship may benefit from recent discussions in civically engaged scholarship.

How Does Feminist Scholarship Improve Women's Lives?

In these chapters, there is much potential for future inquiry beyond the scope of the reports. Marcy Meyer and Laura Shue O'Hara's work relies on feminist ethnography. In addition to their goal of providing an insightful analysis, they explicitly sought to improve women's lives. Yet there is no evidence that the co-researchers' lives are directly improved from this study. Instead, there are many important potential ways in which additional efforts could help in the future, including activism to change federal and state legislation to benefit same-sex couples, fund raising campaigns for events like these that support diverse communities, and development of committees to propose ways of better incorporating the festival into the larger community (thus providing greater consciousness-raising opportunities for the larger community). Patrice Buzzanell sets out an agenda to be used and developed in a particular context to help develop adequate accounts. She also reports her own efforts in encouraging community discussions so that more useful accounts may be generated. Annika Hylmö ends with helpful advice to organizations. Her analysis reveals patterns that may well generalize beyond this particular context to women in many scenarios. However, as is true of the other chapters, there is no evidence that these immediate participants will benefit from this particular study.

Should we expect immediate benefits to participants in research? On one hand, perhaps the greatest contributions are careful, complex analyses that yield insights into problematic patterns and relationships. These analyses become resources for change and improvement. On the other hand, we sometimes articulate an obligation to the particular participants in our studies, but it is difficult to design scholarship so that this promise is necessarily redeemed.

Recent conversations and efforts discussed as civically engaged scholarship may be useful in providing possibilities for more closely aligning particular scholarship with particular participant benefits. Although I cannot summarize this important conversation here (see Ehrlich, 2000), I focus on "genuine partnerships" (W. Sullivan, 2000) as one particular facet that is especially relevant.

As conversations about civic engagement have suggested that higher education has become overly divorced from the public arena in which its mission and identity were historically grounded, institutions have struggled to define and enact civic engagement. One of the important successful means of civic engagement that has emerged from this effort on individual campuses has been forming ongoing partnerships with external entities. In some cases, such unions are developed between the educational institution and the local community. In other cases, smaller, more focused partnerships between small groups or individuals within the educational institution and within the community have been formed. W. Sullivan (2000) discusses the creation of partnerships as it is related to a change from instrumental to practical reasoning and from a positivist assumption of knowledge to an assumption of socially responsive knowledge. In other words, for our purposes, as we turn to theories of knowledge that assume that knowledge evolves from the community through which it is produced, we consider partnerships as the forming of new communities that necessarily also produce new kinds of knowledge. To the extent that inquiry is designed through and for a professional community of scholars, the knowledge produced is most responsive to the expectations of that community. When inquiry is located within "genuine partnerships . . . knowledge and practices evolve cooperatively rather than proceeding in a one-directional way from experts to outsiders" (W. Sullivan, 2000, p. 34).

As groups and institutions have struggled to practice partnerships, we are learning that, as genuine partnerships are enacted, purposes, procedures, and outcomes often are defined in radically different ways from how they are defined through disciplinary scholarship. Put simply, feminist scholars may benefit from forming strong partnerships through which inquiry is formulated, purposes defined, and scholarship proceeds. By formulating inquiry within such partnerships, we may find that scholarship can be designed to more directly benefit women's lives. We may also find that research purposes, processes, and outcomes are radically different from those developed within academic communities. For example, in some cases, the production of scholarly reports may not be a relevant outcome when inquiry is designed through such a union. Such partnerships could radically challenge our understandings of knowledge, purpose, and the relationship between academia and society. The scholarship in these chapters may be understood as representing a historical struggle between producing socially responsive knowledge that benefits women and that simultaneously honors traditional forms of knowledge production. In addition to providing new and complex insights into meaningful material issues as they affect women's lives, these chapters display possibilities that renegotiate the relationship between knowledge production and newly formed hybrid communities through which knowledge is produced.

Part II

Gendering Health

5

Women Cancer Survivors

Making Meaning of Chronic Illness, Disability, and Complementary Medicine

Laura L. Ellingson

The rejection of imperfect bodies in Western cultures is evident in the popular media and manifested in attitudes toward people with disabilities, disfigurements, and others deemed unattractive by social standards (Couser, 1997; Frank, 1991, 1995; Goffman, 1963). The pervasive Western ideology of individualism reinforces the notion that anyone who works hard can succeed in life (including achieving health and physical attractiveness) and thus justifies the rejection of those who do not (Lupton, 1994).

A rapidly growing group of women survive cancer but live with chronic illnesses, impairments, and disfigurements caused either directly by the cancer or as "side effects" of invasive medical treatments. This particular group occupies a position at the intersection of (at least) three marginalizing identities. First, the biomedical model positions patients as helpless and unreliable sources of knowledge about their bodies (Vanderford, Jenks, & Sharf, 1997). Second, women as a group are treated as "other" within the Western health care system, which positions the male as norm and the female as deviant (Wear, 1997). Third, cancer survivors with persistent physical and/or emotional effects of disease and treatment are stigmatized by society and dehumanized by

Author's Note: I wish to thank my co-researchers (who remain anonymous at their request) for sharing their experiences and for listening to mine with warmth and compassion. My thanks also go to Dr. Carolyn Ellis, Dr. Elena Strauman, and James LaPierre for their helpful insights and support.

the medical establishment. Physicians are taught to relentlessly seek to cure patients and consequently feel frustration and failure when managing incurable chronic conditions (Charmaz, 1991). This three-way marginalization serves to diminish or silence many voices despite co-existing marks of privilege, such as high levels of education and middle-class economic status.

Members of this marginalized group, myself included, resist social and medical marginalization, in part, by becoming active in the management of our chronic illnesses, impairments, and disfigurements through researching and using alternative medicine. This chapter explores the meanings of alternative medicine use among women cancer survivors living with impairments or chronic illnesses, offering a preliminary model of a value-centered approach to understanding patients' construction of meaning about health care. I explore theoretical and pragmatic implications of this model for research on health care provider-patient communication and for addressing the marginalized role of alternative medicine in the medical establishment.

Historically, the medical profession has relentlessly policed its borders, lobbying governments, conducting information campaigns, and instituting professional standards within its own governing body (i.e., the American Medical Association) to increase its social power and delegitimize groups and ideas that threaten its dominance (Ehrenreich & English, 1973; Wear, 1997). To contextualize my analysis of participants' experiences with alternative/ complementary and conventional medical care, I explore research on three discourses that are relevant to this process of marginalization: complementary and alternative medicine; chronic illness and disability during and after cancer treatment; and sexism in the medical establishment.

Complementary and Alternative Medicine

Use of alternative medicine is a rapidly growing trend in Western societies (Gürsoy, 1996; S. Williams & Calnan, 1996). Alternative therapies are widely used in the United States (34% of respondents) (D. Eisenberg et al., 1993); Canada (42% of respondents) (Fernandez, 1998; see also Marble, 1998); and Australia (48.5% of respondents) (MacLennan, Wilson, & Taylor, 1996). In 1990, $13.7 billion was spent on alternative medicine in the United States (D. Eisenberg et al., 1993). The mainstream medical community reluctantly is taking alternative medicine more seriously as use increases. Although medical schools do not usually condone alternative medicine or integrate it into their required curriculum, 64% of medical schools surveyed in the United States offered some coverage of alternative medicine, mostly as elective courses (Neimark, 1997). The Office of Alternative Medicine, formed at the National Institutes of Health in 1992 to promote research on the efficacy of alternative therapies, legitimates such practices as worthy of study and yet at the same time rhetorically marks them as separate from and outside of conventional medicine.

A wide range of practices fall under the rubric of alternative medicine, including (but not limited to) acupuncture, acupressure, herbal remedies, meditation, vitamin therapy, rolfing (a type of deep massage), therapeutic touch, therapeutic massage, colonic/enema therapies, certain chiropractic and homeopathic remedies, and chelation. Alternative, holistic, natural, unconventional, unorthodox, complementary, and native are some of the terms used in discussing these treatments (Jonas, 1998). Because the vast majority of people use alternative therapies concurrently with (*not* instead of) conventional medicine (D. Eisenberg et al., 2001; McGregor & Peay, 1996), I will use the term *complementary medicine.* Problematically, people who use both generally do not inform their conventional physicians that they are using complementary medicine (Downer et al., 1994; D. Eisenberg et al., 1993). Patients who do tell their oncologists about complementary medicine use are often disappointed in perceived physician apathy (R. Gray et al., 1997).

Chronic Illness and Disability During and After Cancer Treatment

While undergoing cancer treatment, many patients are disabled by exhaustion, weakness, nausea, pain, and other effects of disease and treatment. Although many of these symptoms go away after recovery, others persist. Female cancer survivors have reported significant incidence of physical, psychological, and social problems (family distress and sexuality problems) long after their treatment ended (Ferrell, Dow, Leigh, Ly, & Gulasekaram, 1995). Relationships between cancer survivors and their loved ones are often affected, and work re-entry difficulties are common (Ferrell et al., 1995). Despite our ongoing suffering, I and other cancer survivors have often been told by medical practitioners that we should just "be happy to be alive" and should not mind living with permanent disfigurements, impairments, and debilitating chronic illnesses. Yet these problems cause physical and emotional pain, affecting our daily lives (Charmaz, 1991).

Women with cancer-related impairments and chronic illnesses are part of a much larger group of women with disabilities. More than half of disabled people are women, and 16% of women are disabled (Wendell, 1992). Women are even more tied to the body as a source of identity than men (e.g., N. Wolf, 1991; Wood, 2001). Thus disabled women suffer more than men from failing to meet the cultural demand for ideal bodies (Wendell, 1992). Unlike the finality of death, chronic illness and progressive disability involves continual loss that requires ongoing or periodic grieving (P. Gordon, 1998; Hewson, 1997; Mairs, 1996). Female cancer survivors who have chronic conditions or impairments are not easily categorized by self or others; they occupy the borderlands between health and illness, ability and disability, wholeness and loss, femininity and "damaged goods" (Hewson, 1997).

Because the participants in this project have damaged bodies that forever identify us as "wounded storytellers" (Frank, 1995), our illness experiences do not have neat beginnings and endings. We continue to struggle with the identity and consequences of being sick in a culture that glorifies health and physical perfection (Frank, 1991). Despite the advances brought about by the Americans With Disabilities Act (1990) in the United States, society continues to be organized around the assumption that people are either completely able and healthy, or they are completely disabled and objects of charity; there is still not enough middle ground (Wendell, 1992).

Sexism in the Medical Establishment

The liminality of women who have survived cancer but continue to cope with chronic symptoms is only one facet of a much larger problem; women's experiences are marginalized in all aspects of conventional health care. Research, education, and practice of diagnosis, treatment, and illness management have focused on the bodies and experiences of men (Harrison, 1992; K. Johnson, 1992; Wear, 1997). Contemporary feminist critics of medical science note:

> First, scientific knowledge (types of data collected, its analysis and the nature and boundaries of scientific paradigms) are found to be biased in a way that sustains male authority and patriarchal power bases. Second, the way science is conducted (the very process of science making) in academic and research institutions is judged to be hostile to women, therefore excluding women's entry and genuine contribution to science. Finally, when women have made contributions within the actual system itself, their work has often been rendered invisible (Gürsoy, 1996, p. 584).

Other scholars, such as Wear (1997), point to the intersection of race, gender, and class oppression within the medical community, which keeps white, upper-class men firmly entrenched in the highest positions within medicine.

Physician-patient communication is an area of particular concern. Although good physician-patient communication is critical to quality health care for women (Ellingson & Buzzanell, 1999; Mann, 1998), research demonstrates that physicians often do not listen to women carefully and will take women's concerns less seriously than men's (Gabbard-Alley, 1995; Todd, 1989). An asymmetrical relationship places physicians in authority over patients, a power dynamic that is exacerbated further when the doctor is male and the patient is female (Borges & Waitzkin, 1995). Physicians are especially distrustful and dismissive of women with vague and chronic symptoms (Strauman, 1997; Wendell, 1992).

This study gives voice to and legitimates patient accounts of marginalized experiences, including making decisions about complementary medicine. Complementary medical practices have their roots in myriad traditions that espouse beliefs and values inconsistent with, and often antithetical to, the biomedical model that still pervades the practice of conventional medicine (D. Morris, 1998). I posed the following research question: What meanings do women cancer survivors living with chronic illnesses and/or impairments construct for their use of complementary medicine? By investigating how women invoke the marginalized discourse of complementary medicine to manage their already marginalized positions in health care, I garner insights into the meanings patients construct of illness and treatment experiences and the values supporting those meanings.

Method

RESEARCH PARTICIPANTS

I participated in three interviews with women cancer survivors who utilized complementary medicine throughout their treatment and who continue to use alternative therapies. Interviews were carried out in fall of 1999 and spring of 2000. I utilized a convenience sample, inviting one friend to participate and using word of mouth to find other participants. To contextualize the findings, I provide brief participant histories.

Liza Stone[1] was diagnosed with non-Hodgkin's lymphoma in 1990. After 2 years of surgery, chemotherapy, and steroid therapy, Liza went into remission. Liza has several prominent surgical scars on her chest. Since her treatment, Liza has suffered from fatigue, fibromyalgia, swelling and numbness in her hands, and hypersensitivity to pollutants and allergens. Charlotte Donnelly was diagnosed in 1984 with cancer of the optic nerve and pituitary gland while she was 7 months pregnant. After delivering a healthy baby, she underwent radiation and steroid therapy followed by surgery. Charlotte was extremely nauseated, weak, and fatigued by treatment. Today, Charlotte continues to struggle with fatigue, metabolic problems, allergies, and migraine headaches, all illnesses resulting from treatment. Her long surgical scar is mostly covered by her hair. Natalie Ford survived metastatic cervical cancer in 1974; she had a total hysterectomy, had parts of her small intestine and abdominal wall removed, and underwent chemotherapy. Because she was not given hormone replacement therapy, Natalie developed severe osteoporosis. She also is undergoing treatment for hepatitis C and has back problems and severe osteoarthritis. Finally, I was diagnosed in 1989 with bone cancer. After chemotherapy, a section of my right femur was replaced with a bone graft. Nine more months of chemotherapy followed, during which a series of infections led to having my bone graft removed; a second graft was inserted after completion of chemotherapy. Nausea, fatigue, suppressed immune system, and pain were primary side effects. Since then, I have had osteoarthritis and narrow range of movement in my leg. My leg is misshapen by swelling, several scars, a muscle graft, and a skin graft.

All of the women who participated in this study are white, middle-class heterosexuals who have attained high levels of education (one participant had a PhD, two had completed master's degrees, and one had a bachelor's degree). The social privileges of our race, class, sexual identity, and education were as much a part of our experience with conventional and complementary medicine as our less-advantageous positions as women with cancer-related chronic illnesses who use complementary medicine.

PROCEDURES

I sought a method that would allow participants to share ideas in a comfortable manner. I was uneasy interviewing others while refusing to share my own story. On the other hand, I also did not want to use my experience as the sole data set. Interactive interviewing enabled me to be both a participant in the study and a facilitator for others' participation. Interactive interviewing does not privilege the researcher over the participant in the manner of traditional interviewing (Ellis, Kiesinger, & Tillmann-Healy, 1997).[2] Researcher and participants share thoughts and question each other in conversation. Consistent with feminist research principles (DeVault, 1990; Reinharz, 1992), interactive interviewing has the potential to be mutually empowering, enabling participants to engage in sensemaking about their experiences. I found the interviews rewarding, and each of my participants reported that they also enjoyed themselves.

The interviews varied in length from one and a half to two and a half hours. I conducted the interviews with each participant individually in private settings (e.g., a participant's home). Interviews were audio-recorded and transcribed. Following DeVault (1990), I sought to represent as faithfully as possible the nuances of our language and did not edit transcripts for grammar or clarity. Interviews were followed by conversations (in person and via e-mail) to further clarify thoughts and to enable participants to give feedback on my findings (Reinharz, 1992).

DATA ANALYSIS

I initially conducted a thematic analysis of the transcripts from these interactive interviews using Owen's (1984) three criteria for assessing themes: recurrence (same meaning, different wording); repetition (same wording); and forcefulness (nonverbal cues that stress or subordinate words or phrases). As the process of data analysis continued, it became apparent that the themes we were discussing related to a core set of values that would serve well as an organizing framework. At this point, I used the value identification in narrative discourse (VIND) process developed by Vanderford, Smith, and Harris (1992). Narrative theorists posit that stories are inherently value-laden (W. Fisher, 1985). Vanderford et al. (1992) extended existing narrative theory by developing guidelines for systematic analysis of characters and actions in participants' discourse designed to reveal their attitudes, beliefs, and values. I used these guidelines to identify the values reflected in our talk.

Results: Values in Complementary Medicine Use

The values of pragmatism, agency, open-mindedness, equality, connection, and harmony with nature were reflected in the interactive interviews. Taken together, these values offer a preliminary model for understanding resistance to marginalization by patients occupying particularly problematic positions vis-à-vis the authority of the medical establishment. In our experience, communication between participants and complementary medical practitioners almost always reflected these values, whereas communication with conventional physicians too often did not. A value-centered approach to communication may prove more helpful in generating alternatives to the biomedical model than approaches that emphasize specific verbal and nonverbal communicative practices (e.g., eye contact, posture) because it focuses on the roots of preferences for particular practices. For ease of discussion, the values are considered here individually; however, in the interviews, two or more values often overlapped.

PRAGMATISM

The first value, pragmatism, is the desire to use strategies that work well. A primary motivation for using complementary medicine was its effectiveness in lessening pain, swelling, and other symptoms. Liza, Charlotte, Natalie, and I sought complementary medicine because it worked where conventional medicine often did not, providing at least partial relief. Liza described the suffering she experienced during her treatment:

> It was a 3-week cycle. I had very high doses of prednisone the first two weeks. Then you go off it completely the next week. . . . And they gave me a drug that was so strong; it was during that time period that I suffered the most nausea and physical pain. Uh, but it wasn't until these problems built up in my system that my withdrawal from the prednisone became much more acute. And the chemotherapy and the toxins built up, and I was in chronic pain.

During her treatment, Liza experimented with a range of herbal and dietary regimens, bee sting therapy, and hydrogen peroxide treatments to treat pain, nausea, and fatigue, and meditation and visualization for stress relief and improved immune system function. Charlotte sought out acupuncture, acupressure, massage therapy, and herbal therapy to alleviate the nausea caused by the radiation and medication. Natalie used visualization, special diets, and herbal treatments to treat chemotherapy symptoms and to enhance her immune system. I used vitamin therapy, visualization, and meditation to treat nausea, fatigue, and suppressed immune function. At the time of the interviews and analysis, we all used various types of complementary medicine to treat our chronic conditions.

Laura: For me, alternative medicine has been so much better at treating those kinds of diffuse, more general symptoms that are harder to treat with allopathic medicine. You know if you tell doctors you're fatigued, they are like, "oh well, yeah."

Natalie: Yeah—"Too bad!"

Laura: Whereas you go to an herbalist or you do research on your own, and there are ways to try to address that. They aren't all going to work, like you said. If they don't work, you move on.

Natalie: What I found, I'm very pragmatic, I am not, like, what you call "New Age-y." What I am is pragmatic. And if whatever the regime it was didn't seem to help, after a period of time, I was on to something else. And I kept on with the visualization through the whole thing—that really felt empowering. I did a low-fat, high-fiber food combination thing, it just made me bloated and gassy, so after a month, I just quit it. I did do [the juicing diet] because it seemed to help. The things that didn't help, I didn't do.

Conventional medical practitioners also valued pragmatism and generally strove to effectively manage diseases and symptoms. However, each of us had been told that some symptoms could not be relieved by current medications and procedures, and we were advised to "live with it." None of us were encouraged by conventional practitioners to seek out complementary medicine to alleviate persistent symptoms, even when conventional treatments were ineffective. Fortunately, Natalie and I also have had more positive experiences with conventional physicians who, although not advocating complementary medicine, were open to discussing it and respected our choices. Charlotte and Liza have not had success finding conventional practitioners open to discussing complementary medicine.

AGENCY

Agency refers to the feeling of control and empowerment we have as agents of our own health. Decisions to obtain effective treatments and discontinue ineffective ones were possible because of our ability to seek out alternatives and to find and form relationships with complementary practitioners. We seized agency, moving from objects of the physician's gaze to active subjects as we engaged in complementary medicine (Couser, 1997; C. Sullivan, 1997). Even the process of learning about complementary medicine gave us a greater sense of control.

Liza: We manage perceptions of our health and of how worthy we are using a variety of tools, including alternative medicine, and there comes a point at which you realize that . . . what matters is your perception of yourself, and there comes a time when you need no audience for that.

Laura: Then you're on a path of healing.

Liza: I still had enough energy to do research, and that was one of the ways I would cope. . . . I familiarized myself with different herbs and their side effects. During my treatment I studied alternative medicine, and it was an extension of my research.

Of course, our middle-class status facilitated our agency; being able to afford complementary treatments was a privilege that many in lower socioeconomic classes do not share. Also, our education gave us research skills that facilitated the gathering and analysis of information.

Not all therapies we explored were useful. Each of us mentioned therapies that we had tried and found unhelpful or too unpleasant. In those cases, we chose to discontinue them and "move on to something else" (Natalie). Much of the agency seemed to come not just from finding relief from symptoms (i.e., pragmatism) but from the process of research, selection, and consumption of complementary medicine. Being complementary medicine users was an integral aspect of our identities; it gave us comfort in the face of judgmental others who accused us of being ill through personal failure. Self-confidence developed as we learned we were capable of making good decisions about our health, a feeling rarely fostered by traditional physicians. This active decision-making process offered hope in a way that conventional treatments often didn't (Stambolovic, 1996), and hope eased some of the pain of day-to-day life.

A sense of agency helped us face the pervasive "blame the victim" mentality. People who have not confronted serious illness tend to believe in a just world in which people get what they deserve: "Our cultural insistence on controlling the body blames the victims of disability for failing and burdens them with self-doubt and self-blame" (Wendell, 1992, p. 72). The achievement of health thus becomes a moral issue, indulgence or failure a sin, and success a virtue and a symbol of one's hard work (Frank, 1991; Lupton, 1994). This social judgment is unrelenting and thus difficult to bear; even children learn to believe in a just universe:

Liza: We treat people who are overweight, who have mental depression, which is increasingly more common, with alcoholism, you name it, as if they deserved these problems somehow. . . . The daughter of one of my friends asked me what did I do to get cancer, and my response was that I didn't know.

Laura: It's frustrating. One of the problems I have is that I don't go a day without having people staring at my leg, or asking me what went wrong. . . . When I get in an elevator, I hate it when someone is standing next to me and decides to put me through the inquisition. . . . I'm called upon to explain my differences.

Liza: I agree. It's funny, it really speaks to how uncomfortable we are with difference, how preoccupied we are with making ourselves feel better by virtue of comparing ourselves to other people. We are supposed to compare ourselves to Kate Moss and other models. . . . That standard . . . that we call good health, and it's so illusory. And yet we buy into it as if it were hard and fast. . . . We don't want to remind ourselves we can't buy that beautiful body, so we blame the victims of bad health. That's really disturbing.

Visible evidence of failure to attain and maintain health marks us as socially deviant (Goffman, 1963). One way of managing negative and victimizing social attitudes was to be active in our own health care through engaging in complementary medicine. While others continued to react negatively to our bodies, our feelings of shame and powerlessness were lessened by our agency. While resisting powerlessness was a major issue for all of us, feelings of stigma were much more of an issue for Liza and me: Natalie and Charlotte felt that they generally succeeded in not allowing negative feedback to affect their self-concept.

OPEN-MINDEDNESS

Another value reflected in our interactive interviews is open-mindedness, which means being willing to try new things, experimenting with treatments and techniques, and embracing the possibilities of the mind/body connection. Charlotte and I discussed the importance of being open-minded about receiving treatment.

Laura: I wonder how much willingness and openness has to do with alternative therapies.

Charlotte: Yeah, it's like you're, you've got to be a receptacle, you've got to be open to all this.

Laura: Yeah, and if you're not, people who don't want to have chemotherapy, who actively resist having it, tend to have worse side effects, more nausea, more headaches, more fatigue, everything. Um, I [think] people who don't believe and are resistant to acupuncture or whatever . . . I wonder if it's less effective for them.

Charlotte: You know, I think it can be 'cause, my ex-husband used to tell me they would give anesthesia to a patient that really didn't want it, and their brain was so strong they could fight it off sometimes, what the medication should be doing for them, because they could just, like, really strong willpower, so they could overcome that medication.

As Charlotte's comment pointed out, open-mindedness was related not only to the success of complementary medicine but to the success of conventional treatments as well. The difference was that complementary practitioners openly embraced the role of the mind/body connection, whereas conventional practitioners were disinclined to discuss it and instead sought to control for or eliminate its effects on patients' attitudes and beliefs. Openness even extended to acknowledging that complementary medicine may have worked at times simply because of the placebo effect.

Laura: Daily living becomes so hard at that point that I think that alternative medicine and practices provide one area of relief even if it's only that, a placebo.

Liza: Well only that's a very powerful effect. They have to randomize drug trials because that placebo effect is so strong. That tells you something. It's a powerful thing [in] your brain, and they're trying to work around it with their drugs. They've had to acknowledge just how strong it is. [Doctors] won't even acknowledge most things. . . . And they had to acknowledge that one because it has a huge statistically significant effect.

We were open to the idea that complementary medicine involved marshaling our inner resources for healing, and we found this intriguing, not threatening.

Natalie: One of the things my mother used to say, "Oh, it's all in your head. You just believe it's going to work, and so it does." And my response was, "What's your point?"

Laura: That's the placebo effect, and it's very powerful.

Natalie: And that's fine. . . . I am totally okay with that. If it's in my head— far out!! All I want is relief of the symptoms, however that happens.

This excerpt illustrates an overlap between pragmatism and open-mindedness; being open-minded was valued, in part, because it could lead to a pragmatic outcome. Moreover, experimenting with different treatments and practices is not only a matter of success and failure, but an exploration that is valuable in and of itself. Being open-minded is a key part of our identities.

Participants' values of pragmatism, agency, and open-mindedness reflected our sense of ourselves as active, powerful, and able to make good decisions for ourselves. However, those decisions also were made in the context of other values that focus on our relationships to others: equality, connection, and harmony with nature.

EQUALITY

Although participants valued empowerment, we also sought to share power. Equality was manifested in equitable and respectful relationships between clients and practitioners. In our experience, conventional physicians generally sought to maintain a position of superiority, even when they exercised benevolent power. We often found conventional practitioners unwilling to really listen to us. Charlotte resented the lack of respect and equality shown to her by conventional practitioners.

Charlotte: Sometimes they think we are stupid, [but] *I know* what's going on with my body and—

Laura: They don't think you do.

Charlotte: —that's exactly it.

Laura: I had this orthopedist, and I had just met him, and he's like contradicting me! And I'm like, excuse me but you've never met me. I have been living with this illness and this leg for now, you know, almost 10 years since the illness started, and you're telling me that I'm wrong about my perceptions of my body and how much pain I'm in.

Charlotte: Yeah, my doctor at the navy hospital was the same way.

Conventional practitioners' communication was often dehumanizing; it denied our knowledge of our bodies, and it reinforced the physician's power.

In contrast, we felt like equal partners with our complementary medicine practitioners. Treatment decisions were made jointly; our knowledge of our bodies was honored, and we valued practitioners' expertise.

Liza brought research to a complementary medicine practitioner to discuss the benefits and risks of various treatments. Unlike her conventional doctor, this practitioner took time to discuss the research, made a recommendation, and then waited for Liza to decide. Charlotte also felt that she was an equal partner with her complementary medicine practitioner. Respect and collegiality were evident not only in what he said to her but how he said it: "It was the way he talked to me, that was the main thing." Natalie also did extensive research, which she discussed with her osteopath and massage therapist, who reacted positively to her efforts to educate herself.

Respect for our time was another component of our interactions with complementary medicine practitioners that reinforced a sense of equality. Conventional physicians routinely kept us waiting for excessive periods of time, often an hour or more. The tendency to have patients wait unreasonable lengths of time is perceived of as a sign of the power and authority of the physician (Ellingson & Buzzanell, 1999). In our experience, an offhand apology was sometimes offered by the physician, but no acknowledgment of the importance of our time was given, thus reinforcing our unequal status as patients. In contrast, complementary medicine practitioners never had us wait for more than a few minutes. Our time was considered as valuable as the practitioners' time, placing us on an equal footing.

Equality is not a value generally upheld by the medical establishment (Wear, 1997). Patients who want a greater role in making health care decisions often have difficulty negotiating a voice at all with conventional physicians. Each woman reported searching for physicians with whom she could communicate from a position of equality.

Natalie: I have had [bad doctors], so I started interviewing before I chose a doctor. . . . I pay the money, the office visit fee . . . to interview them. And I figure out if we are going to be able to work together. And I don't go back if I don't feel we can work together.

Laura: And so you tell them about all the other treatments you are exploring?

Natalie: Absolutely, because how can they treat me effectively if they don't know what I am doing? . . . I feel very confident now and very empowered to advocate for myself and to ask for what I need and to ask questions and to demand answers.

Over time, we have become better at advocating for our needs and forging relationships with physicians who are open to sharing decision-making power with us. Our experiences with complementary medicine practitioners have helped us to develop self-advocacy skills, knowledge, and confidence to develop better relationships with conventional physicians.

CONNECTION

Not surprisingly, being treated as equal by complementary practitioners fostered other positive emotions. Liking our practitioners as individuals and believing that the practitioners "cared what happened to me" (Charlotte) led to a sense of connection. Connection is a value that reflects warmth, caring, and empathy between clients and complementary medicine practitioners and among members of the complementary medicine user community. Illness is often an isolating experience (Charmaz, 1991). Even when we had support from friends and family, the experience of having cancer and of suffering from chronic illness and impairment was in some ways intensely individual. Others offered sympathy and assistance, but it was still the participant who faced the physical manifestation of disease (Frank, 1995). Feelings of isolation often persisted or even escalated when the acute phase of illness ended and the chronic conditions remained.

One way in which connection was established was the blurring of client/ professional boundaries as friendships developed. We felt that our psycho-social needs were often met by complementary medicine practitioners in a way that was not generally found with conventional practitioners. In large part, relationship building was accomplished simply through the practitioners' listening skills. People who have survived trauma need empathetic listeners to hear their stories in order to heal (Brison, 1997; Frank, 1995). Many people feel that alternative medicine practitioners offer more empathy than conventional practitioners (Marble, 1998). In the following excerpt, Charlotte and I discussed the feeling of empathy we experienced with our acupuncturists.

Laura: The acupuncturist . . . [is] very nice, and if I say something hurts, or if I say that thing didn't work as well as the other thing, he listens to me, he nods, he makes eye contact, he does all of the things my other doctors don't do. . . . And that's important to me. Did you feel like you had an ongoing relationship with your acupuncturist?

Charlotte: Absolutely, absolutely. He was just, he was neat. He was so cool. He didn't talk about, like, "your chi isn't flowing." . . . He's just this old Chinese guy, and he was, I guess the word is *nurturing*, which most men aren't. . . . Course, the first time I met him, I was appre-hensive, and I got there, and he just talked to me, and I just started relaxing, and I could tell he really—he cared, you know. It just wasn't a fee, you know.

Being cared about was important to our emotional and physical health. Studies have found that people go to complementary medicine practitioners in part for nurturing (Marble, 1998). Complementary medicine practitioners and users, in our experience, seemed to be more intent on addressing the person, not just symptoms. Complementary medicine is subversive of the dominant modern medicine paradigm because it treats people as whole beings, offering an individualized approach without focusing on a single site of injury or disease, (Stambolovic, 1996).

Each of us also sought out people to talk to about our complementary medicine experiences who were interested in similar treatments or who had similar conditions, and we formed relationships with like-minded people.

Liza: I've seen other relationships develop . . . that's the concept of holistic or alternative medicine providing a sense of community and even a culture.

Laura: I tend to talk to people that—you know, I gave you a copy of Christiane Northrup's [1994] book [*Women's Bodies, Women's Wisdom: Creating Physical and Emotional Health and Healing*] because it meant a lot to me and I thought "it may not do her any good, but we could talk about it" or my aunt who likes to read this sort of thing and we talk about it on the phone . . . and talk about what we read and what we like and don't like.

Liza: Yeah. Some of that serves as a language to communicate with. I don't want to call it an underground, because it isn't really . . . but there's a similar path that's not unfindable. . . . And I think that in that sense the community is incredibly important—having a shared language with somebody that does really care and shares your lived experience.

The complementary medicine community was a source of enjoyment, information and opinions, and social support (Schneirov, 1998). This community was not unlike the community generated within support groups. An important difference is that the practitioners of complementary medicine are part of the community with their clients, instead of apart from it, as conventional physicians usually are.

A final way in which connection was fostered was when conventional practitioners were open to complementary medicine use. Such openness, when it occurred, enhanced the relationship between patient and physician. My current orthopedist and Natalie's current primary physician were willing to discuss a wide range of treatment options, including acupuncture. We were more comfortable communicating with our physicians because they accepted our choices. Charlotte and Liza felt less satisfied with their conventional practitioners.

HARMONY WITH NATURE

The final value reflected in our talk was a desire to feel aligned or in concert with the natural world. The value of harmony with nature is the desire for treatments that involved listening to and being in tune with nature and one's body. Each of us expressed a desire for treatment that works *with* the body. Conventional medicine was often invasive, painful, and involved toxic side effects; complementary medicine was usually less invasive, less (or not) painful, and had fewer (if any) side effects (e.g., Northrup, 1994). Referring to a story about an animal who sought the advice of many other animals in making a decision, Liza said,

> Only at the end he discovers he must craft his own solution—the ability to listen to his own body and determine his own set of values were essential parts of his cure. So there is no right answer out there. None of these things work in and of themselves.

The medical establishment tends to view human bodies through machine metaphors that encourage physicians to fix parts that do not work instead of viewing the body as an integrated system that is intimately connected to its environment. Holistic approaches to healing often involve techniques—such as meditation, breathing exercises, changes in diet, and physical exercise—that recognize the interdependence of the body and are designed to help the body maximize its natural power. Natural substances were also thought to be "more effective and safer" (Charlotte).

Charlotte: And I hate, uh, I hate taking medicine.

Laura: Hmm. And do you feel that way about taking herbs? Like do you not like taking pills in any form, or—?

Charlotte: Oh, no. No, just, what I call, regular prescription medication.

Laura: How do you see that as different from taking herbs?

Charlotte: It's not natural, you know what I'm saying? . . . Because I think, like, herbs and stuff, they *work,* and if you use them right, they're in sync with your body. I don't know, I'm not an herbalist or anything, but if you take herbs right, I don't know of many side effects, I mean, let's face it. But you can take one too many Motrins, and your stomach is just rip roarin'.

Laura: Yeah, that's true. So side effects are definitely a big thing. . . . it appeals to me to be doing something more natural, because I feel like I am working more with my body.

Charlotte: Exactly. . . . And why does it hurt to try it? Cause you're not putting chemicals in your body.

Being in sync with one's body and nature was valued by each of us. Conventional medicine does not see itself as part of nature but *apart* from and even combative with nature. This reflects the patriarchal mindset that encourages domination and control of the environment and, by extension, of bodies (human and otherwise) (Ehrenreich & English, 1973). Historically, harmony with nature has been associated with the feminine, primitive, and barbaric; civilization has meant masculinization, progress, and domination of nature, including domination of those bodies (darker and/or female) deemed uncivilized (Diamond & Orenstein, 1990; Irigaray, 1985). In the same way that "advanced" civilizations justified their colonization of "uncivilized" peoples, Western medicine claims a position of moral authority and technological superiority to colonize bodies, demanding that bodily experiences be defined and mediated through medical language (Zola, 1990). Complementary medicine shifts the focus back to nature—the food we eat, our own embodied sensations, our innate resources for healing—and insists that our bodies are part of nature. Complementary medicine practitioners became "facilitators of natural healing" (Liza).

Discussion and Implications

This study focused on people and practices at the margins of mainstream health care. Woman cancer survivors with permanent impairments or chronic illnesses suffer from physical problems compounded by social stigma. The values reflected in the interactive interviews—pragmatism, agency, open-mindedness, equality, connection, and harmony with nature—underlie our desire to be active in the management of our own health. Complementary medicine use was advantageous to us not only because of the physical benefits but also because we became part of a supportive community and were empowered to act on our own behalf.

Clearly, the participants in this study found complementary medicine satisfying and helpful on a variety of levels. Many people reject claims about the efficacy of complementary medicine because most of the evidence of complementary medicine's effectiveness is anecdotal and/or based on the results of small-scale studies (Boozang, 1998). This study does not claim that others should choose to utilize complementary medicine on the basis of our positive outcomes with it. However, the findings of this study strongly indicate that it is vital for physicians to initiate open dialogue about patients' choices with regard to complementary medicine. In addition to possible danger to patients from interactions (e.g., some herbs and vitamins decrease efficacy of prescription drugs), overt or subtle silencing of patients about their complementary medicine use endangers the physician-patient relationship.

Patients are not usually supported by physicians when they report their use of complementary medicine (R. Gray et al., 1997), and this makes patients reluctant to talk about their choices with physicians (D. Eisenberg et al., 1993). Openness to patients' choices can foster good communication between patients and their physicians, enhancing trust. With open lines of communication, physicians also have the opportunity to provide warnings when they deem appropriate. Given the values evident in the talk of participants in this study, such conversations ideally should include the pragmatics of symptom relief, patients' efforts to research various therapies, patients' feelings about therapies they are using or considering, patients' decision-making processes, and any possible interactions or harms.

Opening communication on complementary medicine between physicians and patients is important, but the findings have wider implications for communication between patients and physicians (and other health care providers). The values reflected in complementary medicine use inherently refute the marginalization of women with disabilities and chronic illnesses (and potentially other groups) in the medical establishment. These values are too often missing from, trivialized by, or even rejected by the Western medical establishment (e.g., Wear, 1997). This study constitutes one more piece of evidence that the organization and culture of Western medicine privileges certain groups at the expense of others. My goal is not to demonize conventional physicians and proclaim all complementary medicine practitioners as effective and empowering. However, there is much that conventional physicians can learn from complementary medicine practitioners about relating to their patients.

Advocates of patient-centered communication between physicians and patients (see, e.g., Brody, 1994) argue that physicians must pay attention to the "voice of the lifeworld," not just the "voice of medicine" (Mishler, 1984). A value-centered approach to improving communication is in keeping with patient-centered approaches; patients' values become central to negotiating a successful partnership. Many studies have demonstrated that communication between patients and physicians is often unsatisfactory to both (e.g., Ellingson & Buzzanell, 1999). Patients' and physicians' values often do not match, making communication and the accomplishment of treatment goals difficult (Vanderford et al., 1992). In value-centered communication, patients and physicians would focus on building communication practices on a foundation of recognized, discussed, and, ideally, shared values. I do not naively assume that agreement will always be reached, but clarification of values can assist in negotiating treatment plans and developing a trusting relationship.

Finally, this study provides implications for methodology. As complementary medicine continues to grow in popularity in our culture, there is public pressure for scientific investigation of these practices. The Office of Alternative Medicine and others are currently conducting clinical trials to investigate the effectiveness and safety of various complementary treatments on specific conditions. Because trials may lead to greater acceptance of complementary medicine by traditional medical practitioners and determination of toxicity levels, possible drug interactions, or other dangers, this type of research is valuable. However, as Audre Lorde (1984) said, "The master's tools will never dismantle the master's house" (p. 110). If we turn to clinical science and statistics as the only source of reliable knowledge of complementary medicine, we undercut the very principles upon which many forms of complementary medicine are based—integration of body, mind, and spirit, and holistic approaches to health.

This study reflects S. Williams and Calnan's (1996) call for holistic research as well as others' calls for patient-centered research (K. Bennett & Irwin, 1997; Vanderford et al., 1997) and for qualitative health research that serves as a "primary source for hearing [patients'] stories and their associated metaphors, caring in relationships, and resisting the colonizing narrative of institutionalized medicine" (W. Miller & Crabtree, 2000, p. 615). This study has the advantage of providing data in the participants' language rather than exclusively from the point of view and language of researchers. Patients' meaning-making processes are at the heart of the research, illuminated via a holistic approach to experiences of health, illness, embodiment, and choice. The multiple intersecting marginalized and privileged positions of the participants are inextricably linked to our experiences with the medical establishment and with complementary practitioners and users. Interactive interviewing enabled a complex rendering of participants' experiences and the values that developed through those experiences.

Interactive interviewing has some limitations, of course. The small number of research participants meant that the study results are not widely generalizable—the narrow inclusion criteria (1. women, 2. cancer survivors, 3. living with impairments or chronic illnesses, 4. who use complementary medicine) generates results (values) that are likely to differ from other groups. Also, the other participants and I enjoy higher than average levels of education that make us particularly appropriate for interactive interviewing; this technique may be less satisfying for people who are less educated, have fewer positive experiences with researchers, or for whatever reason are uncomfortable articulating their ideas in dialogue with a researcher.

Yet, increasingly, people at the margins of health care are speaking out against unfair and uncompassionate treatment, as well as articulating what is empowering for them in health care. Nancy Mairs (1997), a woman writer who lives with multiple sclerosis, explains that for people with chronic illness and disabilities, "speaking out loud is an antidote to shame" (p. 302). By defying the mandate to be silent about our embodied experiences and values, we open the door for more voices to speak out loud the subversive truths of their own experiences of health and illness.

Notes

1. The names of the three participants have been changed to protect their privacy.

2. I do not deny, however, that my voice ultimately is the one in which this chapter is written. It is impossible for me to avoid privileging my perspective because I am acting as interpreter and reporter of discussions in which others took part. I have endeavored to minimize my privilege through collaboration with the other participants in deriving the results, but I acknowledge my inability to achieve equality of representation.

6

The Defining of Menopause

Kelly Quintanilla,
Nada Frazier Cano,
and Diana K. Ivy

onflicting paradigms hamper our understanding of menopause (Voda & George, 1986) because each utilizes its own definition. These definitions support differing, sometimes conflicting, terminology and affect our discussion and understanding of the experience of menopause (Kittell, Mansfield, & Voda, 1998). The purpose of this chapter is to define menopause from the perspective of postmenopausal women. Before we describe this investigation and its findings, we offer an overview of three major paradigms affecting our understanding of menopause: the biomedical, the social/cultural, and the feminist models.

Three Menopause Models

THE BIOMEDICAL MODEL

In this model, menopause is considered physiological. It is a disease or disease-like disorder, sometimes referred to as a "deficiency disease" (Cone, 1993, p. 124). According to this perspective, a deficiency in estrogen results in menopausal symptoms, such as hot flushes/flashes and changes in the breasts, vulva, vagina, cervix, urinary tract, uterus, ovary, and skin (Barbo, 1987). Although the medicalization of menopause originated in the 1930s, it was not until the 1960s that the "deficiency disease" definition of menopause began to receive substantial attention (S. E. Bell, 1987). This timing coincided with unveiling estrogen as a "cure." Estrogen was hailed as "the foundation of youth and beauty." As McCrea (1983) explained, gynecologists "discovered" menopause was a deficiency disease, but promised women that estrogen would remediate the deficiency and keep them feminine forever.

One of the leading advocates of menopause-as-deficiency disease was Brooklyn gynecologist Robert Wilson. During the 1960s, R. Wilson, whose research institute received $1.3 million from pharmaceutical companies, lobbied for redefining menopause as a physiological disorder and for the routine administration of estrogen replacement therapy (ERT), even for women without symptoms. R. Wilson (1966) stressed that ERT would help a woman remain a good wife, a good mother, and a good person in general—value judgments that went beyond conventional views of physiological disorders and related more specifically to sociopolitical views about women's place in society.

The biomedical model is still accepted in the medical community, but it has critics (S. Ferguson & Parry, 1998; Mercer, 1999). A central tenet of the model critiqued by many researchers is that biology is destiny and women are victims of their bodies (Voda & George, 1986). Hall (1999) analyzes the way medical scholars negatively define menopause as, for example, the "cessation of menstruation" or "ovarian failure" (Sheehy, 1998) rather than as a time when women are freed from menstruation and pregnancy. Significant criticism has been leveled at those who would profit from convincing women that they need to take hormones for the remainder of their lives in order to feel "womanly."

Also, early studies advancing the biological model were flawed (S. E. Bell, 1987). First, the samples were biased. Only women whom specialists determined needed medical assistance were included in the studies. Women who did not require medical treatment for menopausal symptoms were not part of the research. Further, obvious ethical questions arise because many of the studies were conducted by physicians who were at the time researching DES, a synthetic estrogen for menopausal women. Physicians who had once held the view that the menopause was natural and normal changed their opinions to believe that all menopausal women had a disease for which DES was the proper treatment. Thus, they simultaneously defined menopause as a disease and introduced the cure for it. By recommending estrogen for all women, these physicians opened the door to an enormous pharmaceutical market.

Since 1975, pharmaceutical companies have worked to identify additional symptoms of menopause that reinforce the biological model. Menopause is now viewed by the medical community as more a syndrome than a disease. According to MacPherson (1985), by defining menopause as a syndrome, "The namers—physicians—are given a wide scope to link disorders such as osteoporosis to menopause without scientific evidence of a direct casual link" (p. 12).

In sum, the biomedical model reduces menopause to a strictly biological event—one, moreover, that has the properties of a disorder rather than a naturally occurring physiological change. This model is supported by scientific evidence; however, critics point out that the evidence is flawed and biased. Nevertheless, this paradigm is accepted by a large circle of medical researchers and practicing physicians and has done much to convince menopausal women, as well as others, that they suffer from an illness.

THE SOCIAL/CULTURAL MODEL

The social/cultural model is primarily promoted by behavioral scientists who claim that menopausal changes are related to the environment and life events (Huffman & Myers, 1999; Mercer, 1999). Biological changes occurring during menopause are viewed as part of aging and as relatively minor in their significance; thus, they are similar to the changes experienced by men as they age. According to this model, most of the changes women experience are socially or culturally, not biologically, based. In Huffman and Myers' (1999) perspective, a biomedical approach to understanding menopause does not exist within a vacuum; rather, it emerged and exists today within a cultural framework from which we derive meaning for menopause.

The social/cultural model counters the reductionistic view of the biomedical model and refutes the idea of women as biologically inferior. This model seeks "to identify societal values or social, political, or economic factors which influence cultural stereotypes of menopause" (Koeske, 1982, p. 7). In this perspective, most of women's menopausal symptoms are not solely the result of hormonal changes. Rather, they are a response to women's position of relative powerlessness in society. For example, at the time of menopause, many women's children leave home. They suffer from the loss of their role as mothers and may have no alternative role. Thus, women feel unfulfilled and many suffer from depression. According to this model, depression results from these feelings and not estrogen deficiency.

For several decades, cross-cultural studies supported the social/cultural model (Im & Meleis, 2000; Mercer, 1999). Flint (1975), one of the leading advocates of this model, claimed that in a youth-oriented culture such as the United States, it was not surprising that menopausal women have negative experiences and become depressed and symptomatic. However, in cultures such as Rajput, India, in which aging corresponds to heightened social prestige, women report no menopausal symptoms. Similarly, Beyene (1986) found that Mayan women from Yucatan, Mexico, who gain status and freedom with age, did not associate menopause with any physical or emotional symptoms. Greek women from Euboea listed such symptoms as hot flashes, cold sweats, headaches, dizziness, insomnia, hemorrhage, irritability, and feeling melancholy. Within Greek culture, "Menopause signifies that they are no longer in the mainstream" (Beyene, 1986, p. 63). Studies of Navajo women and Belgian women also support the social/cultural model, in that women's socioeconomic status within a given culture has a significant impact on their experiences with and views of menopause (Severne, 1982; Wright, 1982).

The social/cultural model has received criticism, however (Koeske, 1982). Critics contend that, just as the first model reduces menopause to a biological event, the social/cultural model reduces it to primarily a social event. Voda and George (1986) argue that proponents of the social/cultural model also perpetuate a reductionistic view by defining women largely in terms of roles they play within a given society. Physiological symptoms may not be taken seriously in this perspective.

If one subscribes to the social/cultural model, much of the research done from the standpoint of the biomedical model is suspect and can be dismissed as not capturing the experience of menopause. Cross-cultural studies have supported the social/cultural model. As noted previously, studies reported that in cultures that value older women, women had few to no menopausal symptoms. On the other hand, in cultures where aging is viewed negatively, women reported a long list of menopausal symptoms. The problem, of course, is that the data thus far are insufficient to warrant establishing symptoms of menopause as exclusively social in origin, even in cultures where women show few physiological manifestations. Furthermore, as mentioned previously, critics claim that this model has as reductionistic a view of menopause as the biomedical model it was designed to replace.

THE FEMINIST MODEL

This model holds that biological changes at the time of menopause are more than coincidental, but that the psychological and social changes that occur simultaneously are of equal consequence to the menopausal women's experience (Berkun, 1986; Carolan, 1994; Koeske, 1982). According to the feminist model, menopause should be viewed as a normal and natural transition for women rather than a disease or illness (Mansfield & Voda, 1993). Gail Sheehy (1998), who wrote one of the most widely read books on the passage of menopause, refers to menopause as a transition, not unlike puberty. She advises women to think back to their experiences in their early teens: "Jolted into menstruating at twelve or thirteen—remember?—we needed five or more years to adjust to our uniquely altered chemistry, while our minds struggled to incorporate our new self-image. So, too, must we readjust to not menstruating" (p. 10).

In a sense, the feminist model includes attributes of the biomedical and the social/cultural approaches to provide an integrative perspective for viewing menopause. As Kaufert (1982) noted, utilizing a framework that is multidisciplinary allows for the explanation of a variety of facets of a phenomenon. Koeske (1982), a supporter of the feminist model, suggested that "to treat all self-reported 'symptoms' as either wholly physiological or wholly sociocultural is to radically distort the complexity and variability of bodily functioning" (p. 12). Berkun (1986) also contended that it is mistaken to view symptoms as all hormonal or all psychosocial.

However, the feminist model does not simply combine the biomedical and the cultural models. For example, the feminist model differs from the biomedical model in its approach to the body. According to Engebretson and Wardell (1997), the biomedical model "is motivated by the imperative to control and direct nature" (p. 260). On the other hand, the feminist model involves "letting the natural material speak to you or allowing it to tell you what to do next" (Engebretson & Wardell, 1997, p. 260). Furthermore, the feminist model grew out of an effort to demedicalize menopause so as to reclaim it and then to rewrite the language used to talk about it and the meaning assigned to it (S. Ferguson & Parry, 1998; Reitz, 1977). As S. Ferguson and Parry (1998) suggest, "By rewriting menopause, women can begin to 'own' menopause and claim a continuum of experiences, attitudes, and interpretations" (p. 38). Feminist scholars call for a new definition of menopause and new language (Engebretson & Wardell, 1997; Gannon & Ekstrom, 1993; Kaufert, 1982; Koeske, 1982; Lippert, 1997; Mansfield, 1990; Sheehy, 1998). The feminist model was developed to provide both.

This model also suggests that menopause in specific, and midlife in general, should be studied from the perspectives of women experiencing it (Banister, 1999; Engebretson & Wardell, 1997; Kittell, Mansfield, & Voda, 1998; McQuaide, 1998; Ricken, 2000; Winterich & Umberson, 1999). According to Engebretson and Wardell (1997), the feminist model "allows for the representation of female perspective and involves examining the social context, with gender as a key aspect of social construction of reality" (p. 255).

By defining menopause as a life transition and examining the psychological and cultural variables influencing women's experiences, the feminist model changes the way menopause is treated and viewed. First, it removes the implication that all women need medical treatment. This does not mean that women with severe experiences should not receive medical assistance. Instead, it means that treatment, if necessary at all, should be tailored to the individual. Second, this definition encourages new perceptions of menopause. It should no longer be viewed as either in need of a cure or as simply a social problem. Each of these changes is discussed below.

Individualized Treatment. As noted earlier, when menopause was defined as a disease, physicians were encouraged to prescribe estrogen replacement therapy (ERT) or hormone replacement therapy (HRT) to all women. Many physicians still follow this practice. From a feminist perspective, this results in inadequate assistance for many women (Cutson & Meuleman, 2000). Sheehy (1998) estimates that 20% of women "sail through" menopause with no problems, about 10% are "temporarily incapacitated," and the remaining 70% "wrestle to some degree with difficulties that come and go over a period of years as we deal with the long transition from our reproductive state" (p. 27). Furthermore, many women experience the transition into menopause as a result of surgery or cancer treatment. As a result of differing experiences, women have differing needs in response to menopause.

Altered Perceptions of Menopause. According to the feminist model, it no longer makes sense to discuss how our reproductive systems have failed. Rather, we should discuss how they have fulfilled their purpose. Menopause is the transition to postmenopausal zest; therefore, language such as "ovarian failure" could be replaced with terms like "ovarian fulfillment" (Sheehy, 1998, p. 243). As Woods (1998) notes, women often describe menopause as "freeing them from reproductive responsibilities to pursue other contributions" (p. 8). This change in language will bring about more positive images of menopause and menopausal women.

By redefining menopause, the often-overlooked stage that follows the ovarian transition, called *post menopause,* would become a more widely and openly discussed topic. If we think of women as diseased, the idea of their finding revitalization seems absurd. However, if we see menopause as a transition, then there must be a period that follows that transition. Margaret Mead did most of her now famous work after her ovarian transition, in the period she referred to as "postmenopausal zest" (Sheehy, 1998, p. 13). According to McQuaide (1998), postmenopausal zest comes to women when their hormones are no longer in flux. It is a highly positive time in women's lives.

As with the other two models, the feminist model has met criticism. Although the feminist model moves away from a reductionist stance and develops a more ontologically based approach to understanding menopause, it is based largely on speculation. This model is also prescriptive in nature. It tells women how to view menopause rather than describing menopause from a menopausal woman's perspective. Although a few studies are consistent with feminist claims (Banister, 1999; Engebretson & Wardell, 1997; Kittell, Mansfield, & Voda, 1998; McQuaide, 1998; Ricken, 2000; Winterich & Umberson, 1999), on the whole, there is little scholarly evidence supporting the paradigm.

Defining Menopause From the Perspective of Postmenopausal Women

As Voda and George (1986) noted, "The construction of women's experiences has never been adequate. Whether that experience has been made trivial or enviable, sanctified or mystified, it has been considered peripheral, described and explained primarily by men and not women themselves" (p. 71). Here we explore the definition of menopause from the perspective of the true experts: postmenopausal women. The following research questions guided our study:

RQ1: What are postmenopausal women's definitions and perceptions of menopause?

RQ2: Which paradigm most accurately reflects menopause according to these definitions?

METHODS

The research design for this study consisted of interviews intended to produce information regarding definitions, insights, and experiences with menopause.

Participants

We initially identified the criteria that would qualify a postmenopausal woman for our study. Specifically, each respondent's postmenopausal status was determined on an individual basis. Because different women have different experiences, the medical definition of cessation of one's menstrual cycle for 1 full year (Mansfield, 1990) was not useful for all respondents. Each respondent was asked how she determined her postmenopausal status. Using the information provided by the respondents, as well as the guideline of 1 year, the following criteria were developed. For women who experience a nonsurgical, non-drug-induced menopause, postmenopausal was defined as not having a menstrual cycle for 1 full year. Women who had drug-induced or surgically-induced (removal of ovaries) menopause were considered postmenopausal if at least 1 year had passed since they began medication and/or underwent surgery. However, for women who had their uteruses removed, but not their ovaries, surgery and the resulting cessation in menstrual cycles cannot serve as an indicator of the onset of menopause. Each of these women reported that they had their doctor monitor their menopausal status via hormone-level testing. They were considered postmenopausal if it had been 1 year since their hormone levels indicated that they were menopausal.

To generate participation in the study, we used a variety of methods, including placing ads in campus and local newspapers, offering small monetary incentives (made possible by an internal grant), placing flyers in our own gynecologists' offices, distributing flyers at community menopause workshops, and running calls for participation in electronic campus announcements. However, most of the participants were generated through word of mouth, meaning that early participants helped us connect with their postmenopausal friends. The final interview group consisted of 35 women who were deemed menopausal by the previously stated criteria. In addition, all the participants had experienced menopause within the last 10 years. Although 10 years is still a fairly broad time frame, this limitation helped ensure that the women recounted reasonably recent experiences. Thirty-one of the 35 participants (88.7%) had gone through menopause within 5 years of the study.

Participants ranged in age from 36 to 63, with an average age of 50. Twenty-one of the women went through natural menopause, 7 had surgically-induced menopause, and 2 experienced drug-induced menopause. Five women had hormone-level testing that determined that they were postmenopausal. Twenty-six of the participants had undergone various forms of hormone replacement therapy during menopause. Four of those 26 were no longer taking hormones.

The participants identified themselves as follows: 85% European American, 12% Hispanic, and the remaining 3% African American. The majority of the respondents identified themselves as middle class. In addition, the participants were generally well educated. All of the women had graduated from high school, some had varying levels of college education, and 3 held doctoral degrees.

Twenty-six (74.3%) of the respondents were employed. Their occupations included university dean, degree counselor, manager, business administrator/secretary, teacher (preschool and elementary), professor, nurse, dietician, probation officer, consultant, and business owner. Of the remaining 9 women, 5 (14.3%) were enrolled as full-time college students, and 4 (11.4%) were full-time homemakers.

Twenty-five (71%) of the respondents were married. Of the remaining respondents, 5 (14%) were divorced, 2 (6%) were in committed lesbian relationships, 2 (6%) were widowed, and 1 (3%) was separated. The respondents had a combined total of 77 children with an average of 2.2 per woman. Specifically, 5 respondents had no children, 5 had 1 child, 12 had 2 children, 8 had 3 children, 2 had 4 children, 2 had 5 children, and 1 respondent had 6 children. Twenty women resided in the Northeastern region of the United States; the remaining 15 participants resided in the Southwest.

Interviews

Interviews enabled participants to describe their experiences with menopause. Their answers provided their definitions as well as explanations of how it affected their self-concepts, communication, and relationships. Kleinman (1988) suggests that qualitative research is an especially effective way to extract the meaning of and an appreciation for an individual's experiences with an illness or biological change. Qualitative approaches have been employed successfully in previous studies of menopause and women's midlife experiences in general (Banister, 1999; Kittell, Mansfield, & Voda, 1998; McQuaide, 1998).

An interview was conducted and audiotape-recorded with each woman participating in the study. The length of each interview varied as a function of the woman's answers; interviews ranged from 40 minutes to 1 hour and 50 minutes. The average length was between 60 and 70 minutes. Each participant was asked a series of open-ended questions; see Table 6.1. As soon as possible after each interview, the tapes were transcribed. All transcripts were compared to the original tapes for accuracy.

The data reported in this chapter were collected as part of a much larger study; therefore, much of the data revealed during the interviews will not be discussed in this chapter. The questions were designed to ensure that topics related to the research questions in this study and the larger study were addressed. The interview schedule was not used to restrict the respondents' recounting of their experiences; rather, it was designed to ensure that all of the participants responded to various issues. Specifically, the interview schedule was utilized more for prompting purposes; the respondents often answered questions without being asked them directly. The first four questions were designed to allow the respondent time to become comfortable with the interviewer, the tape recorder, and so forth. As the participants spoke, the interviewer was trained to allow each woman to tell her story freely.

Research Perspective

After the tapes were accurately transcribed, the data were analyzed from a grounded-theory perspective (Field & Morse, 1985). This approach allows researchers to examine an individual's experience from her or his own words, to elicit the meaning a person applies to a situation, and to describe sensemaking processes (Lynman, 1990; Morse, 1992). As Benoliel (2001) noted, grounded theorists have helped "remedy the deficit" in research on women's health (p. 8). It is important to note that because the research questions addressed in this study focused on exploring definitions and comparing models, a fully integrated theory was not developed. As a result, only selected techniques from the grounded-theory approach were utilized. Grounded-theory techniques were used to identify and code themes and categories describing the data.

Method of Analysis

The goal of the grounded-theory perspective is to establish theoretical themes and categories from data (Charmaz, 1990). Similarities among themes and categories are then examined to identify meaningful relationships. The

(text continues on p. 111)

Table 6.1   Interview Questionnaire

Part I

1. How would you describe yourself?
   a. Can you give examples? Experiences or incidents that reflect your description?

2. Are there other important elements of yourself that are not reflected by the description you just gave?
   a. If so, what?
   b. Do you see these as less central? Less important? Why?

3. To what extent do you think others would agree with your view of yourself?
   a. How do they express agreement?
   b. Do others see you in different ways than you do?
      1) Who?
      2) In what ways?
      3) How do you respond to these varying perceptions?

4. Do you express yourself similarly across situations? Do you exhibit the same characteristics described above with family members, medical professionals, coworkers, etc.?
   a. If so, can you give examples?
   b. If not, what differences are you aware of? Why do these arise?

5. Has your definition of yourself changed since you experienced menopause?

6. Has menopause caused you to re-examine yourself in any way? To re-examine life?
   a. If so, what was the result of the re-examination?

7. Have your priorities changed in any way as a result of menopause? If so, how?
   a. Is this better or worse than before menopause?
   b. Do you still value the same things you did before menopause?

8. If you have undergone a re-examination, what has been the role of others in this re-examination?
   a. Are there particular individuals who have been most important/helpful in this respect?
   b. Why? What were they able to do for you that was helpful?

9. If you have undergone a re-examination, are there people who have been unhelpful in your re-examination of self/life?
   a. Who?
   b. Why?

10. How did or do others respond to your menopause experience?
    a. Did they or do they now treat you differently because of this?
    b. If so, in what ways?
    c. Is this response from others helpful or unhelpful? Why?

11. Have any of the following persons helped you in responding to and/or understanding your experiences with menopause? If so, how, in particular, have the following persons helped you in responding to and/or understanding your experiences with menopause?
    a. spouse/significant other
    b. children
    c. mother
    d. father
    e. siblings
    f. friends
    g. coworkers
    h. physicians
    i. pastor

Part II

1. What were your perceptions of menopause before you experienced it?
    a. Did you have any expectations? If so, what were your expectations?
    b. Did you have any fears? If so, what were your fears?

2. How and when did you first realize you were going through menopause? How did you know?

3. Did you tell anyone else that you were beginning menopause?
    a. Why or why not?
    b. If you did tell someone, whom did you tell?
        1) Describe your conversation(s).
        2) What were his or her reactions?
        3) How did you feel about the reactions?

4. Was there anyone whom you were reluctant to tell that you were beginning menopause?
    a. If so, who were you reluctant to tell?
    b. Why?
    c. Did you tell that person(s)?
    d. What was the reaction?
    e. How did the reaction make you feel?

5. Did other people find out about your experience?
    a. If so, who?
    b. How did they find out?
        1) What were their reactions?
        2) How did their reactions make you feel?

6. Did you go to any medical professionals?
    a. Why or why not?
    b. If you did go to a medical professional, whom did you see?
        1) Describe those experiences.
        2) How did you feel about his/her/their reactions?

Table 6.1 Continued

7. Did you undergo any hormonal treatment?
   a. Why or why not?
   b. How do you feel about your decision?
   c. Did you discuss your decision with others?
   d. Did he/she/they influence your decision?
   e. How did he/she/they react to your decision?

8. What, if any, biological changes occurred during menopause? After menopause?
   a. If changes occurred, cite examples.
   b. If changes occurred, how did you react to these changes?
   c. If changes occurred, how did others react to these changes?
   d. If changes occurred, how did the reactions of others make you feel?

9. What, if any, psychological changes occurred during menopause? After menopause?
   a. If changes occurred, cite examples.
   b. If changes occurred, how did you react to these changes?
   c. If changes occurred, how did others react to these changes?
   d. If changes occurred, how did the reactions of others make you feel?

10. What, if any, social/environmental changes occurred during menopause? After menopause?
    a. If changes occurred, cite examples.
    b. If changes occurred, how did you react to these changes?
    c. If changes occurred, how did others react to these changes?
    d. If changes occurred, how did the reactions of others make you feel?

11. What are your perceptions of menopause now that you have been through the experience?
    a. How would you describe menopause to others?
    b. Complete this statement: "Menopause is like . . ." or "Menopause is . . . ."

12. Do you feel comfortable talking about menopause?
    a. Why or why not?
    b. Under what circumstances?
    c. With which individuals?

Part III

Age:
Race:
Economic Background:
Occupation:
Highest Level of Education Completed:
Marital Status:
Number of Children:
Age and Sex of Each Child:
Date of Your Last Period:

SOURCE: Adapted from the master's thesis of Suto (1994).

text of each interview was examined in an attempt to discover patterns of "persistent words, phrases, themes, and concepts" (Field & Morse, 1985, p. 99). In our case, "persistent" meant that at least 3 participants discussed a given theme.

According to A. Strauss and Corbin (1990), to develop categories data must first be explored for larger themes. For this study, each transcript underwent a line-by-line examination to discover emerging themes within the text. After the themes were identified, statements varying in size from one sentence to a paragraph were cut and pasted under the relevant theme heading. Data under each theme were then analyzed for smaller units of meaning, or categories. The themes were broad enough to allow for the inclusion of individualized experiences. For example, under the theme Menopausal Experiences all menopausal experiences were recorded. After the analysis moved to the category level, the researchers coded individualized experiences. For example, if only one woman noted thinning hair, her experience would be placed into the corresponding category: Biological Menopausal Changes. Relationships within and across themes and categories were examined. The resulting themes and categories were interpreted in light of the two research questions.

After the first coder had analyzed all of the data for major themes and categories, the second coder repeated this procedure. The second analysis was undertaken to ensure that no data had been mislabeled and that no emerging categories had been overlooked during the first analysis. Specifically, the analysis yielded two primary themes: (a) Perceptions and Definitions of Menopause and (b) Menopausal Experiences. There was also a third theme, Other, which contained data that did not fit into the other themes. Various categories emerged from the Other theme; however, they are beyond the scope of this chapter.

RESULTS

To illustrate each respondent's experience with menopause, the following section reviews the data and analysis relevant to the two primary themes. These themes provide valuable information regarding menopause that address our research questions.

Theme One: Perceptions and Definitions of Menopause

These data provide answers to the question "What is menopause?" as well as insight into participants' views and understandings of menopause. Two categories emerged. The first focuses on women's perceptions, fears, and expectations before experiencing menopause, whereas the second deals with definitions and attitudes about menopause after experiencing it.

Definitions Prior to Menopause. Respondents tended to report two types of expectations regarding menopause prior to experiencing it: They either thought that menopause would be a horrible experience or a neutral experience. In many cases, respondents simply had no expectations about menopause because they had not thought about it.

Theresa stated, "I thought it was going to be hell. I thought I was going to be this absolutely raving bitch that people told me that you would become and that your life would end, but it is not true." Similarly, Tammy explained, "I guess I thought it would be hell, but I had a lot of negative perceptions; from whence they came, I do not know." Barbara also thought she "was going to go crazy, seriously insane. I had heard things. If you are not terribly well-balanced when you go through menopause, you will be crazy. And I was worried about it." Julia's perceptions were based on "lots of old wives' tales in terms of night sweats and extremely volatile mood swings." Angelia's expectations about menopause came from "the horror stories that you hear of hot flashes and the night sweats and being a real witch." Similarly, Missy's expectations also came from discussions she overheard:

> My mother and grandmother . . . [would] discuss in hush terms about aunt so-and-so or cousin this-and-that or the neighbor lady or somebody really losing their mind. I never will forget how many times I walked into the kitchen to hear them in hush tones discussing . . . "Miss So-and-So is going through the change, and she is nearly losing her mind."

As examples of neutral expectations, Beth had no clear or specific perceptions of menopause before experiencing it because she "didn't really think about it much. I just thought I would get through it, and there never would be any problems." Haley noted, "I just figured I could sail right through it and not have any discomfort, but I was at such a junction [divorce and returning to school] where life was new for me, [so] I wasn't really that concerned about it." Connie remarked that she had heard menopause is "unspeakable," but beyond that, "I never thought about it. I am not one to think ahead, like, 'I'm in my late 40s and pretty soon I will be going through menopause—I guess I'd better find out about it.'" Kim said, "I just more or less knew what to anticipate because I have been working with women forever. I am in a female-dominated field, so I didn't look forward to it with dread." Dawn stated, "My perception was that all women do this. It's perfectly natural. . . . It was not something that I dreaded by any means." Michelle explained, "The only thing I was determined to do was to have it naturally and that I didn't want it to be treated like a disease, because it is not a disease."

Other respondents thought menopause would be easy; however, their responses were still considered neutral, because they did not think it would necessarily be a positive experience. For example, Heather stated, "My doctor told me at the time [she started taking birth control pills] that I would have a very easy menopause because of it. So I always had that in my mind." Dana claimed, "I was facetious [*sic*] in thinking that if I took really good physical care of myself I won't have any symptoms at all. But I was wrong about that, too. I was naive because of my own self-righteousness about health." Prior to menopause, Stephanie thought it would be easy because she considered all the stories she had heard about menopause "a bunch of hogwash."

Definitions After Menopause. In this category, menopause was portrayed in predominantly positive or neutral terms. Examples of positive experiences included statements describing menopause as "a freeing time for women. It allows them to be people and not just reproductive vessels" (Jessica); "a renewal of life" (Debbie); "great in a lot of respects because it frees" (Pam); "just a change, and it allows you a kind of freedom that you may not have had" (Jessica); "something women should almost look forward to because it is going to be a change for the better" (Tammy); and "a time for you to rest and enjoy" (Theresa). Michelle noted, "I just feel freer and I love it. And I'm taking hormones and that's great. I love it."

Neutral experiences are reflected in the following characterizations: Menopause is "nothing to be feared or nothing to be looked at as a terrible thing, that horrible things are going to happen to you" (Debbie); "a personal experience that is different for everybody; a natural process that occurs within your body" (Cassandra); "[not] the same for everybody; a change in a woman's life that she inevitably has to go through" (Janet); "just like any other change that comes about in your life. It is just like getting married. . . . You deal with it. It is normal" (Cindy); "a natural thing that the body experiences, and it does not mean that you are not a female anymore, that you are not feminine" (Theresa); "a lot easier than having a baby, that's for sure . . . one of those little inconveniences like being overweight when I'm in an airplane seat" (Julia); "overrated. Between childbirth and marriage and death and divorce and work and working families and cars and insurance, that's not on my priority list. Even health wise, it's no biggy" (Nicole).

In addition, there were two negative accounts of menopause. Dana remarked that she thought her divorce was like a roller coaster, and "menopause may have only made the ride that much more scary." Similarly, Stephanie stated, "Menopause is like no control. I didn't have any control over my emotions."

With these two exceptions, all of the respondents characterized menopause as a positive or neutral experience. Although each respondent used slightly different terms, there were similarities across definitions. Specifically, respondents who viewed menopause as a positive experience consistently discussed increased freedom and a feeling of renewal. In regard to the neutral portrayals of menopause, respondents repeatedly stated that menopause was a natural, normal process that varies from woman to woman.

Theme Two: Menopausal Experiences

As illustrated by the first theme, the majority of respondents defined menopause as a natural process of change that has varying biological and psychological effects on women. Thus, for purposes of our continued discussion, any altered physical or psychological states reported by respondents are referred to as *changes,* as opposed to *symptoms,* of menopause. The word *change* is preferred because it is a more neutral term, whereas *symptoms* evokes connotations related to the biomedical perspective.

Theme two encompasses data focusing on the biological and psychological changes of menopause. Four categories emerged from these data:

1. Changes that caused respondents to realize they were beginning menopause

2. Biological changes that respondents experienced throughout menopause

3. Psychological changes experienced throughout menopause

4. Social or environmental changes that occurred in respondents' lives during menopause that were connected to biological and/or psychological changes

Beginning of Menopause. When asked, "How did you first realize you were going through menopause?" the majority of respondents identified biological changes, primarily hot flashes and irregular periods. For example, Debbie reported, "The very first thing was cessation of the periods. I had stopped for about 7 months, which was no problem. It was wonderful. But then after 7 to 8 months, I started with hot flashes, which became uncomfortable. Night sweats—I would be up in the middle of the night, and I never had problems sleeping."

Many of the respondents reported irregular periods. Some noted that their periods were more frequent and/or the flow became increasingly heavy (flooding). Stephanie, like many respondents, had always had a regular cycle, so any variation was an indication that something was changing. Stephanie suspected the onset of menopause "when I started having female problems, which I'd never had in my life. The real big one was my period got erratic, shorter, and weird." Iris recalled that her flooding became so intense she knew something was changing. Although some of the respondents realized they were beginning menopause when their periods became irregular, others did not realize changes in a woman's menstrual cycle were related to menopause. For example, Christy's periods also became irregular, but she did not associate this change with menopause until her doctor gave her a blood test to examine her hormone levels.

As for respondents who had hysterectomies, Jennifer had irregular periods and some vaginal dryness prior to her hysterectomy, whereas Tammy had very heavy bleeding prior to her operation. Beth, on the other hand, did not begin menopause until after her operation, at which time she had hot flashes and "cried for weeks." Cassandra had her uterus removed, so she "started taking [blood] tests every time [she] was at the doctor's." She explained that when she was 51, her doctor told her she was beginning menopause; however, no other changes occurred at that time. Later she realized, "I was probably too busy to recognize anything was happening right away. Probably my first hot flash is when I realized myself, 'Hey, this is it.'"

Both Nicole and Barbara began menopause as a result of their cancer treatment. Nicole explained,

> First of all, 6 months' worth of chemotherapy automatically sends you into menopause, and that's one thing that with breast cancer and everything, all I ever heard was "you're going to lose your hair," "you're going to throw up"—those are the two big things that you always associate with cancer. But nobody ever says "and besides that your fingernails turn yellow, your veins harden, and you go into menopause."

Only 3 respondents listed psychological changes, specifically depression, as indicators of menopause. Jessica "had a hysterectomy, but [she still had her] ovaries, so [she] was still having a normal cycle." When she "started getting real irritable" and "kind of depressed," a girlfriend suggested she was beginning menopause, and her doctor confirmed it via blood tests. As noted previously, following her hysterectomy Beth stated, "I cried for weeks, and I didn't know what was wrong with me." She later realized her depression was part of a hormone imbalance. Dana first realized she was beginning menopause because of depression. She explained,

> I wrote a poem for that one, "Menoporn" I think it was. I had a day when I was really depressed and really down, and I thought, "Oh my God, it's starting." And I got really angry at myself, and I got very depressed.

Biological Menopausal Changes. This category pertains to biological changes that first indicated to respondents that they were beginning menopause but which also continued throughout the experience. For those respondents who did not go through a surgical menopause, cessation of their menstrual cycle was the major biological change associated with menopause. Donna noted, "Periods stopped, which for me was a positive thing. Very positive. That's the single most important thing. I love to tell people that." Similarly, for Nicole,

"That means no more cramps—no more. Oh my God! And that time of the month, no more worrying about carrying tampons and pads."

Those respondents who had full hysterectomies also noted the cessation of their menstrual cycles as a major biological change associated with menopause. Iris reported, "I feel so much better. I think a hysterectomy should be an elective surgery. There is just no sense in putting up with that bologna."

Hot flashes, night sweats, vaginal dryness, skin dryness, hair thinning, hair growth (in unexpected places), headaches, and weight gain also resulted from menopause, as reported by these 35 women. Theresa described her hot flashes in the following way:

> When you are sitting there . . . at the table drinking coffee, and all of a sudden you get very, very hot, and your face turns blood red, and you are ripping your clothes off because you are so hot . . . and you want to shower. . . . You say, "Open the door." And your niece replies, "But Aunt Theresa, it's cold." "Open the door and let me out of here."

Christy stated, "Well, this winter, I noticed I didn't mind the cold as much. I would wake up and have to change my nightgown, which isn't like me. I get cold very quickly." Cassandra explained, "Well, most of my hot flashes occurred at night, so I would kick off the covers. I would be sleeping without blankets, and my spouse would be sleeping with several blankets." Stephanie remarked,

> I bought the fan to blow in my face—on the stand, in my face. Not an oscillating fan, but a steady stream of air all night. And the ceiling fan is on high, and the house is 70 degrees. You could cut meat in my house at night. Literally, you could hang meat and it wouldn't spoil.

Vaginal dryness was another change indicative of menopause reported by respondents. According to Jennifer's experience, "Dryness in the vagina was one big problem that I had with it. The estrogen therapy is supposed to take care of that, but it really doesn't." Regarding her diminished sex drive, Barbara recounted, "You have to have all kinds of jellies and things like that. . . . It is still sometimes painful, so it is not the way it used to be in terms of fun." Other respondents also reported a decreased sex drive: "I didn't have the sexual desire, but that is one of the things I discovered from reading information that happens to you" (Donna).

Only four respondents reported that their hair thinned, whereas many more respondents reported unwanted hair growth. Michelle said, "I started getting some chin hairs." Iris added, "The most horrible physical change is having to watch facial hair. You think you look so cute, and as soon as you get home from a big event you notice the big black hair hanging out of your chin." Missy said, "My hair is thinning . . . in places I don't want it to and growing in places I don't want it to. For instance, my lip. And I have this one wire on my chin, and it drives me crazy.". Stephanie related, "I get facial hair, and I pull it out. I get bloated. I get migraines." A few respondents associated migraines and other types of headaches with menopause.

Respondents commonly bemoaned weight gain as a biological change related to menopause. Cindy noted, "My body is a different shape than it used to be. . . . Clothes that I have worn for years don't fit the same way." Theresa stated that "larger breasts" and a "heavier body" were definitely indicative of menopause. Katie added, "The weight gain, of course—I can see this change in my body shape in the mirror from what it was, say, 10 years ago." Missy explained that she had a "tendency to be more round than I was prior to menopause. Weight doesn't come off as easy. It goes on easy, but it doesn't come off as easy as it did prior to menopause." Iris revealed, "I know that I am real overweight. I think [since menopause] it is just a different shape. I mean, the waist is the deal. What happened to the waist?"

On a positive note, one respondent did report an end of the premenstrual breakout: "My face cleared up. I used to get one of those premenstrual bumps that never had anything in it; it wasn't infectious, it wasn't a blackhead or a whitehead. It was just this huge bump somewhere on my face. Well, I quit getting that, so that was good" (Missy).

Psychological Menopausal Experiences. In addition to biological changes, respondents also reported psychological changes, namely depression, mood swings, and memory loss. In general, fewer women reported psychological changes than biological ones; many respondents were not sure if the psychological changes were a result of menopause. For example, Debbie talked about depression:

> I didn't pay much attention to it, but when I look back there were days when I was moodier, super sensitive. . . . I could almost cry at the drop of a hat, and I never really experienced that much in my lifetime. . . . I kind of figured it was menopause. If it was, I don't know. There might have been something else. I had a lot of stress at that time.

Dana went through a severe depression, about which she remarked, "I felt bad. Again, I think my divorce played a big part in psychological changes." Jessica stated,

> I think I got depressed a little more when it was first starting, but after hormone replacement . . . I don't know if it was that or if it was just me, because I am depressed periodically in my life. It is hard to know.

Angelia revealed that she took antidepressants; other respondents described crying jags. Missy related,

This was one of the worst experiences; I was so embarrassed. I was grocery shopping, I was standing at the meat counter looking at bacon. [The price was] sky high. So I'm standing there looking at a package of bacon and it was $2 or $3, and I just cried. It wasn't that I didn't have the money to buy it. It was just depressing. I cried so much that I couldn't finish shopping.

In addition to depression, many respondents noted that they experienced significant mood swings. "If anything I am just less patient. I just have less patience now that I used to with lots of things" (Katie); "My kids used it as an excuse. I am bitchy, they say. They blame it on menopause" (Morgan); "During menopause I was not calm about anything. When I hit menopause it was like my fuse got real short about things. My husband got my wrath" (Stephanie); "[I became] snippy more than anything" (Julia). Megan explained,

I blew things out of proportion, and I finally had to sit down and say, "Look, I don't know how much of this is due to me being frustrated or whatever, but part of this is the menopause I am experiencing."

Other respondents did not report depression or mood swings. Kari stated, "I could see where it would be a very depressing factor because there is no doubt it is an ending, but again I didn't have the mood swings. I didn't regard it as that, an emotional deal."

Some respondents reported memory loss, which Lynn regarded as "the thing that bothered me the most." She added,

My mind was really busy, so I don't know if that was the problem or if it was a combination. I just couldn't retain anything. I could read a page and you could ask me what I had read, and I couldn't tell you one thing I had read.

Like Lynn, Haley was also unsure whether her memory lapses were the result of menopause, "aging," or her "own anxiety level." Dawn feared her memory loss was a sign of Alzheimer's disease. Susan stated,

For me, the [change] that was most significant, the one that really affected me the most, was memory loss. My memory was like "What I am I coming in this room for? I can't remember." Now, that drove me nuts

A few respondents described positive psychological changes related to menopause. For example, Missy stated, "Psychologically, I probably got healthier because I did not have to work around or through heavy menstrual flows." Similarly, Donna reported she was less paranoid, noting "I was always afraid because I was always flowing so much and I had that paranoia—that, you know, that just uncomfortable feeling." Angelia also described a shorter temper, but she viewed that as a positive change, not a mood swing. She believed,

At this stage of my life if I get aggravated with somebody, I just don't put up with it. . . . When I was young I got along with everyone at all costs, even if it meant not being true to myself. Now if someone gets mad at me and I don't feel that I've done anything wrong, I don't apologize to them.

Social and Environmental Factors. Thirty-three of the 35 respondents reported that significant social or environmental changes occurred in their lives at the time of menopause. None viewed these changes as results or outgrowths of menopause; rather, they noted how life changes intertwined with menopause to introduce additional stress into their lives.

For example, Haley stated, "Moving, children, school. I don't think these things have to do with menopause. It was just the age. I don't think things that were concurrent with menopause were related to menopause." Similarly, Tammy's 94-year-old father-in-law stayed with her family. She professed, "That was a hard time, but I didn't relate that to menopause. It was very depressing because he had me on an emotional roller coaster, but I didn't relate that to my menopause." Cassandra noted,

[My family] had a lot of changes that we both really had to adjust—Bob's [Cassandra's husband's] retirement, David's [Cassandra's son's] finishing up his college career, and my husband being concerned about money matters because he was retiring on disability. I was probably more concerned with the other people around me than basically with what I was going through.

Barbara reported "a lot of pressure from school," as well as pressure from her mother's fight with cancer and her own recuperation from cancer. During menopause, Katie took a new job at the same time that all three of her sons left for college, Dana moved multiple times, Cindy took a new job that was 80 miles from home, and Mary started a job she disliked. Connie was in the middle of a divorce, and she found her life to be "too busy and too full." She explained, "I have too many friends. . . . It is hard to keep up with them. . . . My life has changed for the better, but not necessarily because of menopause." Finally, Iris described the range of occurrences that coincided with her menopause:

I found out that [my son] was gay. I found that out during this period. I was going through life changes, menopause. . . . Then I was shocked when he overdosed on cocaine. There was so much else going on in my life, so a lot of times I couldn't tell what was menopause and what was real-life stress.

DISCUSSION

The response to our first research question is directly reflected in the first theme. The analysis revealed that before experiencing menopause, many respondents perceived it as a negative to neutral experience, with some suggesting that they believed it was going to be "hell." However, after experiencing menopause, all but two comments characterized it as a neutral to positive experience. Some respondents thought they would go through menopause with no problems, and/or they did not give menopause very much thought before it began. No one in this group reported perceiving menopause as a positive change. After experiencing menopause, respondents defined menopause as a natural process that varied among women, an experience that included increased freedom and feelings of renewal. None of the respondents defined menopause as a disease; in fact, several of the respondents specifically emphasized that they did not view it as a disease.

These findings suggest the view of menopause presented by the feminist model. Menopause is one of life's transitions, not a disease or physiological disorder. From this perspective, menopause is a transition that requires individualized responses to women's individualized experiences. In addition, the feminist model acknowledges and supports the view that menopause can be a positive experience.

In each of the 35 interviews, respondents discussed at least one, if not more, biological and/or psychological changes. Changes indicating the beginning of menopause included hot flashes, variation in menstrual cycles, depression, and mood swings. Hot flashes and/or night sweats, vaginal dryness, skin dryness, hair growth, hair thinning, headaches, and weight gain comprised the biological changes participants experienced during menopause, whereas depression, crying jags, mood swings, and memory lapses comprised the psychological changes. The inclusion of biological and psychological changes in the definition of menopause supports both biomedical and feminist models.

Our respondents also experienced many social or environmental changes concurrently with menopause. During their 40s and 50s, respondents described changes in their relationships with significant others brought on by such occurrences as divorce or retirement. Other changes emerged in their relationships with their children, who were in need of less care or who were leaving home. Participants also discussed changes in their relationships with their parents, typically related to an increased need for care or as a result of death. Many respondents indicated that these social/environmental changes added stress to their lives. This stress may or may not have contributed to the biological and/or psychological changes respondents experienced during menopause. These results support both the social/cultural and feminist models.

Some of our findings support the social/cultural model and some support the biomedical model; however, when examined in their entirety, they indicate that the feminist model presents the most accurate and complete definition of menopause. These data closely support the feminist perspective, which recognizes biological and psychological changes as natural events. As noted earlier, the feminist model also assumes that each woman has an individual menopausal experience with highly variable responses.

Further, the feminist model's definition of menopause includes biological, social, and environmental events as they affect each menopausal woman. Both Jennifer and Connie reported severe hot flashes. Both women had full hysterectomies, which is an important factor to consider when deciding to undergo hormone replacement therapy. However, Connie had breast cancer, which made her a high-risk candidate for HRT, whereas Jennifer was not at high risk. Mary and Beth both suffered depression while experiencing menopause, but the differences in the environmental factors affecting their lives were factored into their decisions regarding HRT. Beth was so depressed that she cried all the time and had problems functioning. Other than her recent hysterectomy, Beth had experienced nothing that would account for her depression. Mary, on the other hand, also experienced depression and crying jags at the onset of menopause, but, at that same time, both of her parents became very ill and she began a job that she detested. She believed that her depression was largely a result of these experiences.

CONCLUSION

On the basis of this study, the feminist model best captures the reported experiences of menopausal women. The feminist model provides the most comprehensive, integrative way to explore menopause, encompassing biological symptoms, psychological factors, individual experiences, as well as social and environmental contributors. Recent research recognizes the need for a comprehensive perspective on menopause, one that depicts and captures the real-life experiences of women; however, the biomedical perspective remains in the forefront of research and information on menopause. The fact that most of the evidence still sides with the biomedical perspective continues to be persuasive.

Yet, by shifting from a biomedical or social/cultural paradigm, social perceptions of menopause will change. First, the experience will no longer be polarized as either a disease in need of a cure or as a nonmedical, social problem. Second, the implication that all women need the same treatment will diminish further. Third, exploration of additional methods for responding to menopausal changes will be encouraged. Finally, more women will embrace the notion that menopause and postmenopause are increasingly positive and liberating times in women's lives. That may be the most important result of all.

7

Consuming Breasts

Our Breasts, Our Selves

Patty Sotirin

A feminist perspective on women's health communication must address the politics of women's body knowledge. Wellness, illness, beauty, and aging are aspects of body knowledge that also delimit arenas of struggle among diverse interests, such as medical, pharmaceutical, cosmetic, insurance, governmental, and personal concerns. Knowledge of the female body is a subject not only of personal interest but also of big business, scientific research, and governmental policy. There is much at stake in the question of how women know themselves as embodied because the answer helps determine our under-standing of processes, resources, and beneficiaries of women's health.

In contemporary U.S. society, women often come to know themselves as embodied through sociocultural expectations, popular images, and institutional experts. Rather than knowing our selves through intimate, embodied experience, the dominant sociocultural way of knowing constructs women's bodies as objects or, more specifically, as signs and commodities within an economy of cultural and material capital. In this economy, the quintessential signs of womanly value are breasts. In this chapter, I focus on how having breasts is experienced and exploited. This process occurs in adolescence as women come to define their own value in terms of breast development, in aging when women begin to lose the value of breasts as sexual commodities, and in breast cancer as women are reduced to calculations of life expectancies and treatment costs.

Author's Note: I am grateful to Jennifer Daryl Slack for her unflagging enthusiasm for this piece in all its guises.

In creating efficacious public messages—messages that speak to women in the vernacular of their own experiences and body knowledge—health communication practitioners and scholars must be careful to reflect on the value logics that underwrite those messages. Otherwise, messages can advance interests and ways of knowing that objectify, commodify, and devalue women's bodies and experiences. For example, feminist perspectives value the specificities of the lived body and the networks of care that set our bodies in relation to other bodies. But the value logics of the prevailing capitalist socioeconomic order are the logics of consumption, a set of value logics that place a premium on commodification of the body and the calculation of its value in a market economy. My purpose in this chapter is to critique these value logics and to show how they might be challenged and countered.

I urge feminist advocates to create effective messages about women's health issues by starting from a critical awareness of the prevailing value logics of consumption. I offer two politically productive strategies that advocates might adopt for countering such logics: irony and ambivalence. An *ironic* stance demands that we remain open to the ambiguities, inconsistencies, and differences that constitute women's embodied experiences. A strategy of embracing lived *ambivalences* sensitizes us to the potential for alternative ways of knowing and being embodied. In this chapter, I look for the ironic and ambivalent moments in public messages about everyday experiences of having breasts. I also adopt irony and ambivalence as strategic perspectives for developing my critique and advancing alternatives.

In the first part of the chapter, I use irony to frame my own and other women's anecdotes about the value logics of consumption coding young and old breasts. I also plumb my feelings of ambivalence to call critical attention to the underlying currents of desire and anxiety that are inspired by and simultaneously threaten these logics. In the second part of the chapter, I focus on breast cancer, a disease that palpably draws out our lived ambivalences. Breast cancer is a particularly salient focus because the prevailing popular, medical, and scientific messages and images about this disease are dominated by the logics of consumption. At the same time, cancer survivors, patient advocates, and health activist groups that champion and draw upon women's embodied self-knowledges have vociferously confronted these logics, making the struggle over women's body knowledge particularly visible (Batt, 1994). In the last part of the chapter, I advocate irony and ambivalence as strategies not only for countering the prevailing logics of consumption but for creating alternative ways of knowing ourselves as breasted and for living together as, and valuing the specificities of, breasted bodies.

Irony and Ambivalence

Irony and ambivalence are critical modes of inquiry and writing in this chapter. They serve a threefold analytic purpose: first, as feminist *sensibilities* or ways of knowing and feeling that frame our understandings, feelings, and actions in the world; second, as *ways of critiquing experience* that draw out the "doubleness" of women's lives; and third, as *strategies* for intervention and resistance. Recent endorsements of irony as a feminist sensibility, theoretical framework, and political strategy inform my analysis in this chapter (K. Ferguson, 1993; Haraway, 1985; Trethewey, 1998; Weeks, 1998).

My methodological appropriation of irony and ambivalence expands on common ways of knowing and using these forms. Irony is most familiar as a literary device, used to show that the intended meaning contradicts the literal expression. In this sense, irony is both a practice of encoding that thinly veils the intended meaning and a practice of decoding that reads through the literal message to the intended meaning. But irony can enact feminist sensibilities beyond encoding and decoding because an ironic frame seeks to make sense of women's lives while reveling in the complexities of women's experiences. Similarly, ambivalence is a mode of thinking and feeling in which we vacillate between seemingly diametric alternatives that we value equally. Although ambivalence may be disparaged within a rational-instrumental perspective, feminists often hold that remaining uncertain and open to possibilities can be important cognitive and affective sensibilities for living together and acting politically.

Together, irony and ambivalence offer valuable methods for feminist critique because, as K. Ferguson (1993) contends, they entail being attentive to what she terms the "doubleness" of women's lives. This doubleness appears in many forms: "It can appear as the slippage between what is said and what is meant, or between what is said and what can be understood, or between what is indicated and what is implied or evaded, or between stability and motion" (p. 30). For example, taking an ironic look at the ways women's breasts are represented within the logics of consumption calls attention to the doubleness of women's experiences of their own bodies—that is, the slippage between the commodity value and the embodied experience of breasts.

Such slippages are often marked by ambivalences—for example, feelings of ambivalence about the value of our breasts as commodities. Analytically, ambivalence marks a moment of instability that provides us opportunities for critical insight into the contrarieties of women's lives and the politics of women's body knowledge. In this chapter, I want to demonstrate how pervasive and overwhelming the logics of consumption are by reflecting on how readily co-opted my own and other women's experiences have been. But I couch my observations *ironically* so I can reflect on the ambivalent desires and anxieties that continually unsettle the value logics of the consumed and consuming breast.

Finally, an ironic perspective not only creates a critical awareness of the doubleness of women's embodied experiences but offers strategies of resistance and intervention, and a political ethic as well. K. Ferguson promoted irony as a way to "act politically" in the context of partialities, differences, and endlessly deferred resolutions. We need not resolve differences or ambivalences to resist oppressions and create alternatives. What matters is the ongoing critique of subjects and relations within ordered formations themselves; we must never stop asking who is disadvantaged, marginalized, and silenced, by whom, how, and why. For example, my critique is admittedly situated in a privileged socio-historical location: I am a white, middle-class academic, heterosexual mother. I am painfully aware that my autobiographical premises effect silences and exert their own oppressions. Yet I am equally committed to a feminist politics of embodiment and to contributing, albeit in a partial and inevitably partisan way, to knowing and living through feminist sensibilities. In promoting an ironic feminist perspective and lived ambivalences as political strategies, I contribute to efforts by feminist health advocacy groups like Breast Cancer Action, the Breast Cancer Fund (TBCF), and the Boston Women's Health Collective to recover and embrace the lived ambiguities, anxieties, and desires inherent to women's lived ways of knowing their bodies. As I will show, these embodied fears and dreams are both appropriated and suppressed by the value logics of the prevailing capitalist socioeconomic order.

In summary, as feminist sensibilities, modes of feminist critique, and political strategies, irony and ambivalence serve methodologically and substantively in this chapter to highlight and challenge the dominant logics of body consumption.

EXPERIENCING THE CONSUMED AND CONSUMING BREAST

Those Me-Me Things

I'm in one of the Victoria's Secret shops in the Mall of America, my 7-year-old son a shadow at my side, my almost-3-year-old son in my arms and clinging to my neck. I am determined to do some observations for this analysis. The shop has three chambers, the innermost devoted to bras, the middle occupied in the main with purchases, and the outer chamber, opening to the mall, filled with a variety of lingerie. I have brushed off a perky young saleswoman and passed quickly into the middle chamber in hopes that haste will make us less conspicuous. I look to my left at the two disjointed lines of 20-something buyers holding their selections, spread out in front of the counter that divides buyers from sellers. I feel self-conscious: Am I the oldest woman here? Pinned against the wall to my right is a flock of bras, lacy and bright. My youngest son takes one hand off my neck to point in delight, "There's those me-me things!"

"Me-me"—his name for my breasts. What is the significance of his naming? Is it an act of recognition, my young son's metaphoric identification of himself? An announcement of his place in the patriarchal order—my breasts as his property? His interpellation as a consumer, hailed by the commercialized objectification of the breast? Or is it my own reduction of my breasts to consumable property and my own recognition that age and maternality are incongruous here amid the signs of the sexual breast? I feel the disquieting tension of essentializing dichotomies: sexual/maternal, public/private, young/old, subject/object, masculine/feminine. The tensions of these dichotomies are valuative—they cast the significance of my body and my feelings within a complex of value logics. My questions expose my own ambivalences and confront me, right in the middle of Victoria's Secret, with the ways my breasts are commodified as objects of consumption.

Logics of Consumption

What are the logics of consumption that reduce breasts to commodities? To answer this question, I draw upon the work of the French sociologist Jean Baudrillard in an early collection of his essays, *For a Critique of the Political Economy of the Sign* (1973/1981), which preceded his spin into hyper-reality and simulacra. His position at that time was that, through the work of ideological labor, three logics conspire to produce an object as both commodity and sign: "1) a functional logic of use value, a logic of utility or of practical operations, 2) an economic or market logic of exchange value, a logic of equivalence, 3) a logic of sign value or of status, a logic of difference" (p. 66). These logics intertwine: The logic of exchange value justifies itself in the logic of use value. This functionalist reduction is the condition for exchange value and is immediately inscribed as sign value in a hierarchy of determinate difference: "Today consumption . . . defines precisely the stage where the commodity is immediately produced as a sign, as sign value, and where signs (culture) are produced as commodities" (p. 147). Together, these create sign-commodities addressing and inspiring collective desire and anxiety. As Sawchuk (1986) notes, "The power of late capitalism is in the imaginary, where subjects are maintained in a circuit of desire and anxiety" (p. 71). Baudrillard refers to the "phantasmic organization" of the value process in which desire is fulfilled and anxiety is resolved in the promises and fantasies of sign-commodities (p. 206).

TRAINING BREASTS, TRAINING BRAS:
CONSUMPTION AS SOCIALIZATION

The training bra initiates young women into the circuits of desire and anxiety organized by the logics of utility, equivalence, and significance. My own initiation experiences as an adolescent have become entwined with my current experiences as a parent of two adolescent girls. At Shopko, I buy my 12-year-old daughter a training bra, not for its use value but for its value as a sign in the subculture of preadolescent girls. The circuit of desire and anxiety is nowhere played out more visibly than in the bodily obsessions of puberty. The breast is a fantastical sign-commodity, the promise of womanhood. Artis's (1995) description calls me back to my own pubescent angst:

> We must, we must, we must increase our bust. You remember that? We were going to *die* if we didn't get them. . . . We got our training bras to make them jump into C, E, and double-D cups. Calling them as we saw them like everybody else: boobs, tits, jugs, hooters, headlights, titties, bazooms, knockers, milk duds, and buds. (p. 177)

I wonder now: Aside from its sign value, does a training bra have any functional use? Do breast buds really need training?

I'm relieved to run across a claim for functionality in Stoppard's (1996) owner's manual, *The Breast Book: The Essential Guide to Breast Care and Breast Health for Women of All Ages:* Training bras, she assures readers, are precautions against eventual sagging:

> A girl's breasts can grow quite big very quickly during the adolescent years, producing silvery stretch marks on the skin and stretching suspensory ligaments that will ultimately result in sagging. Once these ligaments lose their tightness, it can never be regained. (p. 52)

The training bra I bought my daughter will protect her irreparable "suspensory ligaments" and the future commodity value of her not-yet-perceptible breasts. There is ideological labor going on here—sagging ligaments are part of a code of sign-exchange value that constitutes what is and is not an aspect of feminine desirability. This is not a matter of mystification. Baudrillard argues that ideology doesn't mystify people—it socializes them (p. 93). My daughter's training bra socializes her to a triad of intertwined relations of value within the logics of consumption:

1. Her training bra initiates her into the *differentiations* of sex/gender—boys don't wear them, girls do; your identity as a girl, at least in junior high school, is secured by your training bra. But my daughter is ambivalent—she is pleased to be mistaken for a boy but wears her training bra fervently—even asking me to wash it at night so she won't miss a day's wear.

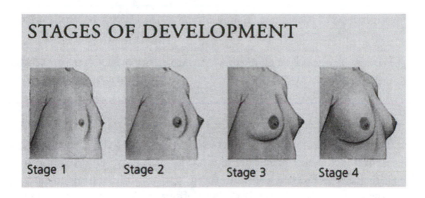

STAGES OF DEVELOPMENT

Stage 1   Stage 2   Stage 3   Stage 4

Figure 7.1

SOURCE: Reprinted with permission from D. K. Images.

2. She is socialized into a *logic of equivalence*—"having breasts" as the standard of exchange in adolescent social relations—and into a logic of difference—that harsh system of differentiations that define social relations among girls—a hierarchy of growth rates, sizes, shapes (see Figure 7.1). Desire and anxiety conjoin in a phantasmic circuitry of need and equivalence: A girl needs breasts to become a woman; being a woman means having/being breasts. The visibility of an adolescent girl's breast development plays out her personal anxieties and desires in public and socializes her into practices of display that present her body as a sign of her womanhood:

> I suppose that for most girls, breasts, brassieres, that entire thing, has more trauma, more to do with the coming of adolescence, with becoming a woman, than anything else. Certainly more than getting your period, although that, too, was traumatic, symbolic. But you could see breasts; they were there; they were visible. Whereas a girl could claim to have her period for months before she actually got it. (Ephron, 1972/1995, p. 7)

3. Finally, the training bra is both a *discipline* of the body—training the body into habits of presentation and desire—and an ideological *interpellation*, a hailing of womanhood as having/being breasts. Young girls are socialized into habits of self-surveillance, self-discipline, and self-objectification (Bordo, 1989; Brumberg, 1998; Trethewey, 2000; I. Young, 1990). They learn to diet and exercise to control body shape and size, to comport their bodies in "feminine" ways, and to master the arts of make-up and fashion so as to display femininity. These practices draw on and contribute to sociocultural ideals of femininity and the feminine body motivated by a pervasive sense of bodily deficiency and abnormality (Cavallaro, 1998; Hollows, 2000). Training bras not only shape, constrain, and display young bodies as feminine, but they shape girls' embodied

experiences of adolescence in terms of bodily deficiencies (too small, too big) and abnormalities (too slow, too soon). The communal surveillance that exerts such intense pressure on teen-aged girls finds its material focus in the training bra as well: who takes it off where, when, and with whom, who wears it and who doesn't. These are not private matters but communal concerns that interpellate girls into the anxieties and desires of having/being breasts.

Young breasts are thus incorporated into the political economy of the breast around an ideological construction of feminine desirability and lived anxieties over deficiency. Ironically, the habits of bodily self-discipline that young girls learn to exercise also train them to a depoliticized understanding of their own possibilities. Trethewey (2000) observes, "Women's concerns with diet, weight, exercise, makeup, and bodily comportment are political concerns, not medical ones" because the political force of disciplinary practices "ultimately narrows the possibilities for women's embodied agency" (p. 115). What appear to be health/medical concerns over stretched ligaments and normal growth patterns are ideological justifications for socializing our daughters to the disciplinary regimens that reproduce the political economy of the breast.

Buying my daughter a training bra may be a sympathetic response to the preteen angst inspired by logics of equivalence and significance; however, ironically, I find myself participating in the ideological labor that engages both of us in practices of self-surveillance, self-discipline, and self-objectification. Still, there are health reasons for wearing training bras, aren't there?

CONSUMED BY AGE: HOW LOW CAN YOU GO?

I'm in my hotel room at a professional conference when, stepping out of the shower, I catch a glimpse of my torso in the mirror. I see my mother's breasts. Gravity-obeying, they are sliding down my chest; once firm, they are droopy pouches now. My breasts are being consumed by age. "How low can you go?" I ask their mirror images.

Paul's (1995) description of her encounter with the aged breast seems to respond to my question. Paul is giving emergency medical treatment to an elderly woman who has collapsed, when she catches sight of the woman's exposed breasts:

The breast I see best is thin and shrunken. It looks more like loose skin than anything else, sucked dry. . . . The nipple is small and pinched. It is pinkish, and clutches itself, a tight, puckered cringe. The ends are an odd yellow color, and I see they are encrusted. Nipples gnawed by old, dirty nightgowns. Sixty years of friction. (p. 115)

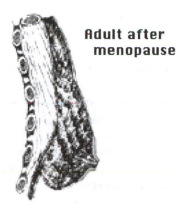

Adult after menopause

Figure 7.2

SOURCE: From Clark, P. "Breast changes over a lifetime," in Boston Women's Health Book Collective, *Our Bodies, Ourselves for the New Century: A Book by and for Women,* copyright © 1998, Touchstone Books. Reprinted with permission.

The Boston Women's Health Book Collective (1998) offers a more abstracted and medicalized explanation of the aged breast: an "involution" of breast tissue occurs with age (p. 605). Estrogen levels affect breast elasticity by maintaining collagen, a protein that makes up most of the connective tissue in the breast. With age, especially after menopause, estrogen levels drop, dehydrating collagen. Once it is dehydrated and inelastic, collagen cannot regain its shape and elasticity (Stoppard, 1996, p. 43). Older breasts do not have as much density, and the breast becomes a mass of fatty tissue with only a fine network of glandular support tissue to give it shape.

The lived upshot is that the measure of value shifts as breasts age. The Boston Women's Health Book Collective (1998) suggests that this shift begins during the middle years of a woman's life:

> Statistically, many of the important losses that women face cluster in the 45-55 year period. Some losses undermine our image of ourselves as young, healthy, even immortal, as when diseases attack the very wholeness of our bodies. Not as serious as threats to our health, but sometimes causing painful feelings of loss, are the surface signs of aging that challenge us to develop a new body image. (p. 552)

This passage describes a shift in the value standards for body self-image, a shift embodied in the changing dynamics of the breast. The aging breast is medicalized rather than sexualized—healthy/unhealthy and normal/diseased become primary standards of value. As they age, breasts "need" more medical and pharmaceutical attention, more insurance coverage (if a woman has insurance), and become the subject of more information about breast problems, diseases, and preventive care. For example, the American Cancer Society advises women under 40 to get a clinical breast examination every 3 years, but women over 40 are advised to have a clinical exam and a mammography every year (American Cancer Society, 2003). Aging breasts are disciplined into an unrelenting dialectic of anxieties and desires: anxieties of loss, threat, and risk; desires for wholeness, health, and normalcy. Like training bras, the recommended regimen of checkups socializes us to habits of body surveillance over imminent threats of disrepair or disease.

It is little wonder that we are demanding and consuming a plethora of messages about women's health issues—from popular media, health organizations, governmental agencies, educational organizations. But as Faraclas (1995) points out,

> What really is being sold to women is not a women's health consciousness but a woman's disease mentality. Women are better informed about diseases . . . but still in the dark when it comes to understanding how their normal, healthy bodies function. . . . Culturally, a taboo still exists which keeps a woman from looking at, touching and knowing her own body. (pp. 57-58)

The Boston Women's Health Book Collective (1998) adds that the variations in how breasts look and feel can create anxiety because "we do not usually have sufficient information about what is normal, either in appearance or in function, to be able to tell when something is abnormal and requires further attention" (p. 604). I notice with surprise that not one of the breast books I have shows pictures of aging breasts, only full, youthful ones—aging breasts are imaged only through medical technologies like photographs of mammograms and medicalized drawings.

Caught between the sexualized and the medicalized models of value—our breasts in the male gaze or the doctor's hands—is it surprising that we resist the recommendation of regular self-exams? The Boston Women's Health Book Collective (1998) reports that 60% of American women do not practice regular self-exams; as one woman admitted,

> I just feel so uncomfortable touching myself there. I'm afraid of what I'll find. . . . I can't stand the thought of having my breast removed. I probably won't find it [a lump] in time, and it will be my fault if I die [because] of it. (p. 605)

Vaughan (1998) suggests that this reluctance to touch ourselves may be an acknowledgment that "women's breasts don't belong to them" (p. 21). We may well feel anxious about our aging breasts, but we are socialized to resolve our anxieties through habits of surveillance and consumption.

CONSUMED BY CANCER

Which woman among us hasn't known a friend, a relative, a grandmother, mother, or sister, who has battled breast cancer? Recently, a colleague told me that a mutual friend was going to go to the doctor to have a lump in her breast checked out. As she told me, our eyes met, and a shared dread enveloped us. Might our bodies, like our friend's body, harbor the threat of disease and death? How will she/we feel if the lump is malignant and the threat is realized? In an interview with *People* magazine (Schindehette, Schneider, & O'Neill, 1998), Linda Ellerbee recalls, "Your first emotion isn't, 'Am I going to lose my breast?' It's, 'Am I going to lose my life?'" (p. 60). My friend wants to know how I would feel if I had to lose one of my breasts to save my life. I turn to the survivors' confessions I've been reading.

Taken together, the breast cancer survivors confess passionate ambivalences. In her *Cancer Journals* (1997), Lorde admits: "I'd give anything not to have cancer and my beautiful breast gone, fled with my love of it. But then immediately after I guess I have to qualify that. . . . I wouldn't give my life." (p. 78). In *Art.Rage.Us.: Art and Writing by Women With Breast Cancer*, Roberts (1998) concludes "A Brief History of My Breasts" with gratitude: "The breast over my heart, the breast that gave me pleasure and nursed two children, is going to sacrifice itself for me. . . . Thank you, my dear left breast, thank you. Go with love" (p. 59). Jordan (1998) speaks of betrayal: "It's very strange when you realize that part of your body could kill you. Something so friendly and familiar is now Enemy No. 1. . . . I never expected to feel so betrayed by my body" (p. 104). Gilchrist (1998) in "Healing" shares a fragment of a conversation with her daughter about her post-cancer breast replacements:

> "What are your breasts filled with now, mommy?" said eight-year-old Elizabeth.
> "Saline, like salt water," I said.
> "Oh," said Elisabeth, after a moment, "you mean like tears."
> "Yes, my darling, my breasts are filled with tears." (p. 121)

There is something about the ambivalences of these breast cancer expressions and experiences that, if only momentarily, exceeds and undermines the logics of value that constitute breasts as sign-commodities. I will return to survivors' confessions later to consider ambivalence as integral to "breasted experience." But first, I want to explore the ways that value logics commodify breast cancer.

Breast cancer is not the leading cause of death among American women. The American Heart Association Web site states bluntly, "One in two women will eventually die of heart disease or stroke, compared with one in 27 who will eventually die of breast cancer" (American Heart Association, 1998). Nonetheless, "Studies show that the average American woman is far more worried about breast cancer than heart disease" (Healthy Bites, 1998, p. 8). Our collective anxiety over the threat of breast cancer is palpable. It consumes us, and we consume for its sake: Breast cancer is a highly commodifiable disease.

Insurance companies, for example, reduce and rationalize the experience of this disease through statistics on cancer risks, treatment effectiveness, and survival rates. Risk charts give weights to the factors that make a difference. There are many different charts with varying numbers of factors depending on the type of chart and the insurance company (Stoppard, 1996; Rosenthal, 1996). Ironically, given that all the known risk factors account for less than 70% of diagnosed breast cancers (Rosenthal, p. 31), these charts render us all at risk—if your risk is high, you should worry; if your risk is low, you should worry. Survival rates invoke a rationalized logic of equivalence as well. Kolker (1996) documents her battle, not only with cancer but with the insurance companies that refused to cover her treatment because the odds of her survival and recovery were not sufficient to mandate coverage.

CONSUMING HOPE: THE IRONY OF *PEOPLE* MAGAZINE

Accounting practices are perhaps obvious places to find the rationalizing effects of exchange logics. So I want to look at one particular presentation of cancer experiences in the popular press where the logics of consumption and cultural anxieties and desires meet. These logics underwrite the message of hope that dominates breast cancer images in a 1998 issue of *People* magazine. Ironically, this message of hope excludes women's lived differences and silences the politics of cancer treatment and research.

The October 26, 1998 issue of *People* magazine included a Special Report on breast cancer survivors. The section begins: "Breast Cancer: The words terrify women of all ages. Yet survivors have proved the disease can be beaten, as scientists gain in the war to end its menace forever" (Schindehette, Schneider, & O'Neill, pp. 52-53). Eleven women, all white but one, all either actresses or well-known public figures, are briefly described through their memories of breast cancer. The tone of the article is upbeat: "Victors Valiant: An actress. An athlete. A Supreme Court justice. They come from many walks of life, but breast cancer made them all simply victims. Happily, they shared the determination and good fortune to conquer their illness" (p. 54). All the photographs show the women in relaxed poses and clothing, and most of them are smiling. They are all shown as "normal bodies" with no outward signs that their bodies may have been mutilated: The clothing of those who lost one breast or both breasts is loose over their chests. All the women are shown in their homes (and analogously, at home in their bodies). One page of the table of contents shows a full-figure view of singer Olivia Newton-John, whose replacement surgery allows her to wear a tight T-shirt.

I do not presume to question the pain and anguish these women suffered. But these high-gloss representations of their experiences obscure their personal struggles over the ambiguities of death, disease, suffering, and healing. Instead, the glossy images offer these survivors as commodity-signs of the triumph of medical technology, the victory of the human spirit, and a return to womanly wholeness. We see composed faces, domestic scenes, and heterosexually desirable bodies. Although 60% of women diagnosed with breast cancer eventually die of the disease (Boston Women's Health Book Collective, 1998, p. 319), the report assures us that there is "Hope at Last: Much remains to be done, but successful new drug therapies and improved surgical techniques raise the possibility that breast cancer may some day be safely and easily cured—even prevented" (O'Neill, 1998, p. 68).

Several of the women featured in the Special Report claim that their encounter with death has enriched their lives; several comment that their cancer made them reflect upon their lives and, as Gloria Steinem notes, "in that sense it's valuable" (Schindehette, Schneider, & O'Neill, 1998, p. 57). I feel ambivalent as I look at these images: I want to buy these assurances, and yet something is missing. I am reminded of Lorde's (1997) encounter with the post-mastectomy support group Reach to Recovery. One of the group's volunteers visited her after her mastectomy to deliver "a very upbeat message" and a pale pink lamb's wool breast-shaped pad for stuffing empty bras. "I wonder if there are any black lesbian feminists in Reach for (sic) Recovery?'" (p. 42) she mused after the visit.

I wonder, too. Perhaps such exclusions and exceptions are the reasons for my ambivalence. The racism and classism of *People's* Special Report are evidenced not only in the absence of women of color and the exclusive focus on famous professional women but in the assumptions that every woman has access to medical treatment, wants medical treatment, and can beat cancer with, in the words of the *People* article, "determination and good fortune" (p. 54). These assumptions ignore the disease's own discriminations and the differences by race and class in the number of women who seek treatment and who can afford or are covered by insurance. For example, according to the Susan G. Komen Breast Cancer Foundation Web site, American Indian women have a lower breast cancer survival rate than women of any other racial or ethnic population, a mortality rate possibly tied to differences in screening practices (Susan G. Komen Breast Cancer Foundation, n.d.). But despite the starkness of such statistical differences, I am drawn to the particularities of the cancer experience. The logics of equivalence that rationalize the experience of breast cancer into statistics and medical techniques and the fashionable depiction of breast cancer as a sign-commodity of faith (in cures, wholeness, order) don't encompass the experiences of this intense and intimate disease.

Countering the Logics of Consumption

CONFRONTATIONS AND ALTERNATIVES

Ironically, the issue of *People* magazine discussed in the previous section offers a popular and widely consumed message about cancer, breasts, and values. But the popular appeal of such messages confronts feminist communicators with a paradox: If we couch messages in nonpedantic and nonpejorative ways that appeal to women as they unreflectively understand themselves, then we risk reproducing the ideological self-alienation that reduces women's knowledge of themselves to the value of their breasts. Further, we risk depoliticizing issues of research, detection, treatment, and survival. Communication about women's health and bodies must be framed from an alternative perspective, informed by feminist theoretical discussions, and responsive to women's own experiences.

I want to demonstrate two strategies for countering the dominant perspective: One is a direct challenge that confronts the valuation of the breast in its own terms of desire and anxiety; the other celebrates women's embodied experiences of self with other. These strategies draw on what K. Ferguson (1993) describes as two distinct feminist projects: an interpretive project that seeks to uncover underlying meanings and construct alternative visions; and a genealogical project that disrupts prevailing orders of meaning and power, unsettling their claims about reality and identity by engaging these claims as sites of political struggle. As she notes, "Both postures are disruptive of established power but in different ways; interpretation subverts the status quo in the service of a different order, while genealogy aims to shake up the orderedness of things" (p. 23).

In the first part of this chapter, I framed stories about my own experiences ironically to reflect on the underlying value logics that co-opt women's experiences of having breasts. As K. Ferguson explains, "Interpretation produces the stories we tell about ourselves, and genealogy insists on interrogating those stories, on producing stories about the stories" (p. 35). The story I set out about the political economy of the breast is one that was interrogated in a recent billboard campaign mounted by the Breast Cancer Fund in San Francisco. This campaign shows how women's health advocates can adopt an ironic sensibility to challenge the prevailing logics that objectify even as they purport to celebrate women's bodies.

STRATEGY OF IRONY: OBSESSED WITH BREASTS

In January 2000, the Breast Cancer Fund launched a controversial public awareness campaign called "Obsessed With Breasts" (see Figure 7.3). This

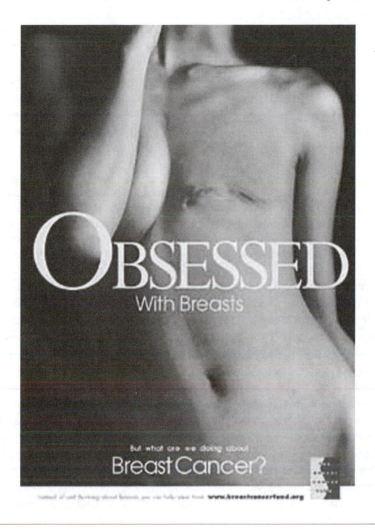

Figure 7.3

SOURCE: Reprinted with permission from The Breast Cancer Fund.

initiative was meant to call critical attention to the irony that, despite our cultural obsession with breasts as symbols of sexuality and nurture, we have collectively failed to face up to the devastating consequences of current attitudes toward and treatments of this epidemic disease. The "Obsessed With Breasts" campaign consisted of three billboard ads, each depicting a conventionally beautiful, thin, young white woman, provocatively posed to simulate each of the following: an ad from a Victoria's Secret lingerie catalog, an ad for Obsession perfume, or a cover on *Cosmopolitan* magazine. Staring out at the viewer, these models present themselves as ideal feminine bodies. But there is a shocking disruption to this presentation: Each one reveals a mastectomy scar in place of one of the perfect breasts we as viewers expect to see.

The goal of this campaign, according to its press statement (Breast Cancer Fund, 2000), was to "increase awareness of this epidemic [breast cancer] and to encourage more public involvement in the issues of breast cancer prevention, treatment and detection." The realities of breast cancer are obscured by popular obsession:

> America is obsessed with breasts. We should be no less obsessed with eradicating the disease that afflicts them. Movies, television, magazines and newspapers are full of images of partially clothed and fully exposed female breasts. TBCF's campaign lifts the polite veil separating these images from breast cancer—like "Saving Private Ryan" lifted the veil on the realities of war—and brings us in touch with the very real consequences of the disease. (The Breast Cancer Fund, 2000)

The locus for the popular obsession with breasts—American culture, the disease itself, popular images, the media, or the American public—is ambiguous, but the inconsistencies between espoused values, popular practices, and lived consequences are clear. This was a campaign aimed at provoking critical awareness and dismantling the established order of American priorities, pleasures, and public concerns.

In this sense, the confrontational audacity of this campaign enacts a feminist deconstruction of the value logics that objectify women's breasts and the conventional stories about breast cancer that instantiate these logics within a message of hope and progress. K. Ferguson (1993) explains that the project of feminist genealogy "employs disruptive and violent rhetorical devices to call our attention to the role that more docile tropes and narratives play in reassuring us of the stability and completeness of familiar interpretive accounts" (p. 26). The role of the docile feminine body in our conventional narratives of femininity and scopophilic consumption is violently disrupted by the presence of the mastectomy scars.

The "Obsessed With Breasts" campaign confronts the dominant consumption logics through a strategy of feminist irony. The posters not only deconstruct the prevailing equation between desire and wholeness but explicitly call into question the reduction of women's value to their breasts. The posters force everyone to admit that they have seen these women through the male gaze of desire that objectifies women's bodies. The scars render the willing surrender of these bodies to that gaze as acts of obscenity, and the atrocity is that we are all caught in unreflective complicity. Too late, we recognize the doubleness of these bodies: desirable and undesirable, whole and mutilated, healthy and diseased, innocent and offensive. The bodies in these posters are parodies of the cultural ideal of feminine beauty and value, and they raise disturbing questions about prevailing values, practices, passions, and policies.

The Breast Cancer Fund, in association with the American Cancer Society, San Francisco Bay Area, and the Susan G. Komen Breast Cancer Foundation, San Francisco Chapter, mounted another striking exhibit of body images by cancer survivors in "Art.Rage.Us.: The Beauty and Outrage of Breast Cancer" (Tasch, 1998). The collection includes paintings, drawings, sculpture, poetry, essays, and journal entries, each with a commentary by the artist about the cancer experience that inspired it. The exhibit premiered in 1998, at the Main Library Gallery in San Francisco, and was photographed for the book *Art.Rage.Us.: Art and Writing by Women With Breast Cancer* (Tasch, 1998), published by the Fund with proceeds donated to cancer research. This exhibit and book take up where the project of deconstruction in the "Obsessed With Breasts" campaign left off: with a re-visioning of the feminine body.

STRATEGY OF PARTICULARITY AND AMBIVALENCE

Women's health advocates can develop interpretive re-visionings by turning to the ambivalences that unsettle representations of the breast cancer experience grounded in the logics of consumption. In the Breast Cancer Fund's book *Art.Rage.Us.* (Tasch, 1998), the journals, artwork, poetry, and stories are by both cancer survivors and women who will not survive their cancers. Together, they articulate values and meanings that are unaccounted for in the dominant political economy of the breast. The survivors' confessions I noted previously express ambivalent feelings toward cancerous breasts—love and anger, sacrifice and betrayal. Their breasts are not objectified as sign-commodities but are integral to personal histories and selves; ambivalence is responsive to the singularity of these contexts. The contrast is explicit in Lorde's (1997) call for a sense (feeling, sensate experience) of the self's value in its own terms:

> Women have been programmed to view our bodies only in terms of how they look and feel to others, rather than how they feel to ourselves, and how we wish to use them. We are surrounded by media images portraying women as essentially decorative machines of consumer function, constantly doing battle with rampant decay. . . . I am personally affronted by the message that I am only acceptable if I look "right" or "normal," where those norms have nothing to do with my own perceptions of who I am. . . . When I mourn my right breast, it is not the appearance of it I mourn, but the feeling and the fact. But where the superficial is supreme, the idea that a woman can be beautiful and one-breasted is considered depraved, or at best, bizarre, a threat to "morale." (pp. 65-66)

What is the beauty of one-breastedness? Lorde's passage suggests the transgressive quality of such beauty—a dynamic beauty of the concrete feel and sense of self. A beauty that cannot be perfect in a conventional sense, in the codes that distinguish acceptable, normal, right beauty from not-beauty that

Figure 7.4   Warrior Woman

SOURCE: Deena Metzger as photographed by Hella Hammid. www.deenametzger.com
<http://www.deenametzger.com>; or e-mail Donnelly/Colt at info@progressivecatalog.com
<mailto:info@progressivecatalog.com>.

is depraved, bizarre, and a threat. The beauty of a one-breasted woman is, in Baudrillard's (1973/1981) sense, a transgression of the prevailing codes of beauty. We can't code such a beauty in a way that would apply to all one-breasted women: It is particular to the relational context that gives rise to its perception.

Baudrillard argues for an ambivalence that "haunts" the ideological and semiological reductions of sign-exchange-use values. Ambivalence exceeds and undermines the semiological restrictions over meaningful relations of exchange. Women's breasts are ambivalent in their simultaneous embodiment of life and death, maternality and sexuality, naturalness and perversity, wholeness and lack. The dominant codes of value reduce the interplay of the terms and relations of these ambivalences, restricting breasts to one or the other. For example, the ambivalence between maternality and sexuality has historically been resolved in favor of one or the other, and even the ambivalences integral to the maternal or the sexual have been resolved, reduced, or denied (Nadesan & Sotirin, 1998). Nevertheless, these rich ambivalences continue to haunt our cultural efforts at resolution and reduction.

In "Sailing," Middlebrook (1998/1996) describes an ambivalence that haunts the message of hope in the current fashionable view of breast cancer. Both her short story and her brief account of the circumstances of its writing (included here) invite us to share in and respond to the ambivalences of her living/dying:

> I can't forget my doctor's casual statement that metastatic breast cancer was "inevitably fatal." . . . "Sailing," which I wrote the summer after enduring that [bone marrow] transplant, was written to bridge the gap between my return to life and my preparation for an early death. Doing both simultaneously is a precarious task. . . . I hope that the reader, like the author, can experience the spectre of death in living terms. (p. 148)

Middlebrook's words speak of ambiguities and ambivalences: return to life/preparation for death; death in living terms. The precariousness of ambivalence haunts the neat and tidy distinctions between living and dying. For Baudrillard, unresolved ambivalence is integral to a relationship of reciprocity in which the meaningful terms of relational exchange are local and concrete, unsettling the codes of equivalence and difference that set the terms of exchange in universalized value logics.

BEYOND VALUE: BREASTED EXPERIENCE

It is possible to build on Baudrillard's relational concept of ambivalence in terms of contemporary feminist arguments about the embodied experience of being women—what I. Young (1990) calls "breasted experience." I. Young admits, "It's hard to imagine a woman's breasts as her own, from her own point of view, to imagine their value apart from measurement and exchange" (p. 192). Maintaining the ambivalence of the breasted body is a political strategy countering the commodification of breast as object. Against the ontology of objects and "thingness" that underwrites the logics of consumption, I. Young posits an ontology of "movement and energy" in which "the nature of things takes its being from the organic context in which they are embedded" (p. 193).

I use this language of ontology to address the consumption of breasted experience by the consuming breast—the ways that being a woman is defined by the objectification of her breasts and that her sense of self is consumed in having/being breasts. In contrast, I. Young's (1990) concept of breasted experience is not satisfied in the consumption of signs and commodities, and it does not respect the distinctions that set the value of the breast in a system of sign-exchange values. Rather, breasted experience is an ongoing, indeterminate, contextually-responsive way of being—the breasted body is "blurry, mushy, indefinite, multiple, and without clear identity" (pp. 192-193).

This disruption of the system of differentiations within which signs as commodities circulate engages a "woman-centered" ontology and epistemology—being breasted and knowing breasted experience in alternative ways to those privileged in the dominant economy. I. Young contrasts the epistemic objectification of the gaze—the distanced knowing through looking—with a sensate way of knowing through the feel and sensitivity of breasts.

Consider the breasted experience of touch. In contrast to the way touch has been exploited in erotica, pornography, and in the popular self-healing literatures, M. Block (1998) expresses her experience of touch as self-knowledge in "Favorite Body Parts." Her words concretize I. Young's concept of touch as intimate, local, sensate knowing:

> If I could effectively enfold myself from behind, I would do it. I would stand behind myself and hold my breasts in each hand, then slowly slide my hands down my slippery smooth skin, feeling my ribs and the space between them, feeling the perfection of the fit of my hands with my hips, the absolute rightness of placing one's hands on one's hips, not in exasperation or consternation, but in perfect harmony. . . . Just me and me. My body. My life. (p. 126)

The reciprocity between sensate experience and the body's textures and symmetries (or asymmetries—this piece was written before her mastectomy) constitutes perfection, absolute rightness in the context of the body and not in terms of an abstracted, fantastical but commodifiable ideal. Feelings in and about breasts define different ways of being a woman not only biologically (the cycles and changes over a woman's life) but culturally and historically as well (see Yalom's excellent *A History of the Breast,* 1997).

Along with touch as epistemic, I. Young (1990) imbues "a womanspace" with ontological significance. She describes a womanspace in terms that resonate to Baudrillard's argument for relational reciprocity (rather than exchange): In such spaces, women go about their everyday activities bare-breasted. I. Young claims that the mundane and constant engagement with their own and each other's breasts "deobjectifies" and "dereifies" the breasts. Breasts are no longer objects coded in dominant value logics as sign-commodities; their meaning is not abstracted from the context of mundane intimacy but rather is immersed in the experience of being in touch with each other: "In a womanspace, with many women walking around bare-breasted, the variability and individuality of breasts becomes salient. I would like to say that in a womanspace, without the male gaze, a woman's breasts become almost like part of her face" (p. 196). This breasted experience in a womanspace is strikingly similar to the experience described by D. Young (1996/1998) after her double mastectomy:

> One Saturday morning, I gathered six of my closest friends and one of their daughters for lunch and a photo session. . . . We found that every woman's breasts are as totally individual as her face. Everyone agreed that my scars didn't look

nearly as bad as what they had expected. After the photos, we were all reluctant to put our blouses and shirts back on since we had all experienced such closeness, honesty, and ease during the shoot. (p. 46)

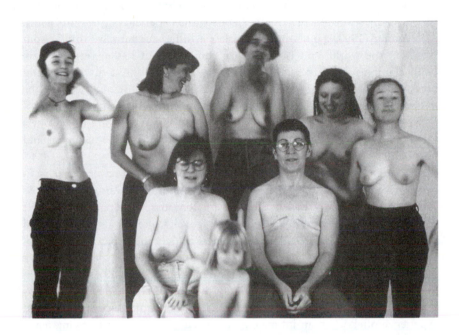

Figure 7.5   One in Eight

SOURCE: Photograph by D. C. Young in J. A. Tasch (Ed.), *Art.Rage.Us.: Art and Writing by Women with Breast Cancer*, copyright © 1998 by Chronicle Books. Reprinted with permission of D. C. Young and The Breast Cancer Fund.

Although D. Young's friends were not encountering each other's breasts in an ongoing, everyday context, they seem to have "deobjectified" each other's breasts and engaged each other's breastedness as an unaffected and intimate way of knowing each other. The mastectomy does not exclude D. Young; her scars, when visible, are acceptable, much more so than when they were hidden. With or without breasts, women's lives and relations are breasted.

REMAINING AMBIVALENT: A STRATEGY OF FEMINIST IRONY

There is a danger of essentialism in calling upon breasted experience, but I agree with Carter (1996), who argues for a strategic deployment of essentialism to emphasize the dynamics of ambivalence. In the case of breastedness, ambivalence entails an incessant movement of meaning that refuses to be fixed within a system of sign-commodity value but casts being/having breasts as dynamically responsive to contexts like age (puberty, old age), social relations (girl, woman, sexual partner, mother), or sensate experiences (pleasure, pain). As I. Young (1990) points out, "It makes a difference how we think about beings in the world, and we can make choices about it that seem to have political implications" (p. 193). We consume breasts as sign-commodities, and breasts as signs consume feminine identities and possibilities. But we have the option of being/feeling ambivalent about these practices and relations of consumption. Ambivalence as a political option is not a failure to act but a way of engaging in relations of reciprocity that constitute the meanings and possibilities of having/being breasted dynamically.

K. Ferguson (1993) calls ambivalence "the painful and rewarding tension between longing for and wariness of" a stable, culturally rewarded identity. As she argued, identity is always an achievement, temporary and partial, "an active corralling of practices, events, desires, contingencies, a regulatory semiotic and material operation"(p. 159). The challenge is to defy the apparent stability of categories of identity like "having breasts" or "breastedness" in ways that "mark their fluidity, their interactiveness, their ambivalences" (p. 169). Categories of identity are themselves achievements, articulations, and accidents riddled by the tensions and vacillations of ambivalence. An ironic perspective on breasted experience offers both an intimate and particularized way of knowing feminine bodies in relation to others and each other. But an ironic perspective is attuned as well to disruptions, exceptions, and breastedness itself as a way of being and knowing.

Conclusion

A feminist perspective on women's health communication must address the politics of women's body knowledge. In promoting irony and ambivalence as feminist perspectives and political strategies, I mean, first, to draw critical attention to the value logics that commodify women's breasts. Second, I urge health communication advocates and scholars to resist re-encoding those logics in their own appeals and to educate people to the oppressions affected through such logics as part of the messages they construct about specific issues of women's health. Finally, I caution feminist health advocates to remain open to the ambiguities, inconsistencies, and differences that constitute women's embodied experiences so that the alternatives we construct and the agencies we mobilize do not create a new order of embodied subjugation.

These recommendations are not meant to offer answers or resolutions; I admit the partialities of my own interpretive and deconstructive efforts. For example, I have highlighted only a few of the moments when breasted experiences reduce the breast to a sign-commodity. I've left out some of the situations that are most central to my own life: the workplace and breast-feeding, especially breast-feeding in the workplace. There are other omissions in this discussion as well. Most obviously, the bodies and practices I describe are drawn upon white, middle-class, U.S. perspectives and not the particular experiences of women of color or women in different class, cultural, and historical contexts. Finally, I didn't talk about the commodification of the sexualized breast in pornography, erotica, and prostitution. But I have shown how readily women's bodies and experiences can be consumed within a set of value logics, and how irony and ambivalence give us perspectives from which to intervene, resist, and re-vision our breasts and ourselves.

My hope is that women will begin to value the ambivalences that they may feel when their own breasted experiences are consumed by the consuming/commodified breast of popular imagery and cultural socialization. As activists, advocates, teachers, scholars, mothers, daughters, lovers, and women, we can engage each other in self-reflective and self-reflexive discussions of our own experiences that admit and embrace our ambivalences. Together, we can engage our ambivalences as strategies for resisting the dominant economy of value logics and for enacting a feminized politics of embodied knowledge.

8

Reframing Communication During Gynecological Exams

A Feminist Virtue Ethic of Care Perspective

Maria Brann and Marifran Mattson

In order to care for a patient, one must begin with caring for the patient.

—Pekkanen (1985)

In this chapter, we give voice to women's concerns about gynecological exams and provide recommendations for communicating those concerns in practical, empowering ways. First, we argue that the patriarchal biomedical model virtually ignores the role of gender in the production and maintenance of women's health. Second, we reframe that model with a feminist ethic of care. Third, we present a preliminary study that examines women's perceptions of gynecological exams. Finally, we offer practical suggestions for both gynecologists and patients to make women's experience of health care more empowering and satisfying.

The Biomedical Model: An Ethic of Justice

Today's health care system is dominated by a biomedical approach to prevention and treatment. Underlying this male-dominated approach to health care is an ethic of justice perspective which is based on several assumptions about how physicians think about and manage encounters with patients (Clement, 1996). Four of these assumptions are particularly relevant to our purposes. An *ethic of justice* (a) assumes objectivity; (b) emphasizes rationality and subsequent reasoning; (c) takes an abstract, generalized approach to all patients; and (d) is male/masculine/masculinist in its orientation to patients.

Previous research suggests several issues pointing to how an ethic of justice pervades women's health care in the United States. These include marginalization of women's health, lack of regard for women's anxiety surrounding the gynecological exam, sources of information about gynecological exams, and preferences for a female gynecologist.

MARGINALIZATION OF WOMEN'S HEALTH

Women and their health needs have been "excluded, overlooked, and understudied" in America's health care system (Rosser, 1994, p. 148). Although health movements have lobbied for women's reproductive rights, the role of women's health care throughout history has consistently been subjugated within a male-dominated, biomedical system. This was especially the case with the medicalization of health care in the latter part of the 19th century (Engel, 1977; D. Morris, 2000; Pauli, White, & McWhinney, 2000). This biomedical approach to health care offers inadequate understanding of health because it encourages physicians to treat illnesses, not women (D. Morris, 2000). As described by Pauli et al. (2000), "The patient . . . becomes a machine; the focus of attention becomes that part of the mechanism that functions or—in the case of disease—does not function according to (bio)engineering prescriptions" (p. 19). Thus, women are not viewed as whole persons but instead are considered as a collection of parts.

Gynecological health care fell prey to an ethic of justice because it is situated in an androcentric health system (Kautz, 1995). Some have even argued that gynecology was promoted as a means for men to control women (Mendelsohn, 1981). Not only has this specialty given men control over women's bodies, but men also control which women's health concerns merit attention. Thus, during the early 19th century, when men became full-time physicians and made medicine a *profession*, medical attention shifted solely to reproduction and ignored other concerns of women (Corea, 1977; Rosser, 1994). A. Haas and Puretz (1992) argue that although the health care system as a whole in the United States is in crisis, health care for women is in especially dire straits because it perpetuates the ideology of women as objects (see also Ehrenreich & English, 1978; Ruzek, 1978). The biomedical model utilized in

America's health care system does not promote an ethic of caring but instead focuses on control through an ethic of justice.

Interestingly, a more feminist, caring approach to women's health was evident during the early 1800s prior to the professionalization of medicine. Midwives treated women holistically by sharing information and support rather than focusing only on the medical condition of the pregnancy. This type of patient-centered care was preferred by most women. However, after the 1800s, a male-dominated system replaced woman-to-woman care with highly specialized, mostly male physicians trained to treat medical conditions rather than persons. As Ehrenreich and English (1978) explain,

> With the elimination of midwifery, all women—not just those of the upper class—fell under the biological hegemony of the medical profession. In the same stroke, women lost their last autonomous role as healers. The only roles left for women in the medical system were as employees, customers, or "material." (p. 88)

Male control over women's reproductive freedom is often detrimental to women (Rosser, 1994). For example, after male physicians drove away midwives and began delivering babies with forceps, more women died during childbirth (Corea, 1977). Because men regulate the study, care, and treatment of women, the specialty of gynecology has tended to focus on male-preferred topics such as procreation and heterosexual activity (Corea, 1977; Rosser, 1994). Unfortunately, females trained in the male-dominated value system of medicine may not be more patient-centered by virtue of their sex (Corea, 1977; Ruzek, 1978).

During the 1960s and 1970s, women's health movements across the country demanded quality health care focusing on the needs of women. One major goal was to improve gynecological care. Women banned together for "abortion rights, reproductive freedom, and dignified health care" (Morgen, 1995, p. 236). They questioned whether men were competent to treat them (Ruzek, 1978). For example, Corea (1977) discussed the preposterous assumption that male physicians should control childbirth: "Men cannot even give birth. Nonetheless, they have taken control of childbearing and now they teach women how to do it properly" (p. 220).

Many women have fought for their reproductive rights because "their health concerns have been neglected by the biomedical research community" (Eidsness & Wilson, 1994, p. 228). However, women's health is still controlled by men because physicians and policymakers are reluctant to respond to a feminist health agenda (D. Morris, 2000; Rosser, 1994). The humanistic health needs of women are not being met (e.g., there has been no end to sexist practices; Fulenwider, 1980), nor can they be met in the existing biomedical system (Fugh-Berman, 1994; Ruzek, 1978).

LACK OF REGARD FOR WOMEN'S ANXIETY

Anxiety is one of the major barriers to women obtaining gynecological care. The gynecological exam is "an unpleasant, uninteresting, and anxiety-producing experience" (Feldmann & Driscoll, 1982, p. 990). According to Domar (1986), the gynecological exam is "one of the most common anxiety-producing medical procedures" (p. 75). Although most women realize that gynecological exams are necessary, they produce more anxiety than other types of medical exams, thus deterring women from seeking gynecological care (C. Frye & Weisberg, 1994; Haar, Halitsky, & Stricker, 1977). Unlike most other preventive health care procedures, gynecological exams have been associated with negative affective, behavioral, and cognitive processes in patients (C. Frye & Weisberg, 1994).

In large part, this fear is attributed to having a male doctor (McDonald, 1997). This has been a concern for women for centuries. Martensen (1994) addresses the history of this issue as follows:

> The situation of the recumbent woman patient, hips and knees flexed and separated, and the seated male practitioner with his hand probing her genitalia and reproductive organs has always been delicate, to use a term favored in the 19th century. (p. 641)

This was not such a delicate situation, however, until men took control of women's reproductive health. For example, when female midwives delivered babies, women would sit upright, which is more comfortable for the woman, and midwives would coax and encourage the woman. This more compassionate approach to childbirth is inconsistent with an androcentric approach to health care, in which it is easier to control a patient because she is lying on her back with her legs in the air (Corea, 1977).

Women's anxiety about gynecological exams may be organized into several emergent themes: discovering pathology, discomfort, embarrassment, and personal intrusion.

Discovering Pathology. According to Settlage (1975), one of the most important concerns women have about gynecological exams is the "fear of discovering pathology" (see also Haar et al., 1977; Weiss & Meadow, 1979). Many women fear that a gynecologist will find some type of disease. Because most women (like men) hold physicians in high esteem and fear death, just the thought of the omnipotent gynecologist discovering an incurable disease, such as cancer, produces anxiety (R. Smith, 2001). Domar (1986) noted an irony regarding this concern: "A consequence of not having regular gynecologic exams is that the likelihood of detecting pathology, such as cervical cancer in its early stages, is vastly reduced" (p. 76). Therefore, it is important that women engage in these exams as a preventive measure, but their anxiety about these exams and the ethic of justice environment in which they occur may be keeping them from consenting to routine exams.

Discomfort. Although discovering pathology appears to be the most serious concern, discomfort during the exam seems to be the most common concern. Whether it is stories heard from someone else or personal memories of previous experiences, women usually anticipate discomfort during a gynecological exam. Domar (1986) stressed that a pelvic exam is physically uncomfortable and suggests that they can be physically traumatizing, which may cause women to postpone future care (see also Millstein, Adler, & Irwin, 1984; Osofsky, 1967; Petravage, Reynolds, Gardner, & Reading, 1979). However, women do not need to experience physical discomfort to have anxiety. As Settlage (1975) suggested, just the expectation of physical discomfort from the procedure is enough to produce anxiety. In addition, the thought of pain (or associated discomfort) increases anxiety, which in turn increases pain, possibly making fear of pain a self-fulfilling prophecy (Millstein et al., 1984).

Further, the discomfort that women are concerned about does not necessarily have to be physical. Haar et al. (1977) found that 36.1% of the women in their study reported emotional discomfort, whereas only 19.2% reported actual physical discomfort. In an attempt to determine why women experienced uncomfortable feelings, Debrovner and Shubin-Stein (1975) suggested that women only intellectually consent to pelvic exams because they recognize the medical need for them, but they never emotionally consent. Therefore, emotional discomfort is as much a contributor to women's anxiety as physical discomfort.

Embarrassment. Although within a health care environment governed by an ethic of justice gynecological exams are supposed to be a "normal" event that women engage in for health maintenance, many women consider them a source of embarrassment (Domar, 1986; Haar et al., 1977; Osofsky, 1967; Wells, 1977). Many women are self-conscious about their bodies; therefore, they are concerned about undressing or being undressed in front of someone else, especially a male gynecologist who often is a stranger. In addition, because they must expose themselves to the gynecologist during the exam, women often become embarrassed and overly concerned about cleanliness. Some of the specific concerns of women during a gynecological exam include whether they are "clean enough for the examination" and if they "would have an odor that the clinician would discover" (Millstein et al., 1984, p. 106).

Personal Intrusion. In addition to experiencing embarrassment, women also consider the need to be undressed an intrusion into their privacy. Women feel anxiety because of the "violation of body privacy by a person who is at best an awesome, friendly stranger" (Settlage, 1975, p. 40). Millstein et al. (1984) found that the invasion of body privacy by a stranger produces psychological discomfort. Some women also fear that the gynecologist will discover "something about [their] sexual practices through the examination" (p. 106). Consequently, heterosexual women often worry about promiscuity, whereas lesbian patients are concerned about being denied treatment because of their sexual orientation. Shinkman (1998) reported that 67% of physicians admitted that they were aware of homosexual patients receiving substandard care because of their sexual orientation.

Another potentially serious anxiety that women expressed regarding personal intrusion is that their genitals will be damaged during the examination (Millstein et al., 1984). According to Settlage (1975), a major concern that women have about gynecological exams is the "exposure and manipulation of a person's genitals" (p. 40). Women rarely overcome the feeling of personal intrusion by the gynecologist during an exam (Debrovner & Shubin-Stein, 1975).

SOURCES OF INFORMATION ABOUT GYNECOLOGICAL EXAMS

Women seek and receive information about gynecological exams from a variety of sources. Early research suggested that women received most of their information about gynecological exams from friends (Millstein et al., 1984; Schrag, 1978). Further, "the most common specific message from peers was that the examination was painful" (Millstein et al., 1984, p. 105). Other sources of information include pamphlets, nurses, magazines, anatomical models, and television (Petravage et al., 1979). Although friends emphasized the pain involved in a gynecological exam, other information sources such as mothers, female relatives, and physicians focused on describing the procedure and its importance (Schrag, 1978). More recently, Lewis (1987) contradicted earlier findings by reporting that young women preferred to gain information about gynecological care from the following sources in this order: "parents, books, films/videos, family planning clinics and friends" (p. 492).

Ironically, much of the existing research on patient care in gynecological practice focuses on how gynecologists can lessen patients' anxiety (see, for example, C. Frye & Weisberg, 1994). However, it is equally important to consider other sources of information in women's networks to address some of the concerns women express about gynecological exams. For example, C. Frye and Weisberg (1994) reported that women sought most of their health information in magazines instead of from physicians because of their distrust with traditional, androcentric health care (see also Halpern & Blackman, 1985).

PREFERENCES FOR A FEMALE GYNECOLOGIST

In an effort to overcome their anxiety about the gynecological exam experience in general and male gynecologists in particular, many women seek out a female gynecologist. Women prefer and seek out a female physician for gynecological care more than in any other health care specialty (Fennema, Meyer, & Owen, 1990; Kerssens, 1997; McGurgan, O'Donovan, & Jones, 2001; Weyrauch, 1990), perhaps because male physicians may dismiss the concerns of female patients more often than women physicians do (C. Frye & Weisberg, 1994). Pointing to the insensitivity of male physicians, Fennema et al. (1990) suggested that "preference for the sex of physician is strengthened in specific clinical settings including visits that require genitalia examinations" (p. 442). When discussing her own distressful experience only a few years ago, Nunneley (1997) asked, "Why are women patients, in 1997, still having to submit to any kind of genital procedure carried out by a male doctor?" (p. 890). She also described how her privacy and care improved after she began to see female physicians who had careful attitudes toward their patients.

Those women who preferred female gynecologists argued that they are more oriented toward helping, caring behaviors and interpersonal relationships (C. Frye & Weisberg, 1994). Further, Lyon (1997) discussed the attitude among patients that "a woman understands me better" (p. 634). The notion that patients prefer female physicians was recorded as early as 1322 (Cockburn & Bewley, 1996). There is overwhelming evidence that patients of both sexes are more satisfied with female physicians, and "female doctors are consistently preferred by women patients" (p. 2). Because female physicians may experience the same concerns as their female patients, it is believed that they better understand and treat women's health concerns. One reason many believe that female gynecologists provide a greater quality of care to women than men do is that female doctors are perceived to be more empathetic and understanding than their male counterparts (Bickell & Earp, 1994; Cockburn & Bewley, 1996; McGurgan et al., 2001; Scully, 1994). In addition, female physicians are more likely to take symptoms seriously and are less likely to believe that an illness is psychogenic (C. Frye & Weisberg, 1994; Scully, 1994).

The empathy and understanding of female physicians is manifest in their communication with patients. Female physicians conduct "longer visits with more total talking by both patient and physician, more positive talk, partnership-building, question-asking, and information-gathering" (Lyon, 1997, p. 635). They also "listen better, offer nondirective counseling, and have longer consultations, allowing more health problems to be presented" (Cockburn & Bewley, 1996, pp. 2-3). Comparatively, male physicians are characterized as hurried (C. Frye & Weisberg, 1994), and they interrupt patients more frequently (Fennema et al., 1990).

Perceptions of empathy, sensitivity, understanding, and communication have been attributed to women's preference for female gynecologists. Studies have shown that "greater satisfaction is found between women patients and women physicians than among other types of physician-patient dyads" (Bickell & Earp, 1994, p. 1651). Based on this perception, women who see a male gynecologist may experience more anxiety and unanswered concerns than women who visit a female physician.

Reframing the Biomedical Model: A Feminist Virtue Ethic of Care

Although previous researchers have provided critical insight into the prevailing medical perspective on gynecological care (Dreifus, 1977; Ehrenreich & English, 1978; Roy, 1990; Weiss, 1977), few have proposed a viable alternative perspective (see Marieskind & Ehrenreich, 1975, for a notable exception). An alternative perspective necessitates a radical shift in how physicians think about and treat women during gynecological exams. The feminist virtue ethic of care perspective (Tong, 1998) provides a constructive framework for creating such a shift. In addition to transforming the ideology of gynecological care, a direct reframing of the interaction between gynecologists and women during these exams must occur.

An ethic of care perspective stands in sharp contrast to the prevailing ethic of justice approach (Johannesen, 1990; Noddings, 1984). Grounded in the writings of Gilligan (1982), Noddings (1984), and Enomoto (1997), an ethic of care perspective accentuates the virtue of caring, which is defined as a genuine concern for the well-being of others. This perspective values the creation of genuine relationships and is committed to do the least harm (Liddell, Halpin, & Halpin, 1992; see also the discussion of harm reduction theory in Mattson, 2000).

The assumptions of an ethic of care counter the assumptions of an ethic of justice (Clement, 1996). The contrasts between justice and caring ethics are particularly evident in four central assumptions:

1. An ethic of justice assumes human separateness or objectivity, whereas an ethic of care assumes human connectedness.

2. An ethic of justice emphasizes reason in performing right actions, whereas an ethic of care stresses the role of emotions in constituting good character.

3. An ethic of justice takes an abstract approach, whereas an ethic of care takes a contextual approach.

4. An ethic of justice is male/masculine/masculinist, whereas an ethic of care is female/feminine/feminist.

In addition to recognizing these contrasts, Tong (1998) complicates the argument by suggesting that the central assumptions in the justice-care debate are limited in their application because they simply offer an ethic of feminism (i.e., caring) as an alternative to an ethic of masculinity (i.e., reasoning). Instead, as Enomoto (1997) observes, the focus should be on a "feminist virtue ethics of care," which "conceptualizes moral maturity as the caring for and sensitivity to the needs of others . . . [and] that is oriented toward the nurturing of relationships and emphasizes one's responsibility to others" (pp. 351, 354) instead of one's power over others. In this way, caring is seen as an innate virtue that guides decisions and actions in everyday life (Hume, 1985; Noddings, 1984). According to Tong (1998), a "feminist virtue ethics of care is the proper moral medicine for much of what ails contemporary health care" (p. 133).

Study Examining Women's Views of Gynecology

One ethic of care value that is especially pertinent in the health care context is voice. Voice includes "the ability both to construct and articulate knowledge and to make choices and act in situations" (Mattson & Buzzanell, 1999, p. 64). It is through genuine voice that patients become empowered. By allowing patients voice on the issue of gynecological care, health care providers may be able to "hear" how the patriarchal medical system influences patients' participation.

Previous research has shown that women fear and avoid gynecological exams. In light of the male-dominated historical backdrop of women's health and the datedness of most of the existing literature on women's concerns about gynecological exams, we wanted to ask contemporary women for their current perceptions. Thus, the following research questions were posed:

RQ1: What concerns do women have regarding gynecological exams?

RQ2: Do women share their concerns with their gynecologists?

RQ3: How do women perceive gynecologists' reactions to their concerns?

PARTICIPANTS, DATA COLLECTION, AND CODING

Seventy-nine women completed our survey. Participants were recruited through a network sample (Frey, Botan, & Kreps, 2000). We gave the surveys to colleagues, family, and friends, and asked many of the participants to refer other people who might be willing to participate. (We recognize that, by using a network sample, the ability to generalize findings from our sample to the population is limited.) The participants voluntarily and anonymously completed the survey and returned it in a self-addressed, stamped envelope.

Table 8.1   Demographics of Sample

Age			Education			Previous Exam			Type of Care		
Years	#	%	Level	#	%[1]	Response	#	%	Type	#	%
18-19	12	15	GED	1	1	Yes	71	90	Private	43	61
20-29	41	52	High			No	8	10	Clinic	27	38
			school	9	11						
30-39	11	14	Some						No		
			college	35	44				response	1	1
40-49	7	9	College								
			degree	33	42						
50-59	5	6	Other	1	1						
60-69	2	3									
70-79	1	1									

1. Note that the total in this column does not equal 100% because of rounding.

Our goal was to reach as many women, and as diverse a sample, as possible. Although precautions were taken to include women of different ages and education levels, due to the nature of the network sample, most of the participants were from the Midwest and the South. Ages ranged from 18 to 71, with a mean age of 29.6 years. Of the 79 participants, 33 had earned a college degree, 35 had some college experience, 9 had a high school diploma, 1 earned her high school vocational diploma in college, and 1 earned her GED. Eight participants had never visited a gynecologist (ages 18, 19, 47, and 53). Of the women who had been to a gynecologist, 43 visited a private physician, 27 sought care at a clinic, and 1 person did not specify the type of care she had received (Table 8.1). Age, educational level, and type of care sought were evaluated to determine if any may have had a significant influence on the concerns women experienced. Twelve participants had not seen a gynecologist in more than a year; the other 59 women had been to a gynecologist within the last 12 months.

Participants were given a 13-question survey that consisted primarily of open-ended questions designed to address the research questions (Table 8.2). By offering an open-ended survey, we sought to empower women to voice their stories (see A. Haas & Puretz, 1992). Demographic questions were also included. Surveys were mailed to potential participants, who were asked to return the completed survey within four weeks.

In addition to coding participants by demographics (Table 8.1), their concerns about gynecological exams were coded into themes (Tables 8.3 through 8.7). Specifically, the analysis process involved separating the data into coding units. A coding unit was defined as a basic unit of text that consisted of a complete idea. Consequently, coding units were phrases, sentences, paragraphs,

Table 8.2   The Survey

The purpose of this questionnaire is to help understand women's feelings about and concerns with gynecological care. Please answer each question and elaborate as much as possible. Attach additional paper, if necessary. Answers will be reported in summary data. All information will remain anonymous, so do not include your name. Please return this form in the envelope provided. Thank you.

1.   Age:

2.   Educational Level (please circle):
     College degree   Some college   High school   Some high   Other:
                                           diploma   school

3. Have you ever been to a gynecologist?	Yes	No
	If yes,	If no,
	go to	go to
	question 4.	question 8.

4.   When was your last appointment?

5.   If it has been more than one year since your last exam, what has prevented you from going?

6.   Is your gynecologist a private physician, or do you visit a clinic?

7.   Why do you usually visit a gynecologist?

8.   Why have you not seen a gynecologist?

9.   What concerns do you have about seeing a gynecologist?

10. Do you have any apprehensions about seeing a gynecologist?	Yes	No

11.   If yes, what are your apprehensions?

12. Do you share your apprehensions with your gynecologist?	Yes	No

13.   If you do share your apprehensions, what reactions do you get from your gynecologist?

     Thank you for your time.

or groups of paragraphs. After the coding units were determined, the first author of this chapter read these units until "threads of meaning that recur" (Baxter, 1991, p. 250) emerged. This discreet reading of the coding units, also referred to as *open coding* (A. Strauss & Corbin, 1998), was conducted to delineate general themes within the data. The general themes of different concerns about gyneco-logical experiences surfaced as meaningful across the women's responses.

Table 8.3   Contemporary Concerns About Gynecological Exams

Concern	# of Women Citing Concern	Percentage
Discomfort	22	31
Discovering pathology	11	16
Sex of gynecologist	10	14
Understanding and communication	10	14
Other (e.g., expense, hours)	17	24

More than half (62%) of the women surveyed expressed some type of concern about seeing a gynecologist. Eighty-nine percent of these women had some college education, with the majority (56%) having earned a college degree. Sixty-one percent of the women surveyed sought care from a private physician; however, of the women who expressed concerns, only 43% visited a private physician. Themes emerged which both supported and contradicted previous research. These themes are discussed according to our research questions.

RQ1: What Concerns Do Women Have About Gynecological Exams?

Although women's concerns in our study generally were consistent with previous research, the ordering of current anxieties was unique (see Table 8.3). We discuss each of the four main concerns in detail.

Discomfort. A theme related to discomfort (Table 8.4) recurred most often among these participants. Primarily women in their 20s expressed concern about discomfort, which initially suggested that this concern may be related to a lack of experience with gynecologists. However, women through their mid-50s also reported experiencing this concern, which suggests other, more systemic or ideological, reasons for this recurrent anxiety. Concern with discomfort also spanned educational levels, from those with high school diplomas to those with college degrees, again suggesting that women with a variety of experiences and sources of information fear discomfort during gynecological exams.

In addition, many women defined discomfort as more than just physical distress. One woman stated, "It is awkward and painful," which denotes emotional as well as physical concern. Another woman described the questions she thinks of when anticipating a gynecological exam. One question reflects her concern with discomfort: "Will he/she be gentle?" Other women elaborated on their sense of discomfort by relating it as the feeling they experienced because their gynecologists seized control during the exam. For example, one woman

Table 8.4   Demographics of the 22 Women Who Cited Discomfort as a Concern

Age			Education			Type of Care		
Years	#	%	Level	#	%	Type	#	%
18-19	2	9	High school	1	5	Private	6	27
20-29	13	59	Some college	8	36	Clinic	16	73
30-39	4	18	College degree	13	59			
40-49	2	9						
50-59	1	5						
60-69	0	0						
70-79	0	0						

stated, "I felt a real lack of personal control, by the physical setup and the doctors' attitudes, which was uncomfortable." Another woman said, "It's personal. You are somewhat vulnerable at that time." These perceptions are consistent with Domar's (1986) research that explained how women sensed a loss of control during their health care because they felt vulnerable to the physician. Further, these responses indicated that the micro-level discomfort women feel about participating in the gynecological exam extends from the macro-level ethic of justice perspective that continues to permeate women's gynecological health care.

Interestingly, the theme of discomfort was related to whether the woman went to a clinic or to a private physician. Seventy-three percent of the women who expressed a concern with discomfort sought care at a clinic rather than with a private physician. Often women who see a private physician have a personal referral or have established better rapport with the physician (Takenaga, Kai, & Ohi, 1985), allowing them to feel more comfortable and more in control. Research shows that more anxiety occurs when unfamiliar gynecologists perform the exam (C. Frye & Weisberg, 1994). Perhaps private physicians more often reflect the tenets of a feminist virtue ethic of care because they have the opportunity to establish unique relationships with their patients, which encourages them to contextualize their approach to patient care.

Discovering Pathology. Most women expressed their concern about discovering pathology as finding something "wrong" (Table 8.5). One woman observed, "I'm nervous to figure out if there is something wrong with me." Another said her concern was that she was "scared something might be wrong." A third was "afraid sometimes they might find a serious problem." Those harboring concern about pathology ranged from a teenager (i.e., 19) to the oldest person surveyed (i.e., 71), implying that age was not a factor in women's concern about disease.

Table 8.5   Demographics of the 11 Women Who Cited Discovering Pathology as a Concern

Age			Education			Type of Care		
Years	#	%	Level	#	%[1]	Type	#	%
18-19	1	9	GED	1	9	Private	3	27
20-29	7	64	High school	1	9	Clinic	8	73
30-39	1	9	Some college	4	36			
40-49	0	0	College degree	5	45			
50-59	1	9						
60-69	0	0						
70-79	1	9						

1. Note that the total in this column does not equal 100% because of rounding.

Only one woman specifically reported what she feared. She stated, "I feel increased concern about cancer, both cervical and breast." Another woman expressed concern, but her anxiety was more that the gynecologist would *miss* the pathology rather than discover it. She said that her concern was "if she [the gynecologist] will know if anything is wrong with my body. If she says everything is normal, and it is not normal." This woman's concern illustrates the complexity of the anxiety produced by a gynecological exam. Not only might women be concerned about having disease but also of incompetent gynecologists not detecting disease.

The biomedical, or ethic of justice, approach to patient care is evident in the theme of discovering pathology. Expressions of this theme illustrate how women see themselves and their respective roles vis-à-vis the gynecologist. From the ethic of justice worldview, gynecologists possess knowledge to diagnose and treat diseases. This objective runs counter to establishing a meaningful relationship with the patient. However, if gynecologists adopted an ethic of care perspective, patients may not be as fearful because, in addition to diagnosis and treatment, they could also expect moral support and humane treatment from their gynecologist.

Sex of the Gynecologist. The sex of the gynecologist was another concern for these women (Table 8.6). Every woman who expressed concern about the sex of the gynecologist preferred a female physician. Several studies indicate that women favor health care from other women (Bickell & Earp, 1994; Cockburn & Bewley, 1996; Fennema et al., 1990; Lyon, 1997; Scully, 1994). Sixty percent of our participants who wanted a female gynecologist were in their 20s. All of the women expressing this preference had some college

Table 8.6   Demographics of the 10 Women Who Cited Sex of the Gynecologist as a Concern

Age			Education			Type of Care		
Years	#	%	Level	#	%	Type	#	%
18-19	1	10	Some college	3	30	Private	5	50
20-29	6	60	College degree	7	70	Clinic	5	50
30-39	2	20						
40-49	0	0						
50-59	1	10						
60-69	0	0						
70-79	0	0						

experience. Unlike the theme of concern with pathology, age and educational level appeared to be associated with participants' desire to seek care from another woman. Younger, college-educated women expressed a preference for a female gynecologist, whereas older women with less education did not indicate a preference, possibly because they were not socialized to expect or desire a choice.

Women who noted a preference thought that female gynecologists would be more understanding. For example, one woman said that the sex of her gynecologist was linked to her comfort level: "So far I've had women gynecologists, but male gynecologists would make me feel very uncomfortable, especially during pap exams." Two other women stated that they thought a female gynecologist would be more understanding. In particular, one woman wrote, "I went to a female gynecologist because I had some questions I thought a woman would be better with." Another woman felt the same way: "I see a female physician, and although I'm not apprehensive at all about seeing a male (from a modesty standpoint), I feel that a female is able to understand more fully any questions or problems I have." It may be an inaccurate stereotype that female physicians understand female patients better. Each woman who addressed this issue reported visiting a female gynecologist only, and she had never experienced being the patient of a male gynecologist for comparison. We suspect that the biomedical socialization of female physicians may predispose them to be similar to male physicians in their ethic of justice ideology and approach to women's health issues.

Understanding and Communication. Most of the comments about understanding and communication involved the desire to have questions answered. One woman wrote, "My concern when seeing my gynecologist is that he answers all of my questions and that he is concerned about my feelings and health."

Another woman wanted to be "comfortable with the physician so I can ask her anything." Another woman stated, "I was apprehensive to ask questions," and someone else expressed a concern with gynecologists "not answering all my questions." Finally, a woman stated that she wanted her gynecologist to provide information with "sensitivity to certain issues, fully explaining if problems or irregularities occur." Gynecologists operating from an ethic of justice perspective do not value interaction with patients other than to transform symptoms into the diagnosis of a physical condition. What these women's comments illustrate is their desire for a gynecologist who values both medical knowledge and physical symptoms but who also contextualizes their symptoms within their unique lives by listening to and responding to all their questions and concerns.

As with the expressed preference for a female gynecologist, all of the women concerned with understanding and communication were in their late teens or 20s and had college experience; only four had not yet achieved their degree (Table 8.7). Taken together, the demographic indicators for these two themes (i.e., sex of the gynecologist, understanding and communication) suggest that these concerns were generation specific. Young, college-educated women may recognize the predominance of the biomedical model, which favors objectivity and abstract reasoning, and attempt to resist the system by favoring female gynecologists.

To achieve the level of care women desire and deserve, a feminist virtue ethic of care, which favors human connectedness through genuine, contextualized relationships, is needed. All gynecologists should practice in this way. Otherwise, women may resist interaction with them for fear their physicians will react negatively to their concerns.

Table 8.7   Demographics of the 10 Women Who Cited Understanding and Communication as a Concern

Age			Education			Type of Care		
Years	#	%	Level	#	%	Type	#	%
18-19	2	20	Some college	4	40	Private	5	50
20-29	8	80	College degree	6	60	Clinic	5	50
30-39	0	0						
40-49	0	0						
50-59	0	0						
60-69	0	0						
70-79	0	0						

RQ2: Do Women Share Their Concerns With Their Gynecologists?

Ironically, although most of the women in this study valued communication with their gynecologist, only 43% of the women reported that they shared their concerns with their gynecologist. The reasons these women did not share their concerns are consistent with the ramifications of an ethic of justice perspective. For example, one woman explained, "I found doctors to be uncaring and patronizing. I don't share concerns/apprehensions with a patronizing person." Many patients echoed the reactions they received from the gynecologist. If positive feedback was received from the gynecologist, the women also were more positive about the situation and experienced less anxiety. However, those women who were not receiving the communication they desired experienced more anxiety and negative emotions during the exam. As the results of this survey suggest, most women's responses to the gynecological exam are influenced by the communication received from the gynecologist. Although Wells (1977) claimed that "airing these fears or concerns is likely to be the best way of dispelling them" (p. 305), and the majority of women in this study who shared their concerns with their gynecologists supported this claim, the reactions women often received when they did share their concerns with their gynecologists intimates that resistance via silence (see Clair, 1998) may prevail unless a feminist virtue ethic of care is adopted by more gynecologists. Perhaps because of negative responses or the expectation of dehumanizing responses, many women simply refrain from sharing their concerns with their gynecologists or resist seeing a gynecologist altogether.

RQ3: How Do Women Perceive Gynecologists' Reactions to Their Concerns?

Women who shared their concerns about the exam with their gynecologists reported a variety of reactions ranging from positive to negative. A few women reported neutral responses from their gynecologists, including responses such as simply receiving "explanations" or "He talks to me." However, even these neutral responses seemed to be imbued with a patriarchal ethic of justice influence because the gynecologists appear to be focusing on quick responses given *to* the women instead of engaging in conversations *with* the women about their concerns.

Fifty-three percent of the women in this study received reassuring feedback when sharing their concerns with their gynecologist. Many of these women noted that their gynecologist was willing to answer questions. Examples included, "She is very open, blunt with me about any questions or statements I make," "My current female gynecologist is very thorough, open, and effective in answering my questions and addressing my concerns," and "I have a wonderful, caring gynecologist who is truly concerned about my well-being. He answers all questions and calms any worries I may have." The notion of calming worries was also expressed by other women, who wrote, "She is extremely supportive and tries to help relax me," "She is very nice and willing to help if something is wrong, reassuring that everything is going to be okay," "He reassures that it is normal and okay to be afraid," and "She is very clear in her explanations and what I need to know to do for any situation that happens to be going on. She is very compassionate and makes you feel comfortable about anything you need to discuss."

One woman mentioned her gynecologist's effective reactions. She wrote that the reactions were "encouraging so far. The gynecologist I visit . . . made the pap exams as relaxing as possible for me, after I shared some amount of apprehension with her. Her good interpersonal skills definitely helped." Upon sharing their concerns, women found that supportive reactions by their gynecologists helped alleviate their concerns. In addition, these positive responses suggest that their gynecologists operated from a feminist virtue ethic of care perspective and so were able to create a unique patient-physician partnership. Women reported that both male and female gynecologists did this.

However, many women reported negative reactions when they shared their concerns. Most of the negative reactions by gynecologists were consistent with the physicians' biomedical training and an ethic of justice perspective. One woman claimed that her gynecologist simply told her "I'm used to this" or "Oh, RELAX!" which she did not find comforting. One woman explained how she does not like to share information with her female gynecologist because the gynecologist becomes angry and has actually yelled at her when she disclosed personal information. Another woman characterized the feedback she received from gynecologists in several ways, including "generally short responses, at times have had no explanations at all, always seem[s] to be in a hurry, not very personable, overall I haven't experienced very positive feedback from any gynecologist I've seen." Negative nonverbal responses also were reported. One woman described being ignored and even laughed at.

Implications

We advocate a radical shift in the treatment of women during gynecological exams. Specifically, we argue for reframing the interaction during these exams, in keeping with a feminist virtue ethic of care (Tong, 1998). A feminist virtue ethic of care accentuates the virtue of caring, values the creation of genuine relationships, and is committed to do the least harm. We are using the phrase *ethic of care* to refer to a set of virtues or values that relate to being a good person and performing right actions (Veatch, 1998). Our study suggests both a theoretical extension of the feminist virtue ethic of care and practical guidance for adopting this perspective.

Although a feminist virtue ethic of care perspective provides an appropriate theoretical framework for reshaping the patient-gynecologist relationship, in its current articulation, it lacks guidance for practical application. Thus, to extend the theory into practice, we argue that a genuine relationship between a patient and a physician is fostered and sustained through communication. And, because relationships are co-created, this entails mutual responsibility.

Using this perspective, gynecologists may be better able to meet the needs of women. Communicating in a caring manner may help alleviate the anxiety women experience before, during, and after gynecological exams. When a woman knows that her gynecologist cares for her, she feels comfortable expressing herself. This empowers women to participate in their health care by voicing their concerns and contributing to decision making.

Recognizing the value of communication in patient-physician interactions, D. H. Smith (1993) discusses two useful issues regarding the communicative value dynamics of ethics, both of which are relevant to our discussion. First, ethical values are expressed through language. According to the feminist virtue ethic of care perspective, the language of the gynecological exam should always reflect feminist values of caring, such as fellow-feeling, interdependence, connection, and benevolence (Enomoto, 1997; Gilligan, 1982; Noddings, 1984; Tong, 1998). Such dialogue fosters caring behaviors that can be woven into the patient-health care provider relationship (Mattson & Buzzanell, 1999).

Second, ethical or value elements are evident in decision making (D. H. Smith, 1993). A feminist virtue ethic of care advocates a caring, participative atmosphere. Mattson and Buzzanell (1999) emphasize voice as promoting participation in decision making. Voice assumes "the ability both to construct and articulate knowledge and to make choices and act in situations" (p. 64). In addition to recognizing the traditionally dominant voice, the concept of voice empowers those who previously have been silenced by the norms of gynecological exams. By adopting a feminist virtue ethic of care perspective, physicians foster an environment in which women's role in decision making about their health is given voice.

PRACTICAL SUGGESTIONS:
GYNECOLOGIST'S RESPONSIBILITY

Seeking a "greater balance of benefits over harms for the patient" should be the primary goal of a gynecologist (Chervenak & McCullough, 1997, p. 91; see also Mattson, 2000). Scholars have long been aware of this objective. Schrag (1978) discussed how women wanted to be respected as individuals and not be patronized (in addition, recall comments regarding patronizing interaction by one of the survey respondents). Each woman uniquely experiences concerns, and ethic of care approaches need to be adapted to fit the needs of the individual patient to help reduce these anxieties (Fertig & Hayes, 1998; C. Frye & Weisberg, 1994; Osofsky, 1967). To adapt to each patient, gynecologists need to spend more time learning about individuals' coping styles. Gynecologists need to "sharpen their sensitivity to and broaden their knowledge of female patients' reactions and changing needs" (Haar et al., 1977, p. 795). Domar (1986) predicted, "Physician sensitivity and awareness of anxiety-producing issues will lead to improved health care" (p. 88). Organizational support (e.g., more time for appointments), however, must also exist to facilitate improved communication, sensitivity, and awareness by gynecologists (Mechanic, 1998; R. Scott, Aiken, Mechanic, & Moravcsik, 1995).

Research shows that women's concerns about pelvic exams are associated with their relationships with their gynecologists. Patients feel that their gynecologists do not treat them with dignity (M. Gray & Meginnis, 1978; Washington, 1999). A woman's dignity must be maintained throughout the examination, especially considering the vulnerable position that women are placed in when they go to the gynecologist. Because of this vulnerable position, it is important for gynecologists to not only maintain the patient's dignity but also to communicate with the patient. This communication should be both verbal and nonverbal, and relevant to the exam process. According to Settlage (1975), saying something as simple as "I understand you are probably a little nervous, at least other patients often are, so let me tell you what I'll be doing" (p. 41) offers tremendous comfort to the patient.

The women in this study explicitly voiced the need for communication with their gynecologists, a concern that M. Gray and Meginnis (1978) also noted more than 20 years ago. More recently, Eidsness and Wilson (1994) found that women still feel frustrated by the lack of meaningful communication they receive during visits with their gynecologists because the language often used by physicians is not responsive to the needs of women for support and understanding (Rosser, 1994).

Women want more interactive health care experiences with their gynecologists (C. Frye & Weisberg, 1994). Nunneley (1997) explained that she not only wanted to be talked to—but also listened to—differently. Women are tired of being talked down to, and much of the communication that they are receiving is not emotionally helpful. Instead, women should be treated as collaborating participants in their health care. Interacting with women in affirming rather than condescending ways can create this collaboration. Communication needs to be open, caring, and encouraging (A. Haas & Puretz, 1992). Valuing a person's emotions and feelings is vital to the ethic of care perspective (Enomoto, 1997). Recognizing the range of emotional responses experienced by women before, during, and after gynecological exams is critical because "emotions are not only morally relevant, but also morally necessary" (Tong, 1998, p. 137; see also Allmark, 1995). Thus, the emotions conveyed by women during gynecological exams should not be dismissed as trivial to the care plan. Instead, women should be listened to and reacted to with understanding and relevant information.

In addition to expressing comforting words, a gynecologist can use non-verbal messages to put patients at ease. The positioning of the gynecologist and the patient throughout the exam is important. For example, during all but the physical examination, gynecologists could interact with patients in a less threatening environment, such as their office, rather than the exam room. In addition, it is critical for gynecologists to maintain eye contact with patients whenever possible (Settlage, 1975). Body movement and personal distance also influence how a patient perceives her physician. During the women's health movement of the 1960s, M. Gray and Meginnis (1978) found that women were becoming increasingly resentful of interpersonal distance, and they desired appropriate, caring touch, such as a consoling pat on the arm when the physician is delivering bad news. Gynecologists work in a professional field devoted to caring, and it is important that they communicate in a way that promotes a caring relationship with their patients.

Although these communication recommendations may seem idealistic, such practices, through repetition, will become embedded in the ideology of a medical system that is reframed to encompass a feminist ethic of care rather than an ethic of justice. In the meantime, adopting such practices, even in the absence of a reframed ideology, may serve to initiate the reframing.

PRACTICAL SUGGESTIONS: PATIENT'S RESPONSIBILITY

Patients, too, bear responsibility for creating more satisfying gynecological exams (A. Haas & Puretz, 1992; Washington, 1999). Patient education is an important way to alleviate anxiety. Increased understanding occurs through a variety of sources, including medically sanctioned teaching tools (e.g., pamphlets, videos) and popular literature and culture—for example, *The Vagina Monologues* (Ensler, 2000). Petravage et al. (1979) discovered that when women had more information about what was going on during the gynecological exam, they were more comfortable. In addition to education about the procedure, education about one's body is also recommended. Settlage (1975) suggests self-exploration, claiming that "self-ignorance aggravates the problems of gynecological and sexual health" (p. 47). By becoming self-educated, women challenge gynecologists to "no longer abuse their power and exploit their patients' ignorance and helplessness" (M. Gray & Meginnis, 1978, p. 175; see also Tong, 1998). Women, instead, become partners with their doctors because they have important information.

Education also inspires confidence. As women become more educated about their bodies and the oppressive dynamics of the health care system, they are demanding that their autonomy be respected and that their input be considered in decision making (Eidsness & Wilson, 1994). According to Chervenak and McCullough (1997), displays of autonomy require gynecologists to present alternatives to women, explain recommendations, and ultimately carry out the patient's preference for care. If gynecologists respect women's autonomy, they will follow the preferences of patients regardless of their own perspective of the consequences (Chervenak & McCullough, 1998; see also Mattson, 2000).

Women also need to communicate better with their gynecologists (Debrovner & Shubin-Stein,1975). Haar et al. (1977) found that women wanted more time with their gynecologists and better communication. One of the authors recalls being told by her female gynecologist, "You sure ask a lot of questions. I don't have much time to be answering these questions." To this she replied, "I guess we'll have to schedule a double appointment time for me from now on." Women must dialogue with their gynecologists and demand the needed time.

Communication can also be used as an important strategy at a more macro level. Because health care exists within a patriarchal system in the United States, it is important to influence legislation to change public policy. Bipartisan support has existed for a patient's bill of rights, which has the goal of offering quality care (Annas, 1998; Dorodny, 1998; Moskowitz, 1999; "President Clinton endorses consumer bill of rights," 1998; Wakefield, 1997). Direct local pressure may also be effective to more immediately create change in a particular health care organization. Invoking patient power through tactics such as utilizing patient advocates, picketing, blacklisting, or even refusing payment provide testament that may aid in advocating for the feminist virtue ethic of *care* in health care.

Ultimately, the message of a feminist virtue ethic of care poses two communication challenges. First, it is not an approach to ethics reserved for women; rather, this perspective is for anyone who wants to reclaim the practice of medicine from those who have rendered it heartless. In other words, it dares health care participants to "at least try to develop caring feelings as well as conscientious desires and empathetic skills" (Tong, 1998, p. 151). Second, it challenges health care participants to counter the oppressive structures of contemporary health care and instead foster genuinely caring relationships.

9

Commentary

Communication and Women's Health

Gary L. Kreps

Communication and Health

The preceding four chapters insightfully examine several important ways that communication influences the health of women. These chapters build upon a large body of research that illustrates the pervasive roles that communication performs in defining health and delivering health care (see reviews of the health communication research literature in Jackson & Duffy, 1998; Kreps, 1988a, 2001). The literature shows that, through formative everyday communication, we learn about what is and what is not healthy, shaping health beliefs (Kreps & Kunimoto, 1994). Communication is also the primary process we use to seek and offer health care (Jones, Kreps, & Phillips, 1995; Kreps, 1988b).

Our ongoing interactions with relevant others, both personally and through the media, influence the development of health beliefs and attitudes, establishing expectations for how we should behave to promote health and seek health care (Kreps & Kunimoto, 1994). For example, Chapter 6, by Quintanilla, Cano, and Ivy, powerfully illustrates the ways communication shapes expectations and responses to menopause. Similarly, Sotirin's provocative Chapter 7 examines the ways socially constructed meanings about women's breasts influence beliefs, attitudes, and behaviors concerning breast health and sexuality.

Author's Note: The ideas presented in this chapter are my own and do not necessarily reflect the official positions of the National Cancer Institute.

Brann and Mattson's fascinating chapter about gynecological health care (Chapter 8) and Ellingson's moving chapter about cancer survivorship (Chapter 5) both show how communication serves as the primary channel for health care delivery, illustrating serious communication problems that influence the ways women are treated within the modern health care system. In this chapter, I expand upon these four chapters by highlighting what I see as several critical communication issues for women and other consumers in the modern health care system that deserve concerted attention and serious redress.

Dysfunction in Modern Health Care

The modern health care system has become increasingly bureaucratic, often making consumers wade through seemingly unending stacks of paperwork, endure unbearably long waiting periods, and sometimes even withstand insensitive and intrusive handling just to access health care (Jones, Kreps, & Phillips, 1995; Kreps, 1996). Worse than the growing bureaucracy and insensitivity within the modern health care system, however, is the fact that the system has also become terribly inequitable for many health care consumers. In many ways, the modern health care system seems to have forgotten how to care (Kreps, 1996).

In essence, health care is a human service process that at a bare minimum must be humane to be effective (Kreps, 1988a, 1996, 1998). Yet, there are serious injustices in the delivery of health care. These injustices are often based upon an inherent imbalance of power in the modern health care system between providers and consumers, which limits consumer participation in and control over their own health care (Kreps, 1998). This power imbalance, which is established and perpetuated through communication, has served to systematically disenfranchise and marginalize many consumers of health care.

The modern health care system is particularly constraining for several marginalized groups of consumers, including health care consumers who are poor, disabled, suffer from stigmatized diseases (such as AIDS and mental illness), as well as many members of minority groups, the ill elderly, and (the largest group of consumers of all) women (Dan, 1994; Fee, 1993; Kreps, 1998). This chapter examines the communication dynamics that underlie the power discrepancies and resulting disenfranchisement of women and other relevant groups of consumers in the health care system. It also identifies several individual-level communication strategies that can be adopted to help equalize power between providers and consumers, empower consumers to take charge of their own health care and, in the process, help to promote social justice within the modern health care system.

Marginalization of Women Consumers of Health Care

There is widespread evidence of profound discrimination and gender bias in the provision of health care for women who are often denied equal access to competent care and treatment. For example, there are many reports that women's health care complaints are often discounted and not taken seriously (Corea, 1977; Thornton, Marinelli, & Larson, 1993). Women are too often patronized by a health care system that minimizes their symptoms, suggests psychosomatic causes for their health problems, and infers that women's health complaints are ploys for getting attention (Chesler, 1972; Franks & Rothblum, 1983; Wallis, 1994). There is a "pervasive stereotype of the woman as complainer, as someone who manifests her mental woes in physical symptoms, such as the hysteric, the neurasthenic, about whom the physician does not have to be too concerned; her headaches or her chest pains are imaginary" (Wallis, 1994, p. 20). This issue is well-illustrated in Chapter 6, which describes how the experience of menopause is misunderstood and trivialized for many women, causing unnecessary guilt, embarrassment, and suffering. Because women's health care complaints are not always taken seriously, especially by health care providers, treatment of their health problems is delayed, and the health problems women experience often get worse through lack of attention. These untreated ailments can become quite serious and may lead to more complex health problems, eventually demanding intensive treatments by many different specialists.

Another clear illustration of the tendency to marginalize women within the health care system is the long-standing predisposition to use men as the standard for establishing clinical research and health care policy (Matroianni, Faden, & Federman, 1994). Male health problems are often taken more seriously than female health problems by the health care establishment, with more concern shown for risks to men's health than to women's health (Mahowald, 1993). Because of this bias against women, the medical establishment is less likely to be proactive in trying to prevent women's health problems. The history of treatment for heart disease is a stark example of this neglect; for years, heart disease was generally considered to be a male disease by the health care establishment (Diethrich & Cohan, 1992; Pashkow & Libov, 1994). The vast majority of all cardiovascular clinical research programs and health promotion efforts were designed for men. Yet, the truth of the matter is that, today, heart disease is a more dangerous and deadly disease for women than it is for men, with deaths from cardiovascular diseases claiming more than half a million women's lives each year (Diethrich & Cohan, 1992).

Perhaps most alarming is the dangerous trend within the U.S. health care system of subjecting too many women to unnecessary and excessive surgical procedures (Fee, 1993; Payer, 1988; S. West & Dranov, 1994). Gynecological and breast surgeries are often questionable, reflecting some of the gendered sensemaking issues concerning female sexual anatomy raised in Chapters 7 and 8. For example, there has been a growing scandal concerning the overuse of hysterectomy as the default, fallback treatment for virtually any reproductive tract complaint (S. West & Dranov, 1994). Thornton, Marinelli, and Larson (1993) note,

> Hysterectomy has classically been treated as an operation of minor significance by the medical establishment even though recent studies suggest tremendous psychological impact including loss of libido, sexual dysfunction, and depression. In France, approximately one-third the rate of hysterectomies are [sic] performed compared to the United States, yet morbidity and mortality rates are similar. (p. 191; see also the Boston Women's Health Book Collective, 1992; Fee, 1993; Payer, 1988; S. West & Dranov, 1994)

It has been estimated that as many as 30% to 40% of all the hysterectomies performed in the United States are not fully warranted because better alternative treatments are available (Ammer, 1989; Boston Women's Health Book Collective, 1992; Lowdermilk, 1995). Similar concerns are brewing in the United States about excessive use of cesarean section surgeries for childbirth deliveries and overuse of radical mastectomy surgeries when less invasive (lumpectomy) procedures are readily available and often warranted (Dan, 1994; Fee, 1993; Thornton, Marinelli, & Larson, 1993). The physiological and psychological toll of these unwarranted and invasive surgical procedures on long-term consumer survivorship and quality of life cannot be overestimated (see the earlier chapters in Part II of this book, particularly Ellingson's Chapter 5 on the many issues concerning successful cancer survivorship).

Communicating to Minimize Marginalization in Health Care

The marginalization of women and other groups of consumers within the health care system is a serious society-wide problem that, to fully address, will certainly demand in-depth, long-term, multilevel, macro-social changes in the delivery of health care. Large-scale interventions to influence cultural norms, government regulations, health care system policies, health promotion strategies, and health care provider educational programs will be needed to make long-lasting changes in engrained patterns of discrimination in health care. However, health care consumers and their advocates can do much as individual health communicators to guard against the detrimental outcomes of marginalization within the modern health care system.

First, to address marginalization on a personal level, health care consumers must stop being passive participants in the health care process. This change is difficult to implement for many health care consumers, who have been socialized for generations to be cooperative and compliant, to listen carefully, and not to interrupt health care providers (Kreps & Kunimoto, 1994; Payer, 1988). Yet, assertiveness is one of the most important communication skills consumers have for getting the most out of health care (Jones, Kreps, & Phillips, 1995). All consumers should recognize and exercise their rights to make decisions about their own treatment and their responsibility to gather valid information for making those decisions competently (Arntson, 1989; Jones, Kreps, & Phillips, 1995).

To be effective, consumers (and their advocates) should communicate strategically and assertively to gather and share relevant health information, using communication to fully participate in health care. This active participation in the health care delivery process is similar to what Arntson (1989) has cleverly referred to as health care "citizenship," becoming a participating citizen of the modern health care system. Citizenship depends upon our abilities to use communication as a tool for identifying and avoiding potential health care system perils, making informed health care decisions, and enlisting cooperation from providers in accomplishing our health care goals.

Health care consumers require information; it is their most important health care resource (Jones, Kreps, & Phillips, 1995; Kreps, 1988a). With relevant health information, they can demystify many of the complexities and ambiguities of illness and improve the quality of their health care decisions. Information can help consumers and providers interpret symptoms of illness to discover the causes of ailments. Relevant health information facilitates accurate diagnoses and helps participants in health care select from among the best and most appropriate available treatment options. Armed with relevant health information, consumers can understand why doctors act as they do, and they can use this information to establish cooperative working relationships with health care providers. Relevant information can also help make it possible to manage the many complex rules, regulations, and procedures that so often get in the way of effective health care delivery.

Human communication is the primary tool health care participants have for gathering relevant health information, and the quality of communication between health care providers and consumers dramatically influences the effectiveness of modern health care. Yet, in current health care practice, human communication is too often underappreciated and poorly utilized (Jones, Kreps, & Phillips, 1995). Consumers and providers can strategically utilize communication to exchange relevant health information, make informed health care decisions, and get the most out of health care.

To achieve their health care goals, health care providers and consumers must be able to work together cooperatively (Kreps, 1988b). Because modern health care often involves a number of different providers—such as doctors with different specializations (general practitioners, surgeons, anesthesiologists, pediatricians, and so forth), nurses, pharmacists, therapists, and even health care system staff members and administrators working with consumers (and often the families and friends of these consumers)—these interdependent individuals must communicate as team members to accomplish their health care goals (Kreps, 1988a). A primary application of health communication knowledge is to use communication to build effective health care teams, in which health care providers, support staff, and consumers share relevant information and coordinate efforts. Sensitive, appropriate, and informative communication must flow among all members of the health care system to promote effective health care delivery.

The consumer should be at the very center of the health care team. The activities of all the interdependent health care providers should revolve around the needs of the consumer, taking a consumer orientation (Kreps, 1996, 1998). Yet, in current practice, the consumer (especially the female consumer) is often left out of the communication loop, and thus left out of the health care team (Kreps, 1998; Mahowald, 1993; Mendelsohn, 1981; Thornton, Marinelli, & Larson, 1993). This is a serious mistake that inevitably limits the effectiveness of health care by blocking the exchange of relevant information from the consumer to the providers and from the providers to the consumer. Consumers should demand to participate in diagnostic and treatment discussions to make informed health care decisions. Their input in these decisions is essential.

Developing meaningful, sensitive, and effective relationships with providers is one of the best ways for consumers to gain access to health care decision making (Jones, Kreps, & Phillips, 1995). Get to know your providers. Let them know you are concerned about your health care and interested in participating fully. Ask questions and demand answers that you can understand. Refuse to be bullied into accepting treatments that you don't fully understand or agree with. The principle of informed consent mandates that consumers must be fully informed about treatment strategies and their implications and must agree to these treatments before they can be implemented. Yet, the concept of informed consent is often honored more in principle than in practice (Jones, Kreps, & Phillips, 1995). Consumers, especially many female consumers, are often intimidated by the health care system, don't stand up for their rights, and don't let their providers know they want to participate actively in their health care (Corea, 1977; Fee, 1993). These consumers are often left in the dark about their health care. They are disenfranchised by the health care system because they do not communicate assertively and strategically.

Conclusion

There is a wide range of personal and professional applications for health communication knowledge and skill to improve the quality of health care delivery, especially for consumers who have been marginalized within the health care system. I encourage health care consumers to carefully examine the roles communication performs in health care, to use communication strategically in their own health care and as advocates for others. I am hopeful that strategic use of health communication will help to guard against the negative effects of marginalization by promoting the development of cooperative relationships between interdependent participants in the modern health care system, encouraging the use of sensitive and appropriate interpersonal communication in health care, enhancing the dissemination of relevant health information, and suggesting adaptive strategies for using health communication to accomplish desired health outcomes. In this way, strategic health communication can empower consumers to take charge of their own health care to overcome systemic forms of marginalization, disenfranchisement, and alienation within the modern health care system.

Part III

Constructing Pedagogy

10

Metaphor in the Classroom

Reframing Traditional and Alternative Uses of Language for Feminist Transformation

Patrice M. Buzzanell

Years ago, when I was a graduate student, I eagerly awaited the birth of my second child. A little more than five months into the pregnancy, I found out that I was having twins. I was still adjusting to that news when I went into premature labor on Thanksgiving Day. After 6 days of labor, I gave birth to two daughters whose total birth weight was less than 3.5 pounds. There were months of testings, operations, specialists' prognoses, and mixed reports, including anticipation of one twin's death. On several occasions, I made funeral plans, which always included a beautiful long white gown (for the parties and proms this child of mine would never experience), white sweetheart flowers, and cremation (so that I could carry this child with me until I found my permanent home). I could never quite figure out how I was going to look at the daughter who was supposed to live without thinking about her identical twin.

As time went on, I realized that these tiny children were going to live and do well despite prognoses. Without consciously choosing to do so, as their stay at the hospital lengthened, I began to think and talk about them as being at a

Author's Note: This chapter is dedicated to my daughters, Sheridan Aileen and Ashlee Marie Sheahan, with love and admiration.

slumber party. In this image, they were with friends—playing and sleeping. I thought of them as physically apart from me but on a temporary basis.

I do not know how I survived those months and the ensuing years of developmental testings. I do know, however, that the metaphor of a future, of hope, of relationships, and of play saved me, nurtured me, and changed my life. I have been blessed, not only by the twins' resilience and unimagined development, but also by the insight that I could choose to frame my life, my losses, my career, and my celebrations.

I often recount this story in my classrooms, speaking engagements, and executive training and development courses to demonstrate the power of language to transform our individual lives and society at large.[1] My slumber party image represents a mundane and temporary event in the lives of many children, but it also signifies trust in the future—these children would come home. Although I could not change the material aspects of my own and my twins' lives, I could sustain hope and normalcy even though this was an extraordinarily difficult time.

Metaphor is a powerful way of reframing experiences in our lifestories—the slumber party is a case in point. The potential to use metaphor in feminist transformation remains underdeveloped. I am surprised that we, as feminist educators, do not use metaphors routinely in our conversations and in our lessons to assist our students in understanding what feminisms are and how women and members of traditionally underrepresented groups are marginalized. This chapter provides both a theoretical basis and practical guide for adopting metaphoric reframing in the classroom, specifically regarding perceptions of gender and feminism. The goal of this pedagogical strategy is to encourage our students to recognize and reframe the negative aspects of traditional gender in their own images and to understand more fully what feminists advocate.

Although research exists on metaphor, lifestories, and standpoints, the integration of these constructs through framing for feminist advocacy in the classroom supplies a unique angle. Framing is "a quality of communication that causes others to accept one meaning over another" (Fairhurst & Sarr, 1996, p. xi). Framing for one single meaning without discussion of multiple interpretations can replicate masculine approaches in the classroom. However, framing events in ways that benefit women and other marginalized members of society while also exploring other possible interpretations can provide our students with complex understandings of historical and contemporary feminisms as well as arguments useful to countering everyday antifeminist portrayals. I begin by talking about research on traditional and feminist approaches to metaphor, move on to the need to reframe the terms *feminist* and *feminisms*, and then conclude with implementation suggestions for instruction.

Traditional and Alternative Research on Metaphor

Although conventional approaches that locate and promote singular metaphorical meanings can prove useful in rallying people around a cause or vision (e.g., visual and verbal metaphors associated with Rosie the Riveter in World War II; see Fairhurst & Sarr, 1996), a different approach that highlights individuals' lifestories, conversations, and standpoints can enable feminist educators to engage in dialogue and, perhaps, persuade students and others.

A TRADITIONAL APPROACH TO METAPHOR

Metaphors are linguistic tools that compare like and unlike phenomena to express our "understanding and experiencing [of] one kind of thing in terms of another" (Lakoff & Johnson, 1980, p. 5).[2] Formal definitions of metaphor link different domains of meaning; specifically, "A is B," with the tenor or target term (A) connecting the vehicle or source term (B). In this equation, the less well-defined object/person/event in A is more clearly delineated through B (see examples in Koch & Deetz, 1981; Lakoff & Johnson, 1980; Owen, 1989). For instance, my experience as a new mother is the A term and my slumber party image is B. A remains the same but B varies across people, time, and culture. The longer we link A and B verbally, cognitively, and behaviorally, the less we notice differences between them.

Researchers collect metaphoric expressions (also known as entailments) through interviews (e.g., Baxter, 1992; Koch & Deetz, 1981; Norton, 1989; Owen, 1985) and surveys (Buzzanell & Burrell, 1997; Jorgensen-Earp & Staton, 1993). In some cases, participants are prompted to provide metaphoric expressions (e.g., Buzzanell & Burrell, 1997; Owen, 1989, 1990). Data-collection methods are significant because researchers often employ context and participants' comments to a limited extent when categorizing images. Researchers typically divide primary metaphors into metaphor families, root metaphors, metaphoric themes, images, schemas, and conceptual metaphors (Baxter, 1992; Burrell, Buzzanell, & McMillan, 1992; Buzzanell & Burrell, 1997; Koch & Deetz, 1981; Lakoff & Johnson, 1980; Morgan, 1993; Owen, 1989; R. C. Smith & Eisenberg, 1987). Analysts uncover primary metaphors through *external systematicity*, the process by which organizational patterns emerge through sorting and structuring metaphoric expressions (e.g., S. Foss, 1996; Hart, 1990; Koch & Deetz, 1981; Lakoff & Johnson, 1980; Owen, 1989; R. C. Smith & Eisenberg, 1987). By this time in the research process, analysts produce themes without referring to the participants or to their comments for explanation but may return to transcripts of what was actually said for examples to support thematic categories.

Adherence to only generalizable approaches limits possibilities for multiple metaphoric meanings. For instance, if we examine McCorkle and Mills's (1992) extension of Hocker and Wilmot's (1991) conflict themes, we find that their metaphorical entailments suggest more than the categories to which the phrases are classified. The metaphor "It was like talking to a brick wall" implies frustration and futility, but this meaning is not captured by McCorkle and Mills's placement of this metaphor in the "one-way communication" categorization and the overall affective descriptor of "negative." Further examples that demonstrate how their attempts to reduce metaphoric entailments to generalizable categories can fail to explore the richness of imagery are: "brain dead" (category: Biologic States); "undertow in water" (Natural Processes); and "circumcised with a dirty butter knife" (Biologic States) (McCorkle and Mills, 1992, p. 61).

Although much conventional metaphoric analysis adheres to stereotypic masculine values, especially by emphasizing generalization and limited contextualization, there are research examples of polysemic metaphoric analyses that explore multiple interpretations of data and that resonate with the values of feminist orientations. An example of metaphoric research that moves in this direction is Owen's (1985, 1989, 1990) research on thematic metaphors in relational communication. Owen summarizes the metaphors in the smallest number of categories, but he also returns to his data to display how tensions, sensemaking, change over time, and connections become manifest. Owen's (1984, 1985) analyses portray how themes can incorporate structural/linguistic devices to display a rich account of romantic partners' feelings, contradictions, and issues. In addition, Owen's (1989) investigation of male and female differences in personal relationship images discusses not only overall categories, such as reactivity and proactivity, but also the ways in which males' and females' linguistic choices portray their views of and feelings about themselves within the total relational context. For example, Owen (1989) found that images of males within personal relationships were primarily proactive, with subthemes of inflexibility and leadership—the male "'coiled spring' uncoils once the male 'decides our plans'" (p. 45). Women are visualized as a "door bell (push button, she reacts)" (p. 44) and as a "'rubber band' because she could be 'twisted and molded' but always returned to her 'unique self' . . . as a flexibly reactive person" (p. 47). Overall, Owen (1989) found that women's metaphors for relationships demonstrated feelings of being subordinate and of needing to respond to others just as the "door bell" waits for the male to activate her.

The limitations of conventional and polysemic metaphoric analyses and the need for a third, feminist, approach to metaphoric analysis can be illustrated with story. One day, I was talking to a neighbor while our daughters attended a birthday party. I remarked that her daughter was talking about her teenage brother's fatal automobile accident and was recalling good times with him. During our conversation, the mother talked about how her family was handling his death. She glossed over aspects I already knew, such as her support system (extensive family and religious community) and the reports that the accident did not involve alcohol or drugs. For the most part, she was matter-of-fact in her conversational style.

At one point, she said that she and her family lived day to day, with ups and downs, and she explicitly used the image of a car gas gauge hovering around empty. There was no reserve; they had hit bottom. There were days when life lightened up a bit, but she did not expect drastic improvements that would extend for long periods of time. She expressed this as a realistic, pragmatic image to discuss her family's grief. She did not separate her own mother's grief from her family's experiences, nor did she describe the emotional phases often found in grief literature (e.g., Kubler-Ross, 1969). Her "car" was not traveling anywhere specific, nor did she expect it to have a destination. She spontaneously introduced the image into conversation and then expanded, without prompting, on what she meant by the metaphor. My reading of this extended metaphor was that she consciously or unconsciously used this image in multiple ways: to engage in conversation, to initiate a topic, to share her feelings, and to "hold the floor" (just as women use compliments to "launch" conversational topics; see C. West, 1995). She wove in details about her daily family life and her knowledge of how the parents of other teenagers who had died were coping after their children's deaths. She was not thinking out loud to explain her coping mechanisms or to summarize her experience (although these may have been secondary conversational goals).[3]

Because we were talking at a noisy children's birthday party and I wanted to respect her privacy, I did not question her image selection. Without knowing her life story, a traditional metaphor analyst would have provided a singular summary statement interpreting her experience; a polysemic analyst would have presented her metaphor and its meaning in a number of different ways. These interpretations might have included: despair (bottom of the gauge); coping mechanism (awareness that things cannot become worse and probably will improve); life orientation as survivor (implicit understanding that this image would continue to dominate her life indefinitely; see Norton, 1989); and passivity (not actively engaging in action to create life change or to attempt to fill the gas tank to full). Both the conventional (categorization) and polysemic (multiple interpretations) approaches are limited in their abilities to fully analyze such a metaphor without knowing the person's lifestory, as is discussed in the next section.

In sum, traditional approaches promote a move to condense metaphoric associations into one categorization or interpretation. In practice, this orientation can be useful because it can unify diversity and promote one agenda (see strategic ambiguity, E. Eisenberg, 1984). However, I have identified another side to metaphoric analysis that explores the polysemy of metaphoric associations. This emphasis on exploring multiple interpretations is consonant with and can be extended by adopting feminist research mandates to develop complex, contextualized analyses. Whereas traditional conceptualizations of and analytic methods for exploring metaphor are tied to stereotypic masculine notions of generalizability, linearity, rationality, efficiency, and control, feminist approaches focus on specificity, connection, nurturing, relational prioritization, and egalitarianism (Buzzanell, 1994; Deaux & Kite, 1993; Marshall, 1993; Wood, 2001). Next, I advance a feminist standpoint approach to metaphoric analysis that extends the polysemic ground of metaphor analysis.

A FEMINIST APPROACH TO METAPHOR

In this section, I develop a feminist approach to metaphor by first discussing its characteristics and providing an example. I then link this approach to lifestories and standpoints.

Characteristics of a Feminist Approach. The "opposite" of a conventional metaphorical approach is one that is relational, embedded in daily communicative practices (such as conversations), and encouraging of diverse purposes and interpretations. This feminine metaphoric approach is grounded in confirmation and personal exchange (see Tannen, 1990) and is aligned with some characteristics of female conversational styles. Rather than promoting condensation and generalizability, these styles include certain qualities: demonstration of interest in others by prompting elaboration and layering personal disclosures, anecdotes, and details; expression of relational responsiveness and vulnerability; integration of ordinary details and topics such as preparing food; and nested narratives, or embedding stories within overarching narrative frameworks (see Condravy, 1993; DeVault, 1990; Eckert & McConnell-Ginet, 1994; K. Gergen & Gergen, 1988; Perry & Geist, 1997; Tannen, 1990; Wood, 2001). Often associated with a feminine style, these communication aspects are used by both men and women, although white middle-class women *may* display greater propensities to these speech and interaction characteristics, particularly in "feminine contexts" (e.g., food preparation, child care; see Wood, Dendy, Dordek, Germany, & Varallo, 1994) or female groups. Rather than extracting the metaphor from surrounding talk, this orientation necessitates the understanding of metaphor within particular contexts and relationships.

Expressions of personal experiences usually take the form of narratives that "reveal insights into the impact of the construction of gender on women's lives, their experiences of oppression and of coping with and resisting that oppression, and their perspectives on what is meaningful in their lives" (K. Foss & Foss, 1994, p. 39). As a result, lifestories are gendered in content and may become feminist in purpose. Lifestories also are gendered in form (Bateson, 1989). In examining autobiographies, M. Gergen and Gergen (1993) have been struck by the progressive, linear, and focused nature of men's narratives and by the shifting, fluid, and embodied nature of women's stories. M. Gergen's (1990, 1992) metaphors for manstories are the arrow and a "song of the self" because story elements focus on career and success as defining who men are. Womanstories are pictured as baskets in which many cognitive, behavioral, affective, and relational elements are interwoven. Women's autobiographies shift toward and away from different topics—success (in which others' assistance often is credited explicitly), emotional interdependencies, and life events. Women's own metaphors for their lives display how "voice, mind, and self were intricately intertwined" as they discover self in connection with others (Belenky, Clinchy, Goldberger, & Tarule, 1986, p. 18). These gendered autobiographical patterns repeatedly and strikingly emerge in lifestories: "The finding that men and women tell their stories differently is so striking that no statistical framework seems necessary once one begins to read for the gendered pattern of narrative form" (M. Gergen, 1990, p. 8). Moreover, diverse groups of women and men may tell their lifestories and personal experiences differently. Riessman (1987) provides a contrast between two narratives of marital separation in which gender congruence could not transcend ethnic and class differences (i.e., a middle-class Anglo interviewer operating in a temporal narrative structure with a working-class Puerto Rican respondent talking in episodic narratives that embedded cultural understandings). Gender, race/ ethnicity, and class may produce different story genres and cultural narratives.

Although lifestories and many expressions of personal experience are discussions of events and individuals who are catalytic in shaping the ways we view ourselves (Belenky et al., 1986; K. Gergen & Gergen, 1988), M. Gergen (1990) has found that these stories are overlooked because they are so ordinary. It is this very ordinariness that makes them so powerful. It is in use of metaphor substantively and structurally that we glimpse the dreams, imagination, and souls of the lifestorytellers.

Metaphor engages truth and fantasy (Swanson, 1979) as well as imagination and heart (Ricoeur, 1979). It is a mechanism for delving into the depths of our being and trying to feel through possibilities. Some time ago, I was talking to a friend when she started describing changes in her life. As she was expressing her pain at a dissolving marriage, she said, "I do not know what I want anymore." Although we were simply conversing on a summer evening, she apologized that her talk was, to her thinking, jumbled and repetitious. She was trying to know who she was again in her life but for the present, she said she was "speaking from . . . [her] wounds." Her metaphor enabled her to share her confusion and pain about changes, such as those in her family, relationships, career, and living arrangements. At times there was a temporal sequence to the episodes she embedded in her talk, but most of our conversation was shaped by the direction her pain took her in her journey of sensemaking and connection. When we talk about things that are important to us, we often tell an unfolding and changeable narrative of important turning points, the ways we made sense of events, what we valued and value, and how we have achieved understanding of our social locations and constrained agency (see Marshall, 1995; O'Brien Hallstein, 1999, 2000).

Creating Change Through Metaphor

Besides personal sensemaking and change, metaphors in lifestories and other personal experience expressions can be catalysts for change in ways other language cannot. When metaphor and metaphoric analysis are embedded within and explore the rich details of women's lives *and* when they are used to advocate for change on behalf of women (and others), then metaphor and its analysis are feminist. In the following example, I display how a white, married woman in her mid to late 40s used an extended metaphor to explain what it is like to have a physical disability in an able-bodied world. She resists others' construction of her identity as deviant; she implies ways that people without physical disabilities can think and act to enable handicapped individuals to be treated as "normal." Her metaphor occurred during a 45-minute interview in which she talked in a straightforward and nonemotional, rather than figurative, fashion about her pregnancy and maternity leave 20 years earlier. She described how a hospital social worker questioned whether she had thought through and was capable of performing her maternal duties. She already had devised an elaborate system, involving wheeling her infant from cribs to low changing tables and using ropes to move from one room of her apartment to another. She did not use figurative language to express her anger and pain at this incident, but her voice trembled.

However, she did use metaphorical language to describe how others saw and treated her on a daily basis. To enable you to understand her image, I need to explain that she worked for a governmental agency and was severely handicapped because of polio. She was rendered "invisible" in the male enclave because of her sex, her disability, and her employment status (secretary). Her pregnancy changed others' interactions with her. She described how others would ask her about her pregnancy (not just how she was doing or feeling but also how she became pregnant!). She said that it took them time to realize that she became pregnant in the usual way. She remarked that male coworkers started talking to her about their families and would provide advice and verbal support. Her pregnancy was similar to their own family situations; therefore, she became "normal." Their recognition that she had the same body with some differences enabled them to speak and look directly at her. Their recognition enabled them to bypass a middle-class U.S. cultural practice—to avoid catching the glance of a handicapped person in an effort to be polite and to avoid an encounter for which there is no common script for appropriate interaction.

Then she took an extended maternity leave. When she returned to paid work, she was once again "invisible." She said that her pregnancy made others see her as a person and not as an "erector set."[4] The erector set image seemed to be her attempt to make sense of the way others treated her. It also was her acknowledgment that others perceived her neither as female/feminine nor male/masculine but, rather, as nonhuman. The erector set was *not* how she identified herself; she did not attempt to distill herself into a single image. Perhaps she did not need to frame herself metaphorically because she already said that she was a normal female.

Many other interpretations of her image choice could be presented. To analyze her metaphorical expression contextually and to uncover directions for change, we can incorporate standpoint analysis. Standpoint analysis of this incident necessitates that we describe her relations with others in detail to situate her image within a specific sociocultural system. Because standpoints celebrate the unique conditions and contexts of specific women's lives, they affirm the variations within and across marginalized groups (see Harding, 1987, 1991; Longino, 1993; Putnam, 1990; Wood, 1992a). They also celebrate standpoints as achievements (Harding, 1991)—that is, our confusion, pain, and exhilaration when we challenge patriarchy. Our standpoints-as-achievements render the consequences of oppression visible through their rich contextualizations and analyses; as such, they assist us in developing feminist epistemologies (Belenky et al., 1986) and in creating theory that addresses the unique conditions of the lives of white women and women of color (e.g., B. Allen, 2000). Our standpoints externalize our struggles to "see beneath the appearances created by an unjust social order to the reality of how this social order is in fact constructed and maintained" (Harding, 1991, p. 127; see Hawkesworth, 1999, for standpoints as an analytic method). Standpoints are, as O'Brien Hallstein (2000) reminds us, political. They provide a richly detailed exploration into the specific conditions of women's lives that raise consciousness and provide directions for change.

Using standpoint analysis, the woman speaking about her pregnancy and maternity leave portrays how she has been unjustly labeled by others and how she has fought against minimization of her abilities and her human dignity, particularly her dignity as a mature female and mother. The power of her metaphor and its placement in her pregnancy story suggests that there is more to this image than would be displayed by classification into a metaphor category. There is a whisper of how we could enable others to look past handicaps by affirming commonalities between handicapped people and able-bodied men and women.

Framing Current Images of Feminists and Feminisms in the Feminist Classroom

Consciousness raising and possible directions for individual and collective advocacy can emerge from our engagement with metaphorical lifestories. Not only are these framing techniques useful in exploring diverse members' experiences, but they also can be used to promote greater understanding of feminisms in our classrooms and everyday conversations.

As readers of this edited collection are aware, feminisms explore the bases and consequences of traditional gender and patriarchy in all aspects of our lives to understand and locate means of transforming our interactions and societies so that women and people who are "different" from the powerful members of our relationships, institutions, and cultures are not disenfranchised and harmed physically, mentally, emotionally, and materially (Buzzanell, 2000b; Calás & Smircich, 1996; Tong, 1989; Wood, 2001). To develop awareness, feminist educators usually incorporate readings, case analyses, and experiential exercises to show how people socially create genders and how arbitrary and changeable the evaluations of these gendered constructions can be (Bem, 1993; Buzzanell, 1993; Flax, 1987, 1990; C. West & Zimmerman, 1987; Wood, 2001). In these discussions, the term *feminist* often is defined in such a way as to counteract the negative associations students accord this label. One premise for these analyses is that it is difficult to unify for change if potential movement members eschew the label.

Even today, the word *feminist* conjures up vivid pictures of a male-hating, bra-burning, no-cosmetics, poorly attired and coiffed, ugly, gray-haired radical of the 1960s (see Ashcraft, 1998; Bulbeck, 2001; Danner & Walsh, 1999; Wood, 2001). The 1970s and 1980s saw white women march off to work in their masculine personas and their dress-for-success bow ties (Harragan, 1977; Pollock, 2000). In contrast, at the beginning of the 21st century, we see the success of women's movements as choice (e.g., electing to flirt or to make oneself masculine for advancement; Pollock, 2000), entitlement to work and education (e.g., Bulbeck, 2001), and "having it all" (e.g., the exhausted career woman who juggles work and family or the female consumerist; Edley, 2001; Faludi, 2001; Posner, 1992). (For some men, the women's movement resulted in the challenge of trying to fulfill an extraordinary number of roles, including breadwinner and actively involved parent; Fagan, 2001; Faludi, 1999). Even in 1995 coverage of the United Nations Fourth World Conference on Women, media reports avoided substance and reinforced stereotypical images of women "bickering," unhappy without marriage and family, and "letting themselves go" physically (Danner & Walsh, 1999).

Other studies indicate that college students attribute some positive characteristics to feminists (e.g., serious, knowledgeable, and intelligent; to a lesser extent, secure, responsible, and sane) but also negative qualities (e.g., stubborn, nontraditional, and angry; to a lesser extent, tense and egotistical), with women evaluating feminists more positively and attitudes toward feminist movements being the best predictor of respondents' judgments of feminists (Twenge & Zucker, 1999). Positive definitions of feminism also have been related to equality and/or rights, with negative definitions centering on females saying that they are superior, and on issues of sexism, being female, and social expectations of women (L. Arnold, 2000). Although men and women appear to hold differing evaluations of feminists and feminist agendas, backlash themes embedded in media and research continue to remind women of double binds and negative consequences associated with nontraditional roles (Faludi, 1991; Hawkesworth, 1999; Jamieson, 1995; P. Sullivan & Turner, 1996, 1999; Twenge & Zucker, 1999). P. Hearn (2000) reminds us that the pull of traditional culture should never be underestimated. Cultural (male) narratives counteract what we do in our classrooms and in women's studies programs.

Because our challenge as feminists in the classroom is twofold—to make visible the way gender influences every aspect of our lives and to frame ourselves and our movement in ways that gain greater support for change—we need to understand the metaphorical underpinnings of our depictions of women and members of other underrepresented groups. We can work with different levels of complexity when using metaphorical analysis as a pedagogical tool in our classrooms. These phases can include: data that are analyzed for entailments and categories (traditional analysis), critiques of "what is missing" that explore emotions and multiple meanings (polysemic interpretation analyses), and standpoint analyses of metaphors embedded in lifestories (feminist metaphorical standpoint analysis).

With regard to the conventional approach, we can illustrate the differences between traditional and alternative approaches by asking students to generate metaphors using simile construction (e.g., Feminists are like _____. Why? ____) in surveys or in taped and transcribed interviews about their experiences with feminists, feminisms, marginalization, and other issues or constructs of importance in our courses.[5] We then can follow the process described in the "Traditional and Alternative Research on Metaphor" section of this chapter. We work with our students to sort entailments, develop categories conceptually and operationally, and return to the data for categorization. We can describe what seems generalizable and what eludes our classifications. By displaying what aspects are missing from a traditional approach, we can demonstrate one effect that feminisms have had on the academy—namely, the serious consideration of individuals' lived experiences in their own words and the development of methods to uncover these experiences. We also can illuminate points of similarity in our students' language choices (although as we discuss the meanings of and background experiences underlying the metaphors, we often find out that students have very different meanings for similar phrases). As we explore linguistic elements, such as nouns and adverbs, we may reveal a lot about the emotions associated with different roles, relationships, situations, or groups of people and with ownership of their opinions.

In addition to comparing and contrasting traditional and polysemic metaphorical analyses, we also can utilize metaphor to frame students' realities. According to sociologists, organization theorists, and organizational communication researchers, numerous people—including top corporate officers, media spokespersons, and public relations professionals—attempt to fuel certain interpretations of events over other meanings (Conger, 1991; Fairhurst & Sarr, 1996; Sussman, 1999). This management of meaning is critical in leadership, particularly in vision creation (Barge, 1994; Pfeffer, 1981; Smircich & Morgan, 1982; Thayer, 1988), although Fairhurst and Sarr (1996) note that *anyone* can use framing techniques.

In framing for particular versions, researchers and practitioners diminish discussion about other possible interpretations. Standpoint analysis and discussions about metaphor embedded in lifestories guard against the essentializing tendencies of traditional framing and metaphorical analytic approaches. Feminist approaches—centered on individuals as members of traditionally underrepresented groups—can help us understand more fully the bases for people's feelings about gender, trivialization, feminists, and feminisms. We can enable them to rewrite their own and others' lifestories in light of different feminisms (for examples of revised stories from the lenses of different feminisms, see Calás & Smircich, 1996; Hawkesworth, 1999).

As students and others envision how we create reality metaphorically and see (or do not even consider) possibilities for change, we reveal much more than we realize. Through our linguistic choices, we indicate whether we feel "stuck" between undesirable or double bind positions (orientational metaphors), whether we are in charge of our own lives (through use of "process" or "state" verbs), and how we can become more active agents in our lives (see Buzzanell & Burrell, 1997). Based on metaphorical orientations, we can use different instructional methods (ranging from discussion for cognitive metaphors, to role playing for orientational metaphors, to linkage to different kinds of images for ontological metaphors (see Buzzanell & Burrell, 1997; Lakoff & Johnson, 1980). For example, we may have a student who says something along these lines: "As a professional woman, I feel as though I am Alice in Wonderland trying to figure out which way to go. The Cheshire Cat is no help, and I don't know if I would want someone else to tell me what to do." Based on other points that this fictitious white student in her early 20s has said, we know that she feels unsure about how to be both professional and feminine, smart and acceptable, feminist and interested in men, celebrating difference and following management's directives about best practices, and so on (see Ashcraft, 1998). She wants a career but worries about media reports that she may have difficulty sustaining a viable pregnancy if she waits too long (see Brenner, 2001). She believes in equal rights but thinks that feminism relates to her own personal transformation and choices (see Hogeland, 2001). She thinks that the women's movement is old news. She sees her life situations as a series of oppositional choices, none of which is fully acceptable. To work through the overall orientational metaphor of being stuck between two places as well as the many possible meanings inherent in her Alice and Cheshire Cat images, we can place her in a role-playing situation where she explores her feelings and responses (for responses to double binds, see Jamieson, 1995; P. Sullivan & Turner, 1996, 1999; Wood & Conrad, 1983).

Finally, we can use metaphor to create conditions where our students can make informed choices about their thinking, behaving, and feelings with regard to gendered interactions and institutions and with regard to feminists and feminisms. Although some feminists would argue against attempts to change people's minds (see S. Foss & Griffin, 1995), a critical point to remember is that *if we do not frame interpretations for what has happened to our students and others, we leave to chance the explanation individuals will believe.* Given the presumption of the status quo, they often subscribe to mainstream rather than feminist perspectives of these events. Jamieson (1995) notes that, when we tell our stories as feminists, we often fear that they may be used by others against us rather than for our benefit. One way of handling this dilemma is to say that we tell our stories anyway, but another way is to say that we actively construct the meanings people have of these narratives through framing.

The woman who used a wheelchair fought to retain her dignity as a human being and as a new mother. Her story offers possibilities for reframing, educating students about difference, and deriving different kinds of change mechanisms. Listeners and readers can rejoice at her feelings of being accepted—when she was pregnant, she became a person with whom others would make eye contact and joke around. As she returns to her usual state of isolation following her maternity leave, listeners feel her frustration and horror at being a nonhuman (erector set)—disappearing once again into crowds of "normal" people and only surfacing in others' consciousness as an object to be avoided. Exploration of her metaphors first in isolation, in multiple interpretations, and then embedded within her lifestory (traditional, polysemic, and feminist standpoint metaphorical analysis, respectively) enable students to conjure up thoughts, feelings, and sensory connections that they may not otherwise describe. The tensions that emerge within and between her self- and other-images and within ourselves as we see our role in creating her isolation cannot help but offer opportunities for change. The important point about reframing, and what makes it "such an effective tool of change is that *once we do perceive the alternative class membership(s) we cannot so easily go back to the trap and the anguish of a former view of 'reality'*" (Watzlawick, Weakland, & Fisch, 1974, p. 99; emphases added).

As our students begin to see that feminisms are not simply about white women burning bras (and other images our students hold), we can create other metaphors for feminists and feminisms.[6] These reframings would be plural to account for the different circumstances in the lives of women and men world-wide who lack voice, opportunity, and safety. These metaphors also could encompass the different phases that seem to occur as women and men develop greater consciousness of women's experiences and movements (Henderson-King & Stewart, 1997). Perhaps through metaphor, we can encourage our students and others to help us transform gender in ways that we ourselves do not even yet envision.

Notes

1. This framing of my story does not mention the anguish I (and others) felt in watching my twins struggle to live. It does not raise bioethical questions surrounding procedures that push back boundaries of infant survival and challenge thinking about life quality (for an examination of such issues, see Klass, 2000).

2. Definitions of metaphor range from "a specialized form of figurative language" to broadly defined terms such as *image*. For my purposes, I do not distinguish among specific figurative language types, such as synecdoche (substituting a part for a whole), personification (attributing human characteristics to animals or inanimate objects), and simile (comparisons using "like" or "as") (S. Foss, 1996; Lakoff & Johnson, 1980). However, I do acknowledge scholarly argument that there are linguistic and usage distinctions among these types (Gibb & Wales, 1990; Mac Cormac, 1985; G. Miller, 1979), just as there are distinctions among *metaphor*, *image*, and related terms (Buzzanell & Burrell, 1997).

Moreover, conventional metaphorical approaches seek to explain why and how individuals produce figurative language. In cognitive orientations, metaphor production and comprehension are examined for information transmission efficiency and effectiveness (e.g., Blasko & Briihl, 1997), with novel metaphors being dependent on interactants' shared experiences (Glucksberg, 1989). Purposes of metaphor other than to label, summarize, or transfer meaning (e.g., to create intimacy or convey feelings) have been considered secondary to cognitive aims or viewed as deviant, inconsequential, and frivolous (Cohen, 1979).

3. A traditional analysis of conversational goals during this example of the mother talking about her teenage son's death in an automobile accident would have focused on what she intended to accomplish through this interaction. In conversational goal research, participants' goals typically are bifurcated into the two broad categories of interaction and discourse (S. Wilson & Putnam, 1990). Interaction goals involve talk and coordination with others to achieve desired end results; discourse goals make communication possible through turn taking, topic initiation and negotiation, and meeting syntactic constraints. In interaction goal research, theorists recognize that

multiple goals emerge dynamically and are purposive, although not necessarily conscious or well-planned (Craig, 1986; S. Wilson & Putnam, 1990). Dillard, Segrin, and Harden (1989, p. 32; see also Schrader & Dillard, 1998) dichotomize primary ("to initiate and maintain the social action") and secondary (to set "boundaries which delimit the verbal choices available to sources") objectives. Primary goals consciously define or bracket the situation, answering the question, "What is the source trying to do?" (e.g., give advice). Primary goals predict cognitive and behavioral planning. Secondary objectives, such as identity, interaction, and arousal strategies, provide interaction content and are derived from motivations consistent with a person's life. Secondary goals act as restraining, countervailing forces on attempts to achieve the primary goal.

Scholars have devoted considerable attention to developing conversational goal typologies (e.g., Canary, Cody, & Marston, 1987; Dillard, 1989, 1990; Rule, Bisanz, & Kohn, 1985). Sheperd (1992, 1998) argues that task and influence orientations neglect the viewpoint that "secondary" or relational concerns also could be the driving, or the defining, goal in communication episodes. Shepherd's point here is well taken, but there is nothing in the primary/secondary goal distinction that denies that identity or relational concerns can become primary goals. For example, a speaker initially may define what is going on in the conversation around an instrumental goal (e.g., acquiring information) but then redefine what is going on as restoring a positive self-identity in the other's eyes (e.g., if the other party seems to believe that the instrumental goal was inappropriate). Thus, primary goals are dynamic and shift among task, relationship, and identity functions in the same conversation (see S. Wilson, 2002). Discourse analysts also focus on task and nontask—that is, identity and relational functions (Tracy & Coupland, 1990; see also research by Tracy, 1984; Tracy & Moran, 1983).

4. An erector set is a creative construction toy consisting of perforated metal plates, rods, bolts, and nuts, in a variety of sizes, shapes, and colors. It is important to also point out that an erector set is a masculine toy generally given to boys. Coworkers of the woman who used a wheelchair were male. She drew on a specifically male toy to try to explain how they saw her. The erector set metaphor is particularly painful because it erases her femininity and embodiment and invokes her wheelchair, which is metal and has screws, rods, and plates like the erector set. When applied to a person, the erector set image implies alienation instead of evoking the sense of play that generally would accompany a toy. Her coworkers see her wheelchair and not her as a person. The evocation of masculinity makes their negation of her femininity even more apparent.

5. We can use feminist interviewing strategies that resemble conversations more than traditional interviewing interactions because the former enhance women's abilities to see and talk clearly about their lives (DeVault, 1990, pp. 100-101). We can approach interviewing and data analyses phenomenologically to empower women by making "clear that which is implied, obscured, and concealed within an experience taken as a concrete whole" (Langellier & Hall, 1989, p. 197).

6. These strategies are useful not only in classes on gender and feminism but also in any communication or women's studies session. Some suggestions based on applied communication contexts follow. In family communication classes, we can explore stereotypic images of entrepreneurial mothers "having it all" (see Edley's Chapter 15) or male abusers in domestic violence intervention programs (see Fink & Tucker's Chapter 17). In health communication seminars, we can contrast metaphors for illness in society with wellness and their gendered implications (see any of the chapters in Part II, "Gendering Health."). In organizational communication classes or training sessions, we can uncover the ways in which we envision our work arrangements (see Hylmö's Chapter 3), workforce diversity and alternative organizing processes (Meyer & O'Hara's Chapter 1), and sexual harassment (Buzzanell's Chapter 2) through exploration of figurative language. In sum, we may be better able to see how we simultaneously (dis)empower ourselves through exploration of metaphor in lifestories (see M. Papa, Singhal, Ghanekar, & Papa, 2000).

11

From Transgression to Transformation

Negotiating the Opportunities and Tensions of Engaged Pedagogy in the Feminist Organizational Communication Classroom

Marcy Meyer

Visualize feminist pedagogy as a box of bright crayons. You open the box and find an array of primary colors that represent core feminist values. Beside these well-worn artistic tools is a rainbow of hues that represent common practices employed by feminist teachers. These shades, derived from the primary colors, enable artists to redraw power relationships in the classroom. As Parry (1996) articulated quite clearly, feminist pedagogy reframes the relationship between students and course material, the relationship between students and instructors, and relationships among students. Toward these ends, feminist pedagogy employs a variety of teaching practices that reconceptualize knowledge, link theory and lived experience, empower students, embrace multiculturalism, and incorporate passion (hooks, 1994). Through these practices, hooks (1994) dared instructors to transgress conventional educational techniques, thereby creating strategies to make the teaching/learning process more dynamic, exciting, and meaningful to students. However, as Rich (1979) noted, redrawing power relationships is a relational process in which students necessarily must consent to drawing outside of the lines. Given that transformation is a dynamic relational process, instructors cannot empower students to claim their education. However, we can facilitate the creation of a culture that questions central assumptions undergirding teaching and learning in traditional classrooms. By cultivating a classroom culture that embodies feminist values, we can create a safe space where students can "speak with authority about their own lives both within contexts that feel like home and those that feel more alienating" (Jenefsky, 1996, p. 352).

Feminist Pedagogy

CORE VALUES

Buzzanell (1993) explored the pedagogical implications of four feminist themes for teaching organizational communication. Derived in response to traditional patriarchal values that are deeply inculcated in American society, alternative feminist themes enable us to transform classrooms into sites of dialogue that foster positive social change. First, Buzzanell encouraged us to stimulate awareness among our students about the ways in which we perpetuate our oppression through competitive ethics, a stance that allows us to revalue cooperation. Second, Buzzanell challenged us to evaluate individualistic and autonomous values, specifically the extent to which they usurp caring and concern for relationships/community. Third, in reaction to the dualism inherent in everyday organizational life (e.g., emotion/reason, masculine/feminine, work/play), Buzzanell invited us to view humans as holistic beings who are capable of simultaneously experiencing thoughts and emotions grounded in their lived experiences. Finally, Buzzanell motivated us to embrace feminist theory, which eschews traditional linear thinking, as a site where creative thinking about possibilities and alternatives is nurtured.

According to Pezzullo and Wood (1999), openness, personal involvement, and a sense of community characterize an effective classroom climate. Openness creates room for students to take risks by letting them know that their feelings, values, and beliefs will not be belittled. Respect for diversity and the equal legitimacy of different identities and points of view are key components of openness. Personal involvement means encouraging students to interact directly with course material to discover how thoroughly intersections among communication, gender, and culture permeate their personal lives and the society in which they live. Instructors who emphasize the importance of social positioning and share their own personal experiences, while acknowledging their resulting biases and limitations, demonstrate their commitment to cultivating a connected learning community.

Perhaps one of the most empowering vehicles for enhancing communication students' involvement in effecting social change is through the process of service learning (O'Hara, 2001). Trethewey (1999) cautions, however, that the traditional service-learning paradigm is limited in that it assumes a positivist epistemology. She contends that a feminist alternative, which combines an action orientation with an understanding of the social construction of identity, reflexivity, the affective components of human interaction, and collaboration, is infinitely more rewarding for students. In her words,

> It is in and through our communicative actions that gender, race, class, and sexuality are constructed and intersect in ways that have very real and material consequences for organizational actors, clients, and communities. Feminist methods offer students the tools to begin to understand the politics of everyday life and the ways in which they might contribute to social changes to enhance the lives of those who have been marginalized inside and outside the walls of contemporary organizations. (Trethewey, 1999, p. 179)

Thus, feminist pedagogy is concerned primarily with effecting social change rather than just problem solving; moreover, it not only focuses on the extent to which desired outcomes are achieved, but it also examines the processes and practices that build meaningful relationships and stronger communities along the way.

COMMON PRACTICES

There are myriad practices that cultivate the core values articulated by feminist teacher-scholars (e.g., Buzzanell, 1993; hooks, 1994; Jenefsky, 1996; Parry, 1996; Pezzullo & Wood, 1999; Rich, 1979; Trethewey, 1999). In fact, if creativity is seen as a feminist hallmark (Buzzanell, 1994), one could argue there are as many pedagogical practices as instructors of feminist courses. Some of the more commonly employed practices include promoting discussion over lecture, enabling student teaching, incorporating journals into classwork and homework, valuing process over product, and creating opportunities for collaboration through group, rather than individual, assignments (Buzzanell, 1993; Motoyama, 1996; Parry, 1996; Pezzullo & Wood, 1999). Although these practices may be implemented in a variety of ways, they all have the same purpose: to foster alternative classroom structures and cultures that promote community, personal involvement, creative and critical thinking, and nonhierarchical power relationships.

OPPORTUNITIES

Pezzullo and Wood (1999) celebrate the practice of feminist pedagogy by identifying several opportunities related to teaching a course in communication, gender, and culture. These include helping students discover how gender is constructed and sustained in cultural life, enlarging students' range of communication competencies to incorporate both masculine and feminine styles of interaction, enhancing students' abilities to participate critically in cultural life, and encouraging students to identify and to take stands on issues that affect their lives. In the words of Rich (1979),

> As women teachers, we can either deny the importance of the context in which women students think, write, read, study, project their own futures; or try to work with it. We can either teach passively, accepting these conditions, or actively, helping our students identify and resist them. (p. 244)

Along these lines, Hedges (1996) identifies critical awareness and empowerment, as well as personalized, experiential learning and appreciation for diversity as valuable outcomes of Women's Studies courses.

TENSIONS

Pezzullo and Wood (1999) note that, realistically, there are a number of tensions that may surface during the process of teaching and learning about gender. First, students may engage in denial, where they resist information that forces them to examine and to question their own gendered values, thoughts, and actions. Second, if students manage to overcome their state of "false consciousness," they may become seriously shaken by the realization of how devalued women are in our society. Finally, in a related vein, the process of questioning worldviews may necessarily involve examining issues that will be personally painful to many students.

In sum, feminist pedagogy offers a number of compelling alternatives to teaching and learning in traditional classrooms. By embracing principles and practices that value community, personal involvement, critical and creative thinking, and nonhierarchical relationships, participants in feminist learning communities create opportunities to transform power relationships inside and outside of the classroom. In the following section, I describe the context and processes in and by which members of a feminist organizational communication seminar (namely, COMM 390 students and I) worked and played to create opportunities for transformation in our learning community.

Transgression and Transformation in COMM 390

Because of the need to examine the exercise of power in everyday life (D. E. Smith, 1987), I use participant observation as the primary means by which I tell the story of transgression and transformation in COMM 390. In telling the story, I intersperse my voice with student narratives drawn from journals, e-mails, course evaluations, and informal discussions that occurred both inside and outside of class over a 4-month period in the fall of 1998. I realize that, like all ethnographies, the tale I tell is not some incontestable truth but, to a certain degree, a fiction (Van Maanen, 1988) written from my perspective—which is, by definition, unique, yet partial, partisan, and problematic (E. Eisenberg & Goodall, 1997). Given these limitations, in this section I attempt to synthesize a variety of perspectives to create a relatively complete, accurate, and coherent representation of the COMM 390 experience.

CONTEXT

Ball State University is situated within the larger context of Muncie, Indiana, which is a relatively homogeneous, conservative Midwestern community (Department of Sociology, 1994, 1998). Ball State University has a Women's Studies minor, not a major; therefore, there is no Department of Women's Studies. In addition, only a limited number of departments on campus (e.g., English, History, Political, Science, Psychology, and Sociology) consistently offer electives for the Women's Studies minor. The Department of Communication Studies does not offer a regular course that focuses exclusively on gender and communication. In short, what I perceived to be a historical lack of institutionalized support for Women's Studies at Ball State was one of the central reasons that I decided to become involved in a faculty development initiative designed to infuse gender into the curriculum.[1]

ORIGINS OF THE COURSE

In the summer of 1997, I attended a curriculum development workshop organized by Ball State's Women and Gender Studies Program. Ten participants from various departments came together to learn more about incorporating gender issues into the curriculum. We became familiar with the goals and objectives of the Women's Studies minor and explored the role of Women's Studies in our disciplines. As a final project, we each developed a course syllabus that could become part of the Women's Studies minor.

During the workshop, I received my first lesson in feminist pedagogy and feminist theory. I read and discussed work written by feminist teacher-scholars (e.g., Donovan, 1992; hooks, 1984; Jaggar & Rothenberg, 1993; Rich, 1979; D. E. Smith, 1987). I talked with other women about their experiences being educated in male-dominated institutions and realized the need to take ownership of my education. (Ironically, this realization came a full year after I had completed my doctoral dissertation.) I began to embark on my education in feminist organizational communication, influenced by the unfailing enthusiasm of Kim Jones-Owen, the Director of Ball State's Women and Gender Studies Program. After a month spent reading work by feminist organizational communication scholars (e.g., B. Allen, 1995; Buzzanell, 1994; Marshall, 1993; Mumby, 1996; Wood, 1992a), I changed the substance and style of the courses I taught. The first product I developed out of this process was a seminar in feminist organizational communication, which I proposed as a special topics honors colloquium.

COURSE PARTICIPANTS

Not only honors students but also students with a Communication major or Women's Studies minor were allowed to take the class. In all, 13 students enrolled: 11 honors students, three Communication majors, and one Women's Studies minor. Although two honors students were also Communication majors, most of the honors students came from a variety of disciplines, such as Theater, English, Sociology, Biology, and Chemistry. Students ranged in age from 19 to 23, and the majority were seniors. Most of the students came from either working-class or middle-class backgrounds, although one student came from a very affluent family. Three of the students were male and 10 were female. The class was composed of 12 European Americans and one African American.

COURSE STRUCTURE AND CULTURE

As I originally explained in the course description that was sent out to both honors and Women' Studies students, COMM 390 was a course designed to generate insights into the consequences of traditional gender interactions on power relationships in the workplace. Students began the semester by becoming familiar with the organizational communication discipline and the history of women in work. Next, students were exposed to a variety of feminist theorists in general (e.g., Rich, 1979; Flax, 1993; M. Frye, 1993) and feminist organizational communication theorists in particular (e.g., Buzzanell, 1994; Mumby, 1996; Wood, 2001). Finally, students explored a number of themes related to feminist organizational communication, including sex differences, diversity, sexual harassment, and gender harassment.[2]

As we covered these topics, I used feminist pedagogy actively to involve students in discussing, learning, and teaching. From the outset, we agreed that we wanted to create a climate in which all the students had an opportunity to have their say and where people weren't afraid to ask questions. Consonant with this agreement, the majority of students adopted a very feminine, affirming style of communication . . . particularly the men. Each week, after we converted the classroom's existing rows of desks into a circle, students took turns facilitating the discussions of the readings. To accomplish this task, facilitators for each Monday's class were asked to prepare discussion questions, which they distributed to class members by 5 p.m. the preceding Friday. Questions ranged in content and depth but generally included basic content questions, critical observations about the readings, and opportunities to share work and personal experiences relevant to the topic at hand. Through discussion, we questioned whether communicative differences were the product of biological factors and/or the fulfillment of sex-role stereotypes, examined our own attitudes and behaviors concerning communication and gender, and explored how gender is communicatively created in various organizational contexts. In the process, students gained an appreciation for the historical, political, social, cultural, and economic dimensions of gendered communication in organizations. More important, as the locus of authority was moved away from me, students took an active role in teaching the course.

Students kept journals in which they wrote about their thoughts or experiences related to gender in organizations. The purpose of this assignment was to validate personal experience as a legitimate way of knowing. Although students had the option of writing critical responses to the readings, people overwhelmingly chose to write about events in their work lives. For example, one student wrote a number of entries about her experience of being repeatedly sexually harassed by an older male patron at a local country club where she worked during the summertime. Although she had not initially labeled the behaviors as sexual harassment, she found her voice over the course of the semester and expressed her anger (in class discussions, as well as in her journal) about his inappropriate behavior and her passive response to the situation.

Toward the goal of emphasizing process over product, students worked on a number of iterations for their final term paper. Each stage of the process, including a proposal, an annotated bibliography, and a rough draft leading up to the final paper, was worth an ascending number of points. This system was implemented to reduce the likelihood that students would procrastinate on the final paper; instead, they could take advantage of the opportunity to receive feedback on their ideas from me and their peers, enabling them to view writing as an interactive, iterative process. Many students mentioned during in-class discussions on "writing workshop days" that they really enjoyed the opportunity to work on their final papers throughout the semester and earn credit for their works in progress.

In addition to the regular seminar, a number of students in the class signed up for an extra credit to conduct collaborative action research about gender in the organization of their choice. This group met weekly, outside of class, for an hour in which we brainstormed and got to know one another (in addition to drinking peppermint tea and eating chocolate products). The practice of "breaking bread" together (or, to be more precise, injecting ourselves with sugar and caffeine) in an informal setting helped promote intimacy. Because our relationships were relaxed and informal, people felt free to self-disclose without being afraid that others would shoot them down. The free exchange of ideas led to collaboration between students, which produced more innovative, valuable insights than people would have generated if they had pursued individual research projects. For example, rather than conducting the organizational case study described in the syllabus, we decided to conduct a survey research project to assess students' perceptions of date rape on the Ball State campus. After the semester was over, one of my students continued to collaborate with me on the project. We revised the final class project into a paper that she went on to present to the Organization for the Study of Communication, Language and Gender at her first academic conference the following fall.

PROCESSES AND PRODUCTS

Opportunities

As Pezzullo and Wood (1999) observed, there are many exciting opportunities related to teaching a course about gendered communication. The opportunities include helping students discover the ways in which gender is constructed and sustained in cultural life, enlarging students' range of communication competencies to incorporate both masculine and feminine styles of interaction, enhancing students' abilities to participate critically in cultural life, and encouraging students to identify and take stands on issues that affect their lives. Although the COMM 390 experience afforded participants the opportunity to learn and grow in a variety of ways, students talked about outcomes primarily in terms of personal discovery and effecting social change.

Discovery. In the spirit of discovery, COMM 390 provided students with the opportunity to reframe their organizational experience from feminist perspectives. In the process, many students developed enhanced critical-thinking skills. As one student put it,

> It was different to have an honors class be treated like an honors class. It was the first time in college (my senior year) that a professor gave us different perspectives of the same issue (i.e., one feminism vs. many feminisms) and expected us to read each critically. The first time! It is too bad that more professors won't encourage critical analysis.

The process of discovery also involved a sense of critical awareness and self-efficacy, evidenced by statements such as, "390 had the power to change my life and raise my consciousness"; "I think that most of us have gained a heightened awareness that will empower us in a positive way in an organizational situation"; and "I really think that this class has given me a greater determination to succeed."

Out of this consciousness-raising experience, students developed an awareness of their ability to make a difference in the lives of those around them. For example, one student mentioned to me that her older sister was in a very controlling romantic relationship with a coworker. After a class in which we discussed the ways in which we perpetuate systems of oppression through our discursive practices, she suddenly understood how her sister was allowing herself to be devalued by her boyfriend. She resolved to share her insight with her sister, who consequently chose to stop participating in the abusive relationship. Another student reflected on the intersection of gender, sexuality, and pregnancy in his girlfriend's work experience:

> Before she realized that she was pregnant, Allison had a great rapport with her managers, but now some of them seem to have misgivings about her work ethic. . . . Some of her managers now seem to resent the fact that she is having a baby because not only does it mean that she may not be able to handle the same workload that she did before (in fact, she does more so that she can leave early), but it also means that she is no longer an appropriate target for sexual advances. It seems to me that some of the people she works with are upset that they are having trouble fantasizing about her and thus feel the need to mistreat her as punishment. I am not sure how to resolve this fundamental problem.

This comment demonstrates a critical awareness of gender issues in the workplace, along with the realization that complex social problems defy easy solutions. Interestingly, these words also suggest an underlying patriarchal assumption that it is his responsibility to solve his girlfriend's problem.

Effecting Social Change. The collaborative social action research project had a number of exciting outcomes for group members, particularly with respect to reframing the ways that students thought about group projects and research in general. Studying something that was personally and socially relevant was a rewarding experience. As one student remarked, "I felt that the research team experience was really positive. I have never worked with a group that was so interested and dedicated to the assignment." Likewise, another student commented, "I'm pleased with our results, as well as their potential impact, and look forward to continuing next semester." In addition, students were pleased with the quality of collaboration on the project, evidenced by statements such as the following: "Although individuals may have missed deadlines or had trouble staying on topic, personality differences and time constraints were always overshadowed by teamwork."

The collaborative research project about date rape had far-reaching implications for the quality of student life at Ball State University. For example, after the final presentation of the group's project to the class, one class member decided to lobby Ball State University's Student Government Association to add a definition of date rape to the student handbook. When her lobbying effort was profiled in the student paper, another student brought in a copy of the article to share with the rest of the class so that we could celebrate her activism. This type of student activism and recognition of excellence is indicative of the progressive, innovative culture of the class, which valued social change and social support.

Tensions

As previously noted, Pezzullo and Wood (1999) observed that tensions, such as denial, shock, frustration, and pain, may surface during a course in gendered communication as students move from resisting information that is dissonant with their existing schema to the realization that they are living in a patriarchal society.

Denial. Students may engage in denial, where they resist information that forces them to examine and question their own gendered values, thoughts, and actions. Denial may be exacerbated in cultural settings where students have been socialized to internalize sexist beliefs. For example, at the beginning of the semester, several students noted that they had been exposed to very negative and stereotypical images of what it meant to be a feminist. As a result, only one student, who had a background in Women's Studies, self-identified as a feminist. In a similar manner, one of the male students in the class expressed skepticism about feminist values:

> Currently, I am at odds with feminist theory in general because I must respect women, yet women don't always seem to respect the work that we [men] do. Equal work and pay for equal qualifications, sure, but only if you can do the job. Can a woman really do the job if she's going to be a mother?

As these observations suggest, reflection and exploration can be difficult when they conflict with deeply held cultural values.

As instructors, we have a responsibility to help students recognize when they are in denial and to encourage them to question their heavily ingrained assumptions about the world. However, in accepting this responsibility, we make three very big assumptions ourselves: first, that these people are in denial; second, that we know the truth; and third, that we have the right to enlighten them. Patai (2000) tells the story of a graduate student who expressed "dismay at being expected to disabuse her students of the notion (with which they all entered class) that they are fully equal to men, and to teach them, instead, that they are oppressed victims" (p. B8). Although most Women's Studies instructors are not likely to label their students explicitly as patriarchs or victims, most feminists would probably agree that we have a responsibility to debunk sexist myths when we hear them from our students. But how do we do this? Although there is no one right way (and sometimes no easy way) to respond to an ignorant remark, what seemed to work best in COMM 390 was the use of a rhetorical question that was prefaced by a relationally sensitive remark. For example, I responded to the young man who was concerned about whether a pregnant woman could "really do the job" by thanking him for asking such an honest question, praising his respect for women, and then reframing his question by replacing the words "woman," "women," and "mother" with male referents. His response, "Point taken," demonstrated that he, like most students, was intelligent and well-intentioned; moreover, that he appreciated the opportunity to question his internalized sexist beliefs.

Frustration. In the process of learning about the ways in which women have been systematically oppressed in our society, many students expressed shock and frustration at the power imbalances that still exist. For example, after a discussion about the intersection of gender and ethnicity, one woman (who was the only African American in the class) expressed her frustration at having to listen to her peers as they demonstrated their ignorance about the African American experience. At the same time, she felt pressured to be the spokesperson for all African American women. As she explained in an e-mail:

> I really do not feel comfortable in this class. I was under the impression that this class would deal mostly with gender issues, but instead this class seems to have become a battleground for emptying one's guts about the myths regarding African Americans. To my surprise, most of the members in this class have a lot of misconceptions regarding African Americans. After the dialogue from last week, I felt like a defender or the sole believer in equality for all African Americans.

In a similar manner, the only self-identified feminist in the class expressed her chagrin at having to play the role of educator and to be the "voice for her people":

> It was really frustrating to be the only women's studies student. Having to re-explain feminist perspectives, listen to those who have never been exposed to gender theories try to work through their misunderstandings, and listen to the rehashing of old myths seemed tedious at times.

Discussing issues that intersect with personal identity can be very difficult and frustrating, particularly for members of minority groups. As instructors, we have a responsibility to support minority students, letting them know that we value their voices and opinions, and that we also respect their choice to remain silent when the task of educating others becomes too much of an emotional burden. Cannon (1990) offers a number of excellent ground rules that instructors can implement to promote open communication across class, race, and gender lines. Adopting such guidelines as a class—and enforcing them through a skillful facilitation process that recognizes differences while acknowledging that our understanding of others will always be limited by our social positioning—can promote a communication climate that minimizes rather than exacerbates frustration caused by existing power differentials in society.

Pain. The process of questioning one's worldview involved examining issues that were personally painful to many students, such as the sexual harassment experienced by the student who worked at the country club. A second example emerged when a student brought up the possibility that some of the respondents to our survey could be survivors of date rape. At that point, one of the group members disclosed that her roommate had gotten drunk and been raped at a fraternity party the previous year and that, personally, it was still a very difficult experience for her to talk about. As a result of this conversation, we decided to include on our surveys contact information for sexual assault counselors at Ball State's Psychological Services and the local domestic violence shelter.

As these stories indicate, asking students to reflect critically on their gendered experience is problematic in that students may have to relive disturbing events that have occurred in their lives. Being an instructor in this situation is much like being a parent in that, instinctively, you want to save your students (as parents want to save their children) from pain. However, sometimes painful introspection is good in that it challenges us to attain a greater level of understanding, which is necessary for personal growth. Toward that end, I provided empathy—as opposed to pity or emotional contagion—and social support to my students who were processing painful life events.

False Consciousness. In addition to experiencing the tensions identified by Pezzullo and Wood (1999), students seemed to have difficulty freeing themselves from deeply ingrained values of competitive individualism, linear thinking, and hierarchical power relations. At the beginning of the semester, some students had a great deal of trouble adjusting to the alternative structure of a seminar because they were used to traditional lecture-format classes. Comments on class evaluation forms indicated that some students were somewhat uncomfortable operating without a hierarchical structure imposed by an authority figure who appeared to have all the answers. For example, one student stated:

> I believe that this class was well organized and put together. However, I would lecture more the first couple of classes, as the class begins with heavy theory. Many students have never been exposed to progressive social theory and would benefit from classes where it is explained by a professor.

Further, some students had a great deal of difficulty living with the ambiguity of the journal writing assignment. Rather than accepting that the journal writing experience was really for their benefit and understanding that they would receive full credit for the assignment no matter what they wrote, some students wanted clear criteria regarding length, content, legibility, and so forth. One student in particular, who was very grade-conscious, left all her journal entries for the end of the semester. She calculated the subtotal of her grade and realized that she had to write only 10 entries to earn a given grade in the class . . . and that's all she wrote. Finally, with respect to the collaborative project, one student expressed discomfort with the process of evaluating her peers:

> On a personal note, I found this peer evaluation extremely difficult. One reason is that although I'm used to receiving evaluations, I'm not accustomed to giving them. Ultimately, I think that you have the best overall knowledge of our performance as individuals.

These responses suggest that students were so well-socialized to succeed in traditional classrooms that they had difficulty adapting to the alternative values of a feminist learning community. As Tompkins (2000) so eloquently wrote in her essay, "Reverie,"

> After babyhood we spend a lot of time learning to sit in rows. Going from unruly to ruled. Learning to write on pages that are lined. Learning to obey. There is no other way, apparently. . . . The habit of learning to sit in rows doesn't leave off when the rows themselves are gone. Having learned to learn the rules, you look for them everywhere you go, to avoid humiliation. You learn to find your seat in the invisible rows. (pp. 47-48)

Those of us who are socialized in a patriarchal system, particularly women, learn to defer to authority. Instructors who endeavor to transform traditional classroom structures and cultures need to be aware that this is no small undertaking; although it's easy to move the desks into a circle, it's not so easy to get students to grant themselves permission to sit outside of the invisible rows.[3] Not only students but also professors find transformative pedagogy difficult. For me, grading was the hardest part.

According to Jenefsky (1996), conventional grading systems are antithetical to the feminist classroom because "as long as the power of grading resides in the hands of teachers, teachers possess the power to punish and reward students, and students are thereby discouraged from taking risks" (p. 346).

Although I understand and, to some extent, identify with Jenefsky's argument, I have a real difficulty in letting go of the control that comes with the authority to assign grades. As a feminist, I realize that grading is problematic because it reifies a hierarchical power structure, in which authority is vested in the instructor's judgment. Nevertheless, I employed a conventional grading system in COMM 390 because I wanted to have a system that was as transparent and as objective as possible; moreover, I wanted to be able to enforce it in a consistent and equitable manner. This decision was congruent with my desire to be perceived as judicious. At the same time, however, I wanted to be supportive and liked, so when students lost points for turning in work that was late, replete with stylistic errors, or otherwise lackluster, I felt badly about grading them down . . . even though I knew that those students had earned the grades that I assigned.

The ambivalent feelings that I experienced related to assigning grades was similar to what Bridge and Baxter (1992) describe as the dialectical tension between judgment and acceptance in workplace friendships. I found that integration, or reframing, was a strategy that allowed me to preserve relational goals with my students at the same time that I upheld academic standards. I made a point of explaining to my students that the grades that they earned reflected the quality of their work—not the quality of their character. In this sense, I communicated to students that their worth as human beings was not contingent upon the grades that they earned in my class. Thus, although I was not capable of relinquishing my position of authority in the hegemonic system that was reinforced through a conventional grading system in COMM 390, I was to some extent able to reframe the importance of grades in the grand scheme of things.

LESSONS LEARNED

Renewal

Throughout the process of developing and participating in COMM 390, I was constantly challenged to rethink my position with respect to the assumptions and discourse of my academic formation. As a graduate student, I was groomed to "know" things in particular ways, and thus to value these ways of knowing. For example, as a doctoral student, I was trained in traditional organizational communication theory and quantitative research methods. I can recall a number of times in my program when organizational cultural studies were devalued (e.g., a senior professor categorized them as "legitimization for qualitative researchers") and qualitative research was dismissed as invalid (because, according to one doctoral student, it pertained to the experience of only "a handful of people that I'll probably never meet"). Doctoral candidates who applied for jobs at teaching colleges rather than research institutions were looked down upon by senior faculty members in the department. Needless to say, feminist scholarship and teaching were marginalized in this learning environment. Given my formation, I experienced a therapeutic liberation in being permitted to "color outside the lines" in prepping and teaching a class that was rooted in critical theory and women's ways of knowing. To paraphrase the words of M. Frye (1993), in granting myself authority as a feminist scholar, I wrote my own emancipation proclamation.

Reflexivity

Given that feminist pedagogy encourages critical introspection, it would be hypocritical for me to refrain from a bit of self-reflection. As Hawes (1994) asserts, reflexivity involves a realization that "all knowledges are mediated through and by others" (p. 7). In this spirit, I must acknowledge how my social positioning may have affected the students' dialogue. For example, as a white, middle-class, heterosexual woman in her 30s who had just graduated from "21st grade," I was older and more educated than all of my students. My social positioning (which, in general, I must admit accords me a number of privileges) may have, at times, influenced the extent to which students were willing to share or to provide honest answers about their perspectives and experiences. In an attempt to reduce the status differential, I downplayed my expert status and promoted nonhierarchical relationships in a number of ways. For example, on the first day of class, after I had introduced myself and described my educational formation and professional credentials, I told students about the social roles that I fulfill as a spouse and a mother, and I encouraged students to call me by my first name. In addition, I disclosed to students that, although I have a PhD, I learned to ride a bike only a few years ago . . . and it was a very scary experience for me. These messages communicate that all human beings are complex, holistic beings who simultaneously hold a variety of social roles; further, that although we may be experts in some areas, we are still novices in others.

Connectedness

Feminist pedagogy's emphases on collaboration and community have important implications for students and instructors on a variety of levels. For example, as I discussed earlier, collaboration between students led to more valuable insights than individuals may have generated on their own. Additionally, collaboration between instructor and students allowed not only for greater insight for all parties, but it also provided an opportunity for reframing power relationships. As a result of this experience, my students and

I had the opportunity to work together as colleagues rather than as teacher and students. Although some students seemed initially reluctant to approach me on a first-name basis, most students were comfortable enough to address me by my given name by the end of the semester. In fact, long after that semester has ended, some of the students in the class still call, e-mail, or stop by my office to catch up over a cup of tea. One student, who taught me a thing or two about feminist theory, paid me the greatest compliment when she came back to visit me and asked if I would be her mentor. hooks (2000) spoke passionately about the importance of this type of connectedness when she said:

> Engaged pedagogy not only compels me to be constantly creative in the classroom, it also sanctions involvement with students beyond that setting. I journey with students as they progress in their lives beyond our classroom experience. In many ways, I continue to teach them, even as they become more capable of teaching me. The important lesson that we learn together, the lesson that allows us to move together within and beyond the classroom, is one of mutual engagement.

In addition to enhancing the quality of relationships that I developed with students, I also experienced a sense of greater connection with other citizens in my academic community. As I mentioned earlier, this course diversified the curriculum of the Department of Communication Studies, which previously did not offer a course in gender. In the process of developing and implementing this course, I established personal and interdepartmental linkages among the Department of Communication Studies, the Women and Gender Studies program, and the Honors College. Looking back with satisfaction on the solid supports we've built, I realize that these interdisciplinary links constitute an informal network of students, faculty, and citizens who are committed to improving the lives of women in our community.

Course By(buy)products

In the beginning of this chapter, I stated that COMM 390 was a curriculum initiative that positioned the Department of Communication Studies to make an important contribution to the intellectual movement to diversify Ball State University. COMM 390 also positioned Ball State University as a player in a much larger national debate about the place of Women's Studies in educational institutions (Hughes, 2000; Patai, 2000) and the Communication discipline (Kramarae, 1996; Varallo, Tracy, Marty, & Tambe, 2001). In this light, it is extremely important to recognize Ball State's position as a state-funded university that is under pressure to cut costs in the current climate of economic slowdowns and budget shortfalls. Because of these economic imperatives, curriculum initiatives at Ball State University—and elsewhere—need to demonstrate not only that they have intrinsic value for enriching students' educational experiences, but also that they can do so in an effective and efficient manner. It follows that the Women's Studies classroom that serves as a training ground for a small number of feminist activists will probably not be as marketable as a Women and Gender Studies course that aims to provide a large number of students with a healthy dose of multicultural education. Unfortunately, employing this logic, many instructors who are committed to feminist pedagogy may feel pressured to water down their course content to make it more palatable to the masses . . . and, consequently, to key stakeholders who count student credit hours as an indicator of success. Although Patai and Koertge (1994) were more concerned about the extent to which feminist proselytizing impinged upon academic freedom when they lamented that "the best instructional efforts have too often succeeded only in subverting both the values of the academy and the goal of improving women's condition" (p. 81), their words are remarkably pertinent to the apparent dilemma that many feminist communication instructors face today.

Until Kramarae's (1996) utopian vision of communication education in a women's university is realized, we have to generate creative strategies to balance the tension between the desire to adhere to feminist pedagogical values and the pressure to sell a product that students and administrators want to buy. In practical terms, this means thinking strategically about how we market ourselves. One strategy that we can employ is to articulate feminist principles that inform our classes in ways that are congruent with university mission statements and stakeholder needs. For me, this meant offering COMM 390 under the umbrella of classes promoted by Ball State University's Diversity Policy Institute[4] and changing the name from "Feminist Organizational Communication" to the more inclusive title "Gender in the Workplace."[5] Another way to balance the tension between "selling ourselves" and "selling out" is to co-opt the university's discourse of accountability and develop assessment tools that evaluate the degree to which courses produce feminist learning outcomes for students in ways that are congruent with departmental learning objectives. The second time that I taught COMM 390, I collaborated with the Women's Studies Curriculum Committee to develop a Women's Studies course evaluation tool, which I administered in addition to the university's standard faculty course evaluation form. This tool gave me valuable information that allowed me to assess students' learning outcomes with respect to critical thinking, effecting social change, and ethical responsibility, as well as to gather process-evaluation data that could be used to improve the course for future students. Employing similar strategies, feminist communication instructors can market the "F-word" (feminism) in our discipline without selling out.

CONCLUSION

In sum, the experience of participating in COMM 390, Feminist Organizational Communication, was a transformative teaching and learning experience. Feminist pedagogical techniques, participant narratives, and critical awareness revealed a number of tensions that participants experienced. Creative communicative responses (e.g., posing rhetorical questions in relationally sensitive ways, adopting ground rules for discussion, communicating empathy and social support, and reframing contradictions) defused tensions and reframed apparent paradoxes. Finally, participants learned a number of important lessons surrounding the importance of renewal, reflexivity, connectedness, and selling ourselves without selling out.

This exploration of feminist pedagogy should not end here. hooks (2000) challenged us to think about education as the practice of freedom:

> The academy is not paradise. But learning is a place where paradise can be created. The classroom, with all its limitations, remains a location of possibility. In that field of possibility we have the opportunity to labor for freedom, to demand of ourselves and our comrades an openness of mind and heart that allows us to face reality even as we collectively imagine ways to move beyond boundaries, to transgress. This is education as the practice of freedom. (p. 177)

In writing this chapter, it is my hope not only to make sense of the COMM 390 experience but also to share this experience with others to demonstrate the advantages of implementing feminist pedagogy in the communication curricula, particularly in those courses that challenge students to engage in critical thinking about issues such as gender, diversity, and power. My experience suggests that the type of student-centered teaching and research described here is a particularly promising way to encourage students and instructors to take ownership of their education and to participate more fully as citizens in their communities.

Notes

1. Although the Women's Studies Program has been offering an interdisciplinary Introduction to Women's Studies course for 30 years, Ball State University still (at the time of this writing) does not offer an undergraduate major in Women's Studies. However, a 36-hour undergraduate major has been approved by Ball State's Undergraduate Education Committee. With the support of university, college, and departmental leaders who are committed to diversity, there is a strong possibility that Ball State will soon have a Women's Studies major (which will include a Symposium in Communication) on the books.

2. L. Miller (1997) defines gender harassment as "harassment that is not sexual, and is used to enforce traditional gender roles, or in response to the violation of those roles" (p. 35).

3. It is not easy for teachers to avoid straightening the invisible rows, either. As a junior faculty member in the fall of 1998, I was trying very hard to do everything right: On one level, that meant following the rules of the Promotion and Tenure committee, demonstrating excellence in teaching, scholarship, and service, so that one fine day I might, as a tenured faculty member, earn the respect of my colleagues and the promise of job security. On another level, following the rules meant trying unsuccessfully to spring free of the Superwoman Trap: I tried to balance my social roles as a woman, mother, spouse, and daughter (my personal life) with my professional role as an assistant professor (a job that never ended). Sometimes, I ended up wondering whether I would ever have a life.

4. The Diversity Policy Institute (DPI) was established at Ball State University in 1999 to increase awareness and knowledge of diversity-related scholarship and to integrate these issues into the curriculum. I served as a DPI fellow in 1999-2000, when I taught a revised COMM 390 course titled "Gender in the Workplace."

5. The decision to change the name of the course from "Feminist Organizational Communication" to "Gender in the Workplace" occurred at about the same time that the Women and Gender Studies Program changed its name to the "Women's Studies Program." This name change symbolized a rebirth of the program, as well as a desire to differentiate itself from the DPI, which had recently proposed a minor with a concentration in gender and sexuality. Although the COMM 390 name change reflected my desire to be more inclusive in the hopes of recruiting students from both programs, I realized that changing the course name from "Feminism" to "Gender" put me smack dab in the middle of a turf battle. To stave off speculation that the COMM 390 name change reflected a concurrent change in allegiance, I explained my rationale for the name change to the director of the Women's Studies Program.

12

Body Shape(ing) Discourse

Bakhtinian Intertextuality as a Tool for Studying Discourse and Relationships

Terri L. Russ

From discussing the trivial to the pivotal, friends rely on each other for guidance, support, and commiseration. In addition to turning to our friends during times of enjoyment, we also turn to our friends to help us make sense of the world and our place in it. Reflecting on my friendships with other women, I noticed a trend in our sensemaking discussions. One topic of discussion repeatedly rose to the top: our bodies, including how we viewed our own and other women's bodies, as well as what we and others were doing to accept or change our bodies. I call these types of discussions *body shape discourse*. This realization prompted a series of questions. Do all women engage in body shape discourse? What cultural, social, and historical forces prompt body shape discourse? Does body shape discourse occur in similar ways across friendships? This chapter presents a theoretical rationale arguing that women's body shape shapes women's friendship discourse as well as the friendship itself[1]—a process that I am calling *body shape discourse*. In addition to this chapter providing rationale for further research into body shape discourse, it also provides a specific method and mode of analysis that can be used within the classroom to analyze body shape discourse as it occurs within students' lives.

As noted by O'Connor (1992), women's friendships have been "systematically ignored, derogated, and trivialized" (p. 9), resulting in a philosophical and theoretical void. One method of filling this void is through an approach grounded in a feminist perspective focused on women's experience as expressed through their voices. Clair, Chapman, and Kunkel (1996) assert that a feminist approach "ought to be founded upon the centrality of women's experience" (p. 245). That is, to "foster new ontological and epistemological understandings of women's realities" (S. Foss & Foss, 1988, p. 9), we should turn to an examination of those realities. There are numerous ways to obtain a greater understanding of women's realities; however, perhaps the most telling is by listening to women's voices. To gain greater insight into the lived experience of women and their bodies, this chapter analyzes the voices of adolescent girls to provide a preliminary study of how adolescent girls enact and live body shape discourse, and it also provides pedagogical approaches to be used in studying and teaching the phenomenon.

I begin with an overview of pedagogical applications. Using body shape discourse as an exemplar, it can be demonstrated that our interpersonal relationships are affected not just by the individuals involved but also by a number of societal forces and images. In addition, analysis of body shape discourse as a discursive genre illustrates how all of our discourse is heteroglot and composed of multiple texts. I provide a brief application and use of body shape discourse within the classroom as a pedagogical tool through the use of personal journals. This initial application is supplemented throughout the chapter with additional suggestions.

The remainder of the chapter presents the theoretical underpinnings of body shape discourse, including specific examples of texts and body shape as discursive genre. To begin, I review women's friendships in general before focusing on female adolescent friendships as the site where body shape discourse initially appears as a prevalent topic. In terms of pedagogical application, the use of adolescent girls provides concrete examples to which college students, only recently out of adolescence themselves, can relate. To provide cultural and historical context to the presence of body shape discourse, I then discuss women being placed in the role of "body," with an emphasis on how media discourses currently enact and disseminate ideal images of the female body. This section concludes with a brief summary of feminist perspectives of the link between the feminine body, media, and culture. To illustrate the specific forms body shape discourse takes within female friendships, I use Bakhtin's theory of intertextuality as a method for analysis of this discourse. Applying this method, I deconstruct body shape discourse to isolate the numerous texts it comprises as well as to show how these texts make up a Bakhtinian discursive genre within the overall friendship discourse. For specific examples, I turn to adolescent girls' voices as embodied in published form.[2] This method and analysis provides an exploratory look at body shape discourse within female friendship. I conclude with a discussion of the implications of this chapter and directions for future research.

Pedagogical Applications and Uses of Body Shape Discourse Analysis

This chapter presents the initial framework for an approach to the study of discourse within personal relationships. The framework provides a tool to determine and demonstrate the numerous texts intertextually present in any specific instance of discourse. Focusing on body shape discourse, this chapter serves as a pedagogical guide for discussing body shape discourse as it occurs within students' lives. Essentially, the format of the chapter provides building blocks that can be combined to form a comprehensive understanding of discourse as it is created and as it operates within relationships. In terms of body shape discourse, these blocks are: female friendship, societal treatment of women and the female body, multiple texts brought into the friendship, and the way discourse forms into genres.

In discussing and analyzing body shape discourse with my students, I ask them to track instances of body shape discourse with their friends, specifically noting each of these building blocks. To prompt thinking about the lived reality of such discourse, I ask students to brainstorm with each other to speculate as to the times and places they are likely to engage in body shape discourse, the individuals they are most likely to converse with, and the most likely reasons. We then discuss these instances as a group to determine how they help to maintain societal control of women and their bodies.

The journals can be used as a starting point for discussion of friendship, the sexualization of women, the ways discourse forms in interpersonal relationships, or any combination of these topics. Although body shape discourse as discussed in this chapter occurs within women's friendships, the phenomenon of discourse formation through intertextuality is not limited to such relationships. Therefore, students can use this method to analyze other specific discursive genres occurring within their lives. For example, it would be interesting to analyze how male students discuss their bodies with their friends. Does their discourse mirror the body shape discourse of women, or is it different?

In addition, the method can be used to analyze discursive genres occurring within intimate relationships, family relationships, or professional relationships, as well as if and how these other discourses act to maintain the status quo. That is, students can begin to see how, through conversation, they intentionally and unintentionally bring societal dictates into their relationship. After students understand this fact, they can explore how to use their relationship conversation to resist such dictates instead of reinforcing them.

The remainder of this chapter discusses the theoretical foundations of body shape discourse before turning to specific examples of such discourse. At the end of each main section, I provide specific pedagogical points of discussion to be used in conjunction with the personal journals.

Friendships Generally and Adolescent Girls' Friendships Specifically

Friendship has been researched and discussed by a multitude of individuals across a variety of disciplines; therefore, instead of presenting a comprehensive review of existing literature in the area of friendships, in this section I provide a summary of the current understanding of the main characteristics of friendship. I then discuss women's friendships specifically and how they are lived and experienced by women. Finally, I present a discussion of female adolescence and female adolescent friendship.

FRIENDSHIP AS PRIVATE RELATIONSHIP IN THE PUBLIC SPHERE

Friendships happen in various ways. Friendships often occur at unexpected times and without the formal ceremony and rituals that we participate in when starting a marriage. A friendship is a private relationship functioning in a public world. It is private in that there are no laws or official requirements for friendships, so friends can communicate and relate to each other as they wish. Among other things, this means that friendship is a wholly voluntary relationship that can be entered into by any individuals wishing to be friends (Friedman, 1993b; O'Connor, 1992; Rawlins, 1992). Although individual friends may desire to do certain things within their friendship—the private—they must also adhere to societal dictates and demands—the public. As clarified by Rawlins (1992), "Friendships are ongoing communicative achievements often pursued in the face of incompatible requirements" (p. 3). These incompatible requirements are often realized as a point of tension within the friendship and result in a "double agency" (Rawlins, 1989, p. 28) in which the individual friends must take on dual roles. For example, the woman who desperately participates in body shape discourse with her friend may find it necessary to put on a face of confidence with others outside the friendship.

Dealing with the public and private within the friendship illustrates what Rawlins (1992) referred to as contextual and interactional dialectics. These dialectics are individually and/or collectively present throughout the cycle of the friendship and present ongoing difficulties that must be managed and negotiated by the individual friends. Rawlins (1983) argues that in managing such dialectical tensions as these, "friends must negotiate the areas of their discourse" (p. 5). That is, as specified by Rawlins and Holl (1987), talk is a function of "structuring a sense of self and relationship with others" (p. 353). We see this function beginning in adolescent friendships. Through discourse, adolescents determine who they are and how they should live in the world.

As shown in the next section, the role of friendship talk has been found to be especially important in female friendships.

FEMALE FRIENDSHIPS

Much of the existing work in the area of women's friendships is fairly sketchy. In attempting to determine the specifics of such friendships, researchers have predominantly taken the existing research on men's friendships and compared women's friendship to men's. However, the groundbreaking work of Smith-Rosenberg (1975) examined the "female world of varied and yet highly structured relationships" (p. 311) found in 19th century women's friendships. These relationships were an "essential aspect of American society" (p. 312) and provided a stabilizing factor in women's lives. The friendship was a site for women to discuss and combat the loneliness inherent in their domestic lives. After Smith-Rosenberg's study, women's friendships continued to be noticeably absent from the academic radar screen; I present here information from the few pertinent studies since conducted that indicate some of the factors currently deemed at play in female friendship.

Female friendship has been characterized as communal or face to face (O'Connor, 1992; Oliker, 1998; Rawlins, 1992). A primary component of this communal nature is that women are self-disclosing and emotionally expressive within their friendships (Oliker, 1998). Like their 19th century counterparts, female friends turn to each other to talk. This talk results in a level of intimacy between female friends that is characterized by a "sharing of emotional experience, mutual self-exploration, and the expression of emotional attachment" (Oliker, 1998, p. 20). O'Connor (1992) asserts that because women's friendships are a form of social integration, any attempt to understand them must note that gender is a social category that will have both a direct and an indirect impact on the friendship. In other words, the public construction of "female" will creep into and act on the private construction of the friendship.

Like O'Connor (1992), B. Fisher and Galler (1988) argue that based on the lesser status afforded to women in American society, all friendships have some sort of "disability." In their words, "Common experience leads to a special sort of sympathetic understanding between women and is basic to women's friendship" (B. Fisher & Galler, 1988, p. 173). This common experience is negotiated through what Gouldner and Symons Strong (1987) term "woman talk." In the universe of discourse, historically, women were separate, so "women turned to their women friends as talking companions" (Gouldner & Symons Strong, 1987, p. 59). The value of a friend then became more than a social value; a friend was also someone to turn to for guidance and support through difficulties. In terms of female friendship, the presence of woman talk initially begins to appear during adolescence.

FEMALE ADOLESCENCE AND FRIENDSHIP

Adolescence is a time of physical change and emotional difficulty. DeBeauvoir (1949/1989), in writing about the problems faced by adolescent girls, noted that "young girls slowly bury their childhood, put away their independent and imperious selves and submissively enter adult existence. . . . Girls stop being and start seeming" (p. 365). Girls experience physical changes that include the beginning of menarche, growth of their breasts, and rounding of their hips. Accompanying these physical changes, cultural and social discourses present dichotomous messages to adolescent girls that indicate on one hand that they are still immature and on the other hand that they are mature. Pipher (1994) has analogized this moment as a Bermuda Triangle of female adolescence. She states that upon entering adolescence, girls "crash and burn in a social and developmental Bermuda Triangle" (p. 19). In entering adolescence, it is as if adolescent girls have boarded a carnival ride, thinking it would be enjoyable like a merry-go-round, and have discovered instead that it is terrifying like the house of horrors. Seemingly overnight, bright, bubbly girls are replaced by dark, moody girl-women. The underlying cause of such changes and difficulties are the many physical changes precipitated by puberty. Although adolescence brings physical maturity, mental and emotional maturity do not simultaneously arrive. This incongruity results in adolescent females thinking like girls but looking like women/girl-women.

Rawlins and Holl (1987) note that in adolescent friendships, talk is a "function of structuring a sense of self and relation with others" (p. 353). Specifically addressing adolescent female friendships, Rawlins (1992) observes that such friendships are "involved—more inclined toward disclosure and discussion of personally involving topics" (p. 73). Discussing personally involving topics is especially important as female adolescents continue to develop physically and become constantly observed by other members of society (Pipher, 1994; Rawlins, 1992). The need for approval, the constant perception of being watched, as well as the physical and emotional turmoil of female adolescence seem to scream for the presence of body shape discourse within female adolescent friendships. As discussed in the next main section, societal placement of women in the role of body reinforces the notion that body shape discourse will be present in friendship talk.

PEDAGOGICAL APPLICATIONS

Friendship offers an extremely fruitful pedagogical tool for discussing relationships. Although not all students will have participated in intimate and/or professional relationships, they usually will have participated in at least one friendship. Friendships can then be used as a starting point for discussing other relationships. Useful questions for students to consider include: What sorts of activities do you participate in with your friends? Do you find that you turn to certain friends for emotional support and other friends for pleasure activities? Are there certain topics of discussion that appear in your personal journal more frequently than others? Are there differences in your friendships with members of the same sex as opposed to members of the opposite sex?

The Feminine Body as Sexualized Object and Homogenized Control

To understand why and how body shape discourse appears in female friendships, it helps first to understand the links between women's body and society. Societal and cultural placement of women in the role of body results in a hypersensitivity to the form female bodies take. Many individual women spend hours focused on the perceived inadequacies they think their bodies exhibit. This focus then manifests in their discourse with other women. Therefore, this section will discuss how women have been placed in the role of body, how the feminine body of most women is perceived as bad, and how striving to achieve the ideal results in reinforcement of patriarchal control.

WOMAN AS BODY

The link among women, their bodies, and society has been advanced by various feminist theorists. DeBeauvoir (1952/1989) spelled out how women have been placed in the role of "body," which allows for a focus on the physical and a sexualization of the feminine form. Placement of women in the role of body results in their being viewed as sexual objects for men's viewing pleasure. Characterizing this sexualization as women's "traditional exhibitionist role," Mulvey (1975/1999) argues that "women are simultaneously looked at and displayed, with their appearance coded for strong visual and erotic impact so that they can be said to connote *to-be-looked-at-ness*" (pp. 62-63). Being or feeling as if they are on display results in women learning that "they must continually watch themselves being watched" (Douglas, 1994 p. 17). Despite the fact that woman has been placed in the role of body, certain ideal bodies are prized whereas bodies less than ideal are considered deviant, as discussed next.

BODY AS BAD

Woman placed in the role of body is not the end of the story; in fact, it is only the beginning. As noted by Trethewey (2000), a woman's relation to her body is a reflection of both the social construction of the feminine form and the response to it. The current social construction of the female body dictates that most bodies in their natural form are inherently bad, as is seen in American culture's homogenization of the female form and the so-called "tyranny of slenderness."

Although we see various women represented in media images, Bordo (1993) has argued that there is an overwhelming homogenization of the feminine form. Even though these various women have minor differences in appearance—hair, skin, and eye color, body size and shape, and others—they are more similar than dissimilar.

Chernin (1981), in discussing her own quest for thinness, termed media portrayal of increasingly thinner, homogenized women as the "tyranny of slenderness." As examined by Seid (1989), the ideal feminine body seen in media images of actresses and models represents the thinnest 5% of all women. Today, the average American woman is 5 feet, 4 inches tall and weighs 140 pounds, whereas the average American model is 5 feet, 11 inches tall and weighs 117 pounds (Eating Disorder Referral and Information Center, 2002).

The tyranny, however, does not end with media images. The thinnest 5% of women are idealized as the beautiful aesthetic that all women should strive to attain. However, with computer enhancements and lighting, these thinnest 5% are more unreal than real. These unreal ideal depictions result in specific negative ramifications and manifestations in women's lives, as demonstrated by S. Turner and Hamilton (1997) in their study gauging the impact of mini-mal exposure to fashion magazines. After a mere 13-minute exposure to the slender (and often anorexic) images in such magazines, the women in the study experienced and exhibited a dramatic increase in body image dissatisfaction (S. Turner & Hamilton, 1997). The proverbial tip of the iceberg, this study does not account for extended and/or repeated exposure to such images. Women, however, are not mere empty receptacles to be filled with media images. Although media images are significant and have a clearly negative effect, they work in conjunction with other aspects of society and culture, as demonstrated in the next section.

BAD AS CONTROL

If woman is in the role of body, and the feminine body in its natural state is bad, then, by extension, woman is bad as well. Recalling Douglas's (1994) assertion that "women learn they must continually watch themselves being watched" (p. 17), the extension of woman as bad not only results in internal-ization of the male gaze identified by Mulvey (1975/1999), but it also results in perhaps the most efficient and effective method of controlling women.

Attempting to achieve the homogenized, ideal, slender form, many women engage in various dieting practices. Starting with negative body image, many women exercise and diet; however, as noted by Eskes and Miller (1998), the end goal of these practices is achievement of the beauty ideal, not health. Often these practices lead to disordered eating practices. In its most basic forms, such disordered eating complicates daily living; in its more extreme forms, it leads to eating disorders such as *anorexia* (the near total abstention from eating) and/or *bulimia* (periods of bingeing followed by periods of purging). Bordo (1993) refers to all of these practices as "normative feminine practices which train the female body in docility and obedience to cultural demands while at the same time being experienced in terms of power and control" (p. 27). Learning to participate in these normative feminine practices often starts when girls are adolescents (Brumberg, 1998; Trethewey, 2000).

Bordo's assertion that participation in these practices results in docility and obedience experienced in terms of power and control becomes clear when examined in light of Foucault's discussion of the prison panopticon (Bartky, 1988; Bordo, 1993; Foucault, 1995). The *panopticon* is a tall tower surrounded by prison cells at its base. Inmates can see the tower but not who or if anyone is occupying it. Inmates quickly realize that they could be on continual surveillance and thus learn to behave accordingly to avoid punishment. Inmates further realize that they must learn to self-monitor to avoid retribution. This self-monitoring is accomplished not with weapons but with a gaze that is internalized by the inmates.

Similar to the inmates discussed by Foucault, many women have internalized a controlling male gaze and act accordingly for fear of the "punishment" that might occur if they don't appear "correctly." Even though there are no federal, state, or local laws mandating physical appearance, many women fear the punishment of scorn and ostracism. Bartky (1988) asserts that this self-monitoring by women not only results in a homogenized feminine form, but it also results in a form of obedience to patriarchy when women force themselves to eat less and exercise more. If the concept of friendship is introduced into the discussion, Bartky's assertion can be further extended. As noted by various authors, women often diet and/or exercise with a friend to maintain motivation and to adhere to the dieting rules of disordered eating (Apter & Josselson, 1998; Brumberg, 1998; Douglas, 1994; Trethewey, 2000). Therefore, not only are individual women self-enforcing patriarchal ideals, but women are also collectively enforcing those ideals. If one thinks of tyranny as absolute power or control, then Chernin's (1981) tyranny of slenderness can be seen as women's removal of power or control from themselves. Talking about this tyranny through body shape discourse does not equal control; however, it does allow women an alternative method of dealing with this aspect of their reality.

PEDAGOGICAL APPLICATIONS

Discussion of the placement of women in the role of body as well as the impact of such placement can take many forms within the classroom. To raise awareness of students' individual body issues, I ask them specifically to record in their journals their feelings about their bodies. I provide guidance by having them think about how food, diet, and exercise are discussed within their families, if they spend time comparing themselves to others, if they exercise for the health benefits or to maintain a certain look, and other topics prompted by class discussion. I then bring several popular magazines to class and have students identify bodies that look like their bodies as well as the bodies they would like to have. I group students into pairs and have each partner identify bodies that look like the bodies of their partner. The pairs are then instructed to discuss differences and/or similarities between the choices of the partners. This exercise usually highlights to students that their own bodies appear differently than they think.

The Shape of Body Shape Discourse

In this section, I explain Bakhtin's theory of intertextuality and discursive genres. I show how the two can be brought together to analyze body shape discourse as realized in women's lives. I then apply this method to discuss and analyze the multiple texts girls bring to body shape discourse as a discursive genre appearing in adolescent female friendships.

THE INTERTEXTUALITY OF DISCURSIVE GENRES

As we ramble through life, we organize our experience through our creation of texts or discourses: "We see the world by authoring it, by making sense of it through the activity of turning it into a text, by translating it into finalizing schemes that can order its potential chaos" (Holquist, 1990, p. 84). The texts that we create, though, are not ours exclusively. Our texts intertextually comprise other texts: "The internally persuasive word is half-ours and half-someone else's" (Bakhtin, 1981, p. 345). *Intertextuality,* then, refers to the interweaving of the myriad texts that occur within every discursive utterance—both written and spoken. A *text* is basically a collection of utterances that are in relation to each other—that is, "any coherent complex of signs—thoughts about thoughts, experiences of experiences, words about words, and texts about texts" (Bakhtin, 1986, p. 103). Each individual text is related to previous texts, "thus creating *intertextual* (or dialogic) relations" (emphasis in original, Todorov, 1984, p. 48). More specifically, each individual text is formed and informed both by texts that came before and texts that will come after it.

The phenomenon of intertextuality becomes clearer when we remember that all of our discourse is social, directed toward the other, and existing among numerous other social discourses. This complexity is explained more intricately in the following:

> Every concrete utterance of a speaking subject serves as a point where centrifugal as well as centripetal forces are brought to bear. The processes of centralization and decentralization, of unification and disunification, intersect in the utterance; the utterance not only answers the requirements of its own language as an individualized embodiment of a speech act, but it answers the requirements of heteroglossia as well, it is in fact an active participant in speech diversity. (Bakhtin, 1981 p. 272)

Caught in the middle of this whirling of centrifugal and centripetal forces, no individual utterance stands alone or is created independently of other utterances. Each utterance is intertextually woven with other utterances, which are woven together into discourse.

The discourses that comprise individual texts form in distinct and repeating ways—discursive genres. We use discursive genres to organize communication on a daily basis. For example, if in passing another I am asked how am I doing, I know to answer with "fine" or some other cursory response. This exchange exemplifies a discursive genre in which we participate in many times in any given day.

In terms of body shape discourse, we see a multiplicity of texts feeding into women's thoughts and discourse. To understand body shape discourse, the first step is to determine the various texts that the discourse comprises. The second step is to analyze the form(s) body shape discourse takes as a discursive genre.

BODY SHAPE TEXTS

Before looking at body shape discourse as a discursive genre in the next section, this section explores the various types of texts that intertextually combine to form the body shape discursive genre. For ease of discussion, I have divided the texts into three categories: print texts, electronic texts, and living texts. Although I have presented these categories as distinct entities, in real life the lines between them are more blurred than clear.

Print Texts

Print texts include those texts that are in some type of print form, such as books, magazines, newspapers, and other written documents. Print texts include written, photographic, and pictorial texts that combine to form an encompassing text. In studying print texts, analysis of the text as an entirety should be made as well as analysis of the individual texts within it.

Illustrations of print texts are prevalent in the works I have chosen to represent adolescent girls' voices. Gottlieb (2000), for example, talks about books that present diets such as "The Effortless Diet" and "Thin in Three Days" (pp. 32-33). In addition to print texts in the form of books, girls' discourse references magazines. Hornbacher (1998) refers to turning to fashion magazines for advice, such as the mandate presented in *Seventeen* magazine that "thighs should not touch" (p. 44). Hornbacher notes that the advice of how one should look is accompanied with suggestions that girls share the tips with their friends.

Magazines are not used only for advice; they are also turned to as a mirror or model that is used to gauge not only what one should look like, but how close (or far) the reader is from the ideal. Browning Smith (1998) exemplifies this use of magazines when she imagines "being skinny like the girls on a run-way or in a magazine" (p. 21). For her, and arguably for many other girls, this elusive and unattainable ideal is "skinny enough" (Browning Smith, 1998, p. 21). Shandler (1999), in her interviews with adolescent girls, relates a different use of fashion magazines. One of her interviewees would "cut out the body parts of models from magazines and piece together her goal body" (Shandler, 1999, p. 4).

In addition to books and magazines, other print texts appear in body shape discourse. Gottlieb (2000) relates that newspaper articles addressing eating disorders lead her to question whether her "problem" was really just a part of larger societal problems (p. 219). She also fondly recalls napkins imprinted with the statement "You can never be too rich or too thin" (Gottlieb, 2000, p. 214) as providing a dieting mantra for her. Shandler (1999) presents a poem that illustrates how even catalogues are sought out for the elusive ideal:

> Searching through catalogues
>
> you wish you could order
>
> the bodies not the clothes. (Bulman, J., as cited in Shandler, 1999, p. 5)

The preceding examples are just a sampling of the types of print texts found in body shape discourse. Undoubtedly, numerous other print texts combine to form the genre.

Electronic Texts

The phrase *electronic texts* indicates texts transmitted by means of some type of electronic media. Included in this category are all forms of television, film, and the Internet, as well as music and video games. These texts provide an especially dangerous influence because they are so readily available. Not all homes have books or magazines, but nearly all homes today do have a television.

Browning Smith (1998) reinforces the power of electronic texts by noting that "rarely" does she turn on either the television or radio without seeing a reference to women and their weight (p. 133). Usually this reference is presented in a negative manner, such as women need to lose weight or exercise more, thereby becoming a continual reminder of not only how girls should look, but also that they do not meet the cultural ideal.

In addition to providing reminders of the need to strive for the ideal, electronic texts also provide specific methods to be used in gauging how close one is to the ideal as well as ways to achieve the ideal. Gottlieb (2000), for example, highlights a commercial for Special K cereal that features a thin woman in a white bathing suit. The commercial ends with the lady asking the audience if they can "pinch an inch" while showing that she cannot because "there's no fat at all" (Gottlieb, 2000, p. 95). The ad, therefore, provides an example of the ideal form and a way to gauge one's own body—pinch an inch. Shandler (1999) presents a section of poem showing an alternate use of electronic texts:

> No one ever taught me how to make myself throw up.
>
> I wish that I was in the movie "Heathers" where my best friend
>
> Would do it for me—
>
> Stick her fingers down my throat . . . (E.G.K.Z., as cited in Shandler, p. 17)

This text is especially interesting in that not only does it provide a specific use of electronic texts, but it also shows a direct link to friendship.

Although not specifically mentioned in any of the references used for this chapter, Internet texts will probably appear in increasing numbers. In the past few years, America has experienced enormous growth in Internet outlets and accessibility options. It would be surprising, therefore, if the Internet was not mentioned in future examinations of body shape discourse. Additionally, the internet provides many unique texts in the form of web sites. Similar to the variety of print texts, the potential exists for numerous other electronic texts to appear.

Living Texts

Living texts refers to those texts involving the living body that are presented in unmediated form. Such texts would include actual conversations as well as those times when conversation is noticeably absent. Also included are the bodies of the individuals involved as well as any and all acts performed individually or jointly. Because I specifically discuss examples of conversation in the next section, I will focus on other examples of living texts in this section.

An interesting text that appears in the body shape discursive genre is silence. As noted by Hornbacher (1998), silence is exceptionally influential when it is parents who are silent. She specifically questions "how could my parents not notice" (Hornbacher, 1998 p. 67) that she was in the midst of bulimic bingeing and purging cycles. Similarly, Browning Smith (1998) wonders why her parents don't realize that she is anorexic and bulimic, and further asks, "Do they think if they don't talk about it that it will just get better or just go away?" (p. 41). The absence of conversation or comment creates a text that acts as a refusal to acknowledge the problem.

Perhaps the most obvious living text is the body of girls, as alluded to in Gottlieb's (2000) pinch an inch discussion in the previous section. Like any other text, the body is created, read, and interpreted in many ways. The body as text intertextually appears in body shape discourse in two ways—through pinching, prodding and poking, and through comparison to other bodies.

Examples of the body as text are prevalent. Reading the body is performed in various ways, including pinching: "My time in front of the mirror, at night, found me pinching my thighs hard" (Hornbacher, 1998 p. 41); "I hate it when I do eat because I think about it all day, pinching the fat on my stomach" (Browning Smith, 1998, p. 27). Gottlieb (2000) presents an even more extreme example of reading the body:

> I could see my collarbone and my ribs, but my stomach still looked fat. Then I checked my butt which was also fat, and my thighs, which looked okay from the side, and made sure my kneecaps still stuck out. That's when I looked below my knees, and this time I actually saw those two separate bones in the bottom of each leg. (pp. 184-185)

In acknowledging the two separate bones in her leg, Gottlieb is referring to a skeletal picture of an anorexic near death. Gottlieb compares her body to that of the anorexic and finds her own body lacking.

Print, electronic, and living texts intertextually combine in various forms within body shape as discursive genre. The foregoing presents an initial deconstruction of the genre and examples of specific texts found within the genre. Future research and pedagogical applications will most likely reveal many other examples. The following section provides specific examples of body shape as discursive genre.

BODY SHAPE AS DISCURSIVE GENRE

Body shape as discursive genre appears in certain repetitive manners: discussion of advice for achieving the ideal and commentary on the shape of the body. Gottlieb (2000) provides an example of the advice form by noting how at lunch she and her friends would discuss her recent method for losing weight, which entailed eating "exactly nineteen flakes of Product 19 cereal, with two ounces of nonfat milk" (p. 90). Hornbacher (1998) references similar discussions when she recalls that she and her friends would sit in the cafeteria "passionately discussing the calories of lettuce, celery, a dinner roll, rice" (p. 102). Browning Smith (1998) explains the purpose of such advice: "Women don't make food choices by desire or taste but by the weight and calories attached to each bite" (p. 147). The body shape discursive genre is a method for sharing this information along with what works and doesn't work. In addition, body shape discourse is a bonding agent for the formation of friendships, such as when Hornbacher (1998) "made a pact with a tall, thin girl who offered to help me lose weight" (p. 106).

Body shape as discursive genre also forms around discourse focused on the shape of the body itself. Because many girls fear an increase in the size of their body (Browning Smith, 1998), their discourse mirrors this fear. For instance, Hornbacher (1998) asserts, "I feel that my butt has magically expanded overnight" (p. 4) or "I look like an elephant" (p. 38). These statements appear to be an alternate form of control—a girl acknowledges her perceived physical inadequacy before it is acknowledged by anyone else.

Acknowledging the perceived inadequacy in their bodies demonstrates Bartky (1988) and Bordo's (1993) panopticon analysis of control and diet. Through discourse, girls acknowledge and take action to correct the perceived lack. Their discursive acknowledgment acts as a point of affinity:

> Women use their obsession with weight and food as a point of connection with one another, a commonality even between strangers. Instead of talking about why we use food and weight control as a means of handling emotional stress, we talk ad nauseum about the fact that we don't like our bodies. (Hornbacher, 1998, p. 283)

Body shape discourse, then, assists in forming and sustaining friendships.

PEDAGOGICAL APPLICATIONS

Body shape discourse can be analyzed as both discursive genre and as intertextually created discourse through students' journal entries. I instruct students to record moments of body shape discourse as it occurs within their friendship talk. I then instruct them to reflect on this discourse and deconstruct it to determine what other texts appear within it. The three categories of text presented in this chapter provide useful guides for students to employ in their analysis. In addition to deconstructing their discourse, students examine it to determine recurring patterns—the various forms (genres) it takes. Combining these findings with examples from our prior class discussions, I ask students to write a personal essay analyzing their own body shape discourse.

Implications and Future Directions

This chapter presented an initial exploration into the phenomenon of how female adolescent friends discuss their bodies with each other—i.e., body shape discourse. By analyzing the journals of adolescent girls recovering from eating disorders, I presented examples of the various texts appearing within body shape discourse as well as the forms the discourse takes. These journals were written by white, middle-class, heterosexual girls, which potentially limits their general applicability. Future research should consider whether body shape discourse is limited to this population or is more pervasive. Additionally, body shape discourse across the life course will probably prove to be a fruitful area of study. Although an adolescent girl is extremely sensitive about her body as it changes during adolescence, the female body experiences numerous other changes throughout the life course. It would be interesting to determine if body shape as discursive genre changes in form and if different texts are present at different stages of life. I am currently studying how college-age women participate in body shape discourse. My initial findings reinforce those reported in this chapter by showing that not only does body shape as discursive genre form in repetitive manners but also that numerous other texts form and inform it.

In addition to providing the theoretical rationale for studying body shape discourse, this chapter presents a specific pedagogical method for analyzing body shape discourse with a class. This method can be used to aid students in understanding not only how body shape discourse operates in their own lives but also how various aspects of society impact both our relationships and our discourse. By studying the intertextual dynamics of their discourse, all students—male and female—can begin to realize how they perpetuate gendered norms. Through this realization, perhaps they can learn how to move beyond these norms and toward greater equality.

Notes

1. By focusing on body shape discourse within women's friendships, I am not stating or implying that such discourse is absent from men's friendships. It is, however, beyond the scope of this chapter. Until very recently, eating disorders were primarily exhibited in women. However, as noted by the Eating Disorder Referral and Information Center (2002), more than 1 million American boys and men are currently struggling with eating disorders. As we see this number increase, we may see a related increase in male body shape discourse. It may, therefore, prove fruitful to examine similar issues within the body of men's friendships.

2. I have specifically used the following sources for examples: Browning Smith (1998); Gottlieb (2000); Hornbacher (1998); Shandler (1999).

13

Aggression in
Interethnic Encounters

Reports by Female and Male Youth
in an Ethnically Diverse School District

Marjorie A. Jaasma

As our world becomes more closely connected through technology, migrations of people, and the globalization of the economy, it becomes increasingly more difficult for us to live our lives without interacting with people who are different from ourselves. This increasing diversity provides interesting and novel experiences but also great challenges. The increasingly diverse elementary and secondary schools of our nation are one context where the challenge of interacting with people from different groups emerges.

This chapter explores one of the ways that sixth-grade students in a multicultural school district deal with troublesome interethnic encounters: aggression, which takes various forms. Little research has focused on the attitudes and experiences of youth that might inform an understanding of interethnic conflict in the schools. This study seeks to identify interethnic encounters that students themselves identify as troublesome and suggest implications for educators.

Theoretical Background

This study draws on several theoretical areas: issues of intergroup relations, discussions of aggression and argumentativeness, and psychological research on aggression in children.

INTERGROUP RELATIONS

Interactions between people of different groups have the potential for creating uncertainty and anxiety, as is explained by Gudykunst's (1995) anxiety/uncertainty management theory. According to Gudykunst, in interactions with someone from a different group, a communicator may experience uncertainty (the inability to predict and explain the other's behaviors) and anxiety (the accompanying feeling of apprehension). In multicultural schools in the United States, students interact with students from different ethnic groups on a daily basis. The uncertainty and anxiety of interacting with people who are different becomes an integral part of the environment. Regulus and Leonaitis (1995) suggest that increasing cultural diversity is a major source of conflict, and "misunderstandings about the different communication and interaction styles as well as values and beliefs systems among racial, ethnic, and social groups can cause conflict that escalates into violence" (p. 41). In fact, fighting and violence are among the biggest problems confronting public schools (Elam, Rose, & Gallup, 1994).

In addition to the uncertainty and anxiety present when students interact with members of different groups, prejudice and discrimination (Aboud, 1988) and intergroup bias (Tajfel, Flament, Billig, & Bundy, 1971) may also be present in multicultural schools. When students in multicultural schools must cope with negative attitudes and intergroup biases as they interact with one another, the results can be misperceptions, exclusion, and conflict (Epstein, 1986; Phinney & Cobb, 1996).

INFANTE'S MODEL OF AGGRESSION

One of the ways students might respond to conflict is with aggression, an understanding of which is found in Infante's (1987) model of aggression. Aggressive behaviors—that is, those that apply force physically and/or symbolically to dominate, damage, defeat, or destroy another—can be either constructive if they facilitate interpersonal communication satisfaction or destructive if they reduce the quality of the relationship.

Infante (1987) identified two forms of constructive aggression: assertiveness and argumentativeness. Assertiveness is "a general tendency to be interpersonally dominant, ascendant, and forceful" (Infante, 1987, p. 164), whereas argumentativeness "predisposes the individual in communication situations to advocate positions on controversial issues and to attack verbally the positions which other people take on these issues" (Infante & Rancer, 1982, p. 72). Researchers have identified a number of benefits of argumentativeness (see Infante and Rancer, 1996, for a review). For example, argumentativeness is constructive, leads to greater relational satisfaction than aggression does, and may prevent violence. In contrast, verbal aggression is destructive, leads to decreased relational satisfaction, and can be a catalyst for violence.

Infante (1987) also identified two destructive forms of aggression: hostility and verbal aggression. Whereas hostility is characterized by negativism, resentment, and suspicion, verbal aggression involves "attacking the self-concepts of others in order to inflict pain, such as humiliation, embarrassment, depression, and other negative feelings about self" (Infante & Rancer, 1996, p. 323).

Because verbal aggression has so many negative consequences, the most serious being that it can be a catalyst for violence, Infante, Trebing, Sheperd, and Seeds (1984) explored explanations for verbal aggression. The argumentative skill deficiency explanation suggests that verbal aggression often stems from a lack of skill in arguing. When individuals are in an argument, they realize they need to defend their own position and attack the position of the other. If they lack skill in refuting the position of the other, they may either attack the opponent's self-concept or perceive that the other person's attack on their position is actually an attack on their own self-concept. In either case, the focus of the attack involves the self-concept rather than the position held.

Argumentativeness and verbal aggression have been found to function differently for females and males. Males appear to be higher in both argumentativeness (Infante, 1982, 1985) and verbal aggression (Nicotera & Rancer, 1994). Females and males also appear to hold different beliefs about arguing. Females perceive arguing as more hostile and dominating than do males (Rancer & Baukus, 1987). Furthermore, when others use verbal aggression, males are more likely to respond with verbal aggression, whereas females are more likely to respond with argumentativeness (Infante, 1989).

Although most studies exploring Infante's (1987) model of aggression have been conducted on interactions between adults, a few have examined the effect of argumentativeness and verbal aggression in parenting. Infante and Rancer (1996) conclude that communication between parents and children is most constructive when it is affirming and low in verbal aggression. They suggest that if parents use affirming communication with low verbal aggression, their children will learn this behavior and, in turn, display this behavior in their own interpersonal conflicts.

PSYCHOLOGICAL RESEARCH ON AGGRESSION IN CHILDREN

Researchers in the field of psychology who conduct research with children view aggression in terms of the destructive end of Infante's (1987) constructive-destructive continuum for aggression. They define aggression as being composed of feelings of anger and the intent to hurt and harm (Crick, Bigbee, & Howes, 1996). This type of aggressive behavior in young people leads to many negative outcomes, from problem behaviors in the early years to violence in adolescence.

Psychological research on aggression in children indicates that males are more aggressive than females (see J. Block, 1983, for a review). Recent research, however, has re-examined the definition of aggression and questioned whether females are indeed less aggressive according to this new definition. Most of the research that identified males as more aggressive focused on overt aggression. More recent studies view overt aggression as containing two types of aggression: physical aggression (e.g., hitting, pushing, or kicking) and verbal aggression (e.g., name calling or threatening to beat up someone). In addition to physical and verbal aggression, this newer research has identified a third type of aggression, called either *relational aggression,* which can be defined as harming through purposeful manipulation and damage of another's peer relationships (Crick & Dodge, 1994) or *indirect aggression,* which involves acts such as telling tales, spreading rumors, persuading others not to play with a person, and so forth (Lagerspetz, Bjorkqvist, & Peltonen, 1988).

Crick and Grotpeter (1995) argue that girls and boys seem to use the type of aggression that will do the most damage to the goals that are respected by the peer group. For girls, who seem to be more interpersonally oriented and more concerned with cooperation and social approval (Crick & Dodge, 1994), the most harm can be inflicted by disrupting a child's friendships or feelings of inclusion in the group. For boys, who appear to be more instrumentally oriented and more concerned about controlling external events and dominating peers (Crick & Dodge, 1994), the most damage can be wrought through physical and verbal aggression. Research conducted in the United States (Crick et al., 1996; Crick & Grotpeter, 1995), in Finland (Lagerspetz et al., 1988), and in Great Britain (Rivers & Smith, 1994) found that overt aggression was used more often by boys and indirect aggression was used more often by girls. Verbal aggression was used equally by girls and boys. In fact, verbal insults were one of the most normative mean (i.e., unkind) behaviors in same-sex interactions for both girls and boys and in girl-boy interactions.

HYPOTHESES AND RESEARCH QUESTIONS

The present study examines the self-reports of troublesome interethnic incidents of sixth-grade students in multicultural schools. Drawing on previous results from psychological research on aggression in children indicating that boys are more physically aggressive than girls, the following hypothesis is proposed:

H1: Male youth will report more physical aggression than female youth in describing troublesome interethnic encounters.

Considering the psychological research on aggression in children that indicates that girls use more indirect aggression than boys, the following hypothesis is put forth:

H2: Female youth will report more instances of indirect aggression than male youth in describing troublesome interethnic encounters.

Finally, on the topic of verbal aggression, the research on Infante's (1987) model of aggression indicates that males are more verbally aggressive than females, but the psychological research on aggression in children shows that girls and boys do not differ in the use of verbal aggression. To explore the topic further, the following research question is posed:

RQ1: Do female and male youth differ in the number of verbal aggression responses reported when describing a troublesome interethnic encounter?

Method

THE SCHOOL SETTING

A pivotal point in youth development comes as youth move from elementary school to secondary school. Not only is there evidence that racial cleavage in friendship patterns increases between the elementary and secondary school years (DuBois & Hirsch, 1990), but other researchers point to adolescence as a pivotal point in development because it is the time in which minority adolescents come to a sense of self as group members, achieving an ethnic identity (Phinney, Ferguson, & Tate, 1997).

Sixth-grade classrooms in California's Central San Joaquin Valley provide an excellent place to conduct research on intergroup relations of multiple ethnic groups. Studying these students provides a look at students prior to the changes that take place in junior high school. In addition, the classrooms are self-contained, which facilitates contact between students. Furthermore, reports indicate that the diversity of this Valley reflects the future diversity of the nation. Projections from the U.S. Census data suggest that minorities will actually be the majority (57%) of children in California schools by 2010 (Braddock, Dawkins, & Wilson, 1995). That diversity has already come to this Valley, which has a mixed rural/urban population, including commuters to the San Francisco Bay Area, European Americans, African Americans, Hispanic residents and migrant workers, and a large number of Southeast Asian refugees, including Cambodians, Lao, and Hmong.

PARTICIPANTS

Participants were 906 sixth graders (ages 11 and 12) in 12 elementary schools in a large, ethnically diverse school district. These 906 students represented the following ethnic backgrounds: 5.3% African American, 2.9% American Indian, 15.4% Asian, 18.0% European American, .7% Filipino, 40.6% Hispanic, 1.2% Pacific Islander, and 13.5% Other. (The remaining 2.4% provided no data on ethnicity.)

QUESTIONNAIRE ADMINISTRATION

During the last month of the school year, participants completed questionnaires that were administered by three graduate students trained in how properly to carry out this task. The questionnaire asked each student to write a response to the following statements:

> Describe the *best* thing that's ever happened to you with a person of another ethnic background.

> Describe the *worst* thing that's ever happened to you with a person of another ethnic background.

On the introductory page of the questionnaire was the heading "Ethnic Background Means" followed by this list of descriptors: American Indian or Alaskan Native, Asian, Black not of Hispanic Origin, Filipino, Hispanic, Pacific Islander, and White not of Hispanic Origin. These were the categories used by the school district to designate ethnic background. The graduate student administering the questionnaire described the term *ethnic background* by reading this list of descriptors with the students prior to their completing the questionnaire. Because the purpose of this study is to understand interethnic experiences from the perspective of the youth without the influence of adult perspectives, students were asked to self-report their identity and to describe interethnic experiences without any adult explanations or predetermined response categories.

DATA ANALYSIS

With 906 students each describing a positive (best) and negative (worst) experience, 1,812 responses were generated. A graduate student in Communication Studies sorted all the positive and negative responses into categories that reflected the same type of occurrence. This process resulted in a total of 36 categories—20 categories for positive experiences and 16 categories for negative experiences.

The 36 categories were reviewed, and the boundaries of each category were identified. These category descriptions were provided to a second graduate student, who (without knowing how the first graduate student sorted the descriptions) sorted the 1,812 responses into the 20 positive and 16 negative categories. Intercoder reliability was determined for these two sorts by computing the percentage of matches of the second coder's categorizations to the first coder's categorizations. The intercoder reliability score for positive was 82% and for negative was 86%.

To assist in analysis of this large number of responses, the QSR NUD•IST (Non-numerical Unstructured Data Indexing Searching and Theorizing) software (Qualitative Solutions and Research Pty Ltd., 1997) was used. All responses were imported into QSR NUD•IST and coded into the 36 categories that were determined by the sort. Reports in the form of plain text documents were made of each category. Each report listed all the responses coded into that category.

The reports were examined to determine the range of responses in each category and to achieve an understanding of the category. The 36 categories were placed on index cards. Through a process of open coding (A. Strauss & Corbin, 1990), the cards (and the categories they represented) were compared and contrasted, and the categories were refined. The refined categories included 8 positive categories and 11 negative categories. Blank responses and those providing no information relevant to positive and negative occurrences were eliminated at this point. The remaining 719 positive responses and 795 negative responses were all checked against the 19 new categories. This process concluded when it was determined that all remaining responses fit into one of the new categories.

This approach resulted in the emergence of three negative categories that described aggressive behavior: Fighting, Verbal Aggression, and Indirect Aggression. In this chapter, these aggression categories are described, and the female and male responses for each category are analyzed.

Results

Of the negative responses in the data set, 57% had to do with aggression (the other 43% of responses were either blank or deemed not applicable to the topic of aggression). Each of the 452 responses in this group—52.2% by females, 47.1% by males (.7% provided no data on sex)—was coded into the three aggression categories: Fighting, Verbal Aggression, and Indirect Aggression. The next section describes the three aggression categories as they emerged from student responses, and the section that follows compares the responses of female and male students.

DESCRIPTION OF THE CATEGORIES

Fighting. The majority of the responses (61.7%) were classified as belonging to the Fighting category. Most of the students did not describe the nature of the fighting but said things like "The worst thing that hapened [sic] to me with a person of another ethnic background was wen [sic] I got on [sic] a fight" (Hispanic male). Although most responses were general responses about getting into fights, 24% of the Fighting responses did specify an act of physical aggression, such as getting beaten up, being jumped, or being hit: "A white boy from another school blind sided me with a sucker punch" (Other male).

Students often gave a cause for the fight, most frequently ethnic differences or slurs, problems while playing, and dislike for each other: "We got into a fight because they hated Asian people" (Asian female). In addition, students often provided the results of fighting. The most frequently cited result of fighting was the loss of friendships, either permanently or for awhile: "The worst thing that's ever happened to me with another ethnic backround [sic] it's [sic] that one day we started fighting and she never wanted to talk with me" (Hispanic female). A few students indicated that they made up after a fight. When they did make up, it was done through talking it out:

> One day I was playing with a person of another ethnic background. I won her friend and she got mad. Then we started to fight, and we both had to stay on the wall. When we were on the wall we began to talk and then we became friends. (Hispanic female)

It is noteworthy that fighting was the only type of aggression for which students mentioned getting punished: "When I got suspended for fighting" (Other male).

Overall, fighting was the most predominant of the three forms of aggression cited by students. Although most described fighting in general terms, about one fourth of them described specific acts of physical aggression. Fighting made an impression on students such that they often gave causes and results of fighting, with interethnic differences being one of the causes.

Verbal Aggression. Verbal aggression was the second most frequently mentioned type of aggression (29.2% of the aggression responses). Verbal aggression occurs when one person directs a verbal attack at another person. Because this study asked students about difficulty in an interethnic encounter, the responses reflected this context. Students most frequently described verbal aggression as racial slurs or name calling:

> Some people from another ethnic [sic] called me a wetback. (Hispanic male)

> Some girls at school who were Mexican always teased me because I was white. They would call me "white trash," and a "white bitch." I finally got really sick of it, and told my parents. (European American female)

Verbal aggression also took the form of one student being made fun of by another, which also reflected cultural differences: "When someone made fun of me because I was black and started calling me a nigger" (African American female). In addition, students described verbal aggression in the context of disagreements and arguments that could lead to physical aggression: "It was when I was playing tether ball and a girl started saying that she was there and then she pushed me and started saying stuff about my family" (American Indian female).

Students rarely gave the causes for verbal aggression; the few who did prefaced their comment by saying it happened during play or because the respondent did not like the other person: "The worst thing that happened to me was when a Mexican girl told me that no whites alowed [sic] and stuff" (European American male).

The results of verbal aggression were strong emotions of hurt and anger, and broken friendships. The upsetting feelings were even recognized by those who were the instigators of verbally aggressive remarks, as this student indicated: "I called somebody a chink or a nigger and they didn't appreciate it and got mad" (Hispanic female). As a result of the verbally aggressive remarks, students most often reported that the two people who argued never spoke again, or the friendship ended: "The worst thing that's ever happened to me with a person from another background is that we got in a bad arguement [sic] and didn't talk to each other again" (Hispanic female). Several students did mention that they were able to repair relationships after verbally aggressive comments had been made: "Worse [sic] my Cambodian friend got mad at me over a boy and because I said something about her I shouldn't have but we worked it out and know [sic] were [sic] friends again" (Other female).

In summary, the Verbal Aggression category was characterized by arguments and disagreements by one person that belittled another person or her or his ethnicity. Ethnic or racial slurs and name calling were ways to inflict pain. Verbally aggressive remarks resulted in strong emotions of hurt and anger, and often the ending of the relationship.

Indirect Aggression. The final aggression category, Indirect Aggression, was mentioned least often (9.1% of the aggression responses). In this study, indirect aggression involved a person damaging another through peer relations and through verbal comments to others, such as spreading rumors, rather than saying something directly to the respondent. The content of what was said to others reflected betrayal, either in terms of revealing secrets, spreading rumors, or telling lies: "They spread rummers [sic] about my rasses [sic]" (Asian female).

The results of indirect aggression were feelings of hurt and the breaking of friendships. As was the case with students who were victims of verbal aggression, students who experienced indirect aggression reported strong feelings, such as anger and embarrassment: "My friend was telling rumors about me and my friend and I hated him so bad and so did my friend" (European American male). The pain caused by indirect aggression appeared to be in the breaking of friendships, both through ostracizing a person from one's group and by breaking the friendship or relationship itself: "My best friend told a lie about me at school and became friends with another group of girls that were the same ethnic background like [*sic*] she is" (Asian female).

Overall, the Indirect Aggression category described harming peer group relationships by going behind a person's back and saying things or spreading rumors about the person. Students felt betrayed, hurt, and angry because indirect aggression led to ostracism and broken friendships.

ANALYSIS OF THE CATEGORIES
FOR FEMALE AND MALE STUDENTS

As previously stated, the Fighting category contained by far the largest percent of the aggression responses: 61.7%. Males reported fighting responses significantly more often than did females, χ^2 (1, $N = 277$) = 4.42, $p = .035$. In the Fighting category, most responses indicated an act of physical aggression, such as getting hit, beaten up, or jumped. Males ($N = 41$) were significantly more likely to report these physically aggressive responses than were females ($N = 24$), χ^2 (1, $N = 65$) = 4.45, $p = .035$.

Verbal Aggression was the category that contained the second-highest number of responses: 29.2%. Females reported this type of response significantly more often than did males, χ^2 (1, $N = 132$) = 12.12, $p < .001$.

Indirect Aggression was the least-mentioned category, appearing in 9.1% of the aggression responses. Females reported indirectly aggressive responses significantly more often than did males, χ^2 (1, $N = 40$) = 8.10, $p = .004$.

Discussion

In this study, sixth-grade students were asked to describe both a positive and a negative interethnic encounter. Of the negative responses, responses reflecting forms of aggression were prevalent (57% of all the negative responses in the study). Analyses of these forms of aggression indicate that differences exist in the forms of aggression reported by female and male youth.

When students think of a negative interethnic encounter, fighting comes to their minds most frequently. (Whereas previous research had referred to overt aggression as physical aggression, when youth were asked to describe their experiences, they chose the term *fighting*, and therefore that category emerged in this study.) Because previous research in the field of psychology on aggression in children indicated that males use more physical aggression than females, hypothesis one proposed that males would report more physical aggression than females. In the current study, males did report fighting significantly more than did females. Because many of the responses did not describe the specific nature of the fighting, it is not possible to determine whether such generally phrased responses referred to physical aggression or to verbal aggression. But for students who did refer specifically to physical aggression, males reported this type of fighting significantly more than did females. In this study, it can be concluded that males reported fighting and acts of physical aggression more than did females, supporting the first hypothesis.

Because previous research found that female youth use indirect aggression more than male youth do, hypothesis two suggested that females would report more instances of indirect aggression. In this study, indirect aggression was reported more by females than by males, supporting hypothesis two. Crick et al. (1996) argue that when researchers consider aggressive behavior, they should include indirect aggression because it involves the same feelings of anger as other types of aggression do. In this study, students did report feelings of anger and hurt for indirect aggression, similar to the feelings expressed for verbal aggression. This study confirms the prevalence and hurtfulness of indirect aggression. This type of aggression had been largely overlooked by researchers, who focused on overt aggression, the type of aggression most seen in male behavior. Research on sex differences has highlighted the importance of also studying female behavior, which has led to the realization that other types of aggression can be just as hurtful as overt aggression. Although indirect aggression is used by females more than by males, it is evident in male responses as well, showing it to be a type of aggression educators must be aware of for both sexes.

The research question asked if verbal aggression is used more by female or male youth to describe a troublesome interethnic encounter. In this study, females reported responses that were classified in the Verbal Aggression category more than did males. This finding must be viewed with caution, however. Many of the students replied that fighting was their most negative experience and did not indicate the specific nature of the fight. These general fighting responses could be referring to verbal attacks or physical attacks. Because some of the responses in the Fighting category could be referring to verbal aggression, it is not possible to definitively conclude that females use verbal aggression more than males, but females did describe negative encounters in ways that were categorized as verbal aggression more than did males.

This study reinforces the importance of considering physical aggression, verbal aggression, and indirect aggression when studying aggressive behavior in youth engaged in interethnic encounters. As previously noted, one possible explanation for the presence of verbal aggression and fighting in youth is provided by Infante et al. (1984) in the argumentative skills deficiency theory, which suggests that verbal aggression may stem from a lack of skill in arguing. If youth are in an argument and lack the skill to defend their position through reasoning, they may attack the self-concept of the other, or they may perceive that the other's reasoned argument is an attack on their own self-concept. One broad area of verbal aggression attack is group membership (Kinney, 1994), a fact that is especially problematic in interethnic encounters, as is evident in the use of racial slurs by students in the current study.

As Infante and Rancer (1996) suggest, verbal aggression can be a catalyst for violence. This, too, was seen in the current study. Students reported that verbally aggressive remarks did lead to acts of physical aggression. This supports the results of Thompson (1996), who found that rumors, gossiping, and name calling (forms of indirect and verbal aggression) were the causes of the majority of fights that led to suspensions at a middle school. Physical aggression appears to be the behavior for which punishment is given, but as the responses of the youth in this study attest, verbal and indirect aggression involve the same strong emotional responses and can be the catalyst for violence. If indirect and verbal aggression are not dealt with, they can escalate to physical aggression.

IMPLICATIONS FOR EDUCATORS

Because aggression was so prevalent in the current study, it is likely that the aggression reported here involves a fairly broad segment of the school population. Educators must implement strategies to prevent all types of aggressive behaviors, not just physical aggression.

A number of studies based on research involving Infante's (1987) model of aggression point to the conclusion that the effects of argumentativeness are constructive and those of verbal aggression are destructive (Infante & Rancer, 1996). Because of the destructiveness of verbal aggression, Infante (1995) calls for training in methods of controlling verbal aggression. Infante's basic premise is that training in arguing (defending and refuting positions on issues) is a way to increase argumentativeness and to decrease verbal aggression.

The ideas of Infante and his colleagues are complemented by efforts to curb aggression in elementary and secondary schools. As aggression and violence are being identified as a major concern in public schools (Elam, Rose, & Gallup, 1994), educators are discussing ways to solve this problem. Their work points to a need for work in three areas: the content of training, the school environment, and the role of teachers.

Training

Programs to curb aggression through training in conflict resolution and peer mediation are becoming widely used in schools. These training programs take two forms: the cadre approach, where a group of peer mediators is trained, and the total student body approach, in which all students are trained in conflict resolution and peer mediation (D. Johnson & Johnson, 1996).

Early positive results of conflict resolution and peer mediation programs were anecdotal in nature (see D. Johnson & Johnson, 1996, for a review). More recent outcome-based studies are offering tentative indications of the successes and benefits of these programs. Dudley, Johnson, and Johnson (1996) trained entire classes of sixth through ninth graders and found that, after being trained, the students showed more positive attitudes toward conflict than they had before they were trained. Moreover, when faced with conflict, the newly trained students chose integrative conflict strategies—that is, ones where they attempted to reach mutually acceptable agreements that maximized mutual benefits. Thompson (1996), using the cadre approach with middle school students, reported reduced incidences of fighting, increased self-esteem scores, enhanced problem-solving skills, and improved school morale. Suspensions decreased by 18.5% the first year and by 50% during the first 2 years. S. K. Bell, Coleman, Anderson, Whelan, and Wilder (2000) similarly found positive results for a cadre approach for sixth through eighth graders. Suspensions for disruptive comments, such as arguments, decreased, and the trained individuals had fewer office referrals than the individual students in a control group who had not received the mediation training. In contrast, Gerber and Terry-Day (1999) found that in a high school cadre-approach program, students rarely used the peer mediators to resolve conflicts, and teachers rarely referred students to the program for conflict resolution. (People had positive attitudes toward the program but did not use it.)

It appears that conflict resolution and peer mediation programs have the following positive results: Students tend to resolve conflicts through integrative means, student attitudes toward conflict and school climate are more positive, psychological health and self-esteem are increased, and discipline problems and suspensions tend to decrease (D. Johnson & Johnson, 1996). If a program is to be successful, however, either all students need to be trained or the program needs to be widely used by students. Rozmus (1997) concludes that students and the entire community must understand and respect the program, and all students must see the program as applying to them.

The contents of the conflict resolution and peer mediation programs are of special interest to communication scholars. These programs teach communication skills—in particular, active listening, perspective taking, clarifying questions, putting feelings into words, and empathy (Angaran & Beckwith,

1999; Rozmus, 1997). These are similar to the skills in argumentation that Infante (1995) proposes for college students. To focus on the issues (argumentativeness),

> [Individuals must] reaffirm the opponent's sense of competence, allow one's opponent to speak without interruption, emphasize attitudes and values shared with the opponent, show an interest in an opponent's views, use a calm delivery, control the pace of the argument, and allow the opponent to save face. (p. 55)

Communication scholars should be encouraged to adapt their training programs to the elementary and secondary levels. The importance of "talk" is reinforced in the current study. When students did mention repairing relationships, it was because they "talked it over." But this type of talk requires the skill development proposed by Infante (1995).

School Environment

Another factor that can contribute to the success of training programs and the lessening of aggression is the school environment. A cooperative context, rather than an individualistic and competitive context, is needed for conflict resolution and peer mediation to succeed (D. Johnson and Johnson, 1996; Wolfe & Spencer, 1996).

Teachers

Teachers can also help teach students how to resolve conflicts without aggression. Just as children are less verbally aggressive when their parents use reasoning with them (Bayer and Cegala, 1992), Dill and Haberman (1995) suggest that teachers who model conflict management behaviors can positively influence their students to use these "gentle responses to aggression" (p. 70). It appears that the total environment of the school, including a cooperative atmosphere, the behavior modeled by teachers, and training programs of conflict resolution and peer mediation, combine to lessen aggression.

Conclusion

This study investigated the types of aggression reported by youth in troublesome interethnic encounters. A limitation of the study is that it is based on the self-reports of pubescent youth on a sensitive topic. Nevertheless, three types of aggression prevalent in troublesome interethnic encounters emerged for both female and male youth: fighting, verbal aggression, and indirect aggression.

In working toward the emotional and physical well-being of youth, educators must address all these types of aggression for both females and males. Research that identifies problematic experiences of both girls and boys provides a wider range of behaviors that require attention than previous work that focused mainly on physical aggression. Educators must consciously work to call attention to verbal and indirect aggression as well as physical aggression and to provide intervention strategies for all types of aggression. Furthermore, educators must be aware of the potential for uncertainty and conflict in interethnic encounters and the possible effects this might have on aggressive behavior. The work on verbal aggression by researchers in the communication field as well as the research on conflict resolution and peer mediation in the schools indicate the importance of communication skills as essential for young people if they are to cope with conflict without resorting to aggression.

14

Commentary

Feminist Classrooms

Richard West

Although we may not often think about it, the communication classroom is rich with student opportunity. Other than in an academic environment, there are limited opportunities for writing to be examined for improvement, or for speaking skills to be assessed for effectiveness. Moreover, students usually are provided frequent opportunities to think openly about their classroom performance and, as Nahavandi (1997), notes, self-reflection can lead to an honest assessment of one's attitudes, values, and behaviors.

The land of educational opportunity, however, is not reserved for students alone. Professors, too, are afforded occasions to make a difference. Consider, for instance, the opportunity teachers have to develop relationships with their students. Without a doubt, the teacher-student relationship is integral to student learning (Frymier & Houser, 2000) and can be a substantial contributor to the educational environment (R. West, 1994).

As most people know, not all teacher-student relationships are valuable or beneficial. Cultivating these relationships, therefore, becomes critical for lasting and positive effects. It seems important, then, for both teachers and students to consider and explore ways to make the teaching and learning process a palatable, enthusiastic, and worthwhile process. Educators need to be prepared to speak, listen, and reflect. They need to be engaged in the process, honoring the diverse voices in the classroom. Finally, the need to look beyond the classroom is paramount. As J. Daly (2002) observed, looking at the "transfer-of-learning" (p. 379) is critical. That is, teachers need to measure the extent to which theory and skills can apply to situations beyond the classroom. In essence, teacher-student relationships are enhanced by these principles, often labeled as feminist.

Looking at teaching from a feminist vantage point is important in several ways. Shrewsbury (1993) eloquently captured the essence of a feminist classroom. She concludes that teachers with a feminist vision have

> a participatory, democratic process in which at least some power is shared. Learners develop independence. The classroom becomes a model of ways for people to work together to accomplish mutual or shared goals, and to help each other reach individual goals. Students are able to take risks in such a classroom. This is an active classroom, where the joy and excitement as well as the hard work of learning provide the kind of positive feedback that magnifies the effort put into learning. . . . Fundamental to a feminist perspective is a commitment to growth, to renewal, to life. (p. 9)

A teacher who adopts feminist principles necessarily honors the individual voice and collective community. Teachers who espouse feminism are concerned with challenging prevailing patriarchal ways of relating. They look uncompromisingly at how the classroom (and its participants) handle real-world issues. As Nelson (2000) personally relates: "Feminism is about fighting, however I can, against stereotypes, sexism, classicism, racism, and any other type of oppression" (p. 27).

Teaching is an applied activity just as learning is one important consequence of that application. Educators, with an armful of theories, skills, and techniques, must be able to inculcate a sense of self-discovery peppered with a sense of self-appraisal and self-respect. With nearly every classroom come doubt, uncertainty, and reflection. It is within this spirit that the feminist educator can help create an atmosphere of tolerance, confidence, and integrity.

Research With a Feminist Purpose

The chapters in Part III of this book reflect an understanding of the teaching-learning process with an infusion of feminist pedagogy. They help us understand that theory and research are not esoteric enterprises. These articles are excellent representations of how the academy has helped us understand the lifestories and life experiences not normally examined by our culture. In this research, we witness thoughtful and compelling ways of showing how feminist principles and practices can illuminate the academic culture. Each chapter also provides us with a glimpse into the culture at large.

The chapters are exemplary in how they intersect the personal with the practical with the theoretical. I wish to address a few noteworthy points about each piece of scholarship and conclude with a call for research directions in how teaching—as applied communication—can be enhanced by adopting a feminist perspective.

Patrice Buzzanell's Chapter 10 attempts to shed light on how a feminist approach can enrich a student's learning experiences. She is quite successful in her goals. Buzzanell frames her thinking using metaphor analysis, a valuable methodological technique employed in instructional communication research (Jorgensen-Earp & Staton, 1993). She challenges feminist educators to unpack the language and life experiences of the powerful in society. Indeed, she is unsettled as she considers that feminist educators have not been consistent in their efforts to understand the journey of unrepresented and marginalized groups in culture. Buzzanell encourages all educators to look at how lifestories can enhance the educational process. Even the mundane stories—so overlooked—can shed light on how individuals are shaped. Through these ordinary tales, Buzzanell tells us that we get a better sense of the "dreams, imagination, and souls of the lifestorytellers." The article's examples, suggestions, and practical advice will assist all educators as they contemplate ways to strengthen the learning opportunities of all students.

Marcy Meyer's Chapter 11 focuses on her individual efforts in conceptualizing, developing, and refining a course pertaining to gender, power, and the workplace. Meyer's work is exceptional in that she aims to shape curricula at a midwestern university in a time characterized by many cultural shifts occurring in and out of the workplace. She is clear in her efforts to consider the communication climate of a classroom and asks students to frame their organizational experiences using a feminist perspective. As a feminist educator, Meyer's personal reflections about her life experiences coupled with her candid personal challenge of trying to reconcile "selling ourselves" and "selling out" help make this research quite meaningful. Her analyses prompt her to conclude that adopting a feminist orientation in the classroom will help students "to take ownership of their education and to participate more fully as citizens in their communities." Who could ask for anything more of students?

In Chapter 12, Terri Russ looks at how body shapes help contribute to the discourse in different interpersonal relationships—namely, women's friendships. Russ asks students to chronicle their feelings about their bodies as these feelings are contextualized in their close relationships with others. This chapter is an excellent example of employing a teaching technique that supports the individual voice and how that voice is influenced by the words and forces in society. Russ embraces an assignment that feminist educators advocate: an exercise that promotes personal and community involvement as well as helps us to understand the hierarchical power relationships everywhere. Educators of all disciplinary stripes should have such activities at their disposal.

Chapter 13, authored by Marjorie Jaasma, examines an overlooked and misunderstood population in instructional communication research: the early adolescent. Employing self-reports, Jaasma's research shows us how sixth graders in an ethnically diverse school district perceive violence in their schools. The research employs a methodological procedure that asks young people to identify their best and worst experiences with a person from an ethnic background. The study provides further evidence of the importance of looking at the influence that a feminist teacher can have on the behavior of her or his students. As Jaasma concludes, educators are in an excellent position to "implement strategies to prevent all types of aggressive behaviors." Jaasma advocates peer mediation programs and classroom environments where conflict is minimized and intervention strategies are embraced. Her research is a feminist call for change.

Calls for a Future Feminist Classroom

The four chapters in Part III present an opportunity for the feminist classroom. Each also prompts a number of calls for future research. I examine four directions below.

First, continuing the excellent scholarship of Buzzanell, Meyer, Russ, and Jaasma, future work might consider how feminist pedagogy and research is carried out across disciplines. It seems particularly fruitful to look at how feminist principles are present in both expected areas of study (e.g., sociology, women's studies, communication, and so forth) and unexpected areas of study (modern languages, criminology, geosciences, and so forth).

Second, looking at feminist pedagogy (or the lack of it) in professional degree programs such as medical sciences, law, nursing, and business would be a valuable area of future work. In particular, it would be quite interesting to examine how our future physicians and nurses practice feminist values in their professional lives.

In addition to looking at feminist teaching across the disciplines, a third course of future scholarship might try to understand the application of feminism out of the classroom. This out-of-class communication (M. K. Nadler & Nadler, 2000) would include faculty-student interactions in advising, office hours, or a number of other important external academic situations. This sort of analysis would help build further evidence of the value of adopting feminist principles beyond classroom walls.

A fourth direction for future research pertains to a type of student that is becoming more and more commonplace in higher education: the returning student. This population, whether women or men, is a unique group that may be the most receptive to a feminist classroom. As they manage adult transitions (e.g., child raising, aging parents, job demands, and so forth), enrolling in classrooms where their lifestories are affirmed, their experiences articulated, and their sense of self recognized, will enhance the learning environment for both teachers and students.

Conclusion

The chapters authored by four feminist scholars illustrate the value of adopting, welcoming, and undertaking feminist thinking in education. We all realize that we have a long way to go before all educators infuse feminism into their class-rooms. In addition, gaining administrative buy-in about the pedagogical value of feminism remains a challenge for us. Yet, we cannot ignore that making the personal relevant, promoting an egalitarian classroom, and becoming a cham-pion of critical and creative thinking will inevitably transform education as we know it. In the feminist academy, all voices should be invited to speak out.

Part IV

Empowering Family

15

Entrepreneurial Mothers' Balance of Work and Family

Discursive Constructions of Time, Mothering, and Identity

Paige P. Edley

Entrepreneurs who work from home encompass a growing number of employed parents. Most of these entrepreneurs start their own businesses to spend more time with their families. For some women, the catalyst is a newborn baby whom they do not want to leave. For others, commuting long distances wastes valuable time that could be spent with children. Still others just want to be their own bosses. What many of these women crave is a way to simultaneously blend work and family responsibilities. They seek to break down the boundaries that separate work/home, public/private, professional/family.

The purpose of this chapter is to explore home-based entrepreneurial mothers' discursive constructions of work-family balance. The term *entrepreneurial mother* simply means women who are mothers who own and operate their own businesses out of their homes. These women make up an invisible population rarely studied in family and organizational communication literature. Up to this point, entrepreneurial mothers have been visible only on the World Wide Web and to each other and their clients.

The Web is full of sites dedicated to entrepreneurial parents—especially entrepreneurial mothers. Many sites are devoted specifically to advising, celebrating, and creating virtual support communities of home-based entrepreneurial mothers. Each site has its own message boards, chat rooms, and e-zines, as well as its own showcase of members, library of advice columns, how-to articles, and home business resources. Such Web sites and e-zines highlight successful work-at-home mothers and offer advice to other entrepreneurial mothers. Their stories of work-family balancing constitute the data for this research project. In their own words, home-based entrepreneurial mothers tell their stories of success, frustration, their negotiation of work-family tensions, and their blurring of boundaries.

The importance of this project lies in understanding the changing lifestyles and work arrangements of employed mothers, their desires to raise families while working in their own home-based businesses, and the community building that they enact online. These women want to be mothers and entrepreneurs simultaneously rather than waiting to have children after establishing their careers or waiting until the children are grown to concentrate on their careers. These women want it all, and they want it all at the same time—no more waiting for the right time for either children or career. These women embrace struggles of negotiating work-family tensions and responsibilities and also may have something to teach employed mothers who do not operate businesses from their homes.

Another key aspect of this research is the data set. These Web-based stories and computer-mediated communications mark not only a viable terrain for work and client interactions, but the online communicative process also enacts a sense of community building and identity construction for these entrepreneurial mothers. Computer-mediated communication has been defined by some scholars as a tool that can enable or constrain workplace communication (see Sproull & Kiesler, 1991), whereas other scholars have focused on online communities, cultures, and individual identities as created and maintained in cyberspace (e.g., Gajjala, 2000, 2002; Hakken, 1999; Markham, 1998; Rheingold, 1993; Turkle, 1995). In his cyberethnography *Cyborgs@cyberspace,* Hakken (1999) suggests that rather than viewing technologies as simply artifacts, "Technologies are best conceived of as networks of interacting human, organizational, and artifactual entities and practices. Particular elements both constitute and are constituted by the networks in which they participate" (p. 23). Similarly Markham (1998) calls for more communication scholarship of online communities and implores that scholars not impose face-to-face communication theories onto the cyber context.

In this research project, I answer Markham's (1998) call "to study online contexts in their own contexts" (p. 210) without imposing my biases and frameworks. I explore the online identities and advice of entrepreneurial mothers' messages on their Web sites, chat rooms, and message boards from a social constructionist perspective without relying on false dichotomies and a priori assumptions. In the following section, I discuss the theoretical grounding that informs this study and pertinent work-family balance literature.

Review of Literature

The project described later in this chapter is grounded in a social constructionist perspective in which meaning—including that of identity, gender, values, relationships, and cultural norms of work and family—is produced and reproduced communicatively through interactions and presentations of self (see Burr, 1995; K. Gergen, 1991; Lannaman, 1995; Leeds-Hurwitz, 1995; Shotter, 1993). In this study, the interactions and self-presentations occur in online contexts such as chat rooms, message boards, and Web sites as entrepreneurial mothers construct meanings of work and family through stories of their experiences. In the next section, I discuss work-family boundaries and movement across them (see S. Clark, 2000; Haraway, 1990, 1991; Hochschild, 1989, 1997; Rakow & Navarro, 1993).

SEPARATION OF PUBLIC AND PRIVATE DOMAINS

Employed mothers often experience both contradictions in their everyday lives and false separations of private and public spheres (Martin, 1992). The creation of the public-private dichotomy constructs false boundaries in human lives (e.g., one never completely exits one realm to enter the other) instead of socially constructed roles and identities situated on a continuum in both realms simultaneously. At work, individuals are located predominantly in the public realm of business and economics but do not shed private roles of parent, significant other, sibling, child, and friend. People do not cast off these private roles and identities, but the traditional organization expects that private matters will not be brought to work. Kanter (1989) discusses this "myth of separate worlds" as "the most prevalent corporate position on work and family" with work and family operating by their own rules (p. 286). Kanter (1977) suggests that organizations require employees to "act as though [they] have no other loyalty, no other life" (p. 15), whereas Martin (1990) argues that family issues in the workplace create "suppressed gender conflict."

Referred to as segmentist (Jorgenson, 2000), segmentation (Nippert-Eng, 1996), the public-private paradigm (Garlick, Dixon, & Allen, 1992), the myth of separate worlds (Kanter, 1989), and public-private divide, or split (for reviews, see S. Clark, 2000; Farley-Lucas, 2000; Martin, 1990, 1994), this mentality of separate spheres and the assumptions that distinguish home and work as separate and gendered realms continue to constrain employed mothers in the 21st century. With flexible work schedules, telecommuting, and home-based businesses, bifurcating the world is complicated greatly. When paid work takes place at home, the boundaries between public and private are blurred.

In the next section, I discuss Hochschild's (1997) depiction of the complexities of work and home as they blend into second and third shifts of unpaid work.

SHIFTS, BORDERS, AND SOCIAL CONTEXTS

Hochschild's (1989, 1997) concepts of the second and third shifts present a complex yet linear picture of family and work. Hochschild (1989) found that working women put in two shifts a day. They did paid work during the day (first shift) and engaged in unpaid labor (second shift) at home. Housework and child care made up the second shift.

In *The Time Bind*, Hochschild (1997) discussed working families engaged in a third shift of relational repair or family maintenance in which working parents "make up" to neglected children and spouses after working long hours and traveling on business. The corporation demands so much time away from home, or requires extra work at home in the home office, that families are not spending enough time together. Hochschild argues that second and third shift work make "home become work and work become home." However, other theorists conceptualize work and home in a less linear, more holistic way.

S. Clark (2000) builds her work-family border theory on Lewin's (1935) concept of "life space—a psychological environment that each individual lives within" (S. Clark, 2000, p. 752). She borrows the notion of separate psychological domains but suggests that different degrees of interaction occur "between the two domains which depends on the strength of the border between them" (p. 752). Clark frames work-family borders in terms of different degrees of permeability, flexibility, and blending, as well as border crossers' ability to influence and identify with the culture and values of the two domains. However, borderlands can be dangerous when domains are extremely different (Anzaldúa, 1987). S. Clark (2000) argues that crossing work-family borders is difficult when the demands and roles of the two domains are so different that they promote a sense of "schizophrenia [in individuals] about their identity and purpose"; however, when domains are similar, "blending can lead to integration and a sense of wholeness" (p. 757). Balance depends on cross-border interaction, identification, and commitment to roles and activities in both domains.

Whereas S. Clark advocates interaction between domains, Jorgenson (1995) suggests abandoning the boundary metaphor altogether. She argues for more theorizing of the complex relationship of work and family by framing boundaries communicatively as social contexts, those "'mutually shared and ratified definitions of situation and . . . the social actions persons take on the basis of those definitions' (Erickson & Schultz, 1977, p. 6)" (p. 204). Jorgenson's research studies professional artists who work at home while raising their children. Like my study of entrepreneurial mothers, Jorgenson's explores the complex and multiple meanings of work and family as interrelated contexts. Home-based artists negotiate tensions of work and family responsibilities in multiple ways at different stages of their children's development. If they create separate workspaces, they also integrate other workspaces elsewhere within or adjacent to family spaces. Furthermore, the women worked around their children's schedules in "the rhythms of work and child care" and alternated their mother-artist roles according to children's schedules (p. 206).

Although it still utilizes the boundary metaphor, Rakow and Navarro's (1993) concept of the parallel shift provides a more accurate depiction of the simultaneity of work-family relationships than Hochschild's linearity does. Rakow and Navarro argue for a parallel view of women who are working parallel shifts rather than the linear, chronologically separate shifts of public and private work. They argue that new technologies have created "remote mothering" in which women manage their home responsibilities while at work. Their participants like being "available to [their] children by having a cellular telephone" (p. 153) in a space between public and private.

Similarly, computer modems and Internet access allow entrepreneurial mothers to bridge the perceived gap between work and home. Home-based entrepreneurs traverse boundaries of work and mothering simultaneously and constantly, at remote client meetings and at home. Technology allows this liminal movement—this betwixt and between bridging of entrepreneurial mothers' worlds. Next, I discuss Haraway's (1990, 1991) concept of the cyborg, an empowered subject that is half-woman and half-machine.

CYBORGS AND ONLINE COMMUNICATION

According to Haraway (1991, 1992), technology allows women to develop cyborg identities—"chimeras, theorized and fabricated hybrids of machine and organism" (1991, p. 150). Cyborgs are empowered constructions of "natural-technical objects of knowledge in which the difference between machine and organism is thoroughly blurred; mind, body, and tool are on very intimate terms" (1991, p. 207). Cyborgs are potent political identities that are "synthesized from fusions of outsider identities" (p. 216) and survive by "seizing the tools to mark the world that marked them as other" (p. 217). Cyborgs have no gender and thus are not marked as *other* by society. A virtual or cyber society is constructed by cyborgs interacting online and engaging in work and identity construction.

Entrepreneurial mothers are represented in the concept of cyborg. Entrepreneurial cyborgs use the "master's tools" (Lorde, 1984)—i.e., the computer—to make their mark on the business world and change women's experiences: "The cyborg is our ontology; it gives us our politics. The cyborg is a condensed image of both imagination and material reality, the two joined centres structuring any possibility of historical transformation" (Haraway, 1991, pp. 149-150). She exists in a postgender world that is no longer structured by artificial, polarized boundaries of public and private. The cyborg "defines a technological polis based partly on a revolution of social relations in the *oikos*, the household" (p. 151). In this world, the cyborg is empowered—she has agency. As Giddens (see Cassell, 1993) argues, agency is in the doing—the capability to do—not in the intention of doing. Cyborgs in cyberspace construct their identities in online interactions with other cyborgs.

Markham (1998) argues that "in text-based spaces, self is constructed through dialogue and . . . on-line or off-line, all of us make sense of our experiences and tell the stories of our lives in self-centered and self-understood ways" (p. 210). She suggests,

> Technologies extend our physical capacities. . . . As an augmentation of the self that is situated outside the body, online communication technology offers a powerful means of control over the text, over the performance of self through the text, and control over Others' capacities as well. (pp. 213-214)

Markham's online ethnography found that participants believe they can control their online self-presentations more than their offline face-to-face interactions: "Control is wielded by the user of the tool, the one writing the text, the one writing the script for the performance—a distinctly non-interactive, non-transactional view of communication" (p. 214). She contends that this control is illusory: "Online, we begin to exist as a persona when others respond to us; being, in this sense, is relational and dialogic"(p. 214). She concludes that the illusion of control is all that is necessary. Even with careful online self-monitoring and constant editing, individuals are still not in control of their own self production. Construction of the self is a dialogic process offline and online.

Thus, as entrepreneurial mothers work out of their homes on their computers—faxing proposals and interacting online—they are co-constructing their identities with their clients, their children, their spouses, and with other entrepreneurial mothers online. They all contribute to the discursive and material construction of the entrepreneurial mother's self. In a more material discussion of entrepreneurs, next, I point out the growing numbers of entrepreneurs who work out of their homes.

WOMEN ENTREPRENEURS

According to a 1998 report by the Small Business Administration's (SBA) Office of Advocacy, women-owned businesses account for more than one third of all businesses in the United States. The SBA (1998) estimates that in

1997 there were 8.5 million women-owned businesses generating $3.1 trillion in revenue. Based on a 1992 U.S. Census report, 36.9 % of the 9 million home-based businesses were owned and operated by women (SBA, 1998). In 2001, the National Foundation for Women Business Owners (NFWBO, 2001) calculated the number of women-owned businesses at 9.1 million with sales totaling $3.6 trillion annually and employee numbers reaching 27.5 million. Communication technology and demand for hand-crafted items have led to an increase in small-scale services and production in home-based businesses (see Jurik, 1998).

The top reasons for working at home are flexibility, the desire to be one's own boss, and wanting to spend time with one's children (Hull, 1994; Jurik, 1998; Rodgers, 1997). In Jurik's (1998) study of self-employed homeworkers, women with small children defined flexibility as having time for child care; whereas women with no children or grown children defined it as "a less stressful work life and more balance among work, leisure, and family" (p. 19). Autonomy and flexibility were important to *all* women.

According to Jurik (1998), "homework" is a "gendered phenomenon" that appeals to women who want to combine paid work with family responsibilities. Beach (1989) found that parents who chose home-based work because of concern for their children were more likely to spend more time during the workday, 9 to 5, with their children than those entrepreneurial parents whose reasons were based on the desire to be their own boss. She also found that entrepreneurial parents with small children tend to use space within the home, such as a kitchen, rather than working in a separate area. She noted that women are more likely to seek flexibility for combining paid work and family care than are men.

Not only do women seek flexibility, they also wish to be their own bosses and thus maintain more control over their schedules. Goffe and Scase (1985) contend that women choose to start their own businesses to escape the *glass ceiling*, an invisible barrier that precludes women from upper-management positions. They also argue that entrepreneurship allows women to challenge patriarchal business systems. Thus, home-based businesses offer women greater chances of advancement, more flexibility, and more satisfying work (Beach, 1989; Edwards & Edwards, 1995).

Women home-based business owners report that they often function as a "virtual corporation" and are just as likely to use communication technology as men home-based business owners (NFWBO, 2000). According to a study conducted by the NFWBO (2000), "Home-based businesses owned by women are providing employment and fostering economic development in their communities, and they owe a lot of their businesses' growth to technology." The study determined that home-based businesses do not just begin in the home as start-up businesses but, in fact, remain home-based businesses.

Furthermore, owners preferred working from home and claimed they would remain home-based indefinitely.

Study of Female Entrepreneurs

I have noted some contradictions in viewing the world as separate private and public spheres. The segmentist view of work-home balance issues is too simplistic to explain the complex lives of work-at-home mothers. The micropractices of everyday life include negotiating time, space, relationships, and identity in responsibilities. Adding in technological dimensions of working from home, researchers find that additional power structures, challenges, and opportunities are woven into balance. Thus, my questions are:

> RQ1: How do home-based entrepreneurial mothers construct their balance of work and family responsibilities?
>
> RQ2: How do they conceptualize time and space for working and for engaging with family, especially children?
>
> RQ3: How do they discursively construct their sense of identity?

METHOD

Participants

Participants consisted of female entrepreneurs who contributed to Web sites that revolved around balancing work-from-home businesses and family concerns. The 78 women whose stories were gathered for this study include those who worked part time and full time in home businesses that ranged from professional services, such as accounting, management consulting, public relations, and freelance writing; to creative arts and crafts positions, such as painting, sculpting, interior decorating, baking and catering, candle and soap making, sewing clothing, and creating home décor projects. Each woman had 1 to 5 children living at home who ranged in age from infants to teenagers. The Web sites and message boards did not list the age, race, or ethnicity of the mothers. Although the Web sites listed names (and these sites exist in the public domain), I masked the women's identities to protect their privacy, especially those who wrote of struggles and conflicts within their work-family balancing.

Procedures

After I registered my name and e-mail address at eight entrepreneur groups' Web sites, I began receiving their e-zines. Once and sometimes twice a week, I automatically received e-zines from each group. The e-zines provide Internet links to articles, message boards, chat rooms, surveys, and contests on their Web sites, as well as links to other Web sites of interest to entrepreneurs and work-at-home parents. I also visited the Web sites of the Bizymoms (www.bizymoms.com); Club Mom (www.clubmom.com); Dot Com Mommies (www.dotcommommies.com); Entrepreneurial Parents (www.en-parent.com/index.htm); Home-Based Working Moms (www.hbwm.com); Mompreneurs (www.ivillage.com/work and www.mompreneursonline.com); Moms Network (www.momsnetwork.com); Moms On-line (www. momsworkingonline.com); NoBoss (www.noboss.com), ParentPreneur Club (www.parentpreneurclub.com); Womenconnect (no longer in business); Work-at-Home Moms (www.wahm.com); Working Divas' Entrepreneur Institute (www.ivillage.com/work/workingdiva/over/articles/0,,187804_ 93345,00.html); the National Foundation for Women Business Owners (www.nfwbo.org), which has since been renamed Center for Women's Business Research; and Mother's Home Business Network (www.homeworkingmom. com).

Over the course of eight months, I printed 554 pages of single-spaced e-zines, Web pages, and message boards. During this time, one Web site and its e-zine ceased operation (www.womenconnect.com). Many of the e-zines to which I subscribed had been in operation less than 18 months. One that focused only on work-at-home mothers was a spin-off of another that had a broader audience of entrepreneurial men and women. I concentrated on Web pages and message boards that showcased entrepreneurs' stories (263 single-spaced pages). Each Web site had a spotlight on success stories that were either transcribed interviews, personal accounts, or stories written by a different author. These data highlight successful entrepreneurial mothers' discourse in their own words.

Data Analytic Techniques

Data were analyzed through discourse analysis. Burr (1995) defines discourse as a "set of meanings, metaphors, representations, images, stories, statements and so on that in some way together produce a particular version of events" (p. 48). In this study, the discourse consisted of the messages and stories written by individual entrepreneurial mothers on Web sites and message boards. The discourse constructed their success stories, challenges and problems, and inspirations for starting their businesses, as well as requests for and offerings of advice for successfully balancing work and family in a home business.

After multiple readings of the data, recurring themes became apparent. These themes consisted of similar ways in which the women's Web sites, biographies, and messages on message boards displayed their sensemaking about working from home and raising a family simultaneously. Using color-coded

Post-it Notes, highlighters, and index cards, I grouped similar descriptions and metaphors of schedules, businesses, children, and ways of balancing, integrating, or separating home-family boundaries. The themes centered on issues such as motivational and community-building discourses. However, the predominant themes were: conceptualizing time, being role models for their children, and constructing professional identities.

RESULTS AND INTERPRETATION

I asked how home-based entrepreneurial mothers (RQ1) constructed their balance of work-family responsibilities, (RQ2) conceptualized time and space for working and engaging with family, and (RQ3) discursively constructed their sense of identity.

I found entrepreneurial mothers' stories to be constructed predominantly around issues of time and identity, both professional and parental. Much of the discourse is autobiographical. The women are relating their own experiences in starting and operating their businesses out of their homes. Many of the messages also involve a type of self-help discourse. These entrepreneurial mothers seek advice and give advice as they enact their own online support group—a virtual community of support. In addition, many "professional" moms, the ones whose business is to offer advice on how to work at home with children, offer help online.

According to Rheingold (1993) and others, the Internet provides instant access to ongoing relationships with a large number of people as well as access to experts on any topic one might need to investigate. These "experts" relate stories of their own experience with the topic, and together the virtual community participants construct what Klein (2001) refers to as a democratic self-help discourse. According to Klein, knowledge sharing is democratic discourse in that it is not strategic but rather allows the information seeker to select whatever parts of the story are relevant to her situation. Furthermore, Klein argues that self-help can be "ideally and realistically an individually empowering and socially proactive force when it exhibits . . . rhetorical characteristics [of] a democratic relationship between the interactants, when it fosters the sharing of knowledge, and when it promotes agency among the interactants" (p. 20). The Web-based interactions of the entrepreneurial mothers exhibited this form of democratic self-help discourse. Women reached out to others in similar situations to help them, offer advice, and, as one young woman suggested, to make a difference in someone else's life, in the same way that starting her business changed her life and brought her family out of poverty. This form of agency and desire to help others succeed is enacted in Web-based messages of democratic self-help.

Entrepreneurial Mothers as Role Models and Agents

Entrepreneurial mothers' discursive constructions of agency were apparent in their stories on the Web. Their Web discourse is filled with messages to their children about their desires to be good role models for them. The messages are filled with strength, power, and implicit feminism. One entrepreneur mentioned that her favorite comment from her 4-year-old daughter was "Girls can be anything . . . except roosters" (Sierra). She also noted, "I believe that seeing me work will provide her this blue-print [sic] for life. It is important that she understands that whatever one dreams, he or she can achieve." Setting a good example is important to these women: "The positive traits that have been handed down to my children through my home career are a work ethic, time management, how to deal with all sorts of people, and knowledge of what it is that mom really does" (Sue). Not only have they instilled pride in their daughters and sons, they also have implicitly instilled self-respect for young girls and respect for women in young boys. They teach their children to be strong and to believe in themselves as well as in their mothers.

Through example, these entrepreneurial mothers build their children's self-esteem and pride in their mothers' accomplishments. In doing so, these role models are making a difference. They are breaking down the patriarchal structures and stereotypes of working mothers as "bad" or "neglectful" mothers who abandon their children. They break down misogynistic attitudes that keep women from realizing their dreams of being their own bosses while simultaneously raising strong, healthy children. In their implicit feminist attitudes and actions, the entrepreneurial mothers enact third-wave feminism (Walker, 1995). Like third wavers, they want it all—children, home, and their own business. Their identity is constructed around multiple roles and responsibilities; they enact agency. One artist described her daughter's pride in her home-based business:

> I recently did a poster for our city-wide anti-violence campaign. My seven year old really loves to point out my posters all over town, saying "Mom you are a famous arteest [sic]!" I think it is important for children to see their parents enjoying what they do—whatever it is. (Abby)

Judy articulated that what she wants most for her son is "for him to see me as a model of self-determination, passion, self-love, and achievement, while still being his loving, considerate mother. That's probably the best gifts [sic] I can give him."

Along with instilling pride in their children, these women are proud of their own accomplishments. Lori, an author and home-based business owner, said,

My greatest home career related achievement was having written my book while I was pregnant with my fourth child, and then having it published while I was caring for an infant and in the throes of moving my family to a new house (in a new state). . . . None of us were half as stressed as the *previous* year when I was working **out**side the home full-time and we were reliant on hired nannies! (emphasis in original)

Maybe becoming a cyborg by merging family and work as she merged her material body with her computer allowed Lori to relieve stress and be more self-reliant. After all, she is a "professional" expert on balancing home-based work and family who is able to give advice to other women. She achieves agency in that she is effecting meaningful change in others' lives and co-constructing entrepreneurial mothers' identity through her support in chat rooms and message boards. As women reach out to each other to build community, they participate in democratic self-help discourse—women reaching out to help others with similar dreams and goals with no race, class, or hierarchical structures (see Klein, 2001).

The entrepreneurial mother sees herself as actively mentoring her children while she serves as role model and active agent in her own and her children's development. She is cyborg, role model, and active agent. Furthermore, her subject positionings are fluid and multiple. She enacts third-wave feminism in her choices of multiple roles and responsibilities. She wants it all, has it all, and makes a difference.

Time—Segmented and Integrated

Entrepreneurial mothers negotiate time and space in a complicated discursive and material dance of shaping and blurring boundaries of public-private and work-family. Their Web discourse of time is constructed in multiple ways. First, they discuss time as choosing to work at home to spend time with their children. Second, time has work-home boundaries or is boundless, with work and child care occurring simultaneously. Third, discourse of time also concerns how to manage one's time.

These three time conceptualizations differ in the ways they involve children. The first concept of time was often constructed as not just being present with children while one is working but also as involving children in one's work. Jane takes an integrated approach to work-family balancing when she describes her children's involvement in her home business. What she enjoys most about working from home is spending time with her family: "I have four children, 13, 8, 5, and 3. They all have 'jobs' with my company, and I often take them with me on business trips." She views work-family as boundaryless and integrated. Thus, Jane's advice is to include family in every step: "Let this be the way your kids earn college money. Teach them everything. . . . My kids are often my inspiration, and I do use their ideas and give them credit for the ideas to my clients."

The tensions between and among work and family must constantly be negotiated with family members and with oneself. The simultaneity and integration of work and family is a complex process that cannot be dichotomized— it is more of a continuum. Entrepreneurial mothers who sometimes segment work and family time fall on one end of the continuum some of the time. Then, when they integrate work and family time, they move along the continuum to the other end. It is rarely an either/or situation but, when it is, it often means discipline and some sort of sacrifice on the part of the entrepreneurial mother. Christina warned mothers working at home with children:

> You have to be disciplined. Yes, you work around your children and include them in as much as possible, but you are still running a business. It's amazing what can be done in 15 minute segments. It may mean getting out of a cozy bed an hour earlier to get work done. . . . It is easy to get relaxed about deadlines and professional standards by saying you want to spend time with your children.

Sonya also advocates working around children's schedules. She includes children in her workspace and manages time by providing toys and activities that are used only while mother is working. She uses nap time or "Mom's Day Out" to make phone calls and run errands. She concludes, "If you work around your kids, rather than expect them to work around you, things run much smoother."

We see both segmentation *and* integration as these entrepreneurial mothers work around their children's schedule rather than imposing a schedule for the children to follow. This perspective on simultaneity ensures family harmony—but what about the mothers' sacrifice? Is she sacrificing sleep or maybe her creativity? She may be sacrificing the ability to network with friends and colleagues. The push and pull of children's needs and the needs of the mother and her business are often at odds. These tensions can only be worked out relationally—by communicating with family members about the mother's needs and desires as well as those of other family members. The entrepreneurial mother cannot be the one who always has to make sacrifices for the family.

Furthermore, some women suggest getting into a work and family rhythm. Deb says, "While at first your focus will be on *separating* your work and family activities, you'll find that *integrating* the two will evolve to create an innovative, work-family, everyday rhythm that is unique to your family alone" (italics in original). Jorgenson (1995) also found a rhythm in the daily activities of home-based artists who were raising small children. Each of the women talked about becoming very disciplined and learning to accomplish a great deal in short amounts of time, such as 15 to 20 minutes.

On the other hand, many of the "professional" work-at-home experts are adamant that family time and work time should be separate. Time for work and for family are bounded and segmented, sometimes by physical separation and other times by outsourcing child care and by letting technology screen telephone calls. The experts suggest hiring baby-sitters or bartering babysitting services with other work-at-home moms. One such professional mom offered this advice in a chat room transcript: "There is definitely a problem with always being at work when you work at home. The best way is to separate is [*sic*] in terms of time. . . . Do your best to stick with them [the time limits you set]" (Linda).

However, in separating her family and work time, the entrepreneurial mother cannot be a cyborg. She can be a border crosser, but her time is segmented, and so is her sense of self. Sometimes she even segments workspace from family space. One entrepreneur said she rented an office because she was always working:

> Sunday mornings I'd get a cup of coffee, glance at the paper and then go into my office. The next thing I knew it was 2:00 in the afternoon. By renting an office I've been able to enjoy my home. (Jan)

By separating time and space for work, these mothers may be perpetuating the patriarchal separation of public and private that many workplaces reproduce in privileging work over family issues (Kanter, 1977; Martin, 1990, 1994).

In addition, on one message board a young mother complained that she and her husband cannot afford extended child care and asked for advice on how to start her business with an infant at home. One entrepreneurial mother advised her to structure her days, trade time with other mothers, make phone calls to clients when her baby naps, and have up-to-date voice mail messages to take calls when children are acting up (Sherry).

Negotiating the tensions of work and family can be frustrating. Because one of the top reasons for starting one's own business is to spend time with children, some work-at-home mothers argue that hiring sitters or putting their children in day care defeats the purpose. Abby, an artist, said that day care is not an option for her: "I really wanted to be here yet I wanted to have an outlet for my creativity. I feel very fortunate to have been able to merge the two." Ann advises, "Remember your priorities. Sometimes I find myself getting upset with the children for interrupting my 'work' and I have to remind myself that the reason I'm working at home is to be with my children!"

Creativity is the key to simultaneous work and child rearing. In her online article, Buske (2000) scoffs at the experts' recommendations to separate work and family: "Over the years I've found such advice taken by itself to be about as effective as telling a tornado to slow down—it just doesn't work that way and it's never that simple" (p. 1).

Buske advocates making time for children when one is not working, being firm that work time is important, preparing children before you begin by "start[ing] with full tummies, things to do, and a promise of time for them when the work is finished" (p. 2).

One might question why a child's entry into workspace would be viewed as an interruption. When we deconstruct this notion of the child, who is both the reason for working at home and an interruption, we see conflicting tensions in identity constructions. Conceptualizing the child as an interruption suggests a sense of role conflict—a tension between the role of mother and that of business owner. With more emphasis on the mother-child relationship rather than on efficiency, perhaps the interruption could be interpreted as taking a break rather than work stoppage. The relational self is one of constant evolution—a self in process. The relational self is constantly being produced and reproduced in the micropractices of everyday life.

Buske (2000) suggests to "always drop what you are doing when the kids really need you" (p. 2). Some creative solutions to soothing a cranky baby during a tight deadline include putting a nap-resistant baby in a baby swing with the vacuum cleaner running nearby. The combination of movement and sound quiets fussy infants. The cyborg mother soothes her child and finishes her project. Her relational and professional selves are in tune as she crosses borders. Her family and work responsibilities are boundaryless. Through technological innovation, she blends and blurs her boundaries.

Thus, attitudes toward blending child care and work are mixed. Some mothers advocated separation and unwittingly perpetuated patriarchal discourses of public and private separation. On the other hand, sometimes they practiced an integrated approach to work-family balance that seemed to disrupt traditional discourses and created a blended, cyborg agent who was independent and self-sufficient. These women's discourses are filled with suggestions of how to be structured, disciplined, and to work around children.

They also agree that being a role model for their children is a very important part of working at home. Next, I discuss the blending of professional and parental identities.

Identity and Perception as Serious Business Owners

Being taken seriously by clients, family, and friends was very important to these entrepreneurial mothers. The professional moms offered advice on how to discourage drop-in neighbors and visits by extended family members during the day. They impressed upon the young entrepreneurial mothers how important it is to never let clients hear crying children in the background of telephone calls. One professional mom counseled others in a chat room about children and use of the telephone. She suggested that, unless the women had clients who were fellow EPs (entrepreneurial parents), they should use phone technologies to avoid sounds of children in the background. Entrepreneurial mothers who work predominantly with other entrepreneurial parents are central participants in both work and family domains (see S. Clark, 2000). The comfort level is high in both domains because their clients understand their lives and experiences. Some mothers learned to laugh when their children answer the phone and make embarrassing announcements, such as telling the caller that Mommy cannot come to the phone because she is on the potty. The discursive blending of professional and maternal identities takes different forms as the women move in and out and among multiple and negotiated discourses of public and private, work and family.

DISCUSSION

This study has important implications for communication and feminist theory, including the enactment of online democratic self-help discourse, the construction of online social support communities, and online enactments of third-wave feminist ideals. The complex lives of home-based entrepreneurial mothers are filled with tensions between work and family responsibilities that seem both normal and exceptional, chaotic and relaxed, and contradictory and complementary. How they blur time and space boundaries between work and family responsibilities is interrelated with their construction of mother/professional identities, their desire to be role models, and their inspiration to instill in their children a sense of self-esteem and pride in their work. They are the cyborgs, active agents who want to make a difference in their children's lives and in business.

This research contributes to communication and feminist theories in several ways. First, the entrepreneurial mothers enacted a form of democratic self-help discourse (see Klein, 2001). The development of this self-help discourse similarly constructed a sense of online community in that the women sought out each other for advice, celebrations, and dialogue regarding common interests, friendship, and identity, just as in any face-to-face network (Gajjala, 2000, 2002; Hakken, 1999; Markham, 1998; Rheingold, 1993). Also, this study follows Hakken's (1999) and Markham's (1998) lead in illustrating the dialogic process of community building and identity construction. Over time, these women advised each other, celebrated accomplishments, and offered emotional support.

The contribution to the work-family balance within organizational and family communication lies in the complexity and constancy of the responsibilities and tensions that pull at employed mothers. There is no right or wrong answer to the question of who should get what they want when they want it. The family as a whole must participate in decision making. Dialogue ensures that *all* voices are raised, heard, and attended to so that consensus takes place.

However, the negotiative process between relational partners is not something that the women discussed explicitly in their Web discourse. Therefore, a suggestion for future research would be to interview entrepreneurial mothers online in their cyber communities of self-help or post questions on Web sites and message boards.

Finally, this study contributes to feminist theory an exemplar of third-wave feminism being enacted online. Although their cyber communities of self-help are not articulated as explicitly feminist in their goals, the entrepreneurial mothers were often in tune with the discourses of third-wave feminism that emphasize women's empowerment, blur boundaries, and celebrate difference. According to Walker (1995), third wavers often "find ourselves seeking to create identities that accommodate ambiguity and our multiple positionalities" (p. xxxiii). This comfort with the ambiguity and contradictions of everyday life, as well as comfort in one's self, is empowering. Third-wave feminists' concentration on individuality rather than collectivity in politics means making one's own choices and feeling good about them. As an example of third-wave philosophy, Lamm (1995) says,

> If there's one thing that feminism has taught me, it's that the revolution is gonna be on my terms. . . . My contradictions can co-exist, cuz they exist inside of me, and I'm not gonna simplify them so that they fit into the linear analytical pattern that I know they're supposed to. (p. 85)

Not only are third-wave feminists independent and self-sufficient, they are selecting and co-constructing their subject positions as strong, independent, nurturing, and loving at the same time. They want it all. These work-at-home moms are neither victims nor ball busters. They do not discuss feminism explicitly. Yet, their discourse is filled with images that can be described as third-wave feminist concepts—self-sufficiency, strength, self-pride, healthy balance between work and family, having it all, and instilling respect for women and the idea that (to restate the words of Sierra's daughter) "girls can be anything" in the next generation. These women do not categorize themselves or anyone else; they embrace the contradictions that family and work place on their busy schedules. Simultaneity works for them. Those who separate work and family achieve their balance in a different way—neither worse nor better than the integrationists—simply different. Furthermore, their comfort with work-family contradictions is also illustrative of S. Clark's (2000) concept of border crossers who identify with and influence both domains and have "greater work-family balance than border-crossers who are not central participants in both domains" (p. 761).

Whether conceived of as border crossers, segmentists, or integrationists, entrepreneurial mothers enact a complex work-family balance. They are constantly negotiating time, space, gender roles, responsibilities, and professional and personal identities based on their own needs, as well as on the needs of their children, spouses, and clients. Negotiation of roles and responsibilities occur with impending work deadlines as well as family emergencies, such as sick children. Some women talked of helpful spouses, whereas others claimed that they "do it all" without aid from others. Negotiating housework and child care is a large part of the work-family balance, whether the approach is separate or integrated.

This blurring of boundaries creates a sense of simultaneity—when work and family are attended to simultaneously and constantly. When and where does the concept of work end and the concept of family begin? For most work-at-home mothers, beginnings and endings are not clear. They blur together in a busy home-working schedule. Entrepreneurial mothers do not take off one hat to don another. They are simultaneously, discursively and physically, temporally and spatially, at home working and working at home. In the case of entrepreneurial mothers, Hochschild's (1997) concepts of second and third shifts and time bind are compelling.

Furthermore, entrepreneurial mothers are indeed cyborgs traversing permeable boundaries between work and home/family both temporally and spatially by utilizing the "master's tools"—the computer, modem, Internet, fax machine, answering machine, and wireless telephone. Entrepreneurial mothers turn Rakow and Navarro's (1993) concept of remote mothering on its head. These women work rather than mother by remote, although some entrepreneurial mothers did engage in remote mothering at the insistence of professional work-at-home mothers, who dish out advice on how to work at home the right way, their way. If they mother by remote control (via telephone to baby-sitters or day care workers), how can they embody the entrepreneurial role model of strength and self-sufficiency for their daughters and sons? In this area, expert advice is problematic. It is the job of responsible parents to be role models for their children. If children always are with baby-sitters, they cannot observe their entrepreneurial mothers in action. They also cannot role-play themselves. They cannot play mail carrier or custodian or even be a board member of Mom's company if they are not present to play those working roles.

The entrepreneurial mother can operate her business through the unbounded realm of cyberspace, where there are no gender, race, physical constraints, or public-private boundaries. Haraway (1991) stipulates that technology subdivides the world "by boundaries differentially permeable to information. . . . The biggest threat to such power is interruption of communication" (p. 164). The computer allows entrepreneurial mothers to develop powerful professional identities without the social biases that constrain them within the politics of gender, race, and class. Technology erases politics of difference just as boundaries blur machine and woman. Potent selves are created in this technological hybrid—the cyborg entrepreneurial mother who lives the liminality of work and home.

And finally, time is not constructed as a commodity but rather as a relational concept that is both bounded and boundless, separate and integrated. Time may be a bounded concept when mothers are unable to relate to the postmodern context of blurring boundaries. Just as K. Gergen's (1991) discussion reveals the lack of a relational language to describe the relational self, we also lack relational language to discuss time. The English language represents life in terms of either/or dichotomies rather than relational, inclusive, and simultaneous, both/and terminology. I argue that entrepreneurial mothers who engage in simultaneous mothering and professional work are comfortable with their blended identities because of their acceptance and acquisition of relational language, a language of simultaneity and, as Jorgenson (1995) suggests, simultaneous social contexts. What is not known is whether entrepreneurial men also experience the same tensions.

In conclusion, these entrepreneurial mothers are all cyborgs. Whether their selves are mediated virtually as they work in cyberspace, shopping and getting paid to surf the Internet, advertising their services and products on the Web, or whether their selves are mediated materially through the products they make and sell over the Internet, they are all cyborgs with shifting subject positions as they negotiate their business identities and their identities as mothers, wives, and daughters. Their shifting subject positions are negotiated virtually, socially, and materially—in a world that is both virtual and real.

16

Playground or Training Ground?

The Function of Talk in African American and European American Mother-Adolescent Daughter Dyads

Barbara A. Penington and Lynn H. Turner

In *The Music Man,* the female residents of River City "Pick-a-Little [and] Talk-a-Little," as they flit about seemingly obsessed with spreading rumor and gossip. Although this song appears harmless in its "humorous" portrayal of women, the message it conveys equates women's talk with superficiality and foolishness. Coates (1996) contends that women's talk is often demeaned as a result of "society's low evaluation of women's cultural practices" (p. 1). The trivialization of women's talk flies in the face of feminist scholarship, which, in a quest for social change, seeks to focus on everyday processes (K. Allen & Walker, 1992). Systematic study of women's talk is not a wasted effort, but rather a necessity for increasing our understanding of how healthy, satisfying relationships are created, maintained, and improved.

Mothers and daughters provide an important context for examining women's talk. The mother-daughter bond has been described as central to the lives of women (Pipher, 1994). Mothers or mother figures often serve as their daughters' first teachers, counselors, and "cheerleaders," providing vital sources of material and emotional support (Diggs, 1999; Lacković-Grgin, Deković, & Opăić, 1994). During the daughter's adolescence, the mother's role becomes even more salient as the daughter begins to develop her own identity. Talk is the mechanism through which mothers and daughters exchange information, advice, and encouragement, and the primary way that mothers and daughters demonstrate mutual care and support. Talk in the mother-adolescent daughter

275

relationship is also important in that it serves to prepare adolescents for interactions outside the family. Trad (1995), for example, suggests that a mother may be a crucial model in showing her daughter how to act in other types of close, personal relationships.

Recognizing the value of studying mother-adolescent daughter talk while ignoring the diversity of mother-adolescent daughter experiences is problematic. Ethnic groups, for example, differ in their perceptions of what constitute strengths, weaknesses, difficult behavior, and acceptable responses to such behavior (McGoldrick & Giordano, 1996a). Yet, researchers have been slow to include culturally diverse populations in their studies. In family communication scholarship, this neglect has been especially glaring. Socha, Sanchez-Hucles, Bromley, and Kelly (1995), for example, found that of 231 articles dealing with family communication, only 5 addressed African American families. Thus, in this chapter we incorporate the experiences of both African Americans and European Americans as we examine the importance and function of talk in mother-adolescent daughter relationships.

Unfortunately, to this point, there is no extensive research literature focusing on talk between mothers and adolescent daughters. Because mothers and daughters are both female, we might expect their talk to exhibit characteristics similar to those found in women's friendships (Coates, 1996). We know that mothers and adolescent daughters, for example, tend to engage in more mutual self-disclosure than any other parent-adolescent family dyad (Noller & Bagi, 1985; Noller & Callan, 1991; Youniss & Smollar, 1985), which supports the notion that women connect through talk.

Because of the kin relationship, age disparity, and power differential, however, talk could also be expected to perform different functions for mothers and adolescent daughters than it performs for female friends. In a study of women's friendships (Coates, 1996), a participant asserted: "Female friendship is unique in offering us an experience of a relationship of equals: 'it's the only [relationship] where you're not playing out parent-and-child'" (p. 43). But if you are a mother or an adolescent daughter, you *are* playing out parent-and-child, at least most of the time.

Talk in the mother-adolescent daughter relationship seems to perform a variety of functions. First, talk is instrumental and communicates important information. Talk is also instructive. Scholars (Fischer, 1986; Haygood, 1991; Ordemann, 1994) have often equated the role of mother with that of a teacher. Even when a daughter moves out of adolescence into adulthood, she may still ask her mother for advice or instruction regarding career choices or child rearing (Fischer, 1983). Talk clearly performs a supportive function. Randall (1995) found that mothers sometimes took the role of "therapist" to their daughters' "client." Talk in this role pairing served a therapeutic function as mothers focused on their daughters' feelings.

Talk within the mother-adolescent relationship enables interactants to learn more about themselves and build self-esteem. Diggs (1999) found that mothers were one of the most important sources of positive feelings for adolescents, regardless of gender. In turn, daughters' comments to mothers are also important in the area of self-esteem. Tolman (1995) found that mothers' feelings of competence and self-worth were often related to their daughters' feedback.

Finally, the dialectic of autonomy and connection is negotiated through talk. This may be an especially important function of talk in the mother-adolescent daughter relationship as daughters attempt to individuate and develop unique identities apart from their parents. Krappman, Oswald, Schuster, and Youniss (1998) studied interaction patterns in mothers and their preadolescent daughters. They found that mother-daughter dyads negotiated connection and autonomy using a variety of strategies as they played a "plan something together" game.

Following McGoldrick, Giordano, and Pearce's (1996) suggestion that "ethnicity patterns our thinking, feeling, and behavior in subtle ways that we are not even aware of" (p. ix), we assume that race affects how African American and European American mothers and adolescent daughters experience and enact their relationships.[1] Daniel and Daniel (1999), for example, contend that African American parents often interact with their children using an imperative mode in part to protect them from a cruel and dangerous world. Tone of voice, physical force, as well as "the look" are nonverbal strategies to keep black children in line. Although European Americans might view these strategies as harsh, the authors contend that they are deemed necessary by black parents, who are adamant about their children's survival and success.

In an interview study that used African American mothers and adolescent daughters as participants, Kizielewicz (1988) found African American daughters were less verbal with their mothers and less likely to show displeasure or anger than European American daughters. Daniel and Daniel (1999) explain that African American parents are often strict, albeit caring, disciplinarians because of the physical and mental challenges they feel their children will encounter due to continued societal racism. Harshness is intended to catch children's immediate attention. There is little tolerance for the child's talking back or attempting to negotiate an alternative action.

Nwoga (1997) examined aspects of African American mother-adolescent daughter talk regarding sexuality. Nwoga found that mothers often shared stories with daughters as a means of teaching them important lessons about sex. Stories were conveyed through use of "double-edged messages, proverbs, metaphors, and wise sayings [which] showed the oral history tradition of the group" (p. ix). Cauce et al. (1996) focused on interactions between African American mothers and their adolescent daughters. An important finding in this study was that a key developmental task for African American daughters was to learn how to live among white people while developing their black identity.

Given the gaps in our understanding of women's talk, especially as it is enacted in the mother-adolescent daughter relationship, and most especially how it might differ by race or ethnicity, the following research questions were examined in this study:

RQ1: What is the nature of talk in the mother-adolescent daughter relationship?

RQ2: Does it differ by race?

Methodology

DESIGN

The current study was part of a larger one designed to examine the mother-adolescent daughter relationship. We employed a feminist approach grounded in the importance of *both* mothers and their adolescent daughters being allowed to voice their own unique perspectives. A key assumption made a priori was that participants would express some commonalities regarding talk in their relationships. Yet, due to such differences as race and age, they would not experience their relationships in the same way and would most likely have different stories to tell. Depth interviews and observations were employed to capture the universality and diversity of how participants experienced talk in their relationships. Data were collected by the first author, who is European American, and an African American research partner to provide insights the first author may have missed (Kochman, 1972). This partnership was geared toward obtaining a comprehensive portrayal of the mother-daughter experience in both cultures.

PARTICIPANTS

Consistent with qualitative methodology, the study used selective rather than random sampling. Ten mother-adolescent daughter pairs—five African American and five European American—participated in the study. Mother-daughter dyads came from both rural and urban midwestern communities within an hour radius of each other. Participants were all designated as middle class. Daughters' ages ranged from 13 to 17 years (mean = 14.8) and they were in the 7th through 12th grades. All of the daughters had an adult male or father-figure in the home. The mothers ranged from 34 to 48 years of age (mean = 41.8); all had full-time employment. Their jobs were in the helping professions, the most popular being social work, followed by teaching/teacher's aide. Three of the African American mothers had bachelor's degrees, and one was a few weeks away from being awarded her master's degree. Two of the African American mothers were high school graduates. Two European American mothers had master's degrees, and three listed high school as their highest level of education.

PROCEDURES

Depth Interviews

Depth interviewing is designed to allow participants to reconstruct their experiences and explore meaning (Seidman, 1991). The interviews in this study were semistructured in that they followed an interview protocol, or outline of questions to be covered, but not in such a way as to interrupt or divert the participant's reconstruction of her own experience. Mothers and daughters were interviewed separately to encourage them to give an honest accounting of their experiences, uninfluenced by the other's presence. Interviews were audiotaped and lasted between 25 minutes and 120 minutes. Immediately after the interviews, audiotapes were transcribed. Daughters' interview transcripts averaged 13 pages, and mothers' averaged 18.5 pages.

Two to six weeks following the initial information-gathering session, the researcher returned to participants' homes to do a follow-up interview. The follow-up interviews represented an opportunity to do member checks, a process whereby participants are asked if the researcher has accurately captured their experience (Lincoln & Guba, 1985).

Joint Interaction Activity

The joint interaction activity involved the mother and daughter discussing the following three topics for approximately 5 minutes per topic:

1. If money were no object, what would the two of you plan for the perfect family vacation—where would you go, in what type of place would you stay, how long would you stay, what would you do, etc.? Come up with as many details as you can.

2. Mothers and their daughters can be both similar to each other as well as very different. In what ways are the two of you similar? In what ways are the two of you different?

3. If you two were asked to help write a book on mothers and teenage daughters, and the editor asked you for the three BEST pieces of advice you could give to help other moms and daughters have a close relationship, what would you say?

The interactions were audiotaped and later transcribed, noting length of pauses, interruptions, and simultaneous speech.

Data Analysis

The data were coded for themes and patterns using the constant comparative method (Glaser & Strauss, 1967; Maykut & Morehouse, 1994), which involves "reconstructing the data into a 'recognizable reality' for the people [who] have participated in the study" (Maykut & Morehouse, 1994, p. 122). Using "talk" as the primary organizing concept, data were examined to illustrate the characteristics and functions of talk in the mother-adolescent daughter dyad and the ways that race affected them.

Results and Discussion

The results are presented with supporting excerpts from interviews or interactions. Whenever a difference based on race was noted, it is included in the discussion of the specific finding. For clarity, participants' names are followed with an "AA" designation for "African American" and "EA" for "European American." In addition, daughters' ages are included.

We found the nature of mother-adolescent daughter talk to be quite complex, and participants indicated that talk was central to their relationships regardless of race. For the purposes of this chapter, the data will be explicated through a discussion of (a) when and where mother-adolescent daughter talk occurs and (b) the primary functions of talk in the relationship.

THE "WHEN AND WHERE" OF TALK

Mothers and daughters acknowledged that it was a problem finding time to talk. Daughters were busy with many activities. Most mothers in this study worked full time, and some were also students or involved in community activities. Despite the time constraints they experienced, most of the mothers shared their need to touch base with their daughters at least once a day to hear how school had gone or ask if their daughters had any concerns they wanted to discuss. Daughters agreed that it was important to find time for talk with their mothers.

For most mothers and daughters, "morning talk" was instrumental, short questions and responses centered on schedules and plans for the day. Dinner was no longer a time for quality conversation because many participants had activities scheduled around the dinner hour. This was especially true of older daughters, who were involved in sports, music, and drama activities, and mothers who worked later hours or went to school themselves.

When and where did substantial interaction between mothers and daughters occur? Many participants reported that the bedroom was the location for their best conversations. African American participants specifically noted that the mother's bed was one of their favorite places to talk. Keesha (AA-15), for example, explained:

> She [mother] may be laying in bed supposedly going to sleep and [she] sits there reading, and she'll ask me, do I want to come in there with her? And I'll go in there, and we'll just be laying there, just reading our books, and we'll talk about our books and stuff, just talking, just relaxing together.

Darcy (AA) also described the mother's bed as a great place to talk:

> When you're sharing heart issues, they're private, they're personal, and you're most comfortable where you're private at—your room where you can lay out and be yourself.

European American participants never mentioned the mother's bed as a favorite location for good conversations, but several noted that they found their daughters' bedrooms a good place to talk.

Although the bedroom was an important location for mother-adolescent daughter conversation, the favorite location for talk regardless of race was the car. Jory (EA-17) participated in a club volleyball league that required a long drive to and from the practice site two times a week. Instead of dreading the drive, both Jory and her mother actually looked forward to it. As Jory explained,

> I'm so busy with school and everything that really, we don't get a chance to talk except in the car. I mean, we talk, but we really don't get *into* things until Mondays and Wednesdays when she comes with me in the car.

Although not mentioned by our respondents, Barker and Watson (2000) suggest that another reason that the car might be perceived as especially conducive to parent-adolescent talk is because when parents drive, they do not have direct eye contact with the adolescent, who may thus feel more comfortable engaging in personal conversation.

FUNCTIONS OF MOTHER-ADOLESCENT DAUGHTER TALK

Talk as Recreation

When queried on what they enjoyed doing most together, the majority of participants indicated "talking," although African American participants' comments were more likely to identify talking as a separate activity, whereas European Americans tended to link talking to other activities such as shopping, doing artwork, or walking. Keesha (AA-15) shared that on weekends when there is nothing to do, "We just sit around, mostly in [Mom's] room and talk about anything." Veronica (AA), Keesha's mother, said she loved "just listening to Keesha talk about anything and everything." Katharine (AA) stated that she and Tanya (AA-13) "laugh and talk; she comes in my bed . . . and we lay there and talk. She tells me what's going on with the other girls." Darlene (EA) said that talking to her daughter, Leslie (EA-16), was "fun" because she had a great sense of humor and "it just feels relaxed."

Humor and joking were clearly important facets of mother-daughter recreational talk for both races. During the joint interaction activity, mothers and daughters frequently laughed and teased, as the following excerpt indicates:

Hope (EA 14):	We both like drama, comedies, then I like—
Bev (EA):	You like plays.
Hope:	Yeah. I like Broadway too, 'cause . . .
Bev:	I'm writing . . . plays . . . coma and dromedy.
Hope:	*Dromedy?* [much laughter]
Bev:	[laughing] Okay, drama, comma, comedy, comma, theater.
Hope:	[still laughing] I'll write it down.

Katharine (AA) told us about an "inside joke" that she and her daughter, Tanya (AA-13), shared. Tanya often calls her mother by a funny nickname. When Tanya uses the nickname, Katharine laughs and asserts, "I'm not answering to that!" "We joke about it," Katharine shared, "but we do it all the time."

Talk as Managing Autonomy/Connection

Baxter (1990) asserts that the dialectical tension between needs for autonomy and connection is central to all close relationships. Pipher (1994) makes the following observation:

> Daughters provoke arguments as a way of connecting and distancing at the same time. . . . They trust their mothers to put up with their anger and to stand by them when they are unreasonable. This is an enormous compliment, but one that's hard for most mothers to accept because it's couched in such hostile terms. (p. 286)

In addition to provoking arguments, daughters in this study used other strategies to demonstrate their autonomy. They asked questions of their mothers and tried to regulate the interactions between them (Hakim-Larson & Hobart, 1987). For instance, in the interaction, Jory (EA-17) and her mother,

Jessica, discuss the idea that parents sometimes push their children into being what they don't want to be. Jory has said all that she wants to say on the subject, but her mother wants to continue the conversation. Jory asserts her autonomy by asking a question which also serves to regulate their interaction:

Jory:	Don't make your child into something that they're not.
Jessica:	Or that you wish you had been?
Jory:	Um hmm.
Jessica:	Makes sense . . . so . . .
Jory:	Are we done?
Jessica:	That's it, we're finished.

When Mary (AA) and her daughter Camille (AA-14) discuss the three pieces of advice they would give to other mothers and adolescent daughters, Mary tries to dismiss one of Camille's ideas. Camille asserts her autonomy as follows:

Mary:	I think sharing interests and hobbies [is good advice] . . . 'cause we do a lot of things together, like going to basketball games, watching volleyball, the sorority . . . you think?
Camille:	You don't have to.
Mary:	You used to come and watch me play volleyball when you were younger.
Camille:	I *said* you don't have to share things. You can be separate. You can do your own thing.
Mary:	[laughs] No . . . now this is advice we want to give somebody, so if you're saying that sharing is *not* one of those things . . . then we shouldn't put it down.
Camille:	But you can be separate too. Put that down.

Interestingly, Camille's comments not only assert her autonomy but summarize a basic tenet of dialectical thinking: Needs for both connection and autonomy must be met to have a satisfying relationship (Baxter, 1988, 1990).

Many participants emphasized the connection needs in their relationships by suggesting that the key to a good relationship was spending time together. Scheduling this was often difficult, however, due to time constraints on both mothers and daughters. Sandy (EA) discussed how she and her daughter Kate (EA-16) used to have long talks when Kate was in middle school. Now that Kate is involved in high school activities and has a steady boyfriend, they don't talk much, and it is Sandy's perception that they are less close than they used to be. She explains:

We had a period this winter where we were the least close we've ever been, and it was really difficult for both of us, and I finally went in to her and just said, "You know, I don't know what's going on, but I really miss you" . . . and she said she'd missed me too, and she just had been busy in school and with her boyfriend and this and that and the other.

This lack of time to talk produced a perceived distance in the relationship, which prompted Sandy to go to Kate to share her feelings in the hope that they could find time to reconnect. Kate's interview supported her mother's assertion that school activities had been interfering with their former closeness: "My mom does get really, really, really, really crabby when I'm very busy, because she doesn't see me." As mothers and daughters negotiated their sense of closeness and distance, talk was both instrumental in managing this dialectic and indicative of how the pair assessed the tension.

Talk as a Training Ground

Participants' interviews and interactions supported the notion that mothers acted as role models and teachers. As Darcy (AA), a probation officer, shared, "We're the record that's being played and they [adolescent daughters] watch or listen to the record, and then they act the record out." Janna (EA), a teacher's aide, is aware of herself as a role model, especially for how to talk. She feels guilty when she swears in front of her daughter, Kari (EA-14). "I tend to swear, and I hate it!" she commented. "I have said [to Kari], 'This is one of my bad habits. Please don't pick it up!'" Janna expresses her concern that Kari will mimic inappropriate speech patterns she observes in her mother.

Although participants' comments suggested many lessons daughters learned, this chapter will discuss only the five that were described most frequently by participants. These include: building self-confidence, becoming other-centered, "doing" conflict, communicating survival skills, and establishing roles. They all provide insights regarding how daughters develop communication competence through interaction with their mothers.

Building Self-Confidence. First, mother-daughter talk was used as a context to teach daughters that they were important and worthy of being heard. Although helping their daughters develop a strong sense of self was important to all mothers in this study, it seemed especially crucial to African American mothers. As our research assistant shared, African American parents know their children have to have "10 times the self-esteem of white kids to make it in life." Self-esteem building was often accomplished through African American mothers' use of proverbs or sayings. Veronica (AA) shared, for example, that she often told her daughter to "reach for the stars" and "be all that you can be." The joint interaction activity also provided insights into how mothers encouraged their daughters to voice their own opinions during decision making. In the interaction between Rhonda (AA) and her daughter Deleasa (AA-14), we see Rhonda asking open-ended questions in an attempt to have her daughter elaborate on her own opinions or feelings:

Rhonda: Okay, in what ways are we similar?
Deleasa: We look alike.
Rhonda: Okay, appearance. All right. [3.0]² I have to agree with that. Um, what other ways?
Deleasa: Like our face.
Rhonda: Facial features?
Deleasa: Facial features. [2.0]
Rhonda: What else?
Deleasa: By our sizes, by the way we're built up.
Rhonda: Body structure. Okay.

Rhonda facilitated her daughter's explanations to promote Deleasa's confidence in speaking for herself. Most African American mothers hoped that the self-confidence developed in adolescence would carry through to other personal and professional interactions, enabling them to one day become successful, self-sufficient women. As Katharine (AA) shared about her daughter Tanya (AA-13), "I let her know that she can do what she sets out to do; don't be a quitter and be—you know—a winner!"

Becoming Other-Centered. A second lesson mothers emphasized through interactions with daughters was the importance of becoming other-centered. As Wood (2001) has suggested, women value relationships and use talk to help to connect with as well as to understand their conversational partners. These objectives require women to develop an other-centered approach. In the following excerpt, we see how the mother, Darlene (EA), guides her daughter, Leslie (EA-17), into considering how others in her family would respond to the question of where to spend the perfect family vacation:

Leslie: [Reads question]. If money were no object, what would the two of you plan for the perfect family vacation?
Darlene: Let's try something. I think of a place that you would say first, and you—
Leslie: Okay, I want to think of one myself.
Darlene: Are you thinking of something I would say?
Leslie: I don't know; you'd probably go anywhere. [laughter] I don't know; you've always wanted to go to Greece, that was my first instinct.
Darlene: No, that's perfect. I don't know if the whole family would want to go.

Leslie: Oh . . . are you asking what I'd want to do with the family?
Darlene: Yeah. The two of us would plan the perfect family vacation. Would
            you want to go to Greece? Would that be all right?

When Darlene asks "Are you thinking of something I would say?" she wants to be sure that Leslie is engaging in the "role reversal" she has suggested and putting herself in her mother's place. Not only does this "connect" the women, but it serves to construct Darlene's role as a teacher as she models empathy or taking another's perspective. As they continue discussing the perfect vacation, Darlene is the one who brings in the father's preferences as well as what must be considered in regard to Jack, the younger brother who has a learning disorder:

Darlene: Well, maybe there's something better. Hawaii?
Leslie: The mountains, the beach; I don't know; I've never been there.
Darlene: I think Dad would like it; he's talked about it before that it would be
            a good place to go. Jack, well I don't know if he'd be into a long, long
            ride. . . . There are some places he would go. Jack does make it hard.
Leslie: Yeah.
Darlene: Jack is hard. So, we probably need to come up with something, settle
            on something to decide where we would stay, what we do.

We see how Darlene works the rest of the family into the deliberations, especially the younger brother, Jack. Leslie hasn't said much, but her first comment was clearly focused on herself; she says "*I* don't know; *I've* never been there." Leslie, however, eventually picks up on the other-centered style that her mother is modeling. As the interaction continues, they discuss going to the Grand Tetons instead of Hawaii:

Leslie: Would Jack like it there better than Hawaii? I think we should stick
            with that.
Darlene: Let's say Hawaii because I know your father would like it and Jack
            would like it once he's down there.
Leslie: Yes, he would.

Here we see that following her mother's example, Leslie now brings Jack into the deliberations and attempts to put herself in her brother's place.

"Doing" Conflict. A third lesson daughters learned from interactions with mothers was how to engage in conflict. There were many sublessons that were emphasized. Mothers implicitly conveyed to daughters, for example, that the

person in authority usually wins. Mothers related stories regarding how they sometimes asserted their power during conflict by making unilateral decisions that their daughters were ultimately not allowed to question. Janna (EA) explained what happened as she and Kari (EA-14) argued about a dance:

> She told me if I chaperoned, she was not going, and then when I found out that they didn't have anybody and couldn't have the dance, I said, "Too bad!" Plus, someone at school, another mother, said, "You're going to let your daughter run the situation? And I thought . . . it is her dance, but at the same time, I'm the mom, I set the rules.

Sometimes, however, mothers inadvertently suggested strategies for circumventing authorities during conflict. Darcy (AA) related that she was often a pushover with her daughter, Chandra (AA-16), and gave the following example:

> I had promised Chandra she could get her nails done, and this was like 2 weeks ago. And then the car problem came up . . . so money was really tight, and I'm like, "Chandra, you know, I'm not going to get the nails done this time even though I did get paid." Right away, "Oh, you promised me," and you know . . . the pouts and the long faces and it's not fair and on and on and on . . . and everybody's upset, everybody's upset. Eventually, I'm like, "All right. Let's go get our nails done. Just get your face up."

Here, Darcy may be teaching her daughter that persistence coupled with pouting and whining can get you what you want.

Mothers also trained daughters to resolve conflict amiably and, again, to be other-centered. Rhonda (AA) for example, said when she has an argument with daughter, Deleasa (AA-14),

> I explain to her why I yelled at her and what my fears are, and if she don't pick these things up, what's gonna happen to her. And then I ask her, what is your input here? What do you feel? Where do you think you're gonna go from here?

Darcy (AA) stated, "I have to say I'm sorry. . . . A lot of times that is hard for a parent to do—to say, I was really wrong, and maybe I shouldn't have done it like that." To teach Chandra (AA-16) to manage conflict in a more positive fashion, Darcy knows that she must be the model.

Communicating Survival Skills. As in Nwoga's (1997) research, stories were used by mothers to convey important lessons; this occurred in both racial groups. The nature of the stories differed somewhat, however. Only the African American mothers seemed to be concerned with teaching their daughters survival skills. The following story shared by Katherine (AA) demonstrates how bluntness, sometimes even fear, served to aid an African American parent in ensuring that her child followed the directions that were given. The purpose of the following story was to teach Tanya (AA-13) to never ride in cars with strangers:

> [Tanya] jumped in the car to ride down the street to her cousin's house. And her dad just blew his top because you don't just jump in a car with nobody! To ride nowhere! And we used the example of the girl, here in the city, who was just riding in a car and two shots were fired and someone was killed. The next day the guys came back to get her! They shot her and killed her because she saw who had shot the person the day before. It was a perfect example of why we say you don't get in anybody's car. We use a lot of things like that as examples.

Daniel and Daniel (1999) suggest that sarcasm can also be used in survival-type messages that are communicated by African American parents to their children. Rhonda (AA) used this strategy in reprimanding her daughter for complaining. She shared,

> Once my daughter Deleasa got mad at me and said, "I wish I could just die!" I said, "You wanna die?" [She said], "I just wish I could die!" I'll never forget that. You see, I've done a lot of tough love with these kids. I said, "Wait a minute. You say you wanna die?" I said, "I ain't got to kill you; there're enough crazy people out there to kill you. Open the door; just go right out there so they can kill you." She looked at me at 11:00 at night, like, "Oh, I ain't going out there!" "But you said you wanted to die! If you wanna die, you go out there and someone will surely kill you, child!"

In this excerpt, Rhonda is teaching her daughter (a) to choose her words carefully and (b) the world can be a dangerous place. Daniel and Daniel (1999) argue that this type of harshness is designed to catch the child's "immediate attention" (p. 31). This tendency toward bluntness and sarcasm with the expectation of immediate response was not shown by the European American participants. And European American mothers did not speak about the survival skills they wished to teach their daughters.

Establishing Roles. A final lesson mentioned by the mothers and daughters focused on teaching role behavior. Family roles are defined by L. Turner and West (2002) as "socially constructed patterns of behavior and sets of expectations that provide us a position in our families" (p. 112). Talk is the vehicle through which these roles are created, sustained, and modified. Participants in this study suggested that they played multiple roles in their relationships. One of these role pairings was that of teacher-student, where mothers taught daughters not only how to make their beds and clean bathrooms but important life lessons as well. Kari (EA-14) learned "kindness" and how to "care for others" from her mother. Jory (EA-17) said her mother taught her "to be herself." Chandra (AA-16) shared that her mother discouraged her from investigating predominantly black colleges, teaching her "you have to learn how to be around everybody . . . to be friends with everybody." In the taped interaction activity, daughters consistently asked mothers for information, especially about locations and activities they might pursue on the perfect family vacation. Daughters seemed very much aware that their mothers' previous life experience and greater knowledge gave them informational power. Daughters seemed very comfortable playing the subordinate role of student, while their mothers functioned as teachers.

Two other role pairings that were suggested from participants' descriptions of their relationships were friend-friend and parent-child. These role pairings occasionally came into conflict. Two friends generally have an egalitarian relationship, whereas the parent-child relationship is more unilateral, with the parent functioning as the authority figure. Moving between these roles was somewhat difficult, and some mothers insisted that it could not and *should* not be done. As Janna (EA) asserted,

> You can't always be friends. It has to be a mother-daughter relationship. And when we first started, I wanted just to be buddies, and you can't be buddies. It doesn't work that way.

Clearly, how one talks to a close friend is not how one talks to a child. Although most mothers admitted acting as friends to daughters, they were also aware that the parent or authoritarian role could not be abandoned. Mary (AA), a social worker, shared,

> I try to be a good friend, but I also let her know that I am the parent. Sometimes we can do buddy-buddy things, but sometimes things are out of place; she might give me a smart crack or something, and I have to let her know that's out of line and it's out of place.

When her daughter starts taking advantage of her mother as "friend," Mary must let her know it is "out of line and it's out of place." Theirs is first and foremost a parent-child relationship in which Mother is in charge. Mary suggests that her change in language and style of talk signals to her daughter that the relationship is no longer in an egalitarian or "friendship" mode. Further, Mary monitors the language and style that her daughter uses with her, admonishing her when it crosses the line.

African American mothers, more so than European American respondents, were clear that playing an authoritarian role in their relationships was a necessity. Although they more often referred to their daughters as their "best friends" than did their European American counterparts, African Americans emphasized that exercising unilateral, parental authority was crucial to their daughters' future success as well as survival. For the most part, African American participants suggested that daughters had strict rules, especially regarding dating and doing schoolwork, and they were not allowed to talk back to parents. European American mothers, in comparison, let their daughters get away with more, especially verbally, which supports Kizielewicz's (1988) research finding that European American daughters were more verbal and showed more displeasure with mothers than did African American daughters. Jory (EA-17), for example, illustrates this behavior with her comments:

> I kind of argue a lot. I argue quite a bit, and I don't know, it's—I think when she [my mother] disciplines me, I don't do well with that, because I don't think she should be disciplining me or anything. I don't like to take anything like that.

Finally, mothers trained adolescent daughters regarding the importance of being flexible in their roles. As stated earlier, mothers and daughters found themselves moving between role pairings, such as from parent-child to friend-friend and back again. Veronica (AA) further described how roles and talk changed in the mother-adolescent daughter relationship:

> I can be a mother to Keesha when I need to be, and I can also be her friend, and I can also be her sister, or I can be her worst enemy! I like being able to be flexible with her. When it's time to be a mother, I say, "You know this is what I want, and this is what you should do," and she respects me for that; then, when it's time to be her friend, where she wants to tell all her little secrets, that's fine. When she wants me to be her sister, we can sit and we giggle, we run, we laugh, we play; when it's time to raise a lot of hell about something she's done that I don't appreciate, she knows I still love her irregardless of where we are—whether we're mother and daughter, sister, friend, whatever.

This flexibility in role enactment was occasionally demonstrated in the joint interactions and was especially common with older adolescents whose relationships with their mothers were generally moving from authoritarian to egalitarian. In the following excerpt, which focuses on the family vacation, Sandy (EA), Kate's (EA-16) mother, is obviously the teacher or the "expert" because she has the information gained from her past experiences in the Bahamas:

Kate: What would we do? We're boring people, we'd probably go there and play cards.

Sandy: No, you can go to the ocean, you can rent like a three-wheel all-terrain vehicle thing and go—ah, there's a lot of stuff to explore there. And Freeport is different from Nassau. Nassau is very, very resort-y; Freeport is not; it's still—OL[3]

Kate: At least it wasn't when you were there.

Sandy: Yeah. Well, it's never been the most popular place to go. People who are looking for more of a tourist thing, like the Las Vegas people, the resort people, would probably find it bland.

Kate: Is it part of the United States?

Sandy: No, plus you need lots of time there because it takes forever to get waited on in restaurants; the pace of life is so slow, it could take you 45 minutes to get a menu and another 25 minutes to order, so you don't go to restaurants when you're really hungry.

In this next excerpt, which followed the previous one by a few minutes, Sandy and Kate are now doing the friend-friend relationship, showing how quickly roles can shift:

Kate: I took a personality thing for speech. It was a temperament test; it was amazing. I just answered all these questions—simple yes or no questions, and it just classified me as "artist," which is like one group of people, "composer," which is a subgroup of the artist, which composed 10% of the population; it described me as being a perfectionist—

Sandy: I would like to take that test.

Kate: Yeah, it was amazing. . . . Then I took a different test, which was by the same people, and came up with the exact same results.

Sandy: Well, I'll have to go to high school and take your speech class.

Kate: You can just go on the Internet; it's on the Internet.

Sandy: Oh . . . see what I mean; you're real aware, you know a lot of stuff. Where to find a lot of stuff; where I just think, it sure would be nice if I knew.

Kate: Yeah, at the same time you take a lot more action than I do. I mean I know where stuff is, but I won't do anything about it; even if you don't know where stuff is, you'll try to find out. And find a way, and make a way, and then do it.

Sandy: I just like to impress you guys.

Playing different roles is frequently required in family relationships as well as in professional ones, where one's boss may also be one's friend. The ability to display behavioral flexibility or to change one's communication to adapt to new situations is vital to achieving success in life. The mother-adolescent daughter relationship gives daughters the opportunity to practice assessing the appropriateness of different styles of talk depending on the situation. In performing this analysis, daughters develop communication competence that will serve them well in the future.

Application

Although mother-daughter talk can function as recreation and play, it performs other highly important tasks, such as serving as a training ground for the daughter's future interactions and relationships. The adolescent daughter's communication competence in displaying empathy or managing conflict in myriad interpersonal situations, for example, may well be linked to the style and quality of talk in her relationship with her mother. Lessons learned in their relationship might well be lessons learned for life. As Deleasa (AA-14) shared,

> [My mother] has taught me what I should do and what I shouldn't do, and, you know, I listen to her and I understand what she taught me. . . . I've followed in her footsteps. . . . Like, if something comes up that I have to make a choice, I'll hear her voice in my head talking to me.

Feminist scholarship, according to K. Allen and Walker (1992), not only seeks to better understand women and their concerns but offers conclusions that will be useful to them as well. Thus, it is prudent to reflect on what women can specifically take from this study. First, it is clear that mother-adolescent talk serves vital functions within the relationship. Therefore, mothers and daughters should be encouraged to take time to talk, wherever and whenever they can, be it in the mother's bed or in the family minivan. Daughters, although they may not all explicitly express it, need to talk with their mothers. As Chandra (AA-16) shared, "If I didn't have my relationship with my mom, it would be like an empty space . . . like a burden on me . . . if we weren't close." Kate also reinforced the importance of talk and connection in her relationship with her mother when she shared,

> But usually, I couldn't go 3 weeks without talking to my mom. . . . She and I have, like, an outlet where it's, like, negative charges and positive charges, and we equalize. It usually ends up working out that way. I usually have to talk to her; otherwise, I get really, really stressed out.

Although a traditional perception is that teen-aged girls do not feel the need to talk to their mothers, our respondents indicated that mother-daughter talk is important and, in a way, the essence of the relationship.

Another key insight to convey to mothers is that the training ground has to be nurturing and safe. Adolescents often see parents as judgmental (Rawlins & Holl, 1988), so mothers should be encouraged to listen without interrupting and refrain from judgment. As Keehsa (AA) stated about her mother, "I can tell her anything, and she doesn't judge me." Knowing she won't be judged, a daughter will most likely exhibit a greater degree of openness.

Participants in this study, especially mothers, indicated that they and their peers who were raising daughters could definitely use additional information, support, and encouragement regarding mother-daughter relationships. They were interested in the results we were developing and requested to read the paper when we had finished. Our results and those of similar studies could ideally be incorporated into school or community workshops and support group programs, providing information and points of discussion for facilitators and participants. Very few scholars have created such programs. A notable exception is Caron (1989), who developed a model for a series of parenting workshops that included both mothers and their middle school or junior high school daughters. Her model focused on the development of adolescent girls, sexuality, mother-daughter relationships in adolescence, family environments best suited to adolescent girls, and contemporary issues with adolescent girls. The model was unique in that it used a biographical and informational approach to learning, which encouraged mothers to reflect on their experiences as adolescents and share these reflections with their daughters.

Finally, these data indicate that mothers and daughters, no matter who they are, share many commonalities, although there are certainly differences as well. For example, although all of the study's mother-daughter pairs valued talk, African American mothers and daughters enjoyed talking in bed, while European American participants did not mention this. African American mothers were more likely than European Americans to characterize their daughters as "best friends," and they were also much more adamant about enacting the role of parental authority. The strategies they used in this role also differed from European Americans. African American mothers had more rules, told stories characterized by bluntness and honesty, and also used more sarcasm in interactions with daughters than did European Americans, who discussed the parental role more in terms of giving punishments *after* rules had been broken. Although both groups of mothers suggested that helping their daughters build self-esteem was important, it was clearly seen as a much more vital task in the African American group. A high degree of self-esteem was deemed a crucial tool for African American daughters who, their mothers felt, might encounter challenges related to discrimination and racism. Further, African American mothers sounded the theme of survival lessons, whereas European American mothers did not mention such lessons as important training for their daughters.

In sum, scholars as well as practitioners must be aware that the mother-adolescent daughter relationship is affected by race as well as a multitude of other variables. We need to acknowledge that the lenses we use to interpret our world may very well differ from those of other women. Understanding rather than evaluating the communication practices and patterns of other cultural groups is clearly a desirable response to differences. Yet, we should not overestimate differences. Both groups in our study valued talk and saw many of its functions similarly.

Although talk between mothers and daughters might sometimes resemble play, that does not mean it is trivial. Coates (1996) suggests,

> Playing provides a context for risk-taking and experimentation. In the playful conversational practices of women friends, we can try out different discourses, different positions in relation to the world ... and through playing with the collaborative strategies which allow us to share the conversational floor, we can jointly move to a new awareness of how things might be. (p. 286)

Through talk, mothers help daughters realize their potential, which may be the first step in changing our world. Is the talk in mother-adolescent daughter relationships playground or training ground? Most likely, they are one and the same.

Notes

1. We recognize that race and ethnicity are different concepts. Ethnicity is commonly thought to mean a common ancestry and cultural heritage (Waters, 2001), whereas race has been considered a social construction based on power as much as physical features (O'Hare, 1996). In this chapter, we are interested in black and white mother-daughter pairs because they are representative of two significant groups within the United States, a country where race matters (C. West, 1993) in many profound ways, ranging from how a child is treated on the playground to the availability of educational and career opportunities.

2. Number in brackets denotes length of pauses in seconds.

3. OL indicates an overlap in turns.

17

Masculinities and Violence Among Intimates

Stories About Male Abusers and Intervention Strategies

Jennifer Fink and Charles Tucker

"You always know that there is domestic violence out there. . . . You just never know how much."

—(Safe Passage, Inc. staff member, whose name could not be revealed for safety reasons; quoted in Grigsby, 1999)

D omestic violence consists of people in established relationships acting in ways that are intended (or perceived as intended) to cause physical pain or injury against other members of their household (Gelles, 1997). Although this definition focuses on physical violence among household members, other

---

Authors' Note: This chapter is dedicated to all those working with men to end violence, including Pam Wiseman, who developed the DeKalb County Domestic Abuse Program at a time when the issues surrounding partner abuse intervention programs were very controversial.

forms of violence involve verbal and emotional assaults against others and often occur simultaneously with physical violence. More inclusive definitions of domestic violence include "acts such as verbal abuse, imprisonment, humiliation, stalking, and denial of access to financial resources, shelter, or services" as well as rape, stalking by current or former relational partners, and physical threats or assaults (Tjaden & Thoennes, 2000, p. 5). These other acts have significant short- and long-term effects for victims and are often viewed by the victims as being more severe than the physical violence itself; therefore, the program's primary energies are focused on the issues of power and control that give rise to all forms of abuse (Bevington, 2001).

More specifically, this chapter presents the story of one man: Dr. Charles Tucker, who answered the feminist call to action by working with others to design and enact a group-centered protocol for change in male abusers. Both authors are members of the domestic violence agency Safe Passage, located in DeKalb, Illinois. This program is one of 62 approved programs in the state of Illinois that are offered at 15 satellite locations (see the Illinois Coalition Against Domestic Violence, n.d.). The first author and interviewer, Jennifer Fink, has worked as a Public Education Coordinator at Safe Passage for several years since completing her graduate degree in communication at Northern Illinois University. The second author and interviewee, Charles Tucker, is an emeritus professor from the same department who has been a volunteer at Safe Passage since the program began. Charles has been involved in a number of programs to create awareness of domestic violence on individual and governmental levels.

This chapter weaves together interview excerpts and stories about abusers, decisions Charles has made during his group counseling, and analyses of masculinities, changing identities, and ongoing social movements. This chapter both celebrates possibilities for change and advocates that readers do more in their training sessions, conversations, classrooms, volunteer activities, and other life experiences to end the thinking and conditions that can produce violence among intimates.

> *Jenn:* Charles, you are a feminist and a volunteer counselor for men who have physically abused their partners. How did you become involved in this work, and how does it fit within your feminist identity?

The short answer to your question is that I was teaching interpersonal communication and feminisms at Northern Illinois University one day when a student asked me directly what I did to change the community. From that day on, I have been a group facilitator at Safe Passage.

However, there also was another reason. The Executive Director of the local domestic violence agency decided to start a partner abuse intervention program. She approached me because I had been studying family communication and interpersonal communication for many years. What she did not know was that I had purposefully avoided all study of domestic violence in my research. I thought of domestic violence as an individual aberration that was best dealt with by abnormal psychologists and social workers. The director provided me with a foot-high stack of literature, several inches of which dealt with studies of the prevalence of domestic violence in America.

The research was dominated by surveys that indicated domestic violence is pervasive—citing such facts as 25% to 50% of women would be subjected to violence by men sometime in their lives.[1] These and other data were contrary to what I believed about domestic violence. As a result, I began to dig into other studies that I felt were more believable. These studies included data from hospital emergency departments for injury and death and other evidence. I became convinced that domestic violence is not an individual aberration but is supported largely by our culture. I felt that the opportunity to work with men convicted of domestic battery, with the state in efforts to change the subculture of the criminal justice system, and with the general public to enhance awareness about violence were needed and meaningful activities.

Since beginning with the partner abuse intervention program, I have been active on the state level with the Male Responsibility Committee,[2] committees for the development of and adherence to the [violence intervention] protocol, and the Illinois Task Force on Domestic Violence and Substance Abuse. Most recently, I have been involved in the formation of a court-monitoring program to examine and address the criminal justice response to domestic violence.

> *Jenn:*   You mentioned that you thought that domestic violence was an anomaly. You examined data and research reports. But how did others become aware of domestic violence?

There have been many changes because of the domestic violence movement in the United States. The domestic violence movement is a grassroots movement based on the notion that our society is patriarchal in that societal members see women as subordinate.

The movement was built from the bottom up by women who were knowledgeably and solidly in the feminist camp and knew the feminist literature.

It originated in the building of safe homes and shelters to provide safety for victims of domestic violence and grew out of a crisis-response orientation to advocacy.[3] At the time these crisis programs were developing, a crucial move for advocates was to classify domestic violence as a crime and to see perpetrators as criminals making the choice to use violence.[4] Domestic violence arises out of the choice one person (typically a man) makes to employ power and control over another person in a relationship. These choices to use violence are culturally supported and embedded in our society. The feminist perspective recognizes that the justification that abusers feel stems from the culture in which they are raised—namely, a patriarchal culture.[5]

Early on, the leaders of the movement committed major resources to encouraging the federal government to pass the Violence Against Women Act of 1994 (see Office on Violence Against Women, n.d.; see also Gelles, 1997, pp. 33-34). Passage of this legislation accomplished the garnering of national resources to programs regarding domestic violence. It established domestic violence as a crime at the national level for all states and all communities. This move established the pattern for the development of this movement.

The movement recognized the existence of a patriarchal system that encouraged the subordination and oppression of women. The patriarchal nature of our country was much more rigid when the movement began than it is now. The shift of women into industry had not yet occurred. The presumption was that advocates in domestic violence would be confronted primarily with the problems of patriarchy—meaning male-dominated courts, male-dominated police, and male-dominated state's attorneys. The whole system was a masculine system, and it was governed by masculine values, which to a large degree considered the family to be a private place. What goes on inside the home could hardly be considered a crime, and therefore there was a great deal of skepticism about family activity as criminal. The people in the movement were prepared for and became immediately engaged in advocacy toward the patriarchal institutions that they had to depend on if domestic violence was going to be treated as a crime. Community-wide task forces and protocols developed, state statutes were refined, and specialized training was provided for law enforcement, medical personnel, and other systems (e.g., Barnett, Miller-Perrin, & Perrin, 1997, pp. 203-207).

Education about the dynamics of domestic violence and its basis in power and control was central to the advocacy that occurred first with law enforcement and prosecution. The idea of domestic violence as a crime grew in support on the national and local levels and was fully legitimized with the passage of the Violence Against Women Act at the federal level.

Jenn: What happened when this act was passed?

As domestic violence was recognized as a crime and law enforcement offi-cers were able to arrest with probable cause, more and more men were being arrested. With the influx of men into the criminal justice system and a lack of space in jails, the system had to examine alternative and appropriate sanc-tions. Domestic violence professionals met to address this need and to ensure the alternatives would be appropriate. Courts were often turning to mental health services or anger management programs to give these men help. Domestic violence professionals were concerned, however, that these were not appropriate. Those services tend not to recognize the power of choice that per-petrators have, and therefore they do not hold them accountable for their actions.

It is crucial here to differentiate between the feminist approach and the perspectives of others who were beginning to address issues of domestic violence.[6] To define domestic violence as a *crime* imputes to the criminal the capacity to make a choice and charges the perpetrator with the failure of mak-ing an appropriate choice for which the community calls. The *mental health community* charges the perpetrator with personal, emotional challenges and does not hold the perpetrator accountable for choice.

Similarly, if you look at domestic violence as an *addiction* that can be addressed by 12-step programs for anger management, you again have a model that does not grant the perpetrator the power of choice. When the courts began to commonly rely on mental health or addictive/anger management type pro-grams, the domestic violence community became alarmed. These mental health or addiction/anger management programs were in direct contradiction to the domestic violence movement's definition of domestic violence as a crime over which the perpetrators have choice. Programs designed specifically to address partner abuse—called Partner Abuse Intervention Programs (PAIPs)—were developed by those in the movement, and standards for these programs fit within the feminist framework.

Jenn: What are the characteristics of these PAIPs?

Partner Abuse Intervention Programs (PAIPs) serve to meet the needs of the criminal justice system as well as to begin to address the societal factors that seem to give men permission to use violence. Most states have developed stan-dards for PAIPs, and most courts now refer men who are arrested to these pro-grams. A crucial guideline for PAIPs to follow is that they be connected to or accountable in some way to a victim's program. This is to ensure against programs that engage in blaming the victim, deny choice for the perpetrator, undermine the victim's program, and place victims at an increased risk for their safety. All state-approved programs are group based and facilitated by male-female teams. To better understand how these programs do their work in a feminist perspective, I'll discuss the DeKalb County Domestic Abuse Program (DCDAP).[7]

The DeKalb program, in existence since 1993, follows the pro-feminist model adopted by the state. The guiding mission of the program and the agency of which it is a part is to end violence. The program adheres to protocol guidelines but has developed its own model of change. The program focuses on men and the steps that are called for in order for them to change and adopt partnership. Central to the model is the goal of partnership.

Men typically transition through four phases before they accept the ideals of partnership.[8] *Phase one* is typical of most men who enter the program. They deny or minimize the choice of violence. They have been arrested for violent acts against their partners but see them as something that was justified or can be blamed on the victim. They deny their responsibility for the violence and minimize its severity. During this phase, the group facilitators invite detailed self-descriptions, starting at a point before anger begins and continuing through to the effects of violence. The detail the facilitators encourage includes the chronology of events, thoughts, emotions, and the participant's own actions.

Phase two is self-understanding and self-responsibility. During self-examination, facilitators strive to get the men to acknowledge their participation. A tool often used is the control log.[9] The men become able to see the situation as their responsibility and as something over which they have choice.

From phase two, men can transition to *phase three*, empathy or understanding a partner's point of view. Common techniques are showing video vignettes of realistic scenarios, having men role-play themselves as well as women and children, and practicing active listening.

The final transition is working as equal partners, *phase four*. Men practice standard conflict resolution by identifying mutual goals, constructing alternative ways both people can be satisfied, and making commitments that can be lived up to and thereby increasing trust. The process of change is self-reflexive, and the goal of partnership is a feminist ideal.

> **Jenn:** These phases sound so simple and linear. But I know that change isn't easy. How do you know that the men are changing and when to change your intervention strategies?

I can best highlight some of the men's transitions by providing a few cases from my own experiences. Although there is no guarantee that the men will change, there are some indications that we can look at that show whether change is likely.

Box 17.1 Case 1

This case involves an African American young man of about 24. He had spent most of his life in a predominantly white community and, like any minority, needed to develop his skills in understanding others. He appeared to be very insightful about other people and their motives, and to have the ability to interpret what underlay their actions and their speech. From the perspective of my cofacilitator and myself, this unusual amount of insight was developed for manipulative purposes that we saw as problematic. The young man's sensitivity to understanding others was developed so that he could better control them, which applied to the women in his life as well as to the men.

This man is characteristic of the type of men we accept into the program. His violence was directed exclusively toward women. He didn't get into any kind of violent trouble with coworkers, in bars, or with buddies. He didn't fight police when he got into trouble with the law. This fact for him, as is the case with many abusers, was very important; he would claim that the only reason he struck out against women was because he couldn't keep from losing his temper. What he hoped to get out of the program was to learn how to control his temper.

His first step was to acknowledge that other people in his world did things that pissed him off just as women did things that pissed him off— but somehow he didn't lose his temper with men. That was the beginning of the move from denial to self-understanding. The next step was to invite him to try to figure out what benefits or drawbacks he saw when he believed he had successfully manipulated the women with whom he lived. We asked him to consider the position in which a woman was placed when he tried to prevent her from thinking what she wanted to think, feeling or disclosing the emotions she wanted to feel, and acting the way she wanted to act.

He viewed women as untrustworthy liars. We proposed that almost all people are honest if they are not fearful of what honesty will produce. If he finds women lying to him, it is likely because they are afraid of him.

(Continued)

Box 17.1 (Continued)

He decided to buy into that. We also proposed that the women with whom he chose to live were enjoyable women—and he agreed to this statement. We asked him to tell story after story after story of what it would be like if a woman he lived with were to disclose to him her true feelings, thoughts, and emotions rather than to skirt around them to keep him pacified. This process of storytelling and self-awareness was a difficult and lengthy phase for him.

Typical of a lot of manipulative people, he had never had occasion to seriously try to think what a nonmanipulative person might do. After that huge step was made, he started changing at a pretty rapid rate. After he could release his own clutch on the necessity to manipulate, he began to understand himself better. When he turned his attention to others, he was able to capitalize on his remarkable ability to understand others in a manipulative manner by changing his focus so that he could understand them empathetically. This was a very exciting time for him.

He started insisting that he was going to come to this group after his 24 weeks were up for at least a year. We had men in the group who had been coming to group for up to 2 years by choice.

The program was very gratifying to him. He would go home and talk to his partner about what went on in group sessions. He was careful not to use what was said in group as a set of commands for her. Instead, he kept focused on what he needed to do. This was a crucial distinction because many men do sit in the group and say, "Aha! That is how that bitch is screwing me over. I'll go home and teach her to stop being so fucked up."

When it came to practicing partnership skills, all of his manipulative background could be turned to good purpose. Of his 24 weeks, about 12 of those weeks were spent working on that first step: examining the motivation and the impacts of being manipulative. In a period of 4 to 5 weeks, he had a central grasp on how to understand having self-understanding and partnership. He did leave the program at the end of 24 weeks and did not continue to come on his own.

The mark of the participant in Case 1 was that he was already contemplative, sensitive, and aware of others and their actions. The mark of the participant in Case 2 is that he is a "male responsibility" person, meaning that he ties his masculine role to being in control of others and the situations in which he finds himself. His work is physical work. His style is nonanalytic and nonsocial.

His primary enjoyment is being with other men and relying on the commonality that men have when they share the same kind of jobs and the same kind of sports. He appeared to be comfortable with the idea that there is no option other than to see women as strange.[10]

Box 17.2 Case 2

Like many men of this "male responsibility" profile, he was heavily dependant on his wife. It was essential to have a wife in order to have the security and the sense of legitimacy that he desired. When they continued to fight seriously and when he found himself beating up on her, he hated it. We talked about the cycle of violence and the honeymoon period in which men express remorse. For many men that expression of remorse is entirely manipulative because she is mad at him and hurt and he wants to get back on her good side. He expresses all kinds of remorse and promises.

For this man the remorse was real, and the threat that he could lose her was very real. His partner went to the local shelter, where she received counseling. She became increasingly convinced that she understood what abuse entailed and that he was abusive. It became clear that his family was seriously at risk.

So he came into the program upset, confused, and anxious, with a huge list of all the ways that she was to blame. He desperately hoped we could provide him with some techniques to make her more manageable. For him the first phase of denial and minimization was not the best starting place.

He had so little experience at self-reflection that our efforts to get him to tell his story in detail referring only to himself kept failing. For him, the starting point was the empathy. He was so confident that she was screwed up that it did not occur to him that she might have a sensible, decent, intelligent perspective on how she was behaving. So, we role-played and role-played.

As facilitator, I would constantly be his wife, and he would constantly be surprised when I would present a picture of her that was believable. The next move was to invite him to role-play his wife, and I would be him. That process became revelatory. When he, to his surprise, discovered that maybe she was not crazy (he did view her as being technically emotionally disturbed), then he was able to look at himself and

(Continued)

Box 17.2 (Continued)

ask, "Why have I been so fixed on her inadequacy or my image of her inadequacy that I couldn't look at myself?" He went from empathy to self-understanding. He remained in the program for more than a year, and it appears to have been successful. I saw him a year after he had left the program. The two of them both proclaimed that they were living a really good life, and she no longer goes to counseling at the shelter.

In these two cases, the participants transitioned through the four phases of change and appeared to be in a place where they were willing to accept the goal of working in partnership in their relationships. The process happened in different ways for the two men. The next case represents a participant who was unable/unwilling to transition to the final phase of partnership.

A great benefit of our program is that it is group based. The men who are glad that they were forced to come commonly testify that they learn more from the other men than they do from the facilitators. I like to hear that. One of the things they then get exposed to is men who are moving from a great deal of self-righteousness to less self-righteousness. They discover that there are alternative ways of looking at things.

Box 17.3 Case 3

The man that I'm thinking about was very surprised to listen to other men make that move into alternative ways of viewing life experiences. Over and over again, a new man would come into the group, and almost always the first thing that the new man would do is explain all the ways in which he blames the woman for his troubles. The man I am thinking about in Case 3 would hear these new men, and he'd buy their stories. He was immediately on the side of the new men. As the new men became more and more flexible, he too would become more and more flexible. He was gratified by this experience.

He did become more flexible about himself. He did acknowledge ways he was being rigid when he didn't need to be rigid. He acknowledged things about which he made a big issue and could afford to

(Continued)

Box 17.3 (Continued)

just let go. He found himself getting angry a lot less often because he became more tolerant of her being different from him. He changed his priorities. He was able to make a list of what was crucial to him and what wasn't so crucial. The list helped because it reduced the frequency and the number of conflicts in which he and his partner engaged.

To look at empathy, we typically do a variety of things. For example, we have video vignettes of disputes that were produced by the Duluth program that are quite realistic.[11] We ask the men to discuss what goes on from the woman's point of view.

This guy just couldn't do it. He could talk about the men and he could talk about how the men may be being overly rigid (that was part of his own self-awareness), but he could not think of any way to look at what the woman was doing without, at the same time, judging what she was doing as either right or wrong, sensible or not sensible. He couldn't lay his judgment aside long enough to see a different point of view in another person.

We often do role playing, where we ask the men to play women and to play men. He wouldn't play women. When men blamed women for doing something because they were trying to "punch their buttons" and make them mad or were being "selfish," we would ask the men to suggest other possible explanations for why the women did something. A lot of the men would be able to come up with other explanations. We call that the beginning of empathy. But this guy couldn't do it.

I still think that the time in the program was well spent because he became less controlling and more flexible than he was. But no woman with whom he became involved could ever expect him to take her point of view.

Jenn: This change process does not sound particularly feminist, yet you have called the program feminist—why?

You're right. The model of change itself is not necessarily feminist. What makes the perspective feminist is that it examines and challenges ideas that are based in patriarchy. Men can generally be described as more competitive and aggressive than women. However, being highly competitive may or may not foster violence.

Patriarchy establishes institutions (i.e., schools, churches) that inculcate men at a very young age with beliefs that value men being in charge and taking control. These beliefs readily lead to a justification for dominance. Our program challenges the beliefs that justify or deny violence against women and tries to insist that men have a special responsibility for their abusiveness.

The DeKalb program is unique in that it is participant-centered as opposed to content-based. The model derives from the experience of working with men through the process of change. The program is a minimum of 24 weeks and is conducted only in a group context. Men have the opportunity to learn from other men, as I said before, as well as to challenge the patriarchal ideas all men encounter.

A benefit of the protocol is that men can learn from other men—they have a credibility that the facilitator can never have. A possible negative outcome is when you have men who establish leadership positions within the group that are contrary to the program. This is a risk in all group work and not exclusive to this type of program. It is the job of the facilitator to be aware of the risk and address the problem.

Groups are cofacilitated by a male-female dyad. It is an intimate activity, and therefore it is essential to have time to process what they are doing and hearing and to maintain compatibility. A risk for male facilitators is that they will collude with the men. A common part of the processing is for the female facilitator to recognize when the male facilitator is collaborating with the men and for him to be responsive to her. A difficulty female facilitators encounter is that the men will commonly decide she is an exceptional woman and therefore she doesn't really count. In this context, the woman's voice is not just an individual voice but is representative of the possibility of equal partnership with women.

> *Jenn:* You mentioned some difficulties in this kind of work. Are there other tough issues with which you deal?

Aside from the challenges of facilitation or group work, PAIPs are faced with several challenges. One main difficulty is that the PAIPs contradict some firmly held beliefs about women and power. These programs have a certain amount of legitimacy because they are supported at the state level. The programs, however, are only one component in the entire system and need support on the local level from the judicial system, law enforcement, and prosecution to thrive.

Many judges are willing to reduce charges or order a suspended sentence when the men complete the program. This presents a problem because domestic violence is a repetitive crime and has implications for other sentences. When an offender is not convicted of domestic battery, it seriously waters down the effectiveness of the criminal justice system. I recall hearing about a Canadian study in which researchers found shockingly low arrest rates (for statistics on police behavior, see Barnett et al., 1997, p. 203). If the seriousness of the crime is reduced, then the system could be hiding numerous crimes.

There is strong evidence that the most reliable, preventative sentence is jail time.[12] Courts often view all sentences as equal, but those working in the field are not convinced. The programs believe in their value as part of the system but rely on the support of other systems to enhance their legitimacy. If men see all the systems around them minimizing the importance of the crime, they are not being given any motivation to change. Courts should view domestic violence as a crime and insist on the same kind of investigation, evidence, interviewing, and prosecution as other crimes.

Editor's Note: As coeditor of this section, I would like to thank Jenn and Charles for their interview and work on behalf of domestic violence victims. We invited them to write this chapter for a couple of reasons. Although our book is titled *Gender in Applied Communication Contexts,* most of the chapters are by and about women. Clearly, "gender" is not simply about women. We wanted to lessen this imbalance by discussing men and masculinities from a feminist point of view. In addition, the issue of violence between intimates has been an ongoing concern for feminist activists but only recently has emerged as an issue in communication literature. As readers of this volume know, in communication, a core feminist goal is to focus on the ways in which discourses and related practices intersect with the real material conditions of people's lives to produce specific situations in which people are both enabled and constrained, empowered and disempowered, and silent and voiced. We wanted to give voice to stories about male abusers and about one male feminist in our field who became involved in the domestic violence movement. We wanted to describe how interventions have been conducted and where controversies continue to exist among people who try to develop the most effective interventions against varied forms of interpersonal and family violence.

Because we wanted to emphasize Charles's and Jenn's voices, we summarized many points about research and theory in endnotes. For the content and differences of opinion that these endnotes may raise, I am solely responsible. I am deeply appreciative of the work of these authors and would also like to thank Steve Wilson of Purdue University for providing a number of references that supplemented my research for these endnotes.

— *Patrice M. Buzzanell*

Notes

1. Statistics on violence against women vary based on the definition of violence used and the specific context in which violence is perpetrated. Lloyd and Emery (2000) summarize findings on physical aggression during courtship relationships. Using the Conflict Tactics Scale developed

by Murray Straus (1979), which has been employed frequently in research of this type, researchers have found that 30% to 36% of men have been physically aggressive, and 31% to 36% of women report that they have been victims of physically violent behaviors (e.g., kicking, beatings, threats, or use of a weapon). When using sexual aggression or unwanted sexual interaction, including attempted rape, as the indicator of violence, between 6% and 39% of surveyed women report being victims, with percentages soaring to 45% to 75% of women when all types of unwanted sexual interaction—including touching and kissing—are included (Lloyd & Emery, 2000, pp. 4-5).

According to data from national surveys of marital violence, 28% of surveyed couples reported marital violence at some point in their marriages (Gelles, 1997, p. 75). Wives who are beaten by their husbands are victimized repeatedly; the average is three beatings per year (p. 75). Lifetime rates of victimization by someone with whom the victim has an intimate relationship range from 9% to 30% for women and 13% to 16% for men (Tjaden & Thoennes, 2000, p. 3).

2. "Male responsibility" means both that men have a choice in or responsibility for their actions as well as that some men use domestic violence as a means of controlling their partners and other family members (i.e., they enact their masculine responsibility to control others; see Parts 3 and 4 in Bevington, 2001).

Although Charles does not mention it here, he was also responsible for protocol development. The protocols he developed have been used by all male batterer programs in the state of Illinois that receive government money.

3. Chapter 2 ("Violence Between Intimates: Historical Legacy—Contemporary Approval") of Gelles (1997) describes the shelter movement and the historical legacy and contemporary issues involved in violence among intimates. In particular, Gelles documents the grassroots movement that drove domestic violence from behind closed doors of homes and into the media, courts, and laws (see pp. 32-34). As a more detailed treatment of the socio-cultural-historical forces, G. Arnold (1995) presents a case study of the battered women's movement in St. Louis, Missouri. G. Arnold illuminates the tensions between feminist ideology and practice that can underlie local pockets of activism.

4. Barnett, Miller-Perrin, and Perrin (1997) describe the lack of police responsiveness to partner abuse in the past as well as specific court challenges to former police policies, current police training, and legal remedies for abuse (pp. 203-207).

5. Contesting and usurping the ways in which dominant group interests have privileged traditional masculinities, public spheres, and rationality have been ongoing feminist concerns. What has happened as a result of feminist and other social movements is that the "legitimation of patriarchy" has crumbled (Connell, 1995, p. 226; italics in original), but the questioning of how and why patriarchy is manifest differently in varied contexts continues. With regard to family communication contexts, particularly violence between intimates, hegemonic masculinity or the maintenance of practices that perpetuate men's dominance over women in every aspect of life—from ordinary conversations to the structuring of standard operating procedures in companies, the emphasis on work rather than home, and postcolonial relationships—creates a sense that male superiority is normal and natural (Acker, 1990; Bird, 1996; Calás & Smircich, 1996; Connell, 1987).

Hegemonic masculinities are sustained through insistence on emotional detachment, construction of competitive individuality, and objectification of women such that men are seen as not only different from, but superior to, women (Bird, 1996). When socialized into varied forms of masculinity that maintain these characteristics as core elements, men and women find themselves in relationships where dialectics of control-dependency, masculine-feminine, concerns of the public (work and economy) realm-concerns of the private (home and family) realm, and so on operate as tensions that can leave both parties confused, unsupportive of the others' needs (such as those needs that fail to fit within male breadwinner roles), or violent (Buzzanell & Turner, 2003; Faludi, 1999; Fine, Weiss, Addelston, & Marusza, 1997; Thompson, 1991; Wood, 1998b, 2001). These dialectics and the tendencies to favor one pole over another mean that some men have been socialized into patterns of thinking, behaving, and feeling that excuse violence in the home as a normal part of male aggression and frustration and that make the private sphere immune to ethics of justice (see Wood, 1998b). However, other men subscribe to different forms of masculinities that are shaped by specific sociohistorical conditions (Mumby, 1998).

6. Lloyd and Emery (2000) review feminist responses to domestic violence. In particular, they note that feminist approaches to partner and courtship abuse center on: (a) analyses of gender and unequal power distributions; (b) patriarchal (i.e., hierarchical systems maintaining rights of men over women) biases in research and theory development; (c) research *for* women that counters both women-as-victim viewpoints, which diminish women's agency and resistance to domination, and women-as-causes for violence perspectives, which blame women for the acts perpetuated against them; and (d) recognition that home is neither a safe haven nor realm of female control and power. Taken together, feminist responses challenge the ways that men's aggression against women and other members of their households has been naturalized in U.S. society.

In contrast to feminist approaches, L. Bennett and Piet (1999) discuss mental health professionals' view of domestic violence as an outcome of interactional or individual deficits. They argue that the conflicts between the views of women's advocates and those of therapists will intensify in years to come because of limited funding for research and programs and because of criticisms leveled against batterer program standards. Critics challenge regulation of these programs based on their arguments that there is a lack of professionalism, a lack of empirical support for effectiveness in prevention or treatment interventions, a lack of authority (meaning that judges and attorneys do what they want regardless of standards), and a lack of regulations based on objective facts rather than ideological beliefs. L. Bennett and Piet (1999) underscore the complexity of the debate between women's advocates and mental health professionals' arguments by providing a case study of the Illinois Protocol. The Illinois Protocol supplies direction to batterer programs through declaration of principles, service coordination, program approaches, standards, staff selection and training recommendations, and maintenance of a database (p. 15).

7. Charles provided some general descriptions of program participants. Typically the men are in the lowest brackets for income. This characteristic is *not* totally representative of those who commit domestic battery; rather, it is a function in part of bias in all phases of the criminal justice system.

The men range between 20 and 45 years of age with modes of 25 and 35. Currently 80% of the men are white and 10% are African-American and Latino. Charles noted that the agency is just beginning a program for Spanish-speaking men and anticipates a slight change in demographics.

8. These four phases are: I: Denial and Minimization; II: Self-Understanding and Self-Responsibility; III: Understanding Partner's Point of View and Empathy; and IV: Working as Equal Partners.

Stage I responses of blame, denial, and minimization by men are outlined in Barnett et al. (1997, p. 237). Different types of treatment and approaches to counseling, including counseling outcomes for group treatments, are presented in Barnett et al. (pp. 246-250). Appropriate and inappropriate interventions, case-by-case resolutions, monitoring, and so on are available in the Illinois Protocol for Partner Abuse Intervention Programs (2001-2002) statute. Copies of this statute are available from the authors and the editor, Patrice Buzzanell.

9. A control log is a dated record in which the male abuser describes his actions (i.e., situations and actions in which he controlled his partner), intents and beliefs, feelings, minimization/denial/blame, effects, past violence, and noncontrolling behaviors (i.e., ideas about what he could have done differently).

10. These cases seem to point to different typologies of male abusers. There are a number of profiles published in the literature. For instance, Holtzworth-Munroe (2000) summarizes the wide array of batterer types and discusses how these subgroups differ along at least two continua: antisociality and borderline personality features. She suggests that people designing interventions should consider batterer subgroup membership. Holtzworth-Munroe, Meehan, Herron, Rehman, and Stuart (2001) refined this typology when they identified four clusters of violent men: family only (FO), borderline-dysphoric (BD), generally violent-antisocial (GVA), and a combined BD-GVA group. Each cluster exhibited fairly predictable patterns that would warrant different treatments.

In yet another study, Jacobson and Gottman (1998) have a popularized version of male batterer typologies in which they dichotomize batterers into two types—cobras, who strike quickly and very violently whenever they want; and pit bulls, who explode after a slow buildup.

11.   The facilitator's manual and vignettes are included in the materials from the National Training Project (NTP) of the Duluth Domestic Abuse Intervention Project. To purchase the Power and Control Curriculum, you must have attended training sponsored by the NTP on the use of the materials and be networking with an advocacy program for battered women. See www.duluth-model.org/catalog.pdf for more information.

12.   Barnett et al. (1997, pp. 204-205) summarize a widely cited series of studies from the 1980s in which arrests deterred acts of marital violence. Since that time, there have been calls for caution and for more research before concluding that the pro-arrest policy is appropriate in *all* cases. Replications funded by the National Institute of Justice indicate that half of the arrests showed some deterrent effects and half did not. The determining factors were whether abusers had something to lose (in which case arrests made a difference), where abusers lived, and what types of individuals these abusers were.

18

Commentary

The Pastiche of Gender and Family Communication

Kathleen M. Galvin

Gender is embedded in all family interactions as a thread or theme, implicit or explicit. This centrality calls for sustained, focused, scholarly attention; the current body of work remains fragmented but is developing. Scrapbooking represents a gendered practice of reflecting on and creating a vision of gendered family life focused on talk. Reminiscent of quilting bees, scrapbooking involves a group of (primarily) females selecting, arranging, and presenting a pastiche of their family experiences in scrapbook pages. Through these efforts they construct and reflect the meaning of family life across time as represented by photos, designs, postcards, journal entries, tickets, ribbons, stencils, greeting cards, and other materials valued for their memories. Thus, the participants create a vision of, and communally reflect on, their family lives.

The three previous chapters serve as artifacts to be glued on pages of a scrapbook reflecting timely concerns; they are positioned in a certain place, next to related artifacts, such as those cited in their references, and surrounded by real and imagined spaces—new pages, new scrapbooks—for future contributions. Eventually, each completed work constructs and reflects the intersections of communication, gender, and family at a point in time. In such scrapbooks, gender is a central ribbon of family life when members connect as parents and children, as siblings, partners, and as extended family members. Examining the scrapbook these chapters encompass, one envisions pages devoted to gendered themes of otherness, talk, culture, boundaries, and choices. Designs of dialectical tensions and bidirectionality border each page.

In this vision, Buzzanell's statement captures the eventual intersection of these pages:

> In communication, a core feminist goal is to focus on the ways in which discourses and related practices intersect with the real material conditions of people's lives to produce specific situations in which people are both enabled and constrained, empowered and disempowered, and silent and voiced. (p. 307 this volume)

Each chapter must be viewed as an artifact unto itself and an element of an ongoing artistic creation.

Parent-Child Interaction

In their analysis of mother-daughter talk in Chapter 16, Penington and Turner examine the function and importance of mother and adolescent daughter interaction within African American and European American dyads, addressing critical issues of gendered talk in parent-child interaction. The authors capture the significance of such studies, arguing that "systematic study of women's talk is not a wasted effort, but rather a necessity for increasing our understanding of how healthy, satisfying relationships are created, maintained, and improved" (p. 275 this volume). These authors add to a latent area of examination for family communication scholars—that of parent-child interaction. This area was referred to as a frontier as recently as the mid-1990s in Socha and Stamp's (1995) groundbreaking work, *Parents, children, and communication*. Later research studies, including those of M. Miller and Day (2002), Prescott and Le Poire (2002), and Lucchetti, Powers, and Love (2002), have extended these conversations.

Consistent with Penington and Turner's feminist approach, Chapter 16 is grounded in the decision to privilege voices and perspectives of both mothers and daughters. Key moments include the generational reversal as a mother reflects on her daughter's skills in Internet searches, and the sharing of ideas. Although limited related research exists, such as that of Saphir and Chaffee (2002), the open space surrounding this piece awaits additional work on bidirectionality or mutual influence of parents and children (Dixson, 1995).

Moments of togetherness and individuality resonate throughout this piece as dialectical tensions emerge when mothers and daughters manage their needs to talk with each other and to pull back, acting as adult parent or independent teenager. The data from both in-depth interviews and joint interaction activities deepen the analysis. This piece contributes to the undervalued discussion of place; the importance of talk sites reinforces the necessity of examining car talk or bed talk between parents and children. One pair's anticipation of talk time during the long drive to athletic practice is consistent with the belief that "the dashboard is becoming the family hearth" (Shellenbarger, 2002, p. B6). Routine car trips represent a significant arena for exploring relational maintenance.

An important contribution results from the authors' decision to include African American and European American mother-daughter pairs, reflecting the role of culture in creating parent-child communication styles and patterns while including a group generally considered "invisible" (Socha, Sanchez-Hucles, Bromley, & Kelly, 1995). Differences noted in the chapter, such as mother's bed as a site of conversation and the use of proverbs to build self-confidence, extend previous understandings of cultural patterns. The African American parental use of the imperative mode (Daniel & Daniel, 1999) or the use of a position-oriented style rather than a person-oriented one (Bernstein, 1971) remains important. In related work, I. Ferguson (1999) foregrounds racism as a pervasive factor in the socialization of African American children because parents must prepare their offspring to respond to racial derogation. This communicative task, unfamiliar to European American parents, is inter-woven with gender in instances of concerns for preparing and protecting male children from law enforcement challenges (Daniel & Daniel, 1999). Class issues interface with these cultural communication concerns as evidenced by Patillo-McCoy's (1999) discussion of flexible boundaries between the black middle and lower classes that impact normative sequences of family formation and interaction.

Mothers and daughters tend to receive more attention in academic literature than other parent-child pairings. Some scholars believe mothers tend to identify with daughters more than with sons; they feel more connected to daughters and experience daughters more as part of themselves (Wood, 2001). If so, differences should emerge in cross-gender studies of talk. Also, it is likely that father-son patterns of closeness may reflect more "doing" or sharing interests than talking (Wood & Inman, 1993). We need counterpart studies examining cross-gender parent-child interactions and father-son interactions.

Work-Family Communication

Through her examination of identity construction and online community building of entrepreneurial mothers in Chapter 15, Edley uncovers new ground both in terms of work-family borders and border crossings, even though communication scholars have been developing work-family studies for more than a decade (Buzzanell, 2000a; Golden, 2001; Jorgenson, 2000; Kirby & Krone, 2002). Arguing that "homework" is a gendered phenomenon, Edley depicts an overlooked, growing population seldom represented in print. Traditionally, only the "stars" who move from the traditional workplace to work from home gain attention (see Conlin, Merritt, & Himelstein, 2002). Major themes emerging in this study reflect the tasks of conceptualizing time, being role models for children, and constructing professional identities. The entrepreneurial mothers in this study work out of their homes and co-construct their identities with clients, children, spouses, and other mothers online, an identity construction process that bears some similarity to a world where the genderless cyborg, unmarked as *other* by society, develops power and agency. Online text construction provides entrepreneurial mothers with control of their personal presentations while providing a sense of agency, respect, and power, but at the price of intense psychological responsibility for managing continually shifting borders.

Edley's chapter serves as a reminder that crossing work-family borders requires tremendous skill, sensitivity, and communicative competence because those who balance work and family were "*pro*active or *en*active as they moved back and forth between their work and family lives, shaping each as they went by negotiation and communicating" (S. Clark, 2000, p. 751). Difficulties arise depending on the similarity or differences of the domains, how persons identify with each domain, and their centrality within each domain. These difficulties may be problematized further. Jorgenson's exploration of separateness and integration within domains provides a valuable counterpoint to consider.

Although the cyborg analogy is thought-provoking, Edley correctly notes that its application is limited; it breaks down in the face of border crossings and segmentation. Just as entrepreneurial mothers struggle with autonomy and connection in relation to family members and clients, they also manage a temporal continuum of integrating and segmenting. Reflecting on the women who make such choices, she concludes, "They want it all." Thoughtful consideration of this goal needs to involve a more nuanced examination, asking to whom, and in which contexts, these findings apply. Issues of gender, class, occupation, family structure, and alternative sources of economic support are the unknowns surrounding the paper or Web site scrapbooks of these entrepreneurial mothers.

Blank pages or hypertext links await depictions of men and their choices, studies that respond to questions such as: If "homework" is gendered, under what conditions do men enact fathering and entrepreneurship? What is the role of men in families with entrepreneurial mothers? Do female entrepreneurs/parents have more agency and power than their traditional male counterparts? In this chapter, women value being role models for their children, breaking down patriarchal structures, and providing their children with positive images of women as well as specific positive images of what Mom does. Under what conditions do children witness the loving father and male model of self-determination, self-love, and achievement?

This chapter depicts a hard-won domain of female agency, where men follow at their peril. Even today, a father is first and foremost expected to provide economic support, thus meeting "macrosocietal expectations that he is the breadwinner while the mother is the primary caregiver" (Kirby & Krone, 2002, p. 55). These beliefs, often unconsciously held (Cose, 1995), restrict male choices both in terms of leaving the traditional workplace for entrepreneurial positions and utilizing work-family benefits within the traditional workplace. Articles in the popular press reflect the reality that work-family issues remain primarily the domain of females because, although corporations expect or tolerate women who seek balance, their male counterparts who do so are viewed as less committed or serious about their work (Grover, 1999; Kleiman, 2000). More women than men leave the traditional workplace to start their own businesses, a reality that may be seen as a gendered option.

Fathers' limited options are evident in the gendered use of work-life benefits. Employees who find that using flexible benefits or leaves are harmful to their careers often choose not to take advantage of the highly touted options, thus following the enacted cultural norms (Perlow, 1997; Perry-Jenkins, Repetti, & Crouter, 2000). In their study of a government organization's field office, Kirby and Krone (2002) report that when women were granted family leave, coworkers were more understanding than they would be for men. This is consistent with previous studies indicating men and career-oriented mothers were less likely to avail themselves of family leave (Bailyn, Fletcher, & Kolb, 1997). Apparently, men have fewer options to leave the workplace and enter the entrepreneurial/parenting borderland; economic and psychological borders restrict their choices. Such restrictions will be noticed by children, who learn about gender by watching who does what (Wood, 2001).

Significant changes occur slowly. S. Clark (2000) argues that identification occurs when individuals internalize domain values; furthermore, when their identity is closely tied with their membership in the domain, their motivation to manage borders and domains increases. Currently, traditional workplaces as well as "homework" appear as differently gendered domains that may be mapped on the already socially constructed gender domains. Pages of Web-based or paper scrapbooks remain unfilled.

Domestic Abuse and Communication

In Chapter 17, Fink and Tucker provide thought-provoking insights into a critical issue and offer a unique view from a site of praxis. In an extensive interview, one subject-author reflects on the feminist call to action. Through reflections on the domestic violence movement, a story of a personal turning point, and abuser case summaries, the authors demonstrate the power of case study research.

A theme of choice resonates throughout this piece, as indicated in the statement from the chapter that "domestic violence arises out of the choice one person (typically a man) makes to employ power and control over another person in a relationship" (p. 298 this volume) and in the explanation that efforts such as mental health services, anger management programs or addiction programs "tend not to recognize the power of choice that perpetrators have, and therefore they do not hold them accountable for their actions" (p. 299 this volume). The authors establish a firm accountability position for gender abuse and suggest that domestic violence is not individual aberration but a choice supported by the culture. Their depiction of the ideal of partnership and its phases, ranging from denying violence to practicing standard conflict resolution, has strong communicative implications. The short narratives of an individual offender's movement through the program are useful but underline the need for extensive case studies that include offenders' words.

Chapter 17 claims a small space on a page of a very large and critical scrapbook as domestic abuse literature continues to explode (Gelles, 1997; J. Miller & Knudsen, 1999). Most family communication scholars are familiar with key marital abuse pieces on topics such as male batterers' emotional states and heart rates (Jacobson & Gottman, 1998), premarital predictors of marital aggression (O'Leary et al., 1989) and gender differences in spousal aggression patterns in early marriage (O'Leary, Malone, & Tyree, 1994). Although isolated communication-oriented studies have contributed to understanding the role of interaction in marital and family abuse (Roloff, 1996; Rogers, Castleton, & Lloyd, 1996; Sabourin, 1996; Sabourin & Stamp, 1995), there is a desperate need for scholar teams to develop large, longitudinal research programs in this area.

The topics of parent-child interaction, work-family communication, and domestic abuse and communication will remain vital areas of research for subsequent decades. In addition, other critical changes that will add to the pastiche are imminent. The family of the future will reflect increasing diversity, including a rise in all-female families; live within four and five generations of familial connection, involving many elderly women; encounter health-related genetic discoveries and medical advances that will necessitate gendered talk and knowledge; face unprecedented technological change that will have gender implications, particularly in areas of reproductive technology; search for new ways to protect and enhance family life, including attention to roles of women (Galvin, 2004). Tomorrow's scrapbookers will fill new pages and books; gender and family communication will continue to engage the minds of creative and committed scholars.

References

Aboud, F. (1988). *Children and prejudice.* New York: Blackwell.

Acker, J. (1990). Hierarchies, jobs, bodies: A theory of gendered organizations. *Gender & Society, 4,* 139-158.

Aden, R. C. (1999). *Popular stories and promised lands: Fan cultures and symbolic pilgrimages.* Tuscaloosa: University of Alabama Press.

Aggarwal, A. P. (1987). *Sexual harassment in the workplace.* Toronto, Canada: Butterworth.

Alarcón, N. (1990). Chicana feminism: In the tracks of "the" native woman. *Cultural Studies, 4,* 248-256.

Allen, B. (1995). "Diversity" and organizational communication. *Journal of Applied Communication Research, 23,* 143-155.

Allen, B. (2000). "Learning the ropes": A black feminist standpoint analysis. In P. M. Buzzanell (Ed.), *Rethinking organizational and managerial communication from feminist perspectives* (pp. 177-208). Thousand Oaks, CA: Sage.

Allen, K. R., & Walker, A. J. (1992). A feminist analysis of interviews with elderly mothers and their daughters. In J. F. Gilgun, K. Daly, & G. Handel (Eds.), *Qualitative methods in family research* (pp. 198-214). Newbury Park, CA: Sage.

Allmark, P. (1995). Can there be an ethics of care? *Journal of Medical Ethics, 21,* 19-24.

American Cancer Society. (2003). *Breast cancer quick facts: Early detection and treatment.* Retrieved February 9, 2003, from www.cancer.org

American Heart Association. (1998). *Know heart and stroke.* Retrieved September 12, 2002, from http://women.americanheart.org/stroke/index.html

Americans With Disabilities Act. 42 U.S.C.A. (1990).

Ammer, C. (1989). *The new A-to-Z of women's health.* New York: Facts on File.

Anderson, J. (1995). When they know who we are. On *Never Assume* [CD]. Durham, NC: TsunamiINC.

Angaran, S., & Beckwith, K. (1999). Peer mediation in elementary schools. *Principal, 78,* 27-29.

Annas, G. J. (1998). A national bill of patients' rights. *New England Journal of Medicine, 338,* 695-699.

Anzaldúa, G. (1987). *Borderlands—La Frontera: The new mestiza.* San Francisco: Aunt Lute Books.

Apter, T., & Josselson, R. (1998). *Best friends: The pleasures and perils of girls' and women's friendships.* New York: Three Rivers Press.

Arnold, G. (1995). Dilemmas of feminist coalitions: Collective identity and strategic effectiveness in the battered women's movement. In M. M. Ferree & P. Y. Martin

(Eds.), *Feminist organizations: Harvest of the new women's movement* (pp. 276-290). Philadelphia: Temple University Press.

Arnold, L. B. (2000). "What is a feminist?" Students' descriptions. *Women and Language, 23*(2), 8-18.

Arntson, P. (1989). Improving citizens' health competencies. *Health Communication, 1*, 29-34.

Arthur, M. B., Inkson, K., & Pringle, J. K. (1999). *The new careers: Individual action and economic change.* London: Sage.

Artis, B. B. (1995). Tidbits. In S. Thames & M. Gazzaniga (Eds.), *The breast: An anthology* (pp. 177-181). New York: Global City Press.

Aryee, S., Wyatt, T., & Stone, R. (1996). Early career outcomes of graduate employees: The effect of mentoring and ingratiation. *Journal of Management Studies, 33*, 95-118.

Ashcraft, K. L. (1998). "I wouldn't say I'm a *feminist,* but . . . ": Organizational micropractice and gender identity. *Management Communication Quarterly, 11*, 587-597.

Ashcraft, K. L. (2001). Organized dissonance: Feminist bureaucracy as a hybrid form. *Academy of Management Journal, 44*, 1301-1322.

Ashcraft, K. L. (in press). Gender, discourse, and organization: Framing a shifting relationship. In D. Grant, C. Hardy, C. Oswick, N. Phillips, & L. Putnam (Eds.), *The handbook of organizational discourse.* Thousand Oaks, CA: Sage.

Ashcraft, K. L., & Pacanowsky, M. E. (1996). "A woman's worst enemy": Reflections on a narrative of organizational life and female identity. *Journal of Applied Communication Research, 24*, 217-239.

Bailyn, L. (1993). *Breaking the mold: Women, men, and time in the new corporate world.* New York: Free Press.

Bailyn, L., Fletcher, J. K., & Kolb, D. (1997). Unexpected connections: considering employees' personal lives can revitalize your business. *Sloan Management Review, 38*, 11-19.

Bakhtin, M. M. (1981). Discourse in the novel. In M. Holquist (Ed.), C. Emerson & M. Holquist (Trans.), *The dialogic imagination* (pp. 259-422). Austin: University of Texas Press.

Bakhtin, M. M. (1986). *Speech genres and other late essays* (C. Emerson & M. Holquist, Eds., & V. W. McGee, Trans.). Austin: University of Texas Press.

Banet-Weiser, S. (1999). *The most beautiful girl in the world: Beauty pageants and national identity.* Berkeley: University of California Press.

Banister, E. M. (1999). Women's midlife experience of their changing bodies. *Qualitative Health Research, 9*, 520-537.

Barbo, D. M. (1987). The physiology of the menopause. *Medical Clinics of North America, 71*, 11-22.

Barge, J. K. (1994). *Leadership: Communication skills for organizations and groups.* New York: St. Martin's Press.

Barker, L. L., & Watson, K. W. (2000). *Listen up: How to improve relationships, reduce stress, and be more productive by using the power of listening.* New York: St. Martin's Press.

Barnett, O. W., Miller-Perrin, C. L., & Perrin, R. D. (1997). *Family violence across the lifespan: An introduction.* Thousand Oaks, CA: Sage.

Bartky, S. L. (1988). Foucault, femininity, and the modernization of patriarchal power. In I. Diamond & L. Quinby (Eds.), *Feminism & Foucault: Reflections on resistance* (pp. 61-86). Boston: Northeastern University Press.

Bartunek, J. M., & Moch, M. K. (1991). Multiple constituencies and the quality of working life: Intervention at FoodCom. In P. J. Frost, L. F. Moore, M. R. Louis, C. C. Lundberg, & J. Martin (Eds.), *Reframing organizational culture* (pp. 104-114). Newbury Park, CA: Sage.

Basch, J., & Fisher, C. D. (2000). Affective events-emotions matrix: A classification of work events and associated emotions. In N. M. Ashkanasy, C. E. J. Härtel, & W. J. Zerbe (Eds.), *Emotions in the workplace: Research, theory, and practice* (pp. 36-48). Westport, CT: Quorum Books.

Bate, B., & Taylor, A. (Eds.). (1988). *Women communicating: Studies of women's talk.* Norwood, NJ: Ablex.

Bateson, M. C. (1989). *Composing a life.* New York: Plume.

Batt, S. (1994). *Patient no more: The politics of breast cancer.* Charlottetown, Prince Edward Island, Canada: Gynergy Books.

Baudrillard, J. (1981). *For a critique of the political economy of the sign* (C. Levin, Trans.). St. Louis, MO: Telos Press. (Original work published 1973)

Baxter, L. A. (1988). A dialectical perspective on communication strategies in relationship development. In S. W. Duck, D. F. Hay, S. E. Hobfoll, W. Iches, & B. Montgomery (Eds.), *Handbook of personal relationships* (pp. 257-273). New York: John Wiley.

Baxter, L. A. (1990). Dialectical contradictions in relationship development. *Journal of Social and Personal Relationships, 7,* 69-88.

Baxter, L. A. (1991). Content analysis. In D. M. Montgomery & S. Duck (Eds.), *Discourse: Studying interpersonal interaction* (pp. 239-252). New York: Guilford Press.

Baxter, L. A. (1992). Root metaphors in accounts of developing romantic relationships. *Journal of Social and Personal Relationships, 9,* 253-275.

Bayer, C. L., & Cegala, D. J. (1992). Trait verbal aggressiveness and argumentativeness: Relations with parenting style. *Western Journal of Communication, 56,* 301-310.

Beach, B. (1989). *Integrating work and family life: The home-working family.* Albany: SUNY Press.

Belenky, M. F., Clinchy, B., Goldberger, N. R., & Tarule, J. M. (1986). *Women's ways of knowing: The development of self, voice, and mind.* New York: Basic Books.

Bell, K. E., Orbe, M. P., Drummond, D. K., & Camara, S. K. (2000). Accepting the challenge of centralizing without essentializing: Black feminist thought and African American women's communicative experiences. *Women's Studies in Communication, 23,* 41-62.

Bell, S. E. (1987). Changing ideas: The medicalization of menopause. *Social Science of Medicine, 24,* 535-542.

Bell, S. K., Coleman, J. K., Anderson, A., Whelan, J. P., & Wilder, C. (2000). The effectiveness of peer mediation in a low-SES rural elementary school. *Psychology in the Schools, 37,* 505-516.

Bem, S. L. (1993). *The lenses of gender: Transforming the debate on sexual inequality.* New Haven, CT: Yale University Press.

Bennett, K. C., & Irwin, H. (1997). Shifting the emphasis to "patient as central": Sea change or ripple on the pond. *Health Communication, 9,* 83-93.

Bennett, L., & Piet, M. (1999). Standards for batterers intervention programs: In whose interest? *Violence Against Women, 5,* 6-24.

Benokraitis, N. V., & Feagin, J. R. (1986). *Modern sexism: Blatant, subtle, and covert discrimination.* Englewood Cliffs, NJ: Prentice Hall.

Benoliel, J. Q. (2001). Expanding knowledge about women through grounded theory: Introduction to the collection. *Health Care for Women International, 22,* 7-9.

Bensimon, H. F. (1997). What to do about anger in the workplace. *Training and Development, 51*(9), 28-32.

Berkun, C. S. (1986). On behalf of women over 40: Understanding the importance of the menopause. *Social Work, 31,* 378-384.

Bernstein, B. (1971). *Class, codes and control: Theoretical studies toward a sociology of language.* London: Routledge & Kegan Paul.

Berryman-Fink, C. (1993). Preventing sexual harassment through male-female communication training. In G. L. Kreps (Ed.), *Sexual harassment: Communication implications* (pp. 267-280). Cresskill, NJ: Hampton Press.

Bevington, C. (2001, November 18). *A special report from KPC News* [8-part series on domestic violence]. Retrieved July 8, 2003, from www.kpcnews.net/special_reports/domestic_abuse

Beyene, Y. (1986). Cultural significance and physiological manifestations of menopause: A biocultural analysis. *Culture, Medicine, and Psychiatry, 10,* 47-71.

Bickell, N. A., & Earp, J. A. (1994). Gynecologists' sex, clinical beliefs, and hysterectomy rates. *American Journal of Public Health, 84,* 1649-1652.

Bingham, S. (1991). Communication strategies for managing sexual harassment in organizations: Understanding message options and their effects. *Journal of Applied Communication Research, 19,* 88-115.

Bingham, S. G., & Burleson, B. R. (1996). The development of the sexual harassment proclivity scale: Construct validation and relationship to communication competence. *Communication Quarterly, 44,* 308-325.

Bird, S. R. (1996). Welcome to the men's club: Homosociality and the maintenance of hegemonic masculinity. *Gender & Society, 10,* 120-132.

Blasko, D. G., & Briihl, D. S. (1997). Reading and recall of metaphorical sentences: Effects of familiarity and context. *Metaphor & Symbol, 12,* 261-285.

Block, J. H. (1983). Differential premises arising from differential socialization of the sexes: Some conjectures. *Child Development, 54,* 1335-1354.

Block, M. (1998). 18 June 1992: Favorite body parts. In J. A. Tasch (Ed.)., *Art.Rage.Us.: Art and writing by women with breast cancer* (p. 126). San Francisco: Chronicle Books.

Bogart, K., & Stein, N. (1987). Breaking the silence: Sexual harassment in education. *Peabody Journal of Education, 64,* 146-163.

Booth-Butterfield, M. (1989). Perceptions of harassing communication as a function of locus of control, work force participation, and gender. *Communication Quarterly, 37,* 262-275.

Boozang, K. M. (1998). Western medicine opens the door to alternative medicine. *American Journal of Law & Medicine, 24,* 185-212.

Bordo, S. (1989). The body and the reproduction of femininity. In A. Jaggar & S. Bordo (Eds.), *Gender/body/knowledge: Feminist reconstructions of being and knowing* (pp. 13-33). New Brunswick, NJ: Rutgers University Press.

Bordo, S. (1993). *Unbearable weight: Feminism, Western culture, and the body.* Berkeley: University of California Press.

Bordo, S. (1999). *The male body: A new look at men in public and private.* New York: Farrar, Straus and Giroux.

Borges, S., & Waitzkin, H. (1995). Women's narratives in primary medical care encounters. *Women and Health, 23,* 1, 29-56.

Boris, E. (1986). *"Right to work" as "women's right": The debate over the Vermont knitters, 1980-1985* (Working paper Series 1, Legal History Program Working Papers, LHP-#1:5). Madison, WI: Institute for Legal Studies, University of Wisconsin-Madison Law School.

Boris, E., & Daniels, C. (Eds.). (1989). *Homework: Historical and contemporary perspectives on paid labor at home.* Urbana: University of Illinois Press.

Boston Women's Health Book Collective. (1992). *The new our bodies, ourselves: A book by and for women.* New York: Simon & Schuster.

Boston Women's Health Book Collective (1998). *Our bodies, ourselves for the new century: A book by and for women.* New York: Simon & Schuster.

Bowers, V., & Buzzanell, P. M. (2002). The space between: Using peer theater to transcend race, class, and gender. *Women and Language, 25*(1), 29-40.

Braddock, J. H., Dawkins, M. P., & Wilson, G. (1995). Intercultural contact and race relations among American youth. In W. D. Hawley & A. W. Jackson (Eds.), *Toward a common destiny* (pp. 237-256). San Francisco: Jossey-Bass.

Breast Cancer Fund (2000). *Obsessed with breasts.* Retrieved July 8, 2003, from www.breastcancerfund.org/campaign_press.htm

Bredin, A. (1996). *The virtual office survival handbook.* New York: John Wiley.

Brenner, M. (2001, August 13). Not their mothers' choices. *Newsweek, 138*(7), 48-49.

Bridge, K., & Baxter, L. A. (1992). Blended relationships: Friends as work associates. *Western Journal of Communication, 56,* 200-225.

Brison, S. J. (1997). Outliving oneself: Trauma, memory, and personal identity. In D. T. Meyers (Ed.), *Feminists rethink the self* (pp. 12-39). Boulder, CO: Westview Press.

Brody, H. (1994). "My story is broken; Can you help me fix it?" Medical ethics and the joint construction of narrative. *Literature and Medicine, 13,* 79-92.

Brown, M. H. (1993). Sex and the workplace: Watch your behind, or they'll watch it for you. In G. L. Kreps (Ed.), *Sexual harassment: Communication implications* (pp. 118-130). Cresskill, NJ: Hampton Press.

Browning Smith, C. (1998). *Diary of an eating disorder: A mother and daughter share their healing journey.* Dallas, TX: Taylor.

Brumberg, J. J. (1998). *The body project: An intimate history of American girls.* New York: Vintage Books.

Bulbeck, C. (2001). Articulating structure and agency: How women's studies students express their relationships with feminism. *Women's Studies International Forum, 24,* 141-156.

Bullis, C., & Stout, K. (2000). Organizational socialization: A feminist standpoint approach. In P. M. Buzzanell (Ed.), *Rethinking organizational and managerial communication from feminist perspectives* (pp. 47-75). Thousand Oaks, CA: Sage.

Burr, V. (1995). *An introduction to social constructionism.* London: Routledge.

Burrell, N. A., Buzzanell, P. M., & McMillan, J. (1992). Feminine tensions in conflict situations as revealed by metaphoric analyses. *Management Communication Quarterly, 6,* 115-145.

Buske, N. T. (2000). Thwarting WAH interruptions. Retrieved March 13, 2000, from www.comsonline.com/jobwise/balancingact/article.asp?key=SS990006

Buzzanell, P. M. (1993). Feminist approaches to organizational communication instruction. In C. Berryman-Fink, D. Ballard-Reisch, & L. H. Newman (Eds.), *Communication and sex role socialization* (pp. 525-553). New York: Garland.

Buzzanell, P. M. (1994). Gaining a voice: Feminist perspectives in organizational communication. *Management Communication Quarterly, 7,* 339-383.

Buzzanell, P. M. (1995). Reframing the glass ceiling as a socially constructed process: Implications for understanding and change. *Communication Monographs, 62,* 327-354.

Buzzanell, P. M. (2000a). The promise and practice of the new career and social contract: Illusions exposed and suggestions for reform. In P. M. Buzzanell (Ed.), *Rethinking organizational and managerial communication from feminist perspectives* (pp. 209-235). Thousand Oaks, CA: Sage.

Buzzanell, P. M. (Ed.). (2000b). *Rethinking organizational and managerial communication from feminist perspectives.* Thousand Oaks, CA: Sage.

Buzzanell, P. M. (2001). Gendered practices in the contemporary workplace: A critique of what often constitutes front page news in the *Wall Street Journal. Management Communication Quarterly, 14,* 518-538.

Buzzanell, P. M., & Burrell, N. A. (1997). Family and workplace conflict: Examining metaphorical conflict schemas and expressions across context and sex. *Human Communication Research, 24,* 109-146.

Buzzanell, P. M., Ellingson, L., Silvio, C., Pasch, V., Dale, B., Mauro, G., et al. (1997). Leadership processes in alternative organizations: Invitational and dramaturgical leadership. *Communication Studies, 48,* 285-310.

Buzzanell, P. M., & Goldzwig, S. (1991). Linear and non-linear career models: Metaphors, paradigms, and ideologies. *Management Communication Quarterly, 4,* 466-505.

Buzzanell, P. M., & Turner, L. H. (2003). Emotion work revealed by job loss discourse: Backgrounding-foregrounding of feelings, construction of normalcy, and (re)instituting of traditional masculinities. *Journal of Applied Communication Research, 31,* 27-57.

Calás, M. B., & Smircich, L. (1996). From "the woman's" point of view: Feminist approaches to organization studies. In S. R. Clegg, C. Hardy, & W. R. Nord (Eds.), *Handbook of organization studies* (pp. 218-257). London: Sage.

Canary, D. J., Cody, M. J., & Marston, P. J. (1987). Goal types, compliance-gaining and locus of control. *Journal of Language and Social Psychology, 5,* 249-269.

Cannon, L. (1990). Fostering positive race, class, and gender dynamics in the classroom. *Women's Studies Quarterly, 18,* 126-134.

Carillo Rowe, A. M. (2000). Locating feminism's subject: The paradox of white femininity and the struggle to forge feminist alliances. *Communication Theory, 10,* 64-80.

Carolan, M. (1994). Beyond deficiency: Broadening the view of menopause. *Journal of Applied Gerontology, 13,* 193-205.

Caron, A. F. (1989). *Model of parenting workshops for mothers of adolescent daughters.* Unpublished doctoral dissertation, Columbia University Teachers College, New York.

Carter, P. (1996). Breast feeding and the social construction of heterosexuality, or "what breasts are really for." In J. Holland & L. Adkins (Eds.), *Sex, sensibility, and the gendered body* (pp. 99-119). New York: St. Martin's Press.

Cassell, P. (Ed.). (1993). *The Giddens reader.* Stanford, CA: Stanford University Press.

Cauce, A. M., Hiraga, Y., Graves, D., Gonzales, N., Ryan-Finn, K., & Grove, K. (1996). African American mothers and their adolescent daughters: Closeness, conflict, and control. In B. J. Ross Leadbeater & N. Way (Eds.), *Urban girls: Resisting stereotypes, creating identities* (pp. 100-116). New York: New York University Press.

Cavallaro, D. (1998). *The body for beginners.* New York: Writers & Readers.

Chapman, P. A. (1993, November). *Tailhook '91: Framing sexual harassment and the myth of desexualized bureaucracy.* Paper presented at the annual conference for the Speech Communication Association, Miami Beach, FL.

Charmaz, K. (1990). Discovering chronic illness: Using grounded theory. *Social Science and Medicine, 30,* 1161-1172.

Charmaz, K. (1991). *Good days bad days: The self in chronic illness and time.* New Brunswick, NJ: Rutgers University Press.

Chernin, K. (1981). *The obsession: Reflections on the tyranny of slenderness.* New York: Harper & Row.

Chervenak, F. A., & McCullough, L. B. (1997). Ethics in obstetrics and gynecology: An overview. *European Journal of Obstetrics & Gynecology, 75,* 91-94.

Chervenak, F. A., & McCullough, L. B. (1998). Ethical issues in gynecology. *Ceska Gynekologie, 63*(2), 103-107.

Chesler, P. (1972). *Women and madness.* New York: Avon.

Clair, R. P. (1993a). The bureaucratization, commodification, and privatization of sexual harassment through institutional discourse: A study of the "Big Ten" universities. *Management Communication Quarterly, 7,* 123-157.

Clair, R. P. (1993b, November). *Four facets of hegemony with implications for sexual harassment.* Paper presented at the annual conference for the Speech Communication Association, Miami Beach, FL.

Clair, R. P. (1993c). The use of framing devices to sequester organizational narratives: Hegemony and harassment. *Communication Monographs, 60,* 113-136.

Clair, R. P. (1997). Organizing silence: Silence as voice and voice as silence in the narrative exploration of the Treaty of New Echota. *Western Journal of Communication, 61,* 315-337.

Clair, R. P. (1998). *Organizing silence: A world of possibilities.* Albany: SUNY Press.

Clair, R. P., Chapman, P. A., & Kunkel, A. W. (1996). Narrative approaches to raising consciousness about sexual harassment: From research to pedagogy and back again. *Journal of Applied Communication Research, 24,* 241-259.

Clair, R. P., & Thompson, K. (1996). Pay discrimination as a discursive and material practice: A case concerning extended housework. *Journal of Applied Communication Research, 24,* 1-20.

Clark, P. (1998). Breast changes over a lifetime. In Boston Women's Health Book Collective, *Our bodies, ourselves for the new century: A book by and for women* (p. 275). New York: Touchstone.

Clark, S. C. (2000). Work/family border theory: A new theory of work/family balance. *Human Relations, 53,* 747-770.

Clement, G. (1996). *Care, autonomy, and justice: Feminism and the ethic of care.* Boulder, CO: Westview Press.

Cleveland, J. N., Stockdale, M., & Murphy, K. R. (2000). *Women and men in organizations: Sex and gender issues at work.* Mahwah, NJ: Lawrence Erlbaum.

Coates, J. (1996). *Women talk: Conversation between women friends.* Cambridge, MA: Blackwell.

Cockburn, J., & Bewley, S. (1996). Do patients prefer women doctors? *British Journal of Obstetrics and Gynecology, 103,* 2-3.

Cohen, T. (1979). Metaphor and the cultivation of intimacy. In S. Sacks (Ed.), *On metaphor* (pp. 1-10). Chicago: University of Chicago Press.

Coleman, G., & Rippin, A. (2000). Putting feminist theory to work: Collaboration as a means toward organizational change. *Organization, 7,* 573-587.

Collins, E. G. C., & Blodgett, T. B. (1981). Sexual harassment: Some see it . . . some won't. *Harvard Business Review, 59*(2), 76-95.

Collins, P. H. (1986). Learning from the outsider within. *Social Problems, 33,* 514-532.

Collins, P. H. (2000). *Black feminist thought: Knowledge, consciousness, and the politics of empowerment* (2nd ed.). New York: Routledge.

Condravy, J. C. (1993). Women's talk: A cooperative discourse. In C. Berryman-Fink, D. Ballard-Reisch, & L. Newman (Eds.), *Communication and sex-role socialization* (pp. 399-431). New York: Garland.

Cone, F. K. (1993). *Making sense of menopause.* New York: Simon & Schuster.

Conger, J. A. (1991). Inspiring others: The language of leadership. *Academy of Management Executive, 5*(1), 31-45.

Conlin, M., Merritt, J. & Himelstein, L. (2002, November 25). Mommy is really home from work. *Business Week,* 101-104.

Connell, R. W. (1987). *Gender and power: Society, the person, and sexual politics.* Stanford, CA: Stanford University Press.

Connell, R. W. (1995). *Masculinities.* Berkeley: University of California Press.

Conquergood, D. (1994). Homeboys and hoods: Gang communication and cultural space. In L. R. Frey (Ed.), *Group communication in context: Studies of natural groups* (pp. 23-55). Hillsdale, NJ: Lawrence Erlbaum.

Cooren, F. (2001). Translation and articulation in the organization of coalitions: The Great Whale River case. *Communication Theory, 11,* 178-200.

Corea, G. (1977). *The hidden malpractice: How American medicine treats women as patients and professionals.* New York: William Morrow.

Cose, E. (1995). *A man's world.* New York: HarperCollins.

Couser, G. T. (1997). *Recovering bodies: Illness, disability, and life writing.* Madison: University of Wisconsin Press.

Cox, A. M. (2001, March 30). A university struggles to oust the professor it hoped would go away: After harassment charges, student complaints, and protests, some ask: What will it take? *Chronicle of Higher Education, 47,* A14-A16.

Craig, R. T. (1986). Goals in discourse. In D. G. Ellis & W. A. Donohue (Eds.), *Contemporary issues in language and discourse processes* (pp. 257-273). Hillsdale, NJ: Lawrence Erlbaum.

Crandall, C. S., Tsang, J.-A., Goldman, S., & Pennington, J. S. (1999). Newsworthy moral dilemmas: Justice, caring, and gender. *Sex Roles, 40,* 187-209.

Crick, N. R., Bigbee, M. A., & Howes, C. (1996). Gender differences in children's normative beliefs about aggression: How do I hurt thee? Let me count the ways. *Child Development, 67,* 1003-1014.

Crick, N. R., & Dodge, K. A. (1994). A review and reformation of social information-processing mechanisms in children's social adjustment. *Psychological Bulletin, 115,* 74-101.

Crick, N. R., & Grotpeter, J. K. (1995). Relational aggression, gender, and social-psychological adjustment. *Child Development, 66,* 710-722.

Cutson, T. M., & Meuleman, E. (2000). Managing menopause. *American Family Physician, 61,* 1391-1400.

Daly, J. A. (2002). After 50: Reflecting on the future. *Communication Education, 51,* 376-382.

Daly, M. (1978). *Gyn/Ecology: The metaethics of radical feminism.* Boston: Beacon Press.

Dan, A. J. (Ed.). (1994). *Reframing women's health.* Thousand Oaks, CA: Sage.

Daniel, J. L., & Daniel, J. E. (1999). African American childrearing: The context of a hot stove. In T. J. Socha & R. C. Diggs (Eds.) *Communication, race, and family:*

Exploring communication in black, white, and biracial families (pp. 25-44). Mahwah, NJ: Lawrence Erlbaum.

Danner, L., & Walsh, S. (1999). "Radical" feminists and "bickering" women: Backlash in U.S. media coverage of the United Nations Fourth World Conference on Women. *Critical Studies in Mass Communication, 16,* 63-84.

Davies, S. A. M. (1998). Women above the glass ceiling: Perceptions on corporate mobility and strategies for success. *Gender & Society,* 12, 339-358.

de Certeau, M. (1984). *The practice of everyday life.* Berkeley: University of California Press.

Deaux, K., & Kite, M. (1993). Gender stereotypes. In F. L. Denmark & M. A. Paludi (Eds.), *Psychology of women: A handbook of issues and theories* (pp. 107-139). Westport, CT: Greenwood Press.

DeBeauvoir, S. (1949/1989). *The second sex.* New York: Vintage Books.

Debrovner, C., & Shubin-Stein, R. (1975). Psychological aspects of vaginal examinations. *Medical Aspects of Human Sexuality, 9,* 163-164.

Deetz, S. (1996). Describing differences in approaches to organization science: Rethinking Burrell and Morgan and their legacy. *Organization Science, 7,* 191-207.

Department of Sociology. (1994). *Ball State Area Studies.* Unpublished manuscript, Ball State University, Ball State, IN.

Department of Sociology. (1998). *Ball State Area Studies.* Unpublished manuscript, Ball State University, Ball State, IN.

DeVault, M. L. (1990). Talking and listening from women's standpoint: Feminist strategies for interviewing and analysis. *Social Problems, 37,* 96-116.

DeVault, M. L. (1999). Liberating method: Feminism and social research. Philadelphia: Temple University Press.

Diamond, I., & Orenstein, G. F. (Eds.). (1990). *Reweaving the world: The emergence of ecofeminism.* San Francisco: Sierra Club Books.

Diethrich, E. B., & Cohan, C. (1992). *Women and heart disease.* New York: Ballantine Books.

Diggs, R. C. (1999). African American and European American adolescents' perceptions of self-esteem as influenced by parent and peer communication and support environments. In T. J. Socha & R. C. Diggs (Eds.), *Communication, race, and family: Exploring communication in black, white, and biracial families* (pp. 105-146). Mahwah, NJ: Lawrence Erlbaum.

Dill, V. S., & Haberman, M. (1995). Building a gentler school. *Educational Leadership,* 52(5), 69-71.

Dillard, J. P. (1989). Types of influence goals in close relationships. *Journal of Social and Personal Relationships, 6,* 293-308.

Dillard, J. P. (1990). A goal-driven model of interpersonal influence. In J. P. Dillard (Ed.), *Seeking compliance: The production of interpersonal influence messages* (pp. 41-56). Scottsdale, AZ: Gorsuch Scarisbrick.

Dillard, J. P., Segrin, C., & Harden, J. (1989). Primary and secondary goals in the production of interpersonal influence messages. *Communication Monographs, 56,* 19-38.

Dixson, M. D. (1995). Models and perspectives of parent-child communication. In T. Socha & G. Stamp (Eds.), *Parents, children, and communication: Frontiers of theory and research* (pp. 433-462). Mahwah, NJ: Lawrence Erlbaum.

Domar, A. D. (1986). Psychological aspects of the pelvic exam: Individual needs and physician involvement. *Women & Health, 10*(4), 75-90.

Donovan, J. (1992). *Feminist theory: The intellectual traditions of American feminism.* New York: Continuum.

Dorodny, V. S. (1998). Security and confidentiality of health information systems: Implications for physicians. *Physician Executive, 24*(3), 32-37.

Dougherty, D. S. (1999). Dialogue through standpoint: Understanding women's and men's standpoints of sexual harassment. *Management Communication Quarterly, 12,* 436-468.

Dougherty, D. S. (2001a). Sexual harassment as (dys)functional process: A feminist standpoint analysis. *Journal of Applied Communication Research, 29,* 372-402.

Dougherty, D. S. (2001b). Women's discursive construction of a sexual harassment paradox. *Qualitative Research Reports in Communication, 2,* 6-13.

Dougherty, D. S., & Krone, K. J. (2000). Overcoming the dichotomy: Cultivating standpoints in organizations through research. *Women's Studies in Communication, 23,* 16-40.

Douglas, S. J. (1994). *Where the girls are: Growing up female with the mass media.* New York: Times Books.

Downer, S. M., Cody, M. M., McCluskey, P., Wilson, P. D., Arnott, S. J., Lister, T. A., & Slevin, M. S. (1994). Pursuit and practice of complementary therapies by cancer patients receiving conventional treatment. *British Medical Journal, 309,* 86-89.

Dreifus, C. (Ed.). (1977). *Seizing our bodies: The politics of women's health.* New York: Vintage Books.

Driscoll, J. B. (1981). Sexual attraction and harassment: Management's new problems. *Personnel Journal, 60,* 33-36, 56.

Droge, D., & Murphy, B. O. (1999). Introduction. In D. Droge & B. O. Murphy (Eds.), *Voices of strong democracy: Concepts and models for service-learning in communication studies* (pp. 1-6). Washington, DC: American Association for Higher Education.

DuBois, D. L., & Hirsch, B. J. (1990). School and neighborhood friendship patterns of Blacks and Whites in early adolescence. *Child Development, 61,* 524-536.

Dudley, B. S., Johnson, D. W., & Johnson, R. T. (1996). Conflict-resolution training and middle school students' integrative negotiation behavior. *Journal of Applied Social Psychology, 26,* 2038-2052.

Dunn, D., & Cody, M. J. (2000). Account credibility and public image: Excuses, justifications, denials, and sexual harassment. *Communication Monographs, 67,* 372-391.

Duxbury, L., Higgins, C., & Neufield, D. (1998). Telework and the balance between work and family: Is telework part of the problem or part of the solution? In M. Igbaria & M. Tan (Eds.), *The virtual workplace* (pp. 218-255). Hershey, PA: Idea Group.

Dwyer, S. I., & Slaybaugh, S. (2001, June). *Women in the Arts and NWMF: Where have we been and where are we going?* Report presented at the 27th Annual National Women's Music Festival, Muncie, IN.

Eadie, W. F. (1994). On having an agenda. *Journal of Applied Communication Research, 22,* 81-85.

Eating Disorder Referral and Information Center. (2002). Retrieved June 30, 2003, from www.edreferral.com

Eckert, P., & McConnell-Ginet, S. (1994). Think practically and look locally: Language and gender as community-based practices. In C. Roman, S. Suhasz, & C. Miller (Eds.), *The women and language debate: A sourcebook* (pp. 432-460). New Brunswick, NJ: Rutgers University Press.

Eder, D., Staggenborg, S., & Sudderth, L. (1995). The National Women's Music Festival: Collective identity and diversity in a lesbian-feminist community. *Journal of Contemporary Ethnography, 23,* 485-515.

Edley, P. (2000). Discursive essentializing in a women-owned business: Gendered stereotypes and strategic subordination. *Management Communication Quarterly, 14,* 271-306.

Edley, P. P. (2001). Technology, employed mothers, and corporate colonization of the lifeworld: A gendered paradox of work and family balance. *Women and Language, 24* (2), 28-35.

Edwards, P., & Edwards, S. (1995). Foreword. In R. Heck, A. Owen, & B. Rowe (Eds.), *Home-based employment and family life* (pp. xiii-xv). Westport, CT: Auburn.

Ehrenhaus, P. (1988). Silence and symbolic expression. *Communication Monographs, 55,* 41-57.

Ehrenreich, B., & English, D. (1973). *Witches, midwives, and nurses: A history of women healers.* New York: Feminist Press.

Ehrenreich, B., & English, D. (1978). *For her own good: 150 years of the experts' advice to women.* Garden City, New York: Anchor Books.

Ehrlich, T. (2000). *Civic responsibility and higher education.* Phoenix, AZ: Oryx Press.

Eidsness, L., & Wilson, A. L. (1994). Women voicing their autonomy: The changing picture of women's health care. *South Dakota Journal of Medicine, 47*(7), 227-229.

Eisenberg, D. M., Kessler, R. C., Foster, C., Norlock, F. E., Calkins, D. R., & Delbanco, T. L. (1993). Unconventional medicine in the United States: Prevalence, cost, and patterns of use. *New England Journal of Medicine, 328,* 246-252.

Eisenberg, D. M., Kessler, R. C., Van Rompay, M. L., Kaptchuk, T. J., Wilkey, S. A., & Appel, S., et al. (2001). Perceptions about complementary therapies relative to conventional therapies among adults who use both: Results from a national survey. *Annals of Internal Medicine, 135,* 344-351.

Eisenberg, E. (1984). Ambiguity as strategy in organizational communication. *Communication Monographs, 51,* 227-242.

Eisenberg, E., & Goodall, H. L., Jr. (1997). *Organizational communication: Balancing creativity and constraint.* New York: St. Martin's Press.

Elam, S., Rose, L., & Gallup, A. (1994). The 26th annual Gallup poll of the public's attitudes toward the public schools. *Phi Delta Kappan, 76,* 41-56.

Ellingson, L. L., & Buzzanell, P. M. (1999). Listening to women's narratives of breast cancer treatment: A feminist approach to patient satisfaction with physician-patient communication. *Health Communication, 11,* 153-183.

Ellis, C., Kiesinger, C. E., & Tillmann-Healy, L. M. (1997). Interactive interviewing: Talking about emotional experience. In R. Hertz (Ed.), *Reflexivity and voice* (pp. 119-149). Thousand Oaks, CA: Sage.

Engebretson, J., & Wardell, D. W. (1997). Perimenopausal women's alienation. *Journal of Holistic Nursing, 15,* 254-270.

Engel, G. W. (1977). The need for a new medical model: A challenge for biomedicine. *Science, 196,* 2129-2136.

Enomoto, E. K. (1997). Negotiating the ethics of care and justice. *Educational Administration Quarterly, 33,* 351-370.

Ensler, E. (2000). *The vagina monologues: The V-day edition.* New York: Villard Books.

Ephron, N. (1995). A few words about breasts. Reprinted in S. Thames & M. Gazzaniga (Eds.), *The breast: An anthology* (pp. 6-14). New York: Global City Press. (Reprinted from N. Ephron (1972). *Crazy Salad.* New York: Alfred A. Knopf, Inc.)

Epstein, J. L. (1986). Friendship selection: Developmental and environmental influences. In E. C. Mueller & C. R. Cooper (Eds.), *Process and outcome in peer relationships* (pp. 129-160). Orlando, FL: Academic Press.

Eskes, T. B., & Miller, E. M. (1998). The discourse of empowerment: Foucault, Marcuse, and women's fitness texts. *Journal of Sport and Social Issues, 22,* 317-345.

Fagan, L. (2001, January 7). Sociologist explores "new maleness." *Lafayette Journal & Courier,* p. C5.

Fairhurst, G. T. (1993). The leader-member exchange patterns of women leaders in industry: A discourse analysis. *Communication Monographs, 60,* 321-351.

Fairhurst, G., & Sarr, R. A. (1996). *The art of framing: Managing the language of leadership.* San Francisco: Jossey-Bass.

Faludi, S. (1991). *Backlash: The undeclared war against American women.* New York: Crown.

Faludi, S. (1999). *Stiffed: The betrayal of the American man.* New York: Perennial.

Faludi, S. (2001, January 8). Don't get the wrong message. *Newsweek, 137*(2), 56.

Faraclas, H. (1995). The healthy breast. In S. Thames & M. Gazzaniga (Eds.), *The breast: An anthology* (pp. 57-66). New York: Global City Press.

Farley-Lucas, B. (2000). Communicating the (in)visibility of motherhood: Family talk and ties: Family talk and the ties to motherhood with/in the workplace. *Electronic Journal of Communication/ Revue Electronique de Communication, 10*(3), retrieved July 18, 2003, from www.cios.org/getfile/farley_V10n3400

Feary, V. M. (2000). Sexual harassment: Why the corporate world still doesn't "get it." In E. Wall (Ed.), *Sexual harassment* (rev. ed., pp. 78-98). Amherst, NY: Prometheus Books.

Fee, E. (Ed.). (1993). *Women and health: The politics of sex in medicine.* Farmingdale, NY: Baywood.

Feldmann, R. J., & Driscoll, C. E. (1982). Evaluation of the patient-centered pelvic examination. *Journal of Family Practice, 15,* 990-993.

Fennema, K., Meyer, D. L., & Owen, N. (1990). Sex of physician: Patients' preferences and stereotypes. *Journal of Family Practice, 30,* 441-446.

Feree, M. M., & Martin, P. Y. (Eds.). (1995). *Feminist organizations: Harvest of the new women's movement.* Philadelphia: Temple University Press.

Ferguson, I. B. (1999). African-American parent-child communication about racial derogation. In T. J. Socha & R. C. Diggs (Eds.), *Communication, race, and family: Exploring communication in black, white, and biracial families* (pp. 45-67). Mahwah, NJ: Lawrence Erlbaum.

Ferguson, K. E. (1993). *The man question: Visions of subjectivity in feminist theory.* Berkeley: University of California Press.

Ferguson, S. J., & Parry, C. (1998). Rewriting menopause: Challenging the medical paradigm to reflect menopausal women's experiences. *Frontiers: A Journal of Women Studies, 19,* 20-41.

Fernandez, C. V. (1998). Alternative and complementary therapy use in pediatric oncology patients in British Columbia: Prevalence and reasons for use and nonuse. *Journal of Clinical Oncology, 16,* 1279-1286.

Ferrell, B. R., Dow, K. H., Leigh, S., Ly, J., & Gulasekaram, P. (1995). Quality of life in long-term cancer survivors. *Oncology Nursing Forum, 22,* 915-922.

Fertig, D. L., & Hayes, D. F. (1998). Psychological responses to tumor markers. In J. C. Holland (Ed.), *Psycho-Oncology* (pp. 147-160). New York: Oxford University Press.

Field, P. A., & Morse, J. M. (1985). *Nursing research: The application of qualitative approaches.* Rockville, MD: Aspen.

Fine, M., Weis, L., Addelston, J., & Marusza, J. (1997). (In)secure times: Constructing white working-class masculinities in the late 20th century. *Gender & Society, 11,* 52-68.

Fine, M. G. (1996). Cultural diversity in the workplace: The state of the field. *Journal of Business Communication, 33,* 485-502.

Fineman, S. (1996). Emotion and organizing. In S. R. Clegg, C. Hardy, & W. R. Nord (Eds.), *Handbook of organization studies* (pp. 543-564). Thousand Oaks, CA: Sage.

Finet, D. (2001). Sociopolitical environments and issues. In F. M. Jablin & L. L. Putnam (Eds.), *The new handbook of organizational communication: Advances in theory, research, and methods* (pp. 270-290). Thousand Oaks, CA: Sage.

Fischer, L. R. (1983). Transition to grandmotherhood. *International Journal of Aging and Human Development, 16,* 67-78.

Fischer, L. R. (1986). *Linked lives: Adult daughters and their mothers.* New York: Harper & Row.

Fisher, B., & Galler, R. (1988). Friendship and fairness: How disability affects friendship between women. In M. Fine & A. Asch (Eds.), *Women with disabilities: Essays in psychology, culture, and politics* (pp. 172-194). Philadelphia: Temple University Press.

Fisher, W. (1985). The narrative paradigm: An elaboration. *Communication Monographs, 52,* 347-367.

Fitzgerald, L. F. (2000). Consensual amorous relationships. In E. Wall (Ed.), *Sexual harassment* (rev. ed., pp. 42-47). Amherst, NY: Prometheus Books.

Fitzgerald, L. F., Shullman, S. L., Baily, N., Richards, M., Swecker, J., & Gold, Y., et al. (1988). The incidence and dimensions of sexual harassment in academia and the workplace. *Journal of Vocational Behavior, 32,* 152-175.

Flax, J. (1987). Postmodernism and gender relations in feminist theory. *Signs: Journal of Women in Culture and Society, 12,* 621-643.

Flax, J. (1990). *Thinking fragments: Psychoanalysis, feminism, and postmodernism in the contemporary West.* Berkeley: University of California Press.

Flax, J. (1993). Women do theory. In A. M. Jaggar & P. S. Rothenberg (Eds.), *Feminist frameworks: Alternative theoretical accounts of the relations between women and men* (pp. 80-85). New York: McGraw-Hill.

Flint, M. (1975). The menopause: Reward or punishment? *Psychosomatic, 16,* 161-163.

Flores, L. A. (1996). Creating discursive space through a rhetoric of difference: Chicana feminists craft a homeland. *Quarterly Journal of Speech, 82,* 142-156.

Fondas, N. (1997). Feminization unveiled: Management qualities in contemporary writings. *Academy of Management Review, 22,* 257-283.

Foss, K. A., & Foss, S. K. (1994). Personal experience as evidence in feminist scholarship. *Western Journal of Communication, 58,* 39-43.

Foss, S. K. (1996). *Rhetorical criticism: Exploration and practice* (2nd ed.). Prospect Heights, IL: Waveland Press.

Foss, S. K., & Foss, K. A. (1988). What distinguishes feminist scholarship in communication studies? *Women's Studies in Communication, 11,* 9-11.

Foss, S. K., & Griffin, C. L. (1995). Beyond persuasion: A proposal for an invitational rhetoric. *Communication Monographs, 62,* 2-18.

Foucault, M. (1995). *Discipline and punish: The birth of the prison.* New York: Vintage Books.

Frank, A. W. (1991). Cancer self-healing: Health as cultural capital in monological society. *Studies in Symbolic Interaction, 12,* 105-222.

Frank, A. W. (1995). *The wounded storyteller: Body, illness and ethics.* Chicago: University Press.

Franks, V., & Rothblum, E. D. (Eds.). (1983). *The stereotyping of women: Its effects on mental health.* New York: Springer.

Fraser, N. (1990-1991). Rethinking the public sphere: A contribution to the critique of actually existing democracy. *Social Text, 25/26,* 56-80.

Frey, L. R. (2000). To be applied or not to be applied, that isn't even the question; but wherefore art thou, applied communication researcher? Reclaiming applied communication research and redefining the role of the researcher. *Journal of Applied Communication Research, 28,* 178-182.

Frey, L. R., Botan, C. H., & Kreps, G. L. (2000). *Investigating communication. An introduction to research methods* (2nd ed.). Boston: Allyn & Bacon.

Friedman, M. (1985). Abraham, Socrates, and Heinz: Where are the women? (Care and context in moral reasoning). In C. B. Harding (Ed.), *Moral dilemmas: Philosophical and psychological issues in the development of moral reasoning* (pp. 25-41). Chicago: Precedent.

Friedman, M. (1993a). Beyond caring: The de-moralization of gender. In M. J. Larrabee (Ed.), *An ethic of care: Feminist and interdisciplinary perspectives* (pp. 258-273). New York: Routledge.

Friedman, M. (1993b). *What are friends for? Feminist perspectives on personal relationships and moral theory.* Ithaca, NY: Cornell University Press.

Frost, P. J., Dutton, J. E., Worline, M. C., & Wilson, A. (2000). Narratives of compassion in organizations. In S. Fineman (Ed.), *Emotions in organizations* (2nd ed., pp. 25-45). London: Sage.

Frye, C. A., & Weisberg, R. B. (1994). Increasing the incidence of routine pelvic examinations: Behavioral medicine's contribution. *Women & Health, 21*(1), 33-55.

Frye, M. (1993). The possibility of feminist theory. In A. M. Jaggar & P. S. Rothenberg (Eds.), *Feminist frameworks: Alternative theoretical accounts of the relations between women and men* (pp. 103-112). New York: McGraw-Hill.

Frymier, A. B., & Houser, M. L. (2000). The teacher-student relationship as an interpersonal relationship. *Communication Education, 49,* 207-219.

Fugh-Berman, A. (1994). Training doctors to care for women. *Technology Review, 97*(2), 34-40.

Fulenwider, C. K. (1980). *Feminism in American politics.* New York: Praeger.

Gabbard-Alley, A. S. (1995). Health communication and gender: A review and critique. *Health Communication, 7,* 35-54.

Gajjala, R. (2000) Negotiating cyberspace/negotiating RL. In A. Gonzalez, M. Houston, V. Chen (Eds.), *Our voices: Essays in culture, ethnicity, and communication* (pp. 63-71). Los Angeles: Roxbury Press.

Gajjala, R. (2002). An interrupted postcolonial/feminist cyberethnography: Complicity and resistance in the "cyberfield." *Feminist Media Studies, 2,* 177-193.

Galvin, K. M. (1993). Preventing the problem: Preparing faculty for the issue of sexual harassment. In G. L. Kreps (Ed.), *Sexual harassment: Communication implications* (pp. 257-266). Cresskill, NJ: Hampton Press.

Galvin, K. M. (2004). The family of the future: What do we face? In A. Vangelisti (Ed.), *Handbook of family communication* (pp. 675-697). Mahwah, NJ: Lawrence Erlbaum.

Gannon, L., & Ekstrom, B. (1993). Attitudes toward menopause: The influence of sociocultural paradigms. *Psychology of Women Quarterly, 17,* 275-288.

Garlick, B., Dixon, S., & Allen, P. (Eds.). (1992). *Stereotypes of women in power: Historical perspectives and revisionist views*. Westport, CT: Greenwood Press.

Gelles, R. J. (1997). *Intimate violence in families* (3rd ed.). Thousand Oaks, CA: Sage.

Gerber, S., & Terry-Day B. (1999). Does peer mediation really work? *Professional School Counseling, 2,* 169-171.

Gergen, K. J. (1991). *The saturated self: Dilemmas of identity in contemporary life*. New York: Basic Books.

Gergen, K. J., & Gergen, M. M. (1988). Narrative and the self as relationship. In L. Berkowitz (Ed.), *Advances in experimental social psychology* (Vol. 21, pp. 17-56). San Diego, CA: Academic Press.

Gergen, M. M. (1990). Baskets of reed and arrows of steel: Stories of chaos and continuity. In S. Srivastva (Ed.), *Symposium: Executive and organizational continuity*. Cleveland, OH: Department of Organizational Behavior, Weatherhead School of Management, Case Western Reserve University.

Gergen, M. M. (1992). Life stories: Pieces of a dream. In G. C. Rosenwald & R. L. Ochberg (Eds.), *Storied lives: The cultural politics of self-understanding* (pp. 127-144). New Haven, CT: Yale University Press.

Gergen, M. M., & Gergen, K. J. (1993). Narratives of the gendered body in popular autobiography. In R. Josselson & A. Lieblich (Eds.), *The narrative study of lives,* (Vol. 1, pp. 191-218). Newbury Park, CA: Sage.

Gibb, H., & Wales, R. (1990). Metaphor or simile: Psychological determinants of the differential use of each sentence form. *Metaphor & Symbolic Activity, 5,* 199-213.

Gilchrist, H. A. (1998). Healing. In J. A. Tasch (Ed.), *Art.Rage.Us.: Art and writing by women with breast cancer* (pp. 120-121). San Francisco: Chronicle Books.

Gill, M. M. (1993). Academic sexual harassment: Perceptions of behaviors. In G. L. Kreps (Ed.), *Sexual harassment: Communication implications* (pp. 149-169). Cresskill, NJ: Hampton Press.

Gilligan, C. (1982). *In a different voice: Psychological theory and women's develoment*. Cambridge, MA: Harvard University Press.

Glaser, B. G., & Strauss, A. L. (1967). *The discovery of grounded theory*. Chicago: Aldine.

Glucksberg, S. (1989). Metaphors in conversation: How are they understood? Why are they used? *Metaphor & Symbolic Activity, 4,* 125-143.

Goffe, R., & Scase, R. (1985). *Women in charge: The experiences of female entrepreneurs*. London: Allen and Unwin.

Goffman, E. (1963). *Stigma: Notes on the management of spoiled identity*. New York: Simon & Schuster.

Golden, A. G. (2001). Modernity and the communicative management of multiple role-identities: The case of the worker-parent. *Journal of Family Communication, 1,* 209-226.

Gordon, J. R., & Whelan, K. S. (1998). Successful professional women in midlife: How organizations can more effectively understand and respond to the challenges. *Academy of Management Executive, 12(1),* 8-23.

Gordon, P. A. (1998). The meaning of disability: How women with chronic illness view their experiences. *Journal of Rehabilitation, 64(3),* 5-11.

Gottfried, H., & Weiss, P. (1994). A compound feminist organization: Purdue University's Council on the Status of Women. *Women & Politics, 14,* 23-45.

Gottlieb, L. (2000). *Stick figure: A diary of my former self.* New York: Simon & Schuster.

Gouldner, H., & Symons Strong, M. (1987). *Speaking of friendship: Middle-class women and their friends.* New York: Greenwood Press.

Gowler, D., & Legge, K. (1989). Rhetoric in bureaucratic careers: Managing the meaning of management success. In M. B. Arthur, D. T. Hall, & B. S. Lawrence (Eds.), *Handbook of career theory* (pp. 437-453). Cambridge, UK: Cambridge University Press.

Grauerholz, E. (1989). Sexual harassment of women professors by students: Exploring the dynamics of power, authority, and gender in a university setting. *Sex Roles, 21,* 789-801.

Gray, M. J., & Meginnis, S. (1978). Role of the gynecologist and the emerging woman. *Clinical Obstetrics & Gynecology, 21,* 173-181.

Gray, R. E., Greenberg, M., Fitch, M., Parry, N., Douglas, M. S., & Labrecque, M. (1997). Perspectives of cancer survivors interested in unconventional therapies. *Journal of Psychosocial Oncology, 15,* 149-171.

Greenhouse, L. (2001, April 24). Suit on sex harassment at work fails to meet high court's test. *New York Times.* Retrieved July 30, 2001, from www.nytimes.com/2001/04/24/national/24SCOT.html

Grigsby, L. (1999, March 4). Battling the battering: Outlets for victims of abuse have become more prevalent and easier to find. Retrieved July 8, 2003, from www3.niu.edu/women/pcsw/Journ1999d.htm

Grover, M. B. (1999, September 6). Daddy stress. *Forbes,* 202-208.

Gudykunst, W. B. (1995). Anxiety/uncertainty management (AUM) theory: Current status. In R. L. Wiseman (Ed.), *Intercultural communication theory* (pp. 8-58). Thousand Oaks, CA: Sage.

Guiniven, J. E. (2001). The lessons of survivor literature in communicating decisions to downsize. *Journal of Business and Technical Communication, 15,* 53-71.

Gürsoy, A. (1996). Beyond the orthodox: Heresy in medicine and the social sciences from a cross-cultural perspective. *Social Science and Medicine, 43,* 577-599.

Gutek, B. (1985). *Sex in the workplace.* San Francisco: Jossey-Bass.

Haar, E., Halitsky, V., & Stricker, G. (1977). Patients' attitudes toward gynecologic examination and to gynecologists. *Medical Care, 15,* 787-795.

Haas, A., & Puretz, S. L. (1992). Encouraging partnerships between health care providers and women recommended for gynecological surgery. *Health Communication, 4,* 29-38.

Haas, T., & Deetz, S. (2000). Between the generalized and the concrete other: Approaching organizational ethics from feminist perspectives. In P. M. Buzzanell (Ed.), *Rethinking organizational and managerial communication from feminist perspectives* (pp. 24-46). Thousand Oaks, CA: Sage.

Haddon, L. (1998). The experience of teleworking: A view from the home. In P. J. Jackson & J. M. van der Wielen (Eds.), *Teleworking: International perspectives from telecommuting to the virtual organisation* (pp. 136-143). London: Routledge.

Haddon, L., & Silverstone, R. (1995). Telework and the changing relation of home and work. In N. Heap, R. Thomas, G. Einon, R. Mason, & H. Mackay (Eds.), *Information technology and society: A reader* (pp. 400-412). London: The Open University.

Hakim-Larson, J., & Hobart, C. J. (1987). Maternal regulation and adolescent autonomy: Mother-daughter resolution of story conflicts. *Journal of Youth and Adolescence,* 16(2), 153-166.

Hakken, D. (1999). *Cyborgs@cyberspace: An ethnographer looks to the future.* New York: Routledge.

Hall, L. L. (1999). Taking charge of menopause. *FDA Consumer, 33,* 17-21.

Halpern, D. F., & Blackman, S. L. (1985). Magazine versus physicians: The influence of information source on intentions to use oral contraceptives. *Women & Health, 10*(1), 9.

Hammid, H. (n.d.). Deena Metzger [photograph]. In M. Yalom's (1997). *A history of the breast* (p. 270). New York: Ballantine Books. (Original from TREE, P.O. Box 186, Topanga, California 90290)

Haney, E. H. (1994). What is feminist ethics? A proposal for continuing discussion. In L. K. Daly (Ed.), *Feminist theological ethics: A reader* (pp. 3-12). Louisville, KY: Westminister John Knox Press.

Haraway, D. (1985). A manifesto for cyborgs: Science, technology, and socialist feminism in the 1980s. *Socialist Review, 15,* 65-107.

Haraway, D. (1990). Manifesto for cyborgs: Science, technology, and socialist feminism in the 1980s. In N. Fraser & L. J. Nicholson. (Eds.), *Feminism/Postmodernism* (pp. 190-233). New York: Routledge.

Haraway, D. (1991). *Simians, cyborgs, and women: The reinvention of nature.* New York: Routledge.

Haraway, D. (1992). The promises of monsters: A regenerative politics for inappropriated others. In L. Grossberg, C. Nelson, & P. Treichler (Eds.), *Cultural studies* (pp. 295-337). New York: Routledge.

Harding, S. (1987). The instability of the analytical categories of feminist theory. In S. Harding & J. F. O'Barr (Eds.), *Sex and scientific inquiry* (pp. 283-302). Chicago: University of Chicago Press.

Harding, S. (1991). *Whose science whose knowledge: Thinking from women's lives.* Ithaca, NY: Cornell University Press.

Harragan, B. L. (1977). *Games mother never taught you: Corporate gamesmanship for women.* New York: Warner.

Harrison, M. (1992). Women health as a specialty: A deceptive solution. *Journal of Women's Health, 1,* 18-23.

Hart, R. P. (1990). *Modern rhetorical criticism.* Glenview, IL: Scott, Foresman.

Harvey, D. (1990). Between space and time: Reflections on the geographical imagination. *Annals of the Association of American Geographers, 80,* 418-434.

Hawes, L.C. (1994). Revisiting reflexivity. *Western Journal of Communication, 58,* 5-10.

Hawkesworth, M. (1999). Analyzing backlash: Feminist standpoint theory as analytical tool. *Women's Studies International Forum, 22,* 135-156.

Haygood, M. S. (1991, October). *Tangled vines: An exploration of the mother-daughter bond through oral history.* Paper presented at the meeting of the Organization for the Study of Communication, Language and Gender, Milwaukee, WI.

Healthy Bites (1998, February). *Quick read: Perspectives.* Seattle, WA: Hope Publications, Hope Heart Institute.

Hearn, J., Sheppard, D. L., Tancred-Sheriff, P., & Burrell, G. (Eds.). (1989). *The sexuality of organization.* London: Sage.

Hearn, P. H. (2000). Young women and success: The most persistent barrier. *Frontiers, 21*(3), 25-37.

Hedges, E. (1996). Curriculum transformation: A brief overview. *Women's Studies Quarterly, 24,* 16-21.

Henderson-King, D., & Stewart, A. J. (1997). Feminist consciousness: Perspectives on women's experience. *Personality and Social Psychology Bulletin, 23,* 415-426.

Hercus, C. (1999). Identity, emotion, and feminist collective action. *Gender & Society, 13,* 34-55.

Hewson, D. (1997). Coping with loss of ability: "Good grief" or episodic stress responses? *Social Science and Medicine, 44,* 1129-1139.

Hickson, M., III, Grierson, R. D., & Linder, B. C. (1990, October). A communication model of sexual harassment. *Association for Communication Administration Bulletin, 74,* 22-33.

Hill, E. J., Hawkins, A. J., Ferris, M., & Weitzman, M. (2001). Finding an extra day a week: The positive influence of perceived job flexibility on work and family life balance. *Family Relations, 50,* 49-58.

Hill, E. J., Miller, B. C., Weiner, S. P., & Colihan, J. (1998). Influences of the virtual office on aspects of work and work/life balance. *Personnel Psychology, 51,* 667-683.

Hochschild, A. R. (1989). *The second shift.* New York: Avon.

Hochschild, A. R. (1997). *The time bind: When work becomes home and home becomes work.* New York: Metropolitan Books.

Hocker, J. L., & Wilmot, W. W. (1991). *Interpersonal conflict* (3rd ed.). Dubuque, IA: Wm. C. Brown.

Hogeland, L. M. (2001). Against generational thinking, or, some things that "Third Wave" feminism isn't. *Women's Studies in Communication, 24,* 107-121.

Hollows, J. (2000). *Feminism, femininity and popular culture.* Manchester, UK: Manchester University Press.

Holquist, M. (1990). *Dialogism: Bakhtin and his world.* London: Routledge.

Holtzworth-Munroe, A. (2000). A typology of men who are violent toward their female partners: Making sense of the heterogeneity in husband violence. *Current Directions in Psychological Science, 9,* 140-143.

Holtzworth-Munroe, A., Meehan, J. C., Herron, K., Rehman, U., & Stuart, G. I. (2001). Testing the Holtzworth-Munroe and Stuart (1994) typology. *Journal of Consulting & Clinical Psychology, 68,* 1000-1019.

hooks, b. (1984). *Feminist theory: From margin to center.* Cambridge, MA: South End Press.

hooks, b. (1994). *Teaching to transgress: Education as the practice of freedom.* New York: Routledge.

hooks, b. (2000). Ecstasy: Teaching and learning without limits. In P. R. Freeman & J. Z. Schmidt (Eds.) *Wise women: Reflections of teachers at midlife* (pp. 173-177). New York: Routledge.

Hornbacher, M. (1998). *Wasted: A memoir of anorexia and bulimia.* New York: Harper Perennial.

Huffman, S. B., & Myers, J. E. (1999). Counseling women in midlife: An integrative approach to menopause. *Journal of Counseling & Development, 77,* 258-266.

Hughes, C. (2000). Review of the book [*Meeting the challenge: Innovative feminist pedagogies in action*]. *Studies in Higher Education, 25,* 246-247.

Hull, C. (1994). Achieving a balance between family and work obligations has become a dominant concern for Americans. Retrieved May 19, 1999, from www3.xls. com/cgi-bin/cwisuite.exe

Hume, D. (1985). *An inquiry concerning human understanding* (C.W. Hendel, Ed.). New York: Macmillan.

Hylmö, A., & Buzzanell, P. M. (2002). The phenomenon of telecommuting and changing organizations: An organizational culture examination. *Communication Monographs, 69,* 329-356.

Illinois Protocol for Partner Abuse Intervention Programs, 89 Illinois Administrative Code § 501, Subchapter a (adopted at 25 Ill. Reg. 6468, effective April 28, 2001; amended at 26 Ill. Reg. 9830, effective June 24, 2002)

Illinois Coalition Against Domestic Violence. (n.d.). *Partner abuse intervention programs.* Retrieved June 16, 2003, from www.ilcadv.org/batterersprogs/default.asp

Im, E., & Meleis, A. I. (2000). Meanings of menopause to Korean immigrant women. *Western Journal of Nursing Research, 22,* 84-102.

Infante, D. A. (1982). The argumentative student in the speech communication classroom: An investigation and implications. *Communication Education, 31,* 141-48.

Infante, D. A. (1985). Inducing women to be more argumentative: source credibility effects. *Journal of Applied Communication Research, 13,* 33-44.

Infante, D. A. (1987). Aggressiveness. In J. C. McCroskey & J. A. Daly (Eds.), *Personality and interpersonal communication* (pp. 157-192). Newbury Park, CA: Sage.

Infante, D. A. (1989). Response to high argumentativeness: Message and sex differences. *Southern Communication Journal, 54,* 159-170.

Infante, D. A. (1995). Teaching students to understand and control verbal aggression. *Communication Education, 44,* 51-63.

Infante, D. A., & Rancer, A. S. (1982). A conceptualization and measure of argumentativeness. *Journal of Personality Assessment, 46,* 72-80.

Infante, D. A., & Rancer, A. S. (1996). Argumentativeness and verbal aggressiveness: A review of recent theory and research. In B. R. Burleson (Ed.) *Communication yearbook 19* (pp. 319-351). Thousand Oaks, CA: Sage.

Infante, D. A., Trebing, J. D., Shepherd, P. E., & Seeds, D. E. (1984). The relationship of argumentativeness to verbal aggression. *Southern Speech Communication Journal, 50,* 67-77.

Irigaray, L. (1985). *The sex which is not one* (C. Porter & C. Burke, Trans.). Ithaca, NY: Cornell University Press.

Ivy, D. K., & Hamlet, S. (1996). College students and sexual dynamics: Two studies of peer sexual harassment. *Communication Education, 45,* 149-166.

Jackson, L. D., & Duffy, B. K. (Eds.). (1998). *Health communication research: A guide to developments and direction* (pp. 1-15). Westport, CT: Greenwood Press.

Jacobson, N., & Gottman, J. (1998). *When men batter women: New insights into ending abusive relationships.* New York: Simon & Schuster.

Jaggar, A. M. (1991). Feminine ethics: Projects, problems, prospects. In C. Card (Ed.), *Feminist ethics* (pp. 78-104). Lawrence: University of Kansas Press.

Jaggar, A. M. (1994). Introduction: Living with contradictions. In A. M. Jaggar (Ed.), *Living with contradictions: Controversies in feminist social ethics* (pp. 1-17). Boulder, CO: Westview Press.

Jaggar, A. M., & Rothenberg, P. S. (1993). *Feminist frameworks: Alternative theoretical accounts of the relations between women and men.* New York: McGraw-Hill.

Jamieson, K. H. (1995). *Beyond the double bind: Women and leadership.* New York: Oxford University Press.

Jansma, L. L. (2000). Sexual harassment research: Integration, reformulation, and implications for mitigation efforts. In M. Roloff (Ed.), *Communication Yearbook 23* (pp. 163-225). Thousand Oaks, CA: Sage.

Jenefsky, C. (1996). Public speaking as empowerment at visionary university. *Communication Education, 45,* 343-353.

Johannesen, R. L. (1990). *Ethics in human communication* (3rd ed.). Prospect Heights, IL: Waveland Press.

Johnson, D. W., & Johnson, R. T. (1996). Conflict resolution and peer mediation programs in elementary and secondary schools: A review of the research. *Review of Educational Research, 66,* 459-506.

Johnson, K. (1992). Women's health: Developing a new interdisciplinary specialty. *Journal of Women's Health, 1,* 14-17.

Jonas, W. (1998). Alternative medicine and the conventional practitioner. *Journal of the American Medical Association, 279,* 708-709.

Jones, A., Kreps, G. L., & Phillips, G. M. (1995). *Communicating with your doctor: Getting the most out of health care.* Cresskill, NJ: Hampton Press.

Jordan, W. (1998). This could kill me [photograph of textile original, 1997]. In J. A. Tasch (Ed.), *Art.Rage.Us.: Art and writing by women with breast cancer* (pp. 104-105). San Francisco: Chronicle Books.

Jorgensen-Earp, C. R., & Staton, A. Q. (1993). Student metaphors for the college freshman experience. *Communication Education, 42,* 123-141.

Jorgenson, J. (1995). Marking the work-family boundary: Mother-child interaction and home-based work. In T. J. Socha & G. H. Stamp (Eds.), *Parents, children, and communication: Frontiers of theory and research* (pp. 203-217). Mahwah, NJ: Lawrence Erlbaum.

Jorgenson, J. (2000). Interpreting the intersections of work and family: Frame conflicts in women's work. *Electronic Journal of Communication/ Revue Electronique de Communication, 10*(3), retrieved July 8, 2003, from www.cios.org/getfile/ JORGEN_V10n3400

Jurik, N. C. (1998). Getting away and getting by: The experiences of self-employed homeworkers. *Work and Occupations, 25,* 7-35.

Kanter, R. M. (1977). *Men and women of the corporation.* New York: Basic Books.

Kanter, R. M. (1989). *When giants learn to dance.* New York: Simon & Schuster.

Kaufert, P. A. (1982). Anthropology and the menopause: The development of a theoretical framework. *Maturitas, 4,* 181-193.

Kautz, E. D. (1995). Gynecologists, power and sexuality in modern texts. *Journal of Popular Culture, 28*(4), 81-91.

Keller, E. A. (2000). Consensual amorous relationships between faculty and students: The constitutional right to privacy. In E. Wall (Ed.), *Sexual harassment* (rev. ed., pp. 21-41). Amherst, NY: Prometheus Books.

Kerssens, J. (1997). Patient preference for the genders of health professionals. *Social Science & Medicine, 44,* 1531-1540.

Keyton, J., & Rhodes, S. C. (1999). Organizational sexual harassment: Translating research into application. *Journal of Applied Communication Research, 27,* 158-173.

Kinney, T. A. (1994). An inductively derived typology of verbal aggression and its association to distress. *Human Communication Research, 21,* 183-222.

Kirby, E. L. (2000). Should I say as you say or do as you do? Mixed messages about work and family. *Electronic Journal of Communication/Revue Electronique de Communication, 10*(3), retrieved September 17, 2002, from www.cios.org/ getfile/kirby_v10n3400

Kirby, E. L., Golden, A., Medved, C., Jorgensen, J., & Buzzanell, P. M. (2003). An organizational communication challenge to the discourse of work and family research: From problematics to empowerment. In P. Kalbfleisch (Ed.), *Communication Yearbook 27* (pp. 1-44). Mahwah, NJ: Lawrence Erlbaum.

Kirby, E. L., & Krone, K. J. (2002). "The policy exists but you can't really use it.": Communication and the structuration of work-family policies. *Journal of Applied Communication Research, 30,* 50-77.

Kittell, L. A., Mansfield, P. K., & Voda, A. M. (1998). Keeping up appearances: The basic social process of the menopausal transition. *Qualitative Health Research, 8,* 618-633.

Kizielewicz, N. (1988). *A study of mothers and adolescent daughters in African American families* (Report No. CG022992). Alexandria, VA: American Association for Counseling and Human Development Foundation. (ERIC Document Reproduction Service No. ED326782)

Klass, P. (2000). The best intentions: Newborn technologies and bioethical borderlines. In M. Garber, B. Hanssen, & T. L. Walkowitz (Eds.), *The turn to ethics* (pp. 65-83). New York: Routledge.

Kleiman, C. (2000, April 4). Family-first dads left dangling on the corporate ladder. *Chicago Tribune,* p. 2.

Klein, K. N. (2001). Toward a model of democratic self-help: Identifying the rhetorical characteristics of a therapeutic and empowering discourse. Unpublished manuscript.

Kleinman, A. (1988). *The illness narratives: Suffering, healing, and the human condition.* New York: Basic Books.

Koch, S., & Deetz, S. (1981). Metaphor analysis of social reality in organizations. *Journal of Applied Communication Research, 9,* 1-15.

Kochman, T. (1972). Toward an ethnography of black American speech behavior. In T. Kochman (Ed.), *Rappin' and stylin' out* (pp. 241-264). Chicago: University of Illinois Press.

Koeske, R. D. (1982). Toward a biosocial paradigm for menopause research: Lessons and contributions from the behavioral sciences. In A. M. Voda, M. Dinnerstein, & S. R. O'Donnell (Eds.), *Changing perspectives of menopause* (pp. 3-23). Austin: University of Texas Press.

Kolker, A. (1996). Thrown overboard: The human costs of health care rationing. In C. Ellis & A. Bochner (Eds.), *Composing ethnography: Alternative forms of qualitative writing* (pp. 132-159). Walnut Creek, CA: AltaMira Press.

Susan G. Komen Breast Cancer Foundation. (n.d.). *Special populations and breast cancer: Survival rates.* Retrieved June 24, 2003, from www.komen.org/bci/bhealth/SpecialPopulationsAndBreastCancer/RacialAndEthnicDifferences.asp

Kompast, M., & Wagner, I. (1998). Telework: Managing spatial, temporal, and cultural boundaries. In P. J. Jackson & J. M. van der Wielen (Eds.), *Teleworking: International perspectives from telecommuting to virtual organisation* (pp. 95-117). London: Routledge.

Kramarae, C. (1992). Harassment and everyday life. In L. Rakow (Ed.), *Women making meaning: New feminist directions in communication* (pp. 100-120). New York: Routledge.

Kramarae, C. (1996). Centers of change: An introduction to women's own communication programs. *Communication Education, 45,* 315-321.

Krappman, L., Oswald, H., Schuster, B, & Youniss, J. (1998). Can mothers win? The transformation of mother-daughter relationships in late childhood. In M. Hofer, J. Youniss, & P. Noack (Eds.), *Verbal interaction and development in families with adolescents* (pp. 11-29). Stamford, CT: Ablex.

Kreps, G. L. (1988a). The pervasive role of information in health and health care: Implications for health communication policy. In J. Anderson (Ed.), *Communication yearbook 11* (pp. 238-276). Newbury Park, CA: Sage.

Kreps, G. L. (1988b). Relational communication in health care. *Southern Speech Communication Journal, 53,* 344-359.

Kreps, G. L. (1993a). Introduction: Sexual harassment and communication. In G. L. Kreps (Ed.), *Sexual harassment: Communication implications* (pp. 1-8). Cresskill, NJ: Hampton Press.

Kreps, G. L. (1993b). Promoting a sociocultural evolutionary approach to preventing sexual harassment: Metacommunication and cultural adaptation. In G. L. Kreps (Ed.), *Sexual harassment: Communication implications* (pp. 310-318). Cresskill, NJ: Hampton Press.

Kreps, G. L. (1996). Promoting a consumer orientation to health care and health promotion. *Journal of Health Psychology, 1*(1), 41-48.

Kreps, G. L. (1998). Social responsibility and the modern health care system: Promoting a consumer orientation to health care. In P. Salem (Ed.), *Organizational communication and change* (pp. 293-304). Creskill, NJ: Hampton Press.

Kreps, G. L. (2001). The evolution and advancement of health communication inquiry. In W. B. Gudykunst (Ed.), *Communication yearbook 24* (pp. 232-254). Thousand Oaks, CA: Sage.

Kreps, G. L., & Kunimoto, E. (1994). *Effective communication in multicultural health care contexts.* Thousand Oaks, CA: Sage.

Kubler-Ross, E. (1969). *On death and dying.* New York: Macmillan.

Kugelmass, J. (1995). *Telecommuting: A manager's guide to flexible work arrangements.* New York: Lexington Books.

Kurth, S. B., Spiller, B. B., & Travis, C. B. (2000). Consent, power, and sexual scripts: Deconstructing sexual harassment. In C. B. Travis & J. W. White (Eds.), *Sexuality, society, and feminism* (pp. 323-354). Washington, DC: American Psychological Association.

Lacković-Grgin, K., Deković, M., & Opăić, G. (1994). Pubertal status, interaction with significant others, and self-esteem of adolescent girls. *Adolescence, 29*(115), 691-700.

Lagerspetz, K. M. J., Bjorkqvist, K., & Peltonen, T. (1988). Is indirect aggression typical of females? Gender differences in aggressiveness in 11- to 12-year-old children. *Aggressive Behavior, 14,* 403-414.

Lakoff, G., & Johnson, M. (1980). *Metaphors we live by.* Chicago: University of Chicago Press.

Lamm, N. (1995). It's a big fat revolution. In B. Findlen (Ed.), *Listen up: Voices from the next feminist generation* (pp. 85-94). Seattle, WA: Seal.

Langellier, K. M., & Hall, D. L. (1989). Interviewing women: A phenomenological approach to feminist communication research. In K. Carter & C. Spitzack (Eds.), *Doing research on women's communication: Perspectives on theory and method* (pp. 193-220). Norwood, NJ: Ablex.

Lannamann, J. (1995). The politics of voice in interpersonal communication research. In W. Leeds-Hurwitz (Ed.), *Social approaches to communication* (pp. 114-132). New York: Guilford Press.

Lannutti, P. J., Laliker, M., & Hale, J. L. (2001). Violations of expectations in social-sexual communication in student/professor interactions. *Communication Education, 50,* 69-82.

LaRocca, M. A., & Kromrey, J. D. (1999). The perceptions of sexual harassment in higher education: Impact of gender and attractiveness. *Sex Roles, 40,* 921-940.

Leatherman, C. (1994, March 16). Fighting back: Professors accused of sexual harassment say their rights have been breached. *Chronicle of Higher Education, 40*(28), A17-A18.

Lee, D. (2001). "He didn't sexually harass me, as in harassed for sex. . . . He was just horrible": Women's definitions of unwanted male sexual conduct at work. *Women's Studies International Forum, 24,* 25-38.

Lee, J. (1999). Leader-member exchange, gender, and members' communication expectations with leaders. *Communication Quarterly, 47,* 415-429.

Lee, J. W., & Guerrero, L. K. (2001). Types of touch in cross-sex relationships between coworkers: Perceptions of relational and emotional messages, inappropriateness, and sexual harassment. *Journal of Applied Communication Research, 29,* 197-220.

Leeds-Hurwitz, W. (Ed.). (1995). *Social approaches to communication.* New York: Guilford Press.

Lengel, L. B. (1998). Researching the "other," transforming ourselves: Methodological considerations of feminist ethnography. *Journal of Communication Inquiry, 22,* 229-250.

Lewin, K., (1935). *A dynamic theory of personality.* New York: McGraw-Hill.

Lewis, H. (1987). Young women's reproductive health survey. *New Zealand Medical Journal, 100,* 490-492.

Liddell, D. L., Halpin, G., & Halpin, W. G. (1992). The measure of moral orientation: Measuring the ethics of care and justice. *Journal of College Student Development, 33,* 325-330.

Lincoln, Y., & Guba, E. G. (1985). *Naturalistic inquiry.* Beverly Hills, CA: Sage.

Lindlof, T. R. (1995). *Qualitative communication research methods.* Thousand Oaks, CA: Sage.

Lindsley, S. L. (1998). Communicating prejudice in organizations. In M. L. Hecht (Ed.), Communicating prejudice (pp. 187-205). Thousand Oaks, CA: Sage.

Lippert, L. (1997). Women at midlife: Implications for theories of women's adult development. *Journal of Counseling & Development, 76,* 16-22.

Lloyd, S. A., & Emery, B. C. (2000). *The dark side of courtship: Physical and sexual aggression.* Thousand Oaks, CA: Sage.

Longino, H. E. (1993). Feminist standpoint theory and the problems of knowledge. *Signs: Journal of Women in Culture and Society, 19,* 201-212.

Lorde, A. (1984). *Sister outsider: Essays and speeches.* Freedom, CA: Crossing Press.

Lorde, A. (1997). *The cancer journals* (special edition). San Francisco: Aunt Lute Books.

Lowdermilk, D. L. (1995). Reproductive surgery. In C. I. Fogel & N. F. Woods (Eds.), *Women's health care* (pp. 629-650). Thousand Oaks, CA: Sage.

Loy, P., & Stewart, L. P. (1984). The extent and effect of the sexual harassment of working women. *Sociological Forces, 17,* 31-43.

Lucchetti, A. E., Powers, W. G., & Love, D. E. (2002). The empirical development of the child-parent communication apprehension scale for use with young adults. *Journal of Family Communication, 2,* 109-131.

Lupton, D. (1994). Consumerism, commodity culture and health promotion. *Health Promotion International, 9,* 111-118.

Lynman, M. J. (1990). Examining support in context: A redefinition from the cancer patient's perspective. *Sociology of Health and Illness, 12,* 169-194.

Lyon, D. S. (1997). Where have all the young men gone? Keeping men in obstetrics and gynecology. *Obstetrics & Gynecology, 90,* 634-635.

Mac Cormac, E. R. (1985). *A cognitive theory of metaphor.* Cambridge: MIT Press.

MacLennan, A. H., Wilson, D. H., & Taylor, A. W. (1996). Prevalence and cost of alternative medicine in Australia. *Lancet, 347,* 569-573.

MacPherson, K. I. (1985). Osteoporosis and menopause: A feminist analysis of the social construction of a syndrome. *Advances in Nursing Science, 7,* 11-22.

Magley, V. J., Hulin, C. L., Fitzgerald, L. F., & DeNardo, M. (1999). Outcomes of self-labeling sexual harassment. *Journal of Applied Psychology, 84,* 390-402.

Maguire, M., & Mohtar, L. F. (1994). Performance and the celebration of a subaltern counterpublic. *Text and Performance Quarterly, 14,* 238-252.

Mahowald, M. B. (1993). *Women and children in health care: An unequal majority.* New York: Oxford University Press.

Mairs, N. (1996). *Waist high in the world: A life among the nondisabled.* Boston: Beacon Press.

Mairs, N. (1997). Carnal acts. In K. Conboy, N. Medina, & S. Stanbury (Eds.), *Writing on the body: Female embodiment and feminist theory* (pp. 296-305). New York: Columbia University Press.

Maiwald, C. R., Pierce, J. L., Newstrom, J. W., & Sunoo, B. P. (1997, July). Workin' 8 p.m. to 8 a.m. and lovin' every minute of it! *Workforce,* pp. 30-36.

Mallia, K. L., & Ferris, S. P. (2000). Telework: A consideration of its impact on individuals and organizations. *Electronic Journal of Communication/Revue Electronique de Communication, 10*(3), retrieved July 8, 2003 from www.cios.org/getfile/mallia_v10n3400

Mann, D. (1998, January 8). Doctors, patients need to talk more. *Medical Tribune (Family Physician Edition), 39*(1), 1, 6.

Mansfield, P. K. (1990). *Menopause: A positive approach.* Unpublished manuscript, Pennsylvania State University, University Park.

Mansfield, P. K., & Voda, A. M. (1993). From Edith Bunker to the 6 o'clock news: How and what midlife women learn about menopause. *Women and Therapy, 14,* 89-104.

Marble, M. (1998, June 29). Alternative medicine used to compliment [*sic*] conventional cancer therapy. *Cancer Weekly Plus,* pp. 2-3. Retrieved October 15, 2002, from www.newsrx.net

Marieskind, H. I., & Ehrenreich, B. (1975, September/October). Toward socialist medicine: The women's health movement. *Social Policy, 62,* 34-42.

Markham, A. N. (1998). *Life online: Researching real experience in virtual space.* Walnut Creek, CA: AltaMira Press.

Marshall, J. (1993). Viewing organizational communication from a feminist perspective: A critique and some offerings. In S. Deetz (Ed.), *Communication yearbook 16* (pp. 122-143). Newbury Park, CA: Sage.

Marshall, J. (1995). *Women managers moving on: Exploring career and life choices.* London: Routledge.

Martensen, R. L. (1994). "To mash a cooked potato": Gynecology and men. *Journal of the American Medical Association, 272,* 641.

Martin, J. (1990). Rethinking feminist organizations. *Gender & Society, 4,* 182-206.

Martin, J. (1992). *Cultures in organizations: Three perspectives.* New York: Oxford University Press.

Martin, J. (1994). The organization of exclusion: Institutionalization of sex inequality, gendered faculty jobs and gendered knowledge in organizational theory and research. *Organization, 1,* 401-431.

Martin, J. R. (2000). *Coming of age in academe: Rekindling women's hopes and reforming the academy.* New York: Routledge.

Massey, D. (1994). *Space, place, and gender.* Minneapolis: University of Minnesota Press.

Matchen, J., & DeSouza, E. (2000). The sexual harassment of faculty members by students. *Sex Roles, 42,* 295-306.

Matheson, K. (1992). Women and computer technology: Communicating for herself. In M. Lea (Ed.), *Contexts of computer-mediated communication* (pp. 66-88). Hemel Hempstead, UK: Harvester Wheatsheaf.

Matroianni, A. C., Faden, R. R., & Federman, D. D. (Eds.). (1994). *Women and health research: Ethical and legal issues of including women in clinical studies.* Wahington, DC: National Academy Press.

Mattson, M. (2000). Empowerment through agency-promoting discourse: An explicit application of Harm Reduction Theory to reframe HIV test counseling. *Journal of Health Communication, 5,* 333-347.

Mattson, M., & Buzzanell, P. M. (1999). Traditional and feminist organizational communication ethical analyses of messages and issues involved in an actual job loss case. *Journal of Applied Communication Research, 27,* 49-72.

Maykut, P., & Morehouse, R. (1994). *Beginning qualitative research: A philosophic and practical guide.* Washington, DC: Falmer Press.

McCorkle, S., & Mills, J. L. (1992). Rowboat in a hurricane: Metaphors of interpersonal conflict management. *Communication Reports, 5,* 57-66.

McCrea, F. B. (1983). The politics of menopause: The discovery of a deficiency disease. *Social Problems, 31,* 111-123.

McDonald, E. (1997). Doctor is god: Male doctors and female patients in Egypt. *Social Biology and Human Affairs, 62*(1), 15-21.

McGoldrick, M., & Giordano, J. (1996). Overview: Ethnicity and family therapy. In M. McGoldrick, J. Giordano, & J. Pearce (Eds.), *Ethnicity and family therapy* (2nd ed.) (pp. 1-27). New York: Guilford Press.

McGoldrick, M., Giordano, J., & Pearce, J. (1996). Preface. In M. McGoldrick, J. Giordano, & J. Pearce (Eds.), *Ethnicity and family therapy* (pp. ix-xiii). New York: Guilford Press.

McGregor, K. J., & Peay, E. R. (1996). The choice of alternative therapy for health care: Testing some propositions. *Social Science and Medicine, 43,* 1317-1327.

McGurgan, P., O'Donovan, P., & Jones, S. E. (2001). The effect of operator gender on patient satisfaction: Does the "Y" in outpatient hysteroscopy matter? *Gynaecological Endoscopy, 10,* 53-56.

McKinney, K. (1990). Sexual harassment of university faculty by colleagues and students. *Sex Roles, 23,* 421-438.

McQuaide, S. (1998). Women at midlife. *Social Work, 43,* 21-31.

Mechanic, D. (1998). Public trust and initiatives for new health care partnerships. *Milbank Quarterly, 76,* 281-302.

Mendelsohn, R. (1981). *Male practice: How doctors manipulate women.* Chicago: Contemporary Books.

Mercer, C. (1999). Cross-cultural attitudes to the menopause and the ageing female. *Age & Ageing, 28,* 12-17.

Meritor Savings Bank v. Vinson, 477 U.S. 57 (1986).

Meyer, J. C. (1997). Humor in member narratives: Uniting and dividing at work. *Western Journal of Communication, 61,* 188-208.

Meyerson, D. E., & Kolb, D. M. (2000). Moving out of the "armchair": Developing a framework to bridge the gap between feminist theory and practice. *Organization, 7,* 553-571.

Middlebrook, C. (1998). Sailing. In J. A. Tasch (Ed)., *Art.Rage.Us.: Art and writing by women with breast cancer* (pp. 148-154). San Francisco: Chronicle Books. (Reprinted from C. Middlebrook (1996). *Seeing the crab: A memoir of dying* (Chap. 11). New York: Basic Books.)

Middletown Area Studies. (1994). (Available from the Department of Sociology, North Quad 205, Ball State University, Muncie, IN 47306)

Middletown Area Studies. (1998). (Available from the Department of Sociology, North Quad 205, Ball State University, Muncie, IN 47306)

Miller, G. A. (1979). Images and models, similes and metaphors. In A. Ortony (Ed.), *Metaphor and thought* (pp. 202-250). New York: Cambridge University Press.

Miller, J. L., & Knudsen, D. D. (1999). Family abuse in violence. In M. B. Sussman, S. K. Steinmetz, & G. W. Peterson (Eds.), *Handbook of marriage and the family* (2nd ed., pp. 705-741). New York: Plenum Press.

Miller, L. (1997). Not just weapons of the weak: Gender harassment as a form of protest for army men. *Social Psychology Quarterly, 60,* 32-51.

Miller, M., & Day, L. E. (2002). Family communication, maternal and paternal expectations, and college students' suicidality. *Journal of Family Communication, 2,* 167-184.

Miller, W. L., & Crabtree, B. F. (2000). Clinical research. In N. K. Denzin & Y. S. Lincoln (Eds.), *Handbook of qualitative research* (2nd ed.) (pp. 607-631). Thousand Oaks, CA: Sage.

Mills, R. S. L., Duncan, K. A., & Amyot, D. J. (2000). Home-based employment and work-family conflict: A Canadian study. In C. B. Hennon, S. Loker, & R. Walker (Eds.), *Gender and home-based employment* (pp. 137-165). Westport, CT: Auburn.

Millstein, S. G., Adler, N. E., & Irwin, C. E. (1984). Sources of anxiety about pelvic examinations among adolescent females. *Journal of Adolescent Health Care, 5*(2), 105-111.

Mirchandani, K. (1998). No longer a struggle? Teleworkers' reconstruction of the work-nonwork boundary. In P. J. Jackson & J. M. van der Wielen (Eds.), *Teleworking: International perspectives from telecommuting to the virtual organisation* (pp. 118-135). London: Routledge.

Mirchandani, K. (1999). Legitimizing work: Telework and the gendered reification of the work-nonwork dichotomy. *The Canadian Review of Sociology and Anthropology, 36,* 87-107.

Mishler, E. G. (1984). *The discourse of medicine: Dialectics of medical interviews.* Norwood, NJ: Ablex.

Mongeau, P. A., & Blalock, J. (1994). Student evaluations of instructor immediacy and sexually harassing behaviors: An experimental investigation. *Journal of Applied Communication, 22,* 256-272.

Moraga, C. (1983). Between the lines. In C. Moraga & G. Anzaldúa (Eds.). *This bridge called my back: Writings by radical women of color* (pp. 105-106). New York: Kitchen Table.

Moraga, C., & Anzaldúa, G. (Eds.). (1983). *This bridge called my back: Writings by radical women of color.* New York: Kitchen Table.

Morgan, G. (1993). *Imaginization: The art of creative management.* Newbury Park, CA: Sage.

Morgen, S. (1995). "It was the best of times, it was the worst of times": Emotional discourse in the work cultures of feminist health clinics. In M. M. Ferree & P. Y. Martin (Eds.), *Feminist organizations: Harvest of the new women's movement* (pp. 234-247). Philadelphia: Temple University Press.

Morris, B. J. (1999). *Eden built by eves: The culture of women's music festivals.* Los Angeles: Alyson Books.

Morris, D. B. (1998). *Illness and culture in the postmodern age.* Berkeley: University of California Press.

Morris, D. B. (2000). How to speak postmodern: Medicine, illness, and cultural change. *Hastings Center Report, 30*(6), 7-16.

Morse, J. M. (Ed.). (1992). *Qualitative health research.* Newbury Park, CA: Sage.

Moskowitz, D. B. (1999). The confidentiality countdown. *Business & Health, 17*(6), 15.

Mossholder, K. W., Settoon, R. P., Armenakis, A. A., & Harris, S. G. (2000). Emotion during organizational transformations: An interactive model of survivor reactions. *Group & Organization Management, 25,* 220-243.

Motoyama, C. T. (1996). Revising an interpersonal communication course. *Women's Studies Quarterly, 24,* 113-117.

Mulvey, L. (1975/1999). Visual pleasure and narrative cinema. In S. Thornham (Ed.), *Feminist film theory: A reader* (pp. 58-69). Washington Square: New York University Press.

Mumby, D. K. (1988). *Communication and power in organizations: Discourse, ideology, and domination.* Norwood, NJ: Ablex.

Mumby, D. K. (1996). Feminism, postmodernism, and organizational communication studies: A critical reading. *Management Communication Quarterly, 9,* 259-295.

Mumby, D. K. (1998). Organizing men: Power, discourse, and the social construction of masculinity(s) in the workplace. *Communication Theory, 8,* 164-183.

Mumby, D. K. (2000). Communication, organization, and the public sphere: A feminist perspective. In P. Buzzanell (Ed.). *Rethinking organizational and managerial communication from feminist perspectives* (pp. 3-23). Thousand Oaks, CA: Sage.

Mumby, D. K., & Putnam, L. L. (1992). The politics of emotion: A feminist reading of bounded rationality. *Academy of Management Review, 17,* 465-486.

Murphy, A. G. (1998). Hidden transcripts of flight attendant resistance. *Management Communication Quarterly, 11,* 499-535.

Nadesan, M. H. (1997). Gender and temporality in interpersonal systems. *Symbolic Interaction, 20,* 21-43.

Nadesan, M., & Sotirin, P. (1998). The romance and science of "breast is best": Discursive contradictions and contexts of breastfeeding choices. *Text and Performance Quarterly, 18,* 217-232.

Nadler, M. K., & Nadler, L. B. (2000). Out of classroom communication between faculty and students: A faculty perspective. *Communication Studies, 51,* 176-188.

Nahavandi, A. (1997). Teaching from the heart. In R. Andre & P. J. Frost (Eds.), *Researchers hooked on teaching* (pp. 197-212). Thousand Oaks, CA: Sage.

National Foundation for Women Business Owners (2000). *Technology boosts growth in home-based businesses.* Retrieved December 11, 2000, from www.nfwbo.org

National Foundation for Women Business Owners (2001, February). The business of America is small business: NAWBO's agenda for continuing our success. *Working Woman,* 35-36, 37.

National Women's Music Festival (2000a). *National Women's Music Festival overview.* Retrieved June 1, 2000, from http://wiaonline.org/nwmf/post02/index02.shtml

National Women's Music Festival. (2000b, June). *National Women's Music Festival program.* Indianapolis, IN: Women in the Arts.

National Women's Music Festival. (2001, June). *National Women's Music Festival program.* Indianapolis, IN: Women in the Arts.

Neimark, J. (1997). On the front lines of alternative medicine. *Psychology Today, 30*(1), 52-55, 67-68.

Nelson, C. M. (2000). The "F" word. *Women's Studies Quarterly, 28,* 26-28.

Nicotera, A. M., & Rancer, A. S. (1994). The influence of sex on self-perceptions and social stereotyping of aggressive communication predispositions. *Western Journal of Communication, 58,* 283-307.

Nilles, J. (1988). *Traffic reductions by telecommuting: A status report. Transportation Research, 22A*(4), 301-317.

Nippert-Eng, C. E. (1996). *Home and work: Negotiating boundaries through everyday life.* Chicago: University of Chicago Press.

Noddings, N. (1984). *Caring: A feminine approach to ethics and moral education.* Berkeley: University of California Press.

Noller, P., & Bagi, S. (1985). Parent-adolescent communication. *Journal of Adolescence, 9,* 125-144.

Noller, P., & Callan, V. (1991). *The adolescent in the family.* New York: Routledge.

Northrup, C. (1994). *Women's bodies, women's wisdom: Creating physical and emotional health and healing.* New York: Bantam.

Norton, C. S. (1989). *Life metaphors: Stories of ordinary survival.* Carbondale: Southern Illinois University Press.

Nunneley, I. (1997). I stopped asking doctors for help. *British Medical Journal, 315,* 890.

Nwoga, I. A. (1997). *Mother-daughter conversation related to sex-role socialization and adolescent pregnancy.* Unpublished doctoral dissertation, University of Florida, Gainesville.

O'Brien Hallstein, D. L. (1999). A postmodern caring: Feminist standpoint theories, revisioned caring, and communication ethics. *Western Journal of Communication, 63,* 32-56.

O'Brien Hallstein, D. L. (2000). Where standpoint stands now: An introduction and commentary. *Women's Studies in Communication, 23,* 1-15.

O'Connor, P. (1992). *Friendships between women: A critical review.* New York: Guilford Press.

O'Hara, L. S. (2001). Service-learning: Students' transformative journey from communication student to civic-minded professional. *Southern Communication Journal, 66,* 251-266.

O'Hare, W. P. (1996). *A new look at poverty in America.* Washington, DC: Population Reference Bureau.

O'Leary, K. D., Barling, J., Arias, I., Rosenbaum, A., Malone, J., & Tyree, A. (1989). Prevalence and stability of physical aggression between spouses. *Journal of Consulting and Counseling Psychology, 57,* 263-268.

O'Leary, K. D., Malone, J., & Tyree, A. (1994). Physical aggression in early marriage: Prerelationship and relationship effects. *Journal of Consulting and Clinical Psychology, 62,* 594-602.

O'Neill, A. (1998, October 26). Hope at last [special report: breast cancer]. *People, 50*(15), 68-78.

Office of the Vice President for Student Affairs. (2000). Fall 2000 *Enrollment Synopsis.* Ball State University, Muncie, Indiana.

Office on Violence Against Women. (n.d.). *Violence Against Women Act of 1994.* Retrieved June 16, 2003, from www.ojp.usdoj.gov/vawo/laws/vawa/vawa.htm

Oliker, S. J. (1998). The modernisation of friendship: Individualism, intimacy, and gender in the nineteenth century. In R. A. Adams & G. Allan (Eds.), *Placing friendship in context* (pp. 18-42). Cambridge, UK: Cambridge University Press.

Olson, M. H. (1988). Organizational barriers to telework. In W. B. Korte, S. Robinson, & W. J. Steinle (Eds.), *Telework: Present situation and future development of a new form of work organization* (pp. 77-100). Amsterdam, Netherlands: Elsevier Science.

Olson, M. H., & Primps, S. B. (1984). Working at home with computers: Work and nonwork issues. *Journal of Social Issues, 40,* 97-112.

Orbe, M. (1998). From the standpoint(s) of traditionally muted groups: Explicating a co-cultural communication theoretical model. *Communication Theory, 8,* 1-26.

Ordemann, J. M. (1994). *Adolescent perceptions: A qualitative study of the descriptions of good parents.* Unpublished master's thesis, Texas Woman's University, Denton.

Osofsky, H. J. (1967). Women's reactions to pelvic examination. *Obstetrics & Gynecology, 149,* 1-4.

"Our stories": Communication professionals' narratives of sexual harassment. (1992). *Journal of Applied Communication Research, 20,* 363-390.

Owen, W. F. (1984). Interpretive themes in relational communication. *Quarterly Journal of Speech, 70,* 274-287.

Owen, W. F. (1985). Thematic metaphors in relational communication: A conceptual framework. *Western Journal of Speech Communication, 49,* 1-13.

Owen, W. F. (1989). Image metaphors of women and men in personal relationships. *Women's Studies in Communication, 12,* 37-57.

Owen, W. F. (1990). Delimiting relational metaphors. *Communication Studies, 41,* 35-53.

Padilla, F. M. (1992). *The gang as an American enterprise.* New Brunswick, NJ: Rutgers University Press.

Paetzold, R. L., & O'Leary-Kelly, A. M. (1993). Organizational communication and the legal dimensions of hostile work environment sexual harassment. In G. L. Kreps (Ed.), *Sexual harassment: Communication implications* (pp. 63-77). Cresskill, NJ: Hampton Press.

Paludi, M. A. (Ed.). (1990). *Ivory power: Sexual harassment on campus.* New York: SUNY Press.

Papa, M. J., Singhal, A., Ghanekar, D. V., & Papa, W. H. (2000). Organizing for social change through cooperative action: The (dis)empowering dimensions of women's communication. *Communication Theory, 10,* 90-123.

Parry, S. C. (1996). Feminist pedagogy and techniques for the changing classroom. *Women's Studies Quarterly, 24,* 45-54.

Pashkow, F. J., & Libov, C. (1994). *The women's heart book.* New York: Plume.

Patai, D. (2000, October 6). Will the real feminists in academe please stand up? *Chronicle of Higher Education, 47*(6), pp. B7-B9.

Patai, D., & Koertge, N. (1994). *Professing feminism: Cautionary tales from the strange world of Women's Studies.* New York: Basic Books.

Patillo-McCoy, M. (1999). *Black picket fences.* Chicago: University of Chicago Press.

Paul, C. M. B. (1995). The threshold. In S. Thames & M. Gazzaniga (Eds.), *The breast: An anthology* (pp. 112-117). New York: Global City Press.

Pauli, H. G., White, K. L., & McWhinney, I. R. (2000). Medical education, research, and scientific thinking in the 21st century (part one of three). *Education for Health, 13,* 15-25.

Payer, L. (1988). *Medicine and culture.* New York: Penguin Books.

Payne, K. (1993). The power game: Sexual harassment on the college campus. In G. L. Kreps (Ed.), *Sexual harassment: Communication implications* (pp. 133-148). Cresskill, NJ: Hampton Press.

Pekkanen, J. (1985). Our no. 1 medical need. *Reader's Digest, 127*(759), 100-106.

Perin, C. (1991). The moral fabric of the office: Panopticon discourse and schedule flexibilities. *Research in the Sociology of Organizations, 8,* 241-268.

Perin, C. (1998). Work, space, and time on the threshold of the new century. In P. J. Jackson & J. M. van der Wielen (Eds.), *Teleworking: International perspectives from telecommuting to virtual organisation* (pp. 40-55). London: Routledge.

Perlow, L. A. (1995). Putting the work back into work/family. *Group & Organization Management, 20,* 227-239.

Perlow, L. A. (1997). *Finding time: How corporations, individuals, and families can benefit from new work practices.* Ithaca, NY: Cornell University Press.

Perlow, L. A. (1998). Boundary control: The social ordering of work and family time in a high-tech corporation. *Administrative Science Quarterly, 43,* 328-357.

Perry, L. A. M., & Geist, P. (1997). Introduction. In L. A. M. Perry & P. Geist (Eds.), *Courage of conviction: Women's words, women's wisdom* (pp. 1-15). Mountain View, CA: Mayfield.

Perry-Jenkins, M., Repetti, R. L., & Crouter, A. C. (2000). Work and family in the 1990s. *Journal of the Marriage and the Family, 62,* 981-998.

Petravage, J. B., Reynolds, L. J., Gardner, H. J., & Reading, J. C. (1979). Attitudes of women toward the gynecologic examination. *Journal of Family Practice, 9,* 1039-1045.

Pezzullo, P. C., & Wood, J. T. (1999). *Teaching gendered lives: A resource book for Wood's "Gendered Lives": Communication, gender and culture.* Belmont, CA: Wadsworth.

Pfeffer, J. (1981). Management as symbolic action: The creation and maintenance of organizational paradigms. *Research in Organizational Behavior, 3,* 1-52.

Phillips, G. M., & Jarboe, S. (1993). Sycophancy and servitude: Harassment and rebellion. In G. L. Kreps (Ed.), *Sexual harassment: Communication implications* (pp. 281-309). Cresskill, NJ: Hampton Press.

Phinney, J. S., & Cobb, N. J. (1996). Reasoning about intergroup relations among Hispanic and Euro-American adolescents. *Journal of Adolescent Research, 11,* 306-324.

Phinney, J. S., Ferguson, D. L., & Tate, J. D. (1997). Intergroup attitudes among ethnic minority adolescents: A causal model. *Child Development, 68,* 955-969.

Pipher, M. (1994). *Reviving Ophelia: Saving the selves of adolescent girls.* New York: Ballantine Books.

Pogue, D. (2000). *ViaVoice Millenium Edition for Macintosh: For a 1.0 version, it's sweet.* Retrieved 5/16/01, 2001, from www.macworld.com/2000/05/reviews/viavoicemillenium.html

Pollock, E. J. (2000, February 7). Deportment gap. In today's workplace, women feel freer to be, well, women. Floppy bow ties give way to more-alluring attire; sex banter has its place. Flirting—or good business? *Wall Street Journal*, pp. A1, A20.

Poole, M. S., & Walther, J. B. (2002). *Communication: Ubiquitous, complex, consequential.* Washington, DC: National Communication Association. Retrieved July 8, 2003, from www.natcom.org/research/monograph.pdf

Popovich, P. M. (1988). Sexual harassment in organizations. *Employee Responsibilities and Rights Journal, 1,* 273-322.

Posner, J. (1992). *The feminine mistake: Women, work, and identity.* New York: Warner.

Prescott, M. E., & Le Poire, B. A. (2002). Eating disorders and mother-daughter communication: A test of inconsistent nurturing as control therapy. *Journal of Family Communication, 2,* 59-78.

"President Clinton endorses consumer bill of rights." (1998). *Journal of Trauma Nursing, 5*(2), 55-56.

Pryor, J. B., & Day, J. D. (1988). Interpretations of sexual harassment: An attributional analysis. *Sex Roles, 18,* 405-417.

Putnam, L. L. (1990, April). *Feminist theories, dispute processes, and organizational communication.* Paper presented at the Arizona State University Conference on Organizational Communication: Perspectives for the 90s, Tempe.

Putnam, L. L., & Mumby, D. K. (1993). Organizations, emotion and the myth of rationality. In S. Fineman (Ed.), *Emotion in organizations* (pp. 36-57). London: Sage.

QSR International. (1999). *QSR NUDIST (Version 4.0).* Melbourne, Australia: QSR International.

Qualitative Solutions & Research Pty Ltd. (1997). *QSR NUDIST 4: User guide.* Thousand Oaks, CA: Sage.

Quina, K. (1990). The victimization of women. In M. A. Paludi (Ed.), *Ivory power: Sexual harassment on campus* (pp. 93-102). Albany: SUNY Press.

Qvartrop, L. (1998). From telework to networking: Definitions and trends. In P. J. Jackson & J. M. van der Wielen (Eds.), *Teleworking: International perspectives from telecommuting to the virtual organisation* (pp. 21-33). London: Routledge.

Rakow, L. F. (1988). Gendered technology, gendered practice. *Critical Studies in Mass Communication, 5,* 57-70.

Rakow, L. F., & Navarro, V. (1993). Remote mothering and the parallel shift: Women meet the cellular phone. *Critical Studies in Mass Communication, 10,* 144-157.

Rancer, A. S., & Baukus, R. A. (1987). Discriminating males and females on belief structures about arguing. In L. B. Nadler, M. K. Nadler, & W. R. Todd-Mancillas (Eds.), *Advances in gender and communication research* (pp. 155-173). Lanham, MD: University Press of America.

Randall, D. (1995). "Doing" mother-daughter: Conversation analysis and relational contexts. In T. J. Socha & G. H. Stamp (Eds.), *Parents, children, and communication: Frontiers of theory and research* (pp. 113-124). Mahwah, NJ: Lawrence Erlbaum.

Rapoport, R., & Bailyn, L. (1996). *Relinking life and work: Toward a better future* [report]. New York: Ford Foundation.

Rawlins, W. K. (1983). Openness as problematic in ongoing friendships: Two conversational dilemmas. *Communication Monographs, 50,* 1-13.

Rawlins, W. K. (1989). Cultural double agency in ongoing friendships and the pursuit of friendship. *Cultural Dynamics, 2*, 28-40.

Rawlins, W. K. (1992). *Friendship matters: Communication, dialectics, and the life course.* New York: Aldine de Gruyter.

Rawlins, W. K., & Holl, M. (1987). The communicative achievement of friendship during adolescence: Predicaments of trust and violation. *Western Journal of Speech Communication, 51*, 345-363.

Rawlins, W. K., & Holl, M. R. (1988). Adolescents' interaction with parents and friends: Dialectics of temporal perspective and evaluation. *Journal of Social and Personal Relationships, 5*, 27-46.

Redding, W. C. (1972). *Communication within the organization: An interpretive review of theory and research.* New York: Industrial Communication Council.

Regulus, T. A., & Leonaitis, K. (1995). Conflict, violence, and cultural diversity. *Update on Law-Related Education, 19*, 41-42.

Reinharz, S. (1992). *Feminist methods in social research.* New York: Oxford University Press.

Reitz, R. (1977). *Menopause: A positive approach.* Middlesex, UK: Penguin.

Rheingold, H. (1993). *The virtual community: Homesteading on the electronic frontier.* New York: Harper Collins.

Rich, A. (1979). *On lies, secrets, and silence: Selected prose, 1966-1978.* New York: Norton.

Ricken, A. (2000). [Review of the book *A disease of housewives? Off the rag: Lesbians writing on menopause*]. *Journal of Lesbian Studies, 4*, 166.

Ricoeur, P. (1979). The metaphorical process as cognition, imagination, and feeling. In S. Sacks (Ed.), *On metaphor* (pp. 141-157). Chicago: University of Chicago Press.

Riessman, C. K. (1987). When gender is not enough: Women interviewing women. *Gender & Society, 1*, 172-207.

Rivers, I., & Smith, P. K. (1994). Types of bullying behavior and their correlates. *Aggressive Behavior, 20*, 359-368.

Roberts, P. (1998). A brief history of my breasts. In J. A. Tasch (Ed.), *Art.Rage.Us.: Art and writing by women with breast cancer* (pp. 58-59). San Francisco: Chronicle Books.

Rodgers, F. (1997, May). The entrepreneurial balancing act: Making the best of a good thing. *Entreworld.org: A world of resources for entrepreneurs.* Retrieved May 19, 1999, from http://entreworld.lycos.com/Perspectives.cfm?ArticleID=8

Rogers, E., Castleton, A., & Lloyd, S. A. (1996). Relational control and physical aggression in satisfying marital relationships. In D. D. Cahn & S.A. Lloyd (Eds.), *Family violence from a communication perspective* (pp. 218-239). Thousand Oaks, CA: Sage.

Roloff, M. (1996). The catalyst hypothesis: Conditions under which coercive communication leads to physical aggression. In D. D. Cahn & S. A. Lloyd (Eds.), *Family violence from a communication perspective* (pp. 20-36). Thousand Oaks, CA: Sage.

Rose, K. (1996, February). The new workforce: Let's be flexible. *HRFocus*, p. 16.

Rosenthal, M. S. (1996). *The breast sourcebook.* Los Angeles: Lowell House.

Rosser, S. V. (1994). *Women's health—missing from U.S. medicine.* Bloomington: Indiana University Press.

Rothschild-Whitt, J. (1979). The collectivist organization: An alternative to rational-bureaucratic models. *American Sociological Review, 44*, 509-527.

Roy, J. M. (1990). Surgical gynecology. In R. D. Apple (Ed.), *Women, health, and medicine in America* (pp. 173-196). New Brunswick, NJ: Rutgers University Press.

Rozmus, K. (1997). Peer mediation programs in schools: Resolving classroom conflict but raising ethical concerns? *Journal of Law & Education, 26*, 69-92.

Rubin, L. J., & Borgers, S. B. (1990). Sexual harassment in universities during the 1980s. *Sex Roles, 23,* 397-411.

Ruether, C., & Fairhurst, G. T. (2000). Chaos theory and the glass ceiling. In P. M. Buzzanell (Ed.), *Rethinking organizational and managerial communication from feminist perspectives* (pp. 236-256). Thousand Oaks, CA: Sage.

Rule, B. G., Bisanz, G. L., & Kohn, M. (1985). Anatomy of a persuasion schema: Target, goals, and strategies. *Journal of Personality and Social Psychology, 48,* 1127-1140.

Russo, T. C. (1998). Organizational and professional identification: A case of newspaper journalists. *Management Communication Quarterly, 12,* 72-111.

Ruzek, S. B. (1978). *The women's health movement. Feminist alternatives to medical control.* New York: Praeger.

Sabourin, T. C. (1996). The role of communicating in verbal abuse between spouses. In D. D. Cahn & S. A. Lloyd (Eds.), *Family violence from a communication perspective* (pp. 199-217). Thousand Oaks, CA: Sage

Sabourin, T. C., & Stamp, G. H. (1995). Communication and the experience of dialectical tensions in family life: An examination of abusive and nonabusive families. *Communication Monographs, 62,* 213-241.

Saphir, M., & Chaffee, S. H. (2002). Adolescents' contributions to family communication patterns. *Human Communication Research, 28,* 86-108.

Sawchuk, K. (1986). A tale of inscription: Fashion statements. In A. Kroker & M. Kroker (Eds.), *Body invaders: Panic sex in America* (pp. 61-77). New York: St. Martin's Press.

Sayer, D. (1991). *Capitalism and modernity: An excursus on Marx and Weber.* New York: Routledge.

Schepp, B. (1990). *The telecommuter's handbook.* Thousand Oaks, CA: Pharos Books.

Schindehette, S., Schneider, K., & O'Neill, A. (1998, October 26). Victors Valiant [special report: breast cancer]. *People, 50,* 15, 52-67.

Schneirov, M. (1998). Technologies of the self and the aesthetic project of alternative health. *The Sociological Quarterly, 39,* 435-451.

Schrader, D. C., & Dillard, J. P. (1998). Goal structures and interpersonal influence. *Communication Studies, 49,* 276-293.

Schrag, K. (1978). The adolescent's first gynecological exam. *Journal of Nurse-Midwifery, 23,* 20-24.

Scott, C. R., & Timmerman, C. E. (1999). Communication technology use and multiple workplace identifications among organizational teleworkers with varied degrees of virtuality. *IEEE Transactions on Professional Communication, 42,* 240-260.

Scott, R. A., Aiken, L. H., Mechanic, D., & Moravcsik, J. (1995). Organizational aspects of caring. *Milbank Quarterly, 73,* 77-95.

Scully, D. (1994). *Men who control women's health: The miseducation of obstetrician-gynecologists.* New York: Teachers College Press.

Seibert, S. E., Kraimer, M. L., & Liden, R. C. (2001). A social capital theory of career success. *Academy of Management Journal, 44,* 219-237.

Seid, R. P. (1989). *Never too thin: Why women are at war with their bodies.* New York: Prentice Hall.

Seidman, I. E. (1991). *Interviewing as qualitative research: A guide for researchers in education and the social sciences.* New York: Teachers College Press.

Settlage, D. S. (1975). Pelvic examination of women. *Practical Psychology for Physicians, 2*(8), 40-47.

Severne, L. (1982). Psychosocial aspects of the menopause. In A. Voda, M. Dinnerstein, & S. R. O'Donnell (Eds.), *Changing perspectives of menopause* (pp. 239-247). Austin: University of Texas Press.

Shandler, S. (1999). *Ophelia speaks: Adolescent girls write about their search for self.* New York: Harper Perennial.

Shapiro, S. B. (1998). *Dance, power, and difference: Critical and feminist perspectives on dance education.* Champaign, IL: Human Kinetics.

Shaw, L. (1996). *Telecommute! Go to work without leaving home.* New York: John Wiley.

Shedletsky, L. J. (1993). Accused of sexual harassment. In G. L. Kreps (Ed.), *Sexual harassment: Communication implications* (pp. 81-89). Cresskill, NJ: Hampton Press.

Sheehy, G. (1998). *The silent passage: Menopause.* New York: Pocket Books.

Shellenbarger, S. (2002, February 13). Americans are spending so much time in cars, living takes a back seat. *Wall Street Journal,* p. B6.

Shelton, J. N., & Chavous, T. M. (1999). Black and white college women's perceptions of sexual harassment. *Sex Roles, 40,* 593-615.

Sheperd, G. J. (1992). Communication as influence: Definitional exclusion. *Communication Studies, 43,* 203-219.

Sheperd, G. J. (1998). The trouble with goals. *Communication Studies, 49,* 294-299.

Shinkman, R. (1998). Specialized primary care. *Modern Healthcare, 28*(40), 36.

Shotland, R. L., & Craig, J. M. (1988). Can men and women differentiate between friendly and sexually interested behavior? *Social Psychology Quarterly, 51,* 66-73.

Shotter, J. (1993). *Conversational realities: Constructing life through language.* Newbury Park, CA: Sage.

Shrewsbury, C. M. (1993). What is feminist pedagogy? *Women's Studies Quarterly, 21,* 8-16.

Sias, P. M., & Cahill, D. J. (1998). From coworkers to friends: The development of peer friendships in the workplace. *Western Journal of Communication, 62,* 273-299.

Small Business Administration's Office of Advocacy (October, 1998). *Women in Business: A report on statistical information about women-owned businesses prepared by the U.S. Small Business Administration's Office of Advocacy.* Retrieved July 7, 2003, from www.sba.gov/ADVO/stats/wib.pdf

Smircich, L., & Morgan, G. (1982). Leadership: The management of meaning. *Journal of Applied Behavioral Science, 18,* 257-273.

Smith, D. E. (1987). *The everyday world as problematic: A feminist sociology.* Boston: Northeastern University Press.

Smith, D. H. (1993). Stories, values, and patient care decisions. In C. Conrad (Ed.), *Ethical nexus* (pp. 123-148). Norwood, NJ: Ablex.

Smith, R. (2001). BMA president warns doctors not to take public esteem for granted. *British Medical Journal, 323,* 70.

Smith, R. C., & Eisenberg, E. N. (1987). Conflict at Disneyland: A root metaphor analysis. *Communication Monographs, 54,* 367-380.

Smith-Rosenberg, C. (1975). The female world of love and ritual: Relations between women in nineteenth-century America. In N. F. Cott & E. H. Pleck (Eds.), *A heritage of her own: Toward a new social history of American women* (pp. 311-342). New York: Simon & Schuster.

Socha, T. J., Sanchez-Hucles, J., Bromley, J., & Kelly, B. (1995). Invisible parents and children: Exploring African-American parent-child communication. In T. J. Socha &

G. H. Stamp (Eds.), *Parents, children, and communication: Frontiers of theory and research* (pp. 127-145). Mahwah, NJ: Lawrence Erlbaum.

Socha, T. J., & Stamp, G. H. (Eds.). (1995). *Parents, children, and communication: Frontiers of theory and research.* Mahwah, NJ: Lawrence Erlbaum.

Spain, D. (1992). *Gendered spaces.* Chapel Hill: University of North Carolina Press.

Spigel, L. (1989). The domestic economy of television viewing in postwar America. *Critical Studies in Mass Communication, 6,* 337-354.

Spitzack, C., & Carter, K. (1987). Women in communication studies: A typology for revision. *Quarterly Journal of Speech, 73,* 401-423.

Sproull, L., & Kiesler, S. (1991). *Connections: New ways of working in the networked organization.* Cambridge: MIT Press.

Stambolovic, V. (1996). Medical heresy—The view of the heretic. *Social Science and Medicine, 43,* 601-604.

Steiner, L. (1997). A feminist schema for analysis of ethical dilemmas. In F. L. Casmir (Ed.), *Ethics in intercultural and international communication* (pp. 59-88). Mahwah, NJ: Lawrence Erlbaum.

Stepp, P. L. (2001). Sexual harassment in communication extra-curricular activities: Intercollegiate debate and individual events. *Communication Education, 50,* 34-50.

Stohl, C., & Cheney, G. (2001). Participatory processes/paradoxical practices: Communication and the dilemmas of organizational democracy. *Management Communication Quarterly, 14,* 349-407.

Stoppard, M. (1996). *The breast book: The essential guide to breast care and breast health for women of all ages.* Toronto: Random House of Canada.

Strauman, E. C. (1997, August). *The exhausted face of illness: A narrative analysis of media accounts of Chronic Fatigue Syndrome.* Unpublished master's thesis, University of South Florida, Tampa.

Straus, M. A. (1979). Measuring intrafamily conflict and violence: The Conflict Tactics (CT) Scale. *Journal of Marriage and the Family, 41,* 75-90.

Strauss, A., & Corbin, J. (1990). *Basics of qualitative research: Grounded theory procedures and techniques.* Newbury Park, CA: Sage.

Strauss, A., & Corbin, J. (1998). *Basics of qualitative research* (2nd ed.). Thousand Oaks, CA: Sage.

Strauss, S. (1988). Sexual harassment in the school: Legal implications for principles. *NAASP Bulletin, 72,* 93-97.

Strine, M. (1992). Understanding "how things work": Sexual harassment and academic culture. *Journal of Applied Communication Research, 20,* 391-400.

Sullivan, C. F. (1997). Women's ways of coping with breast cancer. *Women's Studies in Communication, 20,* 59-81.

Sullivan, P. A., & Turner, L. H. (1996). *From the margins to the center: Contemporary women and political communication.* Westport, CT: Praeger.

Sullivan, P. A., & Turner, L. H. (1999). The Zoe Baird Spectacle: Silences, sins, and Status. *Western Journal of Communication, 63,* 413-432.

Sullivan, W. (2000). Institutional identity and social responsibility in higher education. In T. Ehrlich (Ed.), *Civic responsibility and higher education* (pp. 19-36). Phoenix, AZ: Oryx Press.

Sussman, L. (1999). How to frame a message: The art of persuasion and negotiation. *Business Horizons, 42* (4), 2-6.

Suto, R. (1994). *The narrative reconstruction of self in breast cancer: The role of significant others.* Unpublished master's thesis, The Pennsylvania State University, University Park.

Swanson, D. R. (1979). Toward a psychology of metaphor. In S. Sacks (Ed.), *On metaphor* (pp. 161-164). Chicago: University of Chicago Press.

Tajfel, H., Flament, C., Billig, M., & Bundy, R. (1971). Social categorization and intergroup behaviour. *European Journal of Social psychology, 1,* 149-178.

Takenaga, N., Kai, I., & Ohi, G. (1985). Evaluation of three cervical cancer detection programs in Japan with special reference to cost-benefit analysis. *Cancer, 55,* 2514-2519.

Tangri, S. S., Burt, M. R., & Johnson, L. B. (2000). Sexual harassment at work: Three explanatory models. In E. Wall (Ed.), *Sexual harassment* (rev. ed., pp. 115-132). Amherst, NY: Prometheus Books.

Tannen, D. (1990). *You just don't understand: Women and men in conversation.* New York: William Morrow.

Tasch, J. A. (Ed.). (1998). *Art.Rage.Us.: Art and writing by women with breast cancer.* San Francisco: Chronicle Books.

Taylor, B., & Conrad, C. (1992). Narratives of sexual harassment: Organizational dimensions. *Journal of Applied Communication Research, 20,* 401-418.

Tepper, B. J. (2000). Consequences of abusive supervision. *Academy of Management Journal, 43,* 178-190.

Thayer, L. (1988). Leadership/communication: A critical review and a modest proposal. In G. M. Goldhaber & G. A. Barnett (Eds.), *Handbook of organizational communication* (pp. 231-263). Norwood, NJ: Ablex.

Thompson, K. (Ed.). (1991). *To be a man: In search of the deep masculine.* Los Angeles: Jeremy P. Tharcher.

Thompson, S. M. (1996). Peer mediation: A peaceful solution. *School Counselor, 44,* 151-155.

Thornton, B. C., Marinelli, R. D., & Larson, T. (1993). Ethics and women's health care. In B. C. Thornton & G. L. Kreps (Eds.), *Perspectives on health communication* (pp. 186-195). Prospect Heights, IL: Waveland Press.

Till, F. J. (1980). *Sexual harassment: A report of the sexual harassment of students.* Washington, DC: National Advisory Council on Women's Educational Programs.

Tjaden, P., & Thoennes, N. (2000, July). *Extent, nature, and consequences of intimate partner violence: Findings from the National Violence Against Women Survey* (NCJ 181867). Washington, DC: U.S. Department of Justice, Office of Justice Programs.

Todd, A. D. (1989). *Intimate adversaries: Cultural conflict between doctors and woman patients.* Philadelphia: University of Pennsylvania Press.

Todorov, T. (1984). *Mikhail Bakhtin: The dialogical principle* (W. Godzich, Trans.). Minneapolis: University of Minnesota Press.

Tolman, A. (1995). *Women's experiences as mothers of adolescent children.* Unpublished doctoral dissertation, University of Massachusetts at Amherst.

Tompkins, J. (2000). Reverie. In P. R. Freeman & J. Z. Schmidt (Eds.), *Wise women: Reflections of teachers at midlife* (pp. 47-48). New York: Routledge.

Tong, R. (1989). *Feminist thought: A comprehensive introduction.* Boulder, CO: Westview Press.

Tong, R. (1993). *Feminine and feminist ethics.* Belmont, CA: Wadsworth.

Tong, R. (1998). The ethics of care: A feminist virtue ethics of care for healthcare practitioners. *Journal of Medicine & Philosophy, 2,* 131-152.

Townsley, N. C., & Geist, P. (2000). The discursive enactment of hegemony: Sexual harassment and academic organizing. *Western Journal of Communication, 64,* 190-217.

Tracy, K. (1984). The effect of multiple goals on conversational relevance and topic shift. *Communication Monographs, 51,* 274-287.

Tracy, K., & Coupland, N. (1990). Multiple goals in discourse: An overview of issues. *Journal of Language and Social Psychology, 9,* 1-13.

Tracy, K., & Moran, J. P., III. (1983). Conversational goal relevance in multiple-goal settings. In R. T. Craig & K. Tracy (Eds.), *Conversational coherence: Form, structure, and strategy* (pp. 116-135). Beverly Hills, CA: Sage.

Trad, P. V. (1995). Adolescent girls and their mothers: Realigning the relationship. *American Journal of Family Therapy, 23,* 11-24.

Trelor, D., & Boddy, I. (1996). [Untitled figure]. In M. Stoppard, *The breast book* (p. 41). Toronto: Random House of Canada.

Trethewey, A. (1998). Isn't it ironic: Using irony to explore the contradictions of organizational life. *Western Journal of Communication, 63,* 140-167.

Trethewey, A. (1999). Critical organizational communication theory, feminist research methods, and service-learning: Praxis as pedagogy. In D. Droge, B. O. Murphy, & E. Zlotkowski (Eds.), *Voices of strong democracy: Concepts and models for service-learning in Communication Studies* (pp. 177-189). Washington, DC: American Association for Higher Education.

Trethewey, A. (2000). Revisioning control: A feminist critique of disciplined bodies. In P. Buzzanell. (Ed.), *Rethinking organizational and managerial communication from feminist perspectives* (pp. 107-127). Thousand Oaks, CA: Sage.

Tronto, J. C. (1992). Women and caring: What can feminists learn about morality from caring? In A. M. Jaggar & S. R. Bordo (Eds.), *Gender/body/knowledge: Feminist reconstructions of being and knowing* (pp. 172-187). New Brunswick, NJ: Rutgers University Press.

Tronto, J. C. (1993). *Moral boundaries: A political argument for an ethic of care.* New York: Routledge.

Turkle, S. (1995). Life on the screen: Identity in the age of the Internet. New York: Simon & Schuster.

Turner, L. H., & West, R. (2002). *Perspectives on family communication* (2nd ed.). Boston: McGraw-Hill.

Turner, S. L., & Hamilton, H. (1997). The influence of fashion magazines on the body image satisfaction of college women: An exploratory analysis. *Adolescence (32),* pp. 603-615.

Twenge, J. M., & Zucker, A. N. (1999). What is a feminist? Evaluations and stereotypes in closed- and open-ended responses. *Psychology of Women Quarterly, 23,* 591-605.

Tyler, A., & Boxer, D. (1996). Sexual harassment? Cross-cultural/cross-linguistic perspectives. *Discourse & Society, 7,* 107-133.

Van Maanen, J. (1988). *Tales of the field: On writing ethnography.* Chicago: University of Chicago Press.

Vanderford, M. L., Jenks, E. B., & Sharf, B. F. (1997). Exploring patients' experiences as a primary source of meaning. *Health Communication, 9,* 13-26.

Vanderford, M. L., Smith, D. H., & Harris, W. S. (1992). Value identification in narrative discourse: Evaluation of an HIV education demonstration project. *Journal of Applied Communication Research, 20,* 123-160.

Varallo, S., Tracy, P., Marty, D., & Tambe, A. (2001). Feminism and Communication Studies. In E. L. MacNabb, M. J. Cherry, S. L. Popham, & R. P. Prys (Eds.), *Transforming the disciplines: A Women's Studies primer* (pp. 129-137). New York: Haworth Press.

Vaughan, M. (1998, May 21). A struggle to reconcile double standards. *Herald* (Glasgow), p. 21. Retrieved February 2, 2002, from Academic Universe Search, Lexis-Nexis database.

Veatch, R. M. (1998). The place of care in ethical theory. *Journal of Medicine & Philosophy, 23,* 210-224.

Violanti, M. T. (1996). Hooked on expectations: An analysis of influence and relationships in the Tailhook reports. *Journal of Applied Communication Research, 24,* 67-82.

Voda, A. M., & George, T. (1986). Menopause. *Annual Review of Nursing Research, 4,* 55-75.

Wakefield, M. K. (1997). Protecting health care consumers: A bill of rights and responsibilities. *Nursing Economics, 15,* 315-317.

Waldron, V. R., Foreman, C., & Miller, R. (1993). Managing gender conflicts in the supervisory relationship: Relationship-definition tactics used by women and men. In G. L. Kreps (Ed.), *Sexual harassment: Communication implications* (pp. 234-256). Cresskill, NJ: Hampton Press.

Walker, R. (1995). *To be real: Telling the truth and changing the face of feminism.* New York: Anchor Books.

Wallis, L. (1994). Why a curriculum on women's health? In A. J. Dan (Ed.), *Reframing women's health* (pp. 13-26). Thousand Oaks, CA: Sage.

Washington, H. A. (1999). Your gyn visit. What you don't know can hurt you. *Essence, 30*(2), 83-84, 86, 138, 141, 144-145.

Waters, M. C. (2001). *Optional ethnicities: For Whites only?* In M. L. Andersen & P. H. Collins (Eds.), *Race, class, and gender* (4th ed., pp. 430-439). Belmont, CA: Wadsworth.

Watzlawick, P., Weakland, J. H., & Fisch, R. (1974). *Change: Principles of problem formation and problem resolution.* New York: Norton.

Wayne, J. H. (2000). Disentangling the power bases of sexual harassment: Comparing gender, age, and position power. *Journal of Vocational Behavior, 57,* 301-325.

Wear, D. (1997). *Privilege in the medical academy: A feminist examines gender, race, and power.* New York: Teachers College Press.

Weedon, C. (1987). *Feminist practice and poststructuralist theory.* New York: Basil Blackwell.

Weedon, C. (1999). *Feminism, theory and the politics of difference.* Malden, MA: Blackwell.

Weeks, K. (1998). *Constituting feminist subjects.* Ithaca, NY: Cornell University Press.

Weick, K. E. (1995). *Sensemaking in organizations.* Thousand Oaks, CA: Sage.

Weiss, K. (1977). What medical students learn about women. In C. Dreifus (Ed.), *Seizing our bodies: The politics of women's health* (pp. 212-222). New York: Vintage Books.

Weiss, L., & Meadow, R. (1979). Women's attitudes toward gynecological practices. *Obstetrics & Gynecology, 54,* 110-114.

Wells, G. M. (1977). Reducing the threat of a first pelvic exam. *American Journal of Maternal Child Nursing, 2,* 304-306.

Wendell, S. (1992). Toward a feminist theory of disability. In H. B. Holmes & L. M. Purdy (Eds.), *Feminist perspectives in medical ethics* (pp. 63-81). Bloomington: Indiana University Press.

West, C. (1993). *Race matters.* Boston: Beacon Press.

West, C. (1995). Women's competence in conversation. *Discourse & Society, 6,* 107-131.

West, C., & Zimmerman, D. H. (1987). Doing gender. *Gender & Society, 1,* 125-151.

West, R. (1994). Teacher-student communication: A descriptive topology of students' interpersonal experiences with teachers. *Communication Reports, 7,* 109-118.

West, S., & Dranov, P. (1994). *The hysterectomy hoax.* New York: Doubleday.

Weyrauch, K. (1990). Patient sex role and preference for a male or female physician. *Journal of Family Practice, 30,* 559-562.

Wiley, M. G. (1991). Gender, work, and stress: The potential impact of role-identity salience and commitment. *Sociological Quarterly, 32,* 495-510.

Williams, C. L. (1999). Real-life sexual harassment. In B. Glassner & R. Hertz (Eds.), *Qualitative sociology as everyday life* (pp. 49-57). Thousand Oaks, CA: Sage.

Williams, K. B., & Cyr, R. R. (1992). Escalating commitment to a relationship: The sexual harassment trap. *Sex Roles, 27,* 47-72.

Williams, S. J., & Calnan, M. (1996). The "limits" of medicalization? Modern medicine and the lay populace in "late" modernity. *Social Science and Medicine, 42,* 1609-1620.

Wilson, R. A. (1966). *Feminine forever.* New York: M. Evans.

Wilson, S. R. (2002). *Seeking and resisting compliance: Why people say what they do when trying to influence others.* Thousand Oaks, CA: Sage.

Wilson, S. R., & Putnam, L. L. (1990). Interaction goals in negotiation. In J. A. Anderson (Ed.), *Communication yearbook 13* (pp. 374-406). Newbury Park, CA: Sage.

Winterich, J. A., & Umberson, D. (1999). How women experience menopause: The importance of social context. *Journal of Women & Aging, 11,* 57-73.

Witmer, D. F. (1997). Communication and recovery: Structuration as an ontological approach to organizational culture. *Communication Monographs, 64,* 324-349.

Witteman, H. (1993). The interface between sexual harassment and organizational romance. In G. L. Kreps (Ed.), *Sexual harassment: Communication implications* (pp. 27-62). Cresskill, NJ: Hampton Press.

Wolf, F. R. (2001, April 12). "Telework" would ease the commute: If more employees worked from home using modern technology, roads would be less clogged, says Rep. Frank Wolf. *Washington Post,* p. T5.

Wolf, N. (1991). *The beauty myth: How images of beauty are used against women.* New York: William Morrow.

Wolfe, C., & Spencer, S. J. (1996). Stereotypes and prejudice: Their overt and subtle influence in the classroom. *American Behavioral Scientist, 40,* 176-185.

Wood, J. T. (1992a). Gender and moral voice: Moving from woman's nature to standpoint epistemology. *Women's Studies in Communication, 15,* 1-24.

Wood, J. T. (1992b). Telling our stories: Narratives as a basis for theorizing sexual harassment. *Journal of Applied Communication Research, 20,* 349-362.

Wood, J. T. (1993). Naming and interpreting sexual harassment: A conceptual framework for scholarship. In G. L. Kreps (Ed.), *Sexual harassment: Communication implications* (pp. 9-26). Cresskill, NJ: Hampton Press.

Wood, J. T. (1994). *Who cares? Women, care, and culture.* Carbondale: Southern Illinois University Press.

Wood, J. T. (1998a). Celebrating diversity in the communication field. *Communication Studies, 49,* 172-178.

Wood, J. T. (1998b). Ethics, justice, and the "private sphere." *Women's Studies in Communication, 21,* 125-149.

Wood, J. T. (2001). *Gendered lives: Communication, gender, and culture* (4th ed.). Belmont, CA: Wadsworth.

Wood, J. T., & Conrad, C. (1983). Paradox in the experience of professional women. *Western Journal of Speech Communication, 47,* 305-322.

Wood, J. T., Dendy, L. L., Dordek, E., Germany, M., & Varallo, S. M. (1994). Dialectic of difference: A thematic analysis of intimates' meanings for differences. In K. Carter & M. Presnell (Eds.), *Interpretive approaches to interpersonal communication* (pp. 115-136). Albany: SUNY Press.

Wood, J. T., & Inman, C. C. (1993). In a different mode: Masculine styles of communicating closeness. *Journal of Applied Communication Research, 21,* 270-295.

Woods, N. F. (1998). Menopause: Models, medicine, and midlife. *Frontiers: A Journal of Women Studies, 19,* 5-19.

Wright, A. L. (1982). Variation in Navajo menopause: Toward an explanation. In A. M. Voda, M. Dinnerstein, & S. R. O'Donnell (Eds.), *Changing perspectives of menopause* (pp. 84-99). Austin: University of Texas Press.

Yalom, M. (1997). *A history of the breast.* New York: Ballantine Books.

Young, D. C. (1998). One in eight [15"x19" toned photograph]. In J. A. Tasch (Ed.), *Art.Rage.Us.: Art and writing by women with breast cancer* (pp. 46—47). San Francisco: Chronicle Books. (Original photograph dated 1996)

Young, E. (1989). On the naming of the rose: Interests and multiple meanings as elements of organizational culture. *Organizational Studies, 10,* 187-206.

Young, I. M. (1990). Breasted experience: The look and the feeling. In *throwing like a girl and other essays in feminist philosophy and social theory* (pp. 189-209). Bloomington: Indiana University Press.

Youniss, J., & Smollar, J. (1985). *Adolescent relations with mothers, fathers, and friends.* Chicago: University of Chicago Press.

Zerbe, W. J. (2000). Emotional dissonance and employee well-being. In N. M. Ashkanasy, C. E. J. Härtel, & W. J. Zerbe (Eds.), *Emotions in the workplace: Research, theory, and practice* (pp. 189-214). Westport, CT: Quorum Books.

Zola, I. K. (1990). Medicine as an institution of social control. In P. Conrad & R. Kern (Eds.), *The sociology of health and illness: Critical perspectives* (3rd ed., pp. 398-408). New York: St. Martin's Press.

Zucchermaglio, C., & Talamo, A. (2000). The social construction of work times: Negotiated time and expected time. *Time & Society, 9,* 205-222.

Index

Adolescence, 123, 128, 129
    female, 216
Advancement. *See* Telecommuting,
    promotion
Agency, 35, 40, 87-88, 265, 266
Aggression:
    children and, 233-234
    constructive, 232
    hostility, 233
    indirect, 234, 239-240, 241
    Infante model of, 232-233, 235, 242
    overt, 234, 241
    physical, 234, 241, 242
    relational, 234
    verbal, 233, 238-239, 242
Anderson, J., 22
Ashcraft, K. L., xiv, xv
Autobiographies, 185, 264
Autonomy, 283

Bakhtin, M. M.:
    discursive genres, 224-225
    theory of intertextuality, 216,
        224-225
Ball State University, 5-7, 199
    Department of Women's Studies, 199
    Women's and Gender Studies
        Program, 199
Baudrillard, J., 127, 140, 141
Bem, S. L., xiii
Billability, 52, 66, 72
Biomedical model, 79, 99, 100, 147-148
Bodies:
    as object, 123
    as political canvas, 14

commodification of, 124, 141, 144
control of, 223. *See also* Foucault,
    control
damaged, 82
disciplined, 14, 129
docile, 138
ideals, 81
image, 131, 215
media discourses and, 216
sexualized, 221
"tyranny of slenderness", 222
Body shape discourse, 215, 216
Body shape texts:
    electronic texts, 226-227
    living texts, 227-228
    print texts, 225-226
Bordo, S., 223
Boundaries, 16, 17, 39, 57-58,
    60, 92, 255
    See also Tensions
Breast cancer, 124, 133
    fund, 136-139
    survivors, 134
Breasts, 132
    consumption of, 143
    See also Bodies, commodification of
Browning Smith, C., 227-229
Bureaucracy in health care, 170
Buzzanell, P. M., 196

Care, ethic of. *See* Ethics, of care
Caron, A. F., 293
Childbirth:
    male control of, 149-150
Civic engagement, 74

357

Maguire, M., 5
Martin, J., 49, 51
Marginalization, 4, 17-19, 36, 37, 79, 80,
    96, 171
    See also Voices, marginalized
Maternity leave, 186-188
McCorkel, S., 182
Medicine:
    alternative, 80-81
    as profession, 148-149
    complementary, 81, 83, 85, 87, 89,
        91, 93, 96
    conventional, 89. See also Biomedical
        model
    practitioners, 93. See also Physicians
Menopause:
    as deficiency, 99, 100
    as positive, 104
    as transition, 120
    feminist, 102, 103, 121
    in other countries, 101
    perceptions of, 111-119
Metaphor, 180-192
    feminist/feminine approach, 184
    meanings, 181
    polysemic, 182-183
Methodology:
    feminist ethnography, 7
    interviews, 8, 20, 50, 83, 84, 97, 106,
        107, 278
    participant observation, 8, 20,
        198-199, 278
    survey, 156, 236
    thematic analysis, 85
Middlebrook, C., 140-141
Midwives, 149-150
Mills, J. L., 182
Minority:
    men as, 18, 19
    women as, 55
Mohtar, L. F., 5
Mothers, 275-294
    entrepreneurial 225, 262, 265
    role models, 265, 284
    stereotypes, 265
Multicultural schools, 232, 234
    See also Diversity; Interethinic
        incidents

Narratives, 184-185
National Women's Music Festival, 5, 6
Navarro, V., 259

O'Connor, P., 219
Organization for the Study of
    Communication, Language and
    Gender, 202
Organizational Communication, 21-22,
    196, 200
Other:
    women as, 79
Owen, W. F., 182

Partner Abuse Intervention Programs
    (PAIPs), 299-307
    DeKalb County Domestic Abuse
        Program (DCDAP), 300-307
Paul, C. M. B., 130
Patriarchy, 12, 52, 66
Patient-physician communication. See
    Physician-patient communication
Pedagogy, 188-190, 247
    feminist, 180, 195-212, 248, 250
    journals, 217
Peer mediation programs, 243
    See also Conflict, resolution; Training
People magazine, 133-135
Pezzullo, P. C., 196-198, 202, 204, 206
Physical disability, 186-188
Physician-patient communication, 82,
    91, 96, 165, 168
Physicians:
    gender of, 153, 160-162
    control by, 159
Politics, lesbian, feminist, 12-14, 19
Polysemy, 182-184
Poststructuralism, 34, 35
Praxis, xiv, xvi
Pregnancy, 186-188
Professors, 29, 30
Promotion. See Telecommuting,
    promotion
Public displays of affection, 14-15
Public schools, 242
Public space, 16
    See also Space, public
Public sphere. See Spheres, public

About the Editors

Patrice M. Buzzanell (PhD, Purdue University) is an Associate Professor in the Department of Communication at Purdue University. Her research interests center on feminist organizational communication theorizing and the construction of gendered workplace identities, interactions, and structures, particularly as they relate to career processes and outcomes. Besides teaching courses such as organizational communication, training and development, gender communication, and critical-interpretive methods, she also has taught OBHR at the Eli Broad Graduate School of Management at Michigan State University and at the University of Michigan-Flint and has coadvised an engineering design team focusing on hardware and software for girls aged 9 to 13 years (Institute for Women and Technology team in the Engineering Projects in Community Service at Purdue; IWT-EPICS). She has published in *Human Communication Research, Communication Monographs, Journal of Applied Communication Research,* and other communication journals and edited books. For her edited book, *Rethinking Organizational and Managerial Communication From Feminist Perspectives* (Sage, 2000), she received the Central States Communication Association's Theory Book Award in 2002. She also earned the W. Charles Redding Dissertation Award from the International Communication Association in 1988 and has won several top paper awards. In addition to editing *Management Communication Quarterly,* she has served as chairperson of the Organizational Communication Division of ICA, secretary of the Organizational Communication Division of the National Communication Association (NCA), as President of the Organization for the Study of Communication, Language and Gender (OSCLG), and as a current editorial board member for eight journals and a handbook. For this and other work, she was awarded the Outstanding Member Award from her ICA division, the Alumnus of the Year Award from the School of Interpersonal Communication at Ohio University, the Teacher-Mentor Award from OSCLG, and the Violet Haas Award for promoting the advancement of women at Purdue University. *pbuzzanell@sla.purdue.edu*

Helen Sterk (PhD, University of Iowa) is Professor of Communication Arts and Sciences and Director of the Gender Studies minor at Calvin College. She was appointed to Calvin College's William Spoelhof Teacher Scholar Chair in 1997. Dr. Sterk has written widely on rhetoric, feminism, gender, and popular culture. She has coauthored or coedited several books, including her most recent collaboration, *Who's Having This Baby? Perspectives on Birthing* (Michigan State University Press, 2002), as well as *Differences That Make a Difference* (edited with Lynn Turner; Bergin & Garvey, 1994) and *Constructing and Reconstructing Gender* (edited with Linda A. M. Perry and Lynn Turner; State University of New York Press, 1992). Her work has been published in journals such as the *Western Journal of Communication* and the *Journal of Communication,* and in edited collections such as *Evaluating Women's Health Messages: A Resourcebook* (Sage, 1996). She currently edits the *Journal of Communication and Religion* and serves on three editorial boards. She also has served as President for the Organization for the Study of Communication, Language and Gender and the Religious Communication Association, as Chapter President for the American Association of University Professors (AAUP), and as a member of the state executive board for the AAUP (Michigan). She has earned awards for her outstanding articles and dissertation work. *hsterk@calvin.edu*

Lynn H. Turner (PhD, Northwestern University) is an Associate Professor in Communication Studies at Marquette University. Her research areas of emphasis include interpersonal, gender, and family communication. She is the coauthor or coeditor of several books, articles, and chapters, most of which focus on intersections between communication and gender. Her articles have appeared in many journals, including *Management Communication Quarterly, Journal of Applied Communication Research, Women and Language,* and *Western Journal of Communication.* Her books include *From the Margins to the Center: Contemporary Women and Political Communication* (coauthored with Patricia Sullivan; Praeger, 1996; recipient of the 1997 Best Book Award from the Organization for the Study of Communication, Language and Gender [OSCLG]) and *Perspectives on Family Communication* (coauthored with Richard West; McGraw-Hill, 2002). She was the recipient of the College of Communication Outstanding Research Award in 1999. She has served in a number of different positions: Director of Graduate Studies for the College of Communication at Marquette University. President of OSCLG, President-Elect of Central States Communication Association (CSCA), and Chairperson of the Family Communication Division for the National Communication Association. She has planned several conferences for OSCLG and CSCA. *lynn.turner@marquette.edu*

About the Contributors

Maria Brann (PhD, University of Kentucky) is an Assistant Professor in the Department of Communication Studies at West Virginia University. Her research interests include ethical health issues such as confidentiality breaches, gynecological care, body image, gender construction, organizational values, and drug and alcohol use. Her publications include articles in *Health Communication, Communication Studies, Health Care Analysis,* and *MD Computing.* She has served the profession by assisting as panel facilitator, presenter, representative, paper reader, and planning committee member for the National Communication Association as well as regional and state associations. She also serves as a reviewer for *Communication Studies. maria.brann@mail.wvu.edu*

Nada Frazier Cano (BA, Texas A&M University-Corpus Christi, with Highest Honors) is a Board-Certified Legal Assistant in Personal Injury Trial Law, Texas Board of Legal Specialization, currently working as a paralegal for the law firm of Sapp & White, P.C. in Austin, Texas. Ms. Cano aspires to complete her master's degree in Counseling. Her research interests are communication, women and gender studies, and law-related subjects. Her publications and papers include: guest author, Epilogue Chapter, "The Impact of Social Movements on Gender Communication: You Must Know Where You've Been to Know Where You're Going" in *Exploring GenderSpeak: Personal Effectiveness in Gender Communication* (2nd ed. by Ivy & Backlund, 2000); paper co-presenter with Quintanilla and Ivy at the conference for the Organization for the Study of Communication, Language and Gender, held in Milwaukee, Wisconsin (October 2000): "The Defining of Menopause"; and paper presenter at the sixth annual conference for the Study of Women and Politics, held at the Carrie Chapman Catt Center at Iowa State University (October, 1998): "First Lady Hillary Rodham Clinton: Challenging the Cultural Confines of the White House's Glass Ceiling." *ncano@austin.rr.com*

Paige P. Edley (PhD, Rutgers University) is an Assistant Professor in the Department of Communication Studies at Loyola Marymount University. Her research examines the intersections between work-family concerns, feminist transformation, and technology, as well as alternative organizing and women-owned businesses. She is currently involved in the International Communication Association Feminist Scholarship Division's research and advocacy group MAP (Media Associations Project). She has published in *Management Communication Quarterly, Women & Language,* and *Argumentation and Advocacy.* She currently serves as an elected Board Member for the Organization for the Study of Communication, Language and Gender. *pedley@lmu.edu*

Laura L. Ellingson (PhD, University of South Florida) is an Assistant Professor in the Department of Communication at Santa Clara University. Her research interests include physician-patient communication, interdisciplinary communication on health care teams, and feminist theory and methodology. Her publications include articles in *Health Communication, Women's Studies in Communication, Communication Studies, Journal of Applied Communication Research,* and *Journal of Aging Studies.* She has served the profession as a board member of the Organization for the Study of Communication, Language and Gender, and as Vice President of the Ethnography Division of the National Communication Association. She teaches courses in qualitative research methods, health communication, communication and gender, and public speaking. *lellingson@scu.edu*

Jennifer Fink (MA, Northern Illinois University) is employed at Safe Passage, Inc., as the Resource Coordinator. She previously served as the Community Relations and Volunteer Coordinator and a legal advocate. She copresented the paper "Enlarging Public-Private Boundaries—Letitia Westgate" at the 1999 International Communication Association conference and presented "Reaching the End of the Road: Phillip Morris' Fight for Legitimacy" at the 1997 Central States Communication Association conference. She served as the Editorial Assistant for *Management Communication Quarterly* from 1998 through 1999. *jenn_fink@hotmail.com*

Kathleen M. Galvin (PhD, Northwestern University) is a Professor of Communication Studies and a graduate of The Family Institute's Two Year Training Program in Family Therapy. Her research interests are family boundary management, especially as it relates to international adoption and step-families; her courses include Family Communication, Theories of Relational Communication, and Introduction to Family Therapy. She is author or co-author of eight books, including *Family Communication: Cohesion and Change* (sixth edition) and *Making Connections: Readings in Relational Communication* (third edition). She has published in a range of communication journals. Her 26-video telecourse in Family Communication currently appears on the PBS

Adult Learning Satellite Service. She recently won the National Communication Association's award for contributions to the area of family communication, has appeared on the *Today Show*, and has been cited in numerous local and national media outlets. *k-galvin@northwestern.edu*

Annika Hylmö (PhD, Purdue University) is an Assistant Professor in the Communication Studies Department at Loyola Marymount University. Her research interests center on the tensions between being a part of and apart from organizational contexts by focusing on organizational discourse, identity construction, and organizational culture. She studies changing and boundary-less careers, such as telecommuting, expatriates, and independent contractors; Third Culture Kid identity communication; student communication about their educational experiences, and identity representations of Native Americans. Her award-winning work has been published in anthologies and journals such as *Communication Monographs. ahylmo@lmu.edu*

Diana K. Ivy (PhD, University of Oklahoma) is a Professor in the Department of Communication and Theatre at Texas A&M University-Corpus Christi. Her research interests include gender communication, with a special emphasis on gender representations in language and media; interpersonal communication; and nonverbal communication. She has coauthored two textbooks, *GenderSpeak: Personal Effectiveness in Gender Communication* (3rd ed.) and *Communication: Principles for a Lifetime* (2nd ed.). She has served the profession as a longstanding member of the National Communication Association, of which she is a past Chair of the Women's Caucus, and has served as Secretary for the Instructional Development Division, and as a member of the Western States Communication Association; the Organization for Women and Communication; and the Organization for the Study of Communication, Language and Gender. She frequently teaches introduction to communication, gender communication, nonverbal communication, interpersonal communication, and public speaking. *diana.ivy@mail.tamucc.edu*

Marjorie A. Jaasma (EdD, University of the Pacific) is a Professor in the Communication Studies Department at California State University, Stanislaus. Her research interests are issues of gender and diversity in educational settings. Her publications include articles in *Communication Education, Women's Studies in Communication, Pacific Education Research Journal,* and *Communication Reports.* She teaches courses in the areas of gender communication, intercultural communication, and communication education. *mjaasma@csustan.edu*

Gary L. Kreps (PhD, 1979, University of Southern California) is Chief of the Health Communication and Informatics Research Branch at the National Cancer Institute (NCI), where he plans, develops, and coordinates major new national research and outreach initiatives concerning risk communication, health promotion, behavior change, technology development, and information dissemination to promote cancer prevention and control. Prior to joining the NCI, he was the Founding Dean of the School of Communication at Hofstra University, and, before that, Executive Director of the Greenspun School of Communication at the University of Nevada, Las Vegas. He has also served in faculty and administrative positions at Northern Illinois, Rutgers, Indiana, and Purdue Universities. His areas of expertise include health communication/promotion, information dissemination, organizational communication, information technology, multicultural relations, and applied research methods. He is an active scholar who has produced more than 20 books and 160 articles and chapters examining communication, health, and society. He has received numerous honors, including the Future of Health Technology Institute's *2002 Future of Health Technology Award*, the Ferguson Report's *2002 Distinguished Achievement Award for Outstanding Contributions in Consumer Health Informatics and Online Health*, the *2000 Outstanding Health Communication Scholar Award* from both the International Communication Association and the National Communication Association, and the *1998 Gerald M. Phillips Distinguished Applied Communication Scholarship Award* from the National Communication Association.

Marifran Mattson (PhD, Arizona State University) is an Associate Professor in the Department of Communication at Purdue University. Her research and teaching interests include exploring the intersection of health communication and organizational communication by considering the relationship between communication processes and problems related to human health and safety. Publications include articles in *Communication Monographs, Journal of Applied Communication Research, Health Communication, Journal of Health Communication, Communication Studies, Management Communication Quarterly, American Journal of Health Behavior,* and *American Journal of Pharmaceutical Education;* a chapter in the *Handbook of Health Communication;* and other book chapters. She has served the profession as chair of the National Communication Association's Health Communication Division, as an editorial board member for *Communication Studies,* and as an ad hoc reviewer for several communication journals. *mmattson@purdue.edu*

Marcy Meyer (BS, Georgetown University; MA, PhD Michigan State), a native of New Hampshire, is an Associate Professor in the Department of Communication Studies at Ball State University, where she teaches classes in organizational communication and research methods, and serves as the faculty advisor for the student group Feminists for Action. A winner of the 1996 Charles W. Redding Dissertation Award, Marcy conducts research in the areas of organizational innovation, gender, diversity, and feminist theorizing. Her articles have appeared in *Human Communication Research, Journal of Communication, Communication Studies, Journal of Business Communication,* and *Preventive Medicine. mmeyer@bsu.edu*

Laura Shue O'Hara (PhD, Ohio University) is an Associate Professor in the Communication Studies Department at Ball State University. Her primary areas of research are organizational and intercultural communication with an emphasis on gender and power in organizations. She has recently received a grant to develop a course using digital communication to create a global classroom for the study of intercultural communication in real-world business contexts. Her partner for the project is Pontifical Universidad Catolica de Rio Grande do Sul, (PUCRS), Porto Alegre, Brazil. *lohara@bsu.edu*

Barbara Penington (PhD, Marquette University) is an Assistant Professor in the Department of Communication at the University of Wisconsin-Whitewater and currently serves as the Graduate Program Coordinator for her department. Her research interests include family communication, listening, and culture and communication. She teaches courses in Fundamentals of Speech, Listening Behavior, and Cross-Cultural Communication. Her articles have appeared in the *Wisconsin Communication Association Journal, Let's Talk: A Cognitive Skills Approach to Interpersonal Communication,* and several editions of *Swap Shop,* a publication of the International Listening Association. Barbara is the mother of a former adolescent daughter, Caitlin, and also has two sons, Eric and Mark. *peningtb@uww.edu*

Kelly Quintanilla (PhD, Pennsylvania State University) is an Associate Professor and Chair in the Department of Communication and Theatre at Texas A&M University-Corpus Christi. Her research interests include organizational communication, with a special emphasis on organizational culture and public relations; and health communication. Publications include "Exploring the Effects of Organizational Change in an Organizational Subculture" in the *New Jersey Journal of Communication* and "Nonverbal Communication: A Fashion Alert" in *Readings in Gendered Text.* She has served as a communication consultant and trainer throughout the Coastal Bend. Her teaching interests include organizational communication, public relations techniques, communication theory, interviewing, small group communication, and public speaking. *kelly.quintanilla@mail.tamucc.edu*

Terri L. Russ (JD, DePaul University; PhD, Purdue University) is an Assistant Professor in the Department of Communication Studies at Bridgewater College. Her research interests are discourse and social power, female friendships, Bakhtin, feminist theory and practices, and ethnography as transformative praxis. Her publications include articles in *Res Gestae* and *DePaul Women's Law Journal. truss@bridgewater.edu*

Patty Sotirin (PhD, Purdue University) is an Associate Professor of Communication in the Humanities Department at Michigan Technological University. Her research interests are feminist theory, workplace talk, and gender representations in popular culture. Her publications include articles in *Text and Performance Quarterly; Organization: The International Journal of Organization, Theory, and Society;* and *Journal of Popular Film and Television;* and book chapters in such collections as *Animations (of Deleuze and Guattari)* (J. Slack, ed.) *Women and Work: A Handbook* (K. Borman & P. Dubeck, eds.) and *Gender and Conflict* (A. Taylor, ed.). She has served as President of the Organization for the Study of Communication, Language and Gender (OSCLG), Secretary of the Ethnography Division of the National Communication Association (NCA), and Book Review Editor for *Women and Language. pjsotiri@mtu.edu*

Charles Tucker (PhD, Ohio State University) is a Professor Emeritus in the Department of Communication Studies at Northern Illinois University. He has published *Talking About Relationships* (Waveland) and essays about management style and leadership in journals such as the *Central States Speech Journal.* Until recently, he was a consultant for partner abuse intervention programs for the Illinois Department of Human Services and a contract consultant for the same agency. *tucker@niu.edu*

About the Commentators

Connie Bullis (PhD, Purdue University) is an Associate Professor in the Department of Communication at the University of Utah. She has served as chair of her department at the University of Utah and on a number of editorial boards. She has published on feminist organizational communication theory, organizational identification, relational turning points, and ways of reconceptualizing socialization in journals including *Management Communication Quarterly, Communication Monographs, Western Journal of Communication, Human Communication Research,* and *Communication Studies,* as well as in Patrice Buzzanell's edited book, *Rethinking Organizational and Managerial Communication From Feminist Perspectives* (Sage, 2000). *bullis@admin.comm. utah.edu*

William F. Eadie (PhD, Purdue University) is Director of the School of Communication at San Diego State University, where he is responsible for leadership of a large program (2,300 student majors, 125 faculty) that encompasses all aspects of communication, media, and journalism. Prior to joining the SDSU faculty in 2001, he was Associate Director of the National Communication Association (NCA), in Washington, DC, where he worked with the discipline's researchers and promoted communication research to a variety of audiences. His other faculty appointments have been at Ohio University and California State University, Northridge, and he has served as an adjunct or visiting faculty member at the University of Minnesota, Twin Cities; the University of Maryland, College Park; the University of California, Los Angeles; and California State University, Los Angeles. He served as the first editor of the *Journal of Applied Communication Research* after it became an NCA publication. He has also served as President of the Western States Communication Association. His scholarship has focused on how interpersonal rhetoric affects the development of relationships. He has also been an advocate for the application of communication research in ways that affect ordinary people's lives. He has received the NCA Golden Anniversary Award for an outstanding article published in the field's journals. He has also been elected a member of Phi Kappa Phi, Golden Key, and Phi Beta Delta, all national honorary societies. *weadie@mail.sdsu.edu*

Kathleen M. Galvin (PhD, Northwestern University) is a Professor of Communication Studies at Northwestern University. She is also a graduate of The Family Institute's Two Year Training Program in Family Therapy. Her research interests are family boundary management, especially as it relates to international adoption; her courses include Family Communication, Theories of Relational Communication, and Introduction to Family Therapy. She is the author or coauthor of eight books, including *Family Communication: Cohesion and Change* (with Carma Bylund and Bernard Brommel), now in its 6th edition, and *Making Connections: Readings in Relational Communication* (with Pamela Cooper), in its 3rd edition. Her articles have appeared in a range of communication journals. Her 26-video telecourse in Family Communication currently appears on the PBS Adult Learning Satellite Service. She recently won the National Communication Association's award for contributions to the area of family communication, has appeared on *The Today Show*, and has been cited in numerous local and national media outlets. *k-galvin@northwestern.edu*

Gary L. Kreps (PhD, University of Southern California) is Chief of the Health Communication and Informatics Research Branch at the National Cancer Institute (NCI), where he plans, develops, and coordinates major new national research and outreach initiatives concerning risk communication, health promotion, behavior change, technology development, and information dissemination to promote cancer prevention and control. His areas of expertise include health communication and promotion, information dissemination, organizational communication, information technology, multicultural relations, and applied research methods. He is an active scholar who has published many articles in journals such as *Health Communication, Journal of Health Communication, Journal of Health Psychology, Journal of Applied Communication Research, Public Health Reports, Patient Education and Counseling, The American Behavioral Scientist, Family and Community Health, Journal of the American Medical Informatics Association,* and *Communication Studies.* He has also published (along with a number of esteemed coauthors) many books, including *Health Communication: Theory and Practice; Perspectives on Health Communication; Communication and Health Outcomes; Communicating Effectively in Multicultural Health Care Settings; Communicating With Your Doctor: Getting the Most Out of Health Care; Qualitative Research: Applications in Organizational Life; Interpreting Communication Research: Introduction to Research Methods; Sexual Harassment: Communication Implications;* and *Organizational Communication: Theory and Practice.* He has edited special issues of several journals: the *Electronic Journal of Communication/La Revue Electronique de Communication,* issue on "Health Communication and

Information Technology"; the *Journal of Health Psychology,* issue on "E-Health: Computer-Mediated Health Communication"; the *Journal of the American Medical Informatics Association,* issue on "Critical Issues in Consumer Health Informatics"; *Patient Education and Counseling,* issue on "Advancing Consumer/Provider Health Communication Research"; and the *American Behavioral Scientist,* issue on "Communicating to Promote Health." Dr. Kreps has received numerous honors, including the Future of Health Technology Institute's 2002 Future of Health Technology Award, the Ferguson Report's 2002 Distinguished Achievement Award for Outstanding Contributions in Consumer Health Informatics and Online Health, the 2000 Outstanding Health Communication Scholar Award from both the International Communication Association and the National Communication Association, and the 1998 Gerald M. Phillips Distinguished Applied Communication Scholarship Award from the National Communication Association. *gary.kreps@nih.gov*

Richard West (PhD, Ohio University) is a Professor in the Department of Communication at the University of Southern Maine in Portland. He received his BA and MA from Illinois State University. Rich has been teaching since 1984, and his teaching and research interests range from family diversity to teacher-student communication. He is the recipient of various teaching and research awards at USM, including the College of Arts and Sciences Outstanding Teacher-Scholar and the Faculty Senate Award in Social Science Research. He is a past recipient of the Outstanding Editing]Alumni Award in Communication Studies at both Illinois State University and Ohio University. He is the co-author (with Lynn Turner) of *Gender and Communication* (3rd Ed.), *Perspectives on Family Communication* (2nd Ed.), and *Introducing Communication Theory* (2nd Ed.). His publications include articles published in *Communication Education, Communication Reports, Day Care and Early Education,* and the *Journal of Communication Studies.* He remains grateful and proud of the feminist thinking instilled in him over the years by his mother, Beverly, and grandmother, Lucille. *rwest@usm.maine.edu*